Valuing Diversity in Early Childhood Education

Valuing Diversity in Early Childhood Education

Lissanna Follari

University of Colorado

Colorado Springs

PEARSON

Boston   Columbus   Indianapolis   New York   San Francisco   Upper Saddle River
Amsterdam   Cape Town   Dubai   London   Madrid   Milan   Munich   Paris   Montreal   Toronto
Delhi   Mexico City   São Paulo   Sydney   Hong Kong   Seoul   Singapore   Taipei   Tokyo

Vice President and Editorial Director:
Jeffery W. Johnston
Senior Acquisitions Editor: Julie Peters
Editorial Assistant: Andrea Hall
Executive Marketing Manager: Krista Clark
Production Project Manager:
Laura Messerly
Operations Specialist: Michelle Klein
Senior Art Director: Jayne Conte
Cover Designer: Jennifer Hart

Cover Art: Lissanna Follari; Mairim Saavedra;
Benjamin LaFramboise/Pearson; Carla
Mestas/Pearson
Media Project Manager: Tammy Walters
Full-Service Project Management:
Mansi Negi, Aptara®, Inc.
Composition: Aptara®, Inc.
Printer/Binder: LSC Communications
Cover Printer: LSC Communications
Text Font: ITCGaramondStd

Credits and acknowledgments for material borrowed from other sources and reproduced, with permission, in this text appear on the appropriate page within the text.

Every effort has been made to provide accurate and current Internet information in this text. However, the Internet and information posted on it are constantly changing, so it is inevitable that some of the Internet addresses listed in this text will change.

Photo Credits: Mairim Saavedra, pp. 3, 28, 56, 76, 109, 116, 207, 288; Mahmoud Rahall/Fotolia, p. 6; David Kostelnik/Pearson Education, pp. 11, 84, 89, 112, 122; Lissanna Follari, pp. 14, 42, 47, 60, 63, 70, 154, 159, 170, 173, 187, 197, 201, 211, 216, 246, 249 (b), 261, 266; Katelyn Metzger/Merrill Education/Pearson Education, p. 18; Niyazz/Fotolia, p. 35; Jen Ensign, p. 40; Carla Mestas/Pearson Education, pp. 44, 93, 105, 134; Laura Bolesta/Merrill Education/Pearson Education, p. 66; Jaren Wicklund/Fotolia, p. 80; Benjamin LaFramboise/Pearson Education, pp. 128, 138, 145, 249 (t), 255; Noam/Fotolia, p. 164; Jasmin Merdan/Fotolia, p. 167; Lissanna Follari, p. 176; Glenda Powers/Fotolia, p. 191; Denys Kuvaiev/Fotolia, p. 222; Merrill Education/Pearson Education, pp. 224, 229, 234, 271.

Library of Congress Cataloging-in-Publication Data

Follari, Lissanna M.
   Valuing diversity in early childhood education / Lissanna M. Follari,
Colby-Sawyer College.—First edition.
         pages cm
   ISBN-13: 978-0-13-268721-8
   ISBN-10:   0-13-268721-6
   1. Early childhood education. 2. Cultural pluralism—Study and teaching (Early childhood)
   3. Child development. 4. Children with disabilities—Education (Early childhood) I. Title.
   LB1139.23.F665   2015
   371.9'0472—dc23   2013043155

ISBN 13: 978-0-13-268721-8
ISBN 10:   0-13-268721-6

Preface

In today's increasingly diverse world, it is essential that teachers develop competence in three key areas:

- Understanding important differences among people
- Seeing and appreciating differences as strengths within families, communities, and programs
- Making decisions about care and education that reflect cultural competence

This book is a part of this important evolution in the professional preparation and development of teachers.

This text takes new and experienced early childhood educators on a reflective journey to explore personal attitudes and values related to human diversity and culturally competent teaching. It also identifies and explains effective strategies for supporting and celebrating diverse children and families.

Three facets serve as overarching themes throughout the text: *self*, *others*, and *group*. Reflective activities prompt readers to understand their own biases, background experiences, and values, while interactive experiences prompt readers to explore the similarities and differences of others. A final piece of the three-part puzzle encourages readers to practice instructional strategies that promote belonging and partnership among groups of children, professionals, and families in various early childhood settings.

The purpose of this text is to support professionals as they develop awareness and an appreciation of differences and the confidence to apply culturally competent teaching practices to ensure success for each child and family.

Features of the Text

A key feature of this text is the use of individual stories about diverse family contexts (In My Family) and classroom experiences (Classroom Story Corner). Each story brings a genuine and real-world aspect to the text, offering important glimpses into the unique experiences of individual children, families, and teachers as a way of emphasizing the differences and similarities among us. Each chapter also includes robust practical strategies for applying instructional practices that are culturally relevant and validating both in the classroom

(Curricular Connections) and in partnership with families (Family Partnerships). Videos are woven through each chapter of the Pearson eText to help students understand the content, issues and teaching applications.

Each chapter wraps up with a series of critical thinking discussion prompts and activities to promote self-reflection and interactive perspective-taking. Through these culminating activities, readers are guided to examine their personal ideas and background in the context of the richly diverse world in which we live and work.

Guiding Concepts

First and foremost, this book is wholly focused on the belief that our individual differences and diverse family contexts are tremendous assets to our communities. Beginning from a place of truly valuing, honoring, and celebrating our differences, we can then layer in the important and meaningful ways in which we share similarities. Only from a place of valuing differences and validating similarities can we truly form connected, reciprocal partnerships with colleagues, children, and families, partnerships that are equitable and promote in each and every member a sense of belonging and inclusiveness.

Acknowledgments

I wish to offer my heartfelt appreciation to all my students, past and present. It is for you that I undertook this project. I hope that the inspiration and collegiality we share in our classes continue to fuel your work as they do mine. And for my much-appreciated colleagues across the country: It continues to be an honor to travel this road together. I wish you all a successful and nourishing journey.

I would like to thank Maria Montano and Andrea Gunkel for sharing their practice as model professionals; Shannon Gallagher, Meggan Gonyo, and Kendra Hotchkiss for their tireless work during internship semesters; and very heartfelt appreciation to Julie Peters and Andrea Hall at Pearson for their continued support and valuable feedback. This project is stronger for your thoughtful, dedicated involvement.

I would like to thank the following reviewers for their helpful comments: Helen Bond, Howard University; Camille Catlett, University of North Carolina at Chapel Hill; Patricia Doelitzsch, Los Angeles Pierce College; Shanna L. Graves, University of Houston–Clear Lake; Cathy Gutierrez-Gomez, University of New Mexico; Kim A. Horejs, Fox Valley Technical College; Grace Ibanez Friedman, St. John's University; Patricia Mendez, Oxnard College; and Katherine Norris, West Chester University.

A very special thank you also goes out to the dedicated teachers and families at the Windy Hill Lab School at Colby–Sawyer College. Your relentless commitment to child-centered play-based practice is truly an inspiration to me and the countless students who are fortunate enough to learn from you all.

Finally, I lovingly dedicate this project to Greisan, the motivation behind it all.

Brief Contents

Contents

Chapter 2 • THE DEVELOPMENT *OF* CULTURAL IDENTITY   28

Chapter 3 • THE SPECTRUM *OF* RESPONSES *TO* DIVERSITY   54

PART II   FACETS OF HUMAN DIVERSITY

Chapter 4 • RACE *AND* ETHNICITY 76

Chapter 5 • LANGUAGE *AND* NATIONALITY 104

Chapter 6 • SOCIOECONOMIC FACTORS 128

Chapter 7 • RELIGION   154

Chapter 8 • FAMILIES 186

Chapter 9 • ABILITIES 216

PART III   BRINGING IT ALL TOGETHER

Chapter 10 • SUPPORTING INDIVIDUAL LEARNERS 246

Chapter 11 • TEACHING *IN A* DIVERSE WORLD 266

1

The What, Why, *and* How *of* Exploring Diversity

In every city, town, neighborhood, and classroom there exists a rich array of diversity. At first glance around at the faces in your classroom this might not seem so; the people around you might all appear to reflect a similar background. Or perhaps thinking about the children and families you work with, you are nodding and thinking "There sure is a mix in my room!" Statistically, in many schools and centers the cultural makeup of the children and families comprises more people of color than White, and classrooms are generally evenly split between boys and girls. Yet the vast majority of early childhood teachers are White females (see Figure 1.1).

FIGURE 1.1 *Early Childhood Teacher Workforce by Race/Ethnicity*

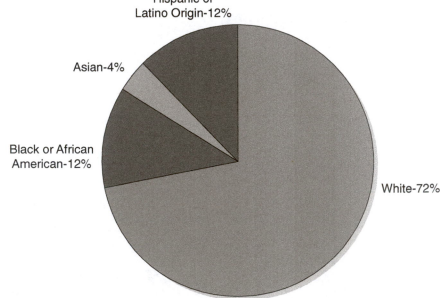

Statistics on demographics of educators show that the early childhood teacher workforce is largely White and 98% female (BLS, 2012). For elementary and middle schools, the teacher workforce is 83% White and 76% female (NCES, 2012).

More than two-thirds of children in full-day child care arrangements nationally represent people of color (including people identifying as having Hispanic origins, or as Black, Asian, American Indian/Alaska Native, and multiracial); clearly a mismatch exists between the make-up of children and families using early care and education and the make-up of the professionals working in those arrangements (NCES, 2010).

This discord between student demographics and teacher demographics can pose significant challenges that negatively impact children's outcomes. This is especially true when teachers are not well-prepared to appropriately interact with children, families, and colleagues from diverse backgrounds and with widely varying abilities. Many teachers are unaware of how to develop these skills (part of cultural competence), or how to acknowledge differences without further alienating groups.

It all starts with knowledge and awareness, which can grow into attitude and action. As you become aware of diverse perspectives and are willing to walk in another's shoes, you create opportunities every day to act in ways that perpetuate fairness and equity. Finding and using everyday moments to explore and value diversity takes study and practice. Even more important, it takes a personal commitment to the belief that each and every individual—infant, child, adult—is a unique person worth celebrating for all the colorful ways in which he or she is different *and* alike. This book is designed to be a catalyst, an inspiration, a guide, a tool for self-discovery, and a practical resource to provoke this messy, complicated, worthy, and joyful journey.

LEARNING OUTCOMES
· · · · · · · · · · · · · · · · · ·

● Explore the purpose of studying diversity

● Identify key concepts in the study of diversity

● Define *diversity* and related terms, including *culture, identity, ethnicity, cultural competence, equity, social justice*, and more

● Practice strategies to build cultural competence

Today's classrooms robustly represent the increasingly diverse and complex lives of children and families, and it is essential that teachers value these complexities.

Exploring Diversity

The beauty of our human differences really lies in its closeness to our sameness. At the heart of our human experience are the things that unify us all, with relatively subtle characteristics and dynamics that add vivid color to our world. Valuing diversity is about using our common threads as a way to highlight all the wondrous ways that we are different. For example, bookstores and early childhood supply catalogs include children's books containing photographs illustrating different forms of a common item shared by people around the world—like *homes, bread,* and *families.* Most children are familiar with these concepts; we all have these things in common. Yet families with children might live in cars, apartments, modest homes, or expensive homes; eat pita, lavosh, or challah breads; and children might live in families with one adult or relative, two adults, siblings, or several generations of adults. The concept of these books is the essence of today's approach to diversity, inclusion, and multicultural education, putting the focus on our sameness and celebrating our diversity through everyday moments and experiences.

Diversity might well feel like a topic of the moment. It is the focus of a great deal of professional research, discourse, and policy, and is a reality of daily teaching practice. We hear and read about *diversity* related to many different concepts, settings, and practices. For many teachers and most people in general, these ideas and terms are vaguely defined and often not part of a shared concept or definition. But answering the question, "What is diversity?" is not simple. What diversity really means is highly complex, personal, and rooted in personal and shared history. The concept holds different meanings for individuals and groups. On the surface, diversity is basically about differences, uniqueness, and the ways people are unlike one another, including culture (which is defined and discussed more below) as well as differences in abilities. Our concept of our own identity is what makes us aware of how someone else is different than us. Because we tend to recognize differences in others in comparison to ourselves, we may respond to someone who seems different from us personally, or in a negative way, and this might be uncomfortable. Awareness of others and our own responses to people who might be different are important parts of the process of valuing diversity. In the next section, take a few minutes to honestly assess your experiences related to diversity.

DIVERSITY INVOLVES COMPARISONS

Beliefs and reactions to definitions, labels, and realities of diversity are very personal and can reveal within us potentially hurtful biases. We often feel unprepared and insecure when faced with an individual, family, or colleague who is different than us in some obvious or subtle way. We may either worry that we will appear biased, or we may be consciously biased

ATTITUDE TO ACTION, BELIEF TO BEHAVIOR 1.1

My Identity and Values

Exploring your own identity, values, expectations, and culture is an essential part of becoming more culturally aware. Use the following questions to prompt self-reflection and collegial discussion about your own identity and your beliefs.

When prompted (on job applications or for the census), I indicate my race as	
My first language is	
Other languages that I am at least a little familiar with are	
I have or have had friends who were/are classified as having a documented diverse ability (such as an IEP in school)	
If I come across someone with a diverse physical ability or using an assistive device, my initial thought is	
I am aware of what researchers call the *achievement gap*	
My definition of a *family* is	
My definition of *marriage* is	

and prefer our own way of doing or thinking. Our insecurity or bias will influence how we respond to and interact with people in these situations, sometimes influencing us in ways we don't realize but which can have negative consequences.

"Most of us initially define ourselves as nonbiased. When we look more deeply, however, we all find areas where bias exists" (Williams & Cooney, 2006, p. 76). **Biases** are simply the ways we are inclined to think about things. Our biases are a natural part of our own upbringing, values, identity, customs, and socialization. The processes that socialize each of us to internalize certain values begin in both direct and indirect ways before we are even born. Our families, caretakers, and communities have their own deeply ingrained values that are passed along through overt and subtle messages from the very beginning of our lives.

Consider the widespread tradition, sometimes referred to as *instinct*, for parents-to-be to "nest" and prepare a space in the home for a new baby. It might feel like a mainstream custom to create space and select materials based on the gender of the baby. I have heard from parents who decided not to find out their baby's gender before birth and were consequently scolded and met with outright anger from relatives who insisted they could not

Infant care-taking routines, including choices about sleeping and feeding, are often a big part of family culture and traditions, but traditions like infant ear piercing, circumcision, and clothing are also connected to family culture.

prepare for the baby or purchase gifts without knowing the gender. These parents felt attacked for their choices and were met with a clear dominant bias. But beyond thinking about pink ruffled dresses, blue-striped wallpaper borders, or gender-themed baby showers, also think about how messages of cultural identity expectations are shared throughout moments of daily life. Families of different economic status, family/extended-family structure, and different lifestyles prepare for the birth of a baby in their own ways, but all with decisions that imply certain values and expectations of both family and child. A co-sleeper next to mom's bed; a crib in a separate room; a dresser drawer lined with a blanket; a swaddling board; a sheepskin hide in a corner of a shared hut; or a separate living arrangement where baby will stay with a nonparental caretaker: these all are physical cues of a family's or society's values and indicate different expectations of children and adults.

We often consider normal the certain messages and expectations we are familiar with, and anything that deviates from our perceptions is judged to be abnormal, strange, or wrong (Gonzalez-Mena, 2008). Some culture-study researchers even point out that "all contemporary Americans, to some extent, regardless of their national origin or ancestry (often mixed), participate in a common culture (patterned ways of behaving and thinking)" (Kottak & Kozaitis, 2008, p. 10). This shared common culture can serve to unify people but also can cause conflict and distress for individuals who are either new to this country or are met with hostility for not conforming. Biases can be entrenched preferences which lead us to value one way over all others. While it might be a natural reaction to think of our own ways of doing and thinking as normal because they are more familiar, the first step in exploring and learning about what diversity means in education is to become aware of the implications of our biases. When our biases lead to value judgments about what is normal, better, or right, the result will be individuals and, potentially, entire groups of families who we marginalize, dismiss, or try to correct to do things our way. Negative responses to people or groups who are perceived of as "other" by a more dominant group have historically created a vast and painful difference of power between dominant values and subordinate groups (Hyun, 2007).

This domination and marginalization are not part of the important role and ethical obligation that early childhood professionals have to the children and families we work with. At the very core of our professional ethical duty is to do no harm and to support and respect children and families. We begin the journey toward meeting this charge by opening our minds and hearts to a critical exploration of ourselves and others. Your task in this exploration (and in reading this book) is to be honest with yourself; to deeply examine your own background, perspectives, experiences, and reactions; and to recognize the values and biases these elements have instilled in you. In essence, studying diversity involves learning about yourself as much as it involves learning about people and groups who are different than you in some way. Most of all, exploring diversity is about reprogramming how we respond to our own biases—from actions that perpetuate a dominant or one-way-is-better view toward a more pluralistic practice that emphasizes many equally valid ways also exist. As you watch this **video**, consider examples of individual differences that you have experienced.

Why Study Diversity?

The study of diversity is a three-fold endeavor requiring that you explore definitions of *others*, *self*, and *we*. It involves learning about people you might think of as being different than you, reflecting on yourself and your values, and thinking about what makes a group of people collaboratively construct a community of *we*. Studying diversity is about a culture of listening, transformation, and change. It is about committing to the ongoing work of meaningfully co-constructing new cultures together within each new group (class, neighborhood, school, family, team, office, and more) that reflect authentic individual identities of members as well as a dynamic shared concept of *group*. The exploration and ultimate skill of communicating across cultures requires looking inward to examine our own backgrounds and personal histories while looking outward to listen to and understand those of other individuals (Trumbull, Rothstein-Fisch, & Hernandez, 2003).

JOURNEY CAREFULLY

This important journey has some potential dangers. First and foremost, it is imperative to understand and emphasize that looking at differences can lead us to generalize or define people into groups and make assumptions about *all* people we categorize in that group. There can be great harm in using generalized themes to make stereotypes or assumptions about all people who share one or more characteristics. We must be sensitive to the ways that some people feel similar to others but also to how people with some shared characteristics differ.

Here is one example of the more critical approach we need to take in exploring diversity. I often hear in media and research that "Americans raise their children to be independent and to focus on individual achievement." Some behaviors and messages might validate this observation, but a deeper and more critical reading of this statement has to prompt us to wonder which Americans does this refer to and what does it mean to be *American*? The Americas are a large geographic area made up of two continents, many countries, and vastly different people across and within each country (North America, Central America, South America). Many of us reading this book might agree with those parenting values, and many might immediately think "Well, I don't think that way, and I live in the United States." Some might think of the ways that we encourage our children to collaborate or to socialize in an interdependent group, or ways that we were raised to support shared achievement, which is quite different than a sole focus on independent achievement.

Consider the implications of thinking that children with disabilities are special, fragile, and need protection. Children with diverse abilities are sometimes treated unfairly or abusively, certainly. However, both this statement

IN MY FAMILY

Maria's Family Tradition of Oral Storytelling

I am a college student and am completing my degree part-time while I work as a preschool teacher's aide part-time. As a Mexican American, English is my second language, but I am fluently bilingual. My early childhood college classes involve a lot of reflection and dialogue, which was a little hard for me at first. I guess I was more used to keeping quiet and doing my work. My professor really prompts us to think a lot about our own background as we develop into professionals. One area that we have talked a lot about is the emphasis on literacy in early childhood.

At first when we talked about our personal memories of our own early literacy development or when the professor read us children's books and asked if we know the story, I was embarrassed. In my home we never had books. Partly because we were so poor (we didn't even have running water), but partly because education wasn't an important thing in my home. My mother stayed at home, and my father worked as a laborer. Only for Christmas did I ever see books. That was when my aunt, who was a teacher, gave me books as a present.

Still, my mother and grandmothers didn't read them to me. I do remember lots of the old stories and fairy tales though, because my one grandmother would always be telling me stories from her memory—like a storyteller. I have clear memories of sitting at her feet while she rocked in an old, creaky chair telling me all these old stories, the same ones from children's books. In my college class now we talked about how storytelling is a powerful way to strengthen and build children's language development, knowledge of stories, and imagination.

I don't have the same memories of a mom reading bedtime stories or shelves lined with books in my bedroom like a lot of other students in my classes. But I have come to realize that I do have my own memories of experiences that were important ways my family helped build my language development. And here I am—a college student with a 3.95 GPA coming from a dirt-poor, uneducated, immigrant family. Now I am glad I am asked to reflect on my own culture and upbringing in relation to my work as a teacher, and I'm the first one to share personal stories in class!

and the term *disabilities* or *special needs* imply that children with diverse abilities are less capable or needier than other children. Moving around in a wheelchair, using a speaking device or sign language, or receiving food through a feeding tube does not make a person less capable than others; rather the child simply moves, communicates, or eats in a different way.

The more we think about it, the more we may feel boxed in by a narrow label or perhaps insulted by a limiting definition (such as "women are the weaker sex"). This is the risk in learning about defined groups. It is ultimately valuable to learn about some of the characteristics that might be shared by groups of people who may associate themselves with these characteristics. Indeed, expanding our knowledge of various cultures, traditions, and styles is an essential element of becoming a culturally responsive professional. But we should always remember that each person has an individual background that shapes her or him. Our job is to acknowledge and understand group and individual differences as we journey to valuing and celebrating the diversity among us.

Benefits of Studying Diversity

Studying the complex issues, challenges, and opportunities involved in living in a diverse world is more than about keeping up with "hot" topics, being politically correct, or about a passing trend. Diversity involves individual uniqueness, group affiliation, social justice, and striving for equity. It is about valuing each other and both what we share as humans and what makes us unique. It is about being a competent, ethical professional engaged in high-quality practice. What we hear people say is true—times are changing; the realities of family life in the United States are different today than they were years ago. But the makeup of family structures, societies and communities, and population demographics have always been dynamic and changing. Perhaps what feels new today is the wider awareness of the need for stronger policies and practices designed to ensure equity (fairness) and equality (equal access) among people.

BEING CULTURALLY COMPETENT

Exploring the many facets of diversity as they relate to you and how to work with other people has tremendous benefits to you personally. First and foremost, understanding differences among people provides you with a window into communicating better and accomplishing more with others. Being knowledgeable about how differences serve as strengths and being prepared to maximize those strengths toward ultimate common goals (such as ensuring healthy development for children) makes your job easier and more satisfying. Consider the benefits of cultural competence in this **video**. When you are open to and skilled at fostering family participation in children's care and education in all families, you cultivate allies which make your workload lighter. Being more effective in your work prompts you to become a much more confident and successful early childhood professional. Knowledge of diversity really is good for you and good for your students: a win–win!

Teacher Education Standards Relating to Diversity

In addition to your personal commitment to developing your knowledge base about people with diverse backgrounds, proficiency in meaningful engagement of all children is included in state and national teaching standards. Being a culturally competent educator able to teach to diverse learning styles, dual language learners (those learning English in addition to home language), children with diverse abilities and from vastly different family backgrounds is considered a professional expectation as you enter the field of teaching. Professional educator associations unanimously recognize the importance of professional preparation that clearly recognizes and values diverse populations.

The Council for the Accreditation of Educator Preparation (CAEP), formed in 2010 as a merger of the National Council for the Accreditation of Teacher Education (NCATE) and the Teacher Education Accrediting Council (TEAC) and representing both bodies, has developed draft standards for new teacher practice (http://caepnet.org). At the time of publication, the draft standards were still under review and open for comment with finalized standards forthcoming. The draft of five standards includes an overarching statement defining the inclusive and encompassing perspective on student diversity with the following note: "In this report, the term 'all students' is defined as children or youth attending P-12 schools including students with disabilities or exceptionalities, who are gifted, and students who represent diversity based on ethnicity, race, socioeconomic status, gender, language, religion, sexual identification, and geographic origin" (CAEP, 2012, p. 19).

Standard 1 includes additional specific reference to a commitment to promote equity through self-reflection and culturally competent practice: "Candidates reflect on their personal biases and access resources that deepen their own understanding of cultural, ethnic, gender, sexual orientation, language, and learning differences to build stronger relationships and to adapt practice to meet the needs of each learner" (CAEP, 2012, p. 16).

The Interstate New Teacher Assessment and Support Consortium (InTASC) has likewise identified 10 standards that every new teacher should practice and know proficiently. Each broad standard includes specific indicators for performance. Standard 2 addresses teacher competence in working with students of diverse backgrounds: "The teacher uses understanding of individual differences and diverse cultures and communities to ensure inclusive learning environments that allow each learner to reach his/her full potential" (CCSSO, 2011, p. 11). This standard includes key performance, knowledge, and disposition indicators clarifying teacher beliefs and behaviors. Indicators include valuing individual differences, knowledge of exceptionalities and resources, knowledge of language acquisition processes, and belief in the potential in all students.

Of particular interest to early childhood professionals is the widely accepted benchmark of best practices in early childhood education, the *Developmentally Appropriate Practice* (DAP) statement from the National Association for the Education of Young Children (NAEYC). The most recent updates to this continually reviewed and evolving document include an emphasis on the significant demographic changes in the populations of children served in early childhood education settings. In particular, the statement underscores the increases in linguistically, culturally, and economically diverse families participating in early childhood programs as well as the value of supporting inclusive settings for children of varying ability levels. This pivotal DAP framework is founded on three core values that are the basis for all early childhood practice:

1. What is known about ***child development and learning***—referring to knowledge of age-related characteristics that permits general predictions about what experiences are likely to best promote children's learning and development.

2. What is known about ***each child as an individual***—referring to what practitioners learn about each child that has implications for how best to adapt and be responsive to that individual variation.

3. What is known about the ***social and cultural contexts in which children live***—referring to the values, expectations, and behavioral and linguistic conventions that shape children's lives at home and in their communities that practitioners must strive to understand in order to ensure that learning experiences in the program or school are meaningful, relevant, and respectful for each child and family (Copple & Bredekamp, 2009, emphasis added).

Using these three essential foundational building blocks for all professional practice, NAEYC provides research-based recommendations and strong emphasis on individually and culturally constructed teaching. In addition to the DAP, NAEYC has

Inviting families into the classroom for social gatherings is a meaningful way to learn more about children's varied backgrounds and is an important part of welcoming and valuing families.

published position statements in support of antidiscrimination policies and practices in teacher employment and children's access to programs and services, as well as focused recommendations for working with children and families with linguistic and cultural diversity (NAEYC, 1995, 2005).

The national standards of these associations demonstrate just how important it is for all educators to develop both knowledge of diverse individuals and proficiency in skillfully and successfully interacting with and meaningfully engaging all learners. All of these standards and statements are freely available online and should become familiar resources for all early childhood professionals.

Defining Diversity and Important Related Terms

One challenge we face on this journey of exploring diversity is right at the start: defining what we mean by the word *diversity* and what diversity means conceptually in teaching practice. As with all effective interpersonal communication, it is important that we start out by creating shared meaning and orient ourselves to the same guideposts for the purposes of the current exploration. Throughout this book the following terms and concepts will be explored in more depth separately and as they interrelate. They are presented in overview here to provide shared background knowledge and to facilitate reflection and dialogue.

DIVERSITY

In its simplest definition, **diversity** is about variety, or the ways people or things are different. In child development and education usage, definitions of diversity are more layered, referring to "the human differences between people including, but not limited to, shape, size, ability, gender, age, skin color, sexual orientation, family background, spiritual beliefs, and political affiliation" (York, 2003, p. 262). In working with teachers and college students in various areas across the United States, I often hear comments that reflect the assumption that diversity refers only or primarily to skin color or geographic origins. However, keep in mind the heart of the definition— simply, *different*. "In short, [diversity] includes whatever we think distinguishes us" (Bucher, 2010, p. 26). This book emphasizes the more broad view and encompasses elements that shape how individuals within a society perceive their individual identity. The attributes that we may think of as being part of our identity or something that distinguishes us can include:

- Economic/social class
- Sex (having male or female genitalia)

- Gender identity
- Age
- Nationality/geography
- Race/ethnicity
- Religion
- Ability
- Body shape or appearance
- Language
- Thinking/learning style
- Family composition

This book will explore all of these aspects of human identity within the scope of valuing diversity. Individual chapters will provide general background knowledge as appropriate, with stories from individuals and ideas for helping ensure successful learning and developmental outcomes for all children.

CULTURE

Definitions of **culture** can include references to excellence of taste in socially valued artifacts and works in fine arts, humanities, and sciences; it can also refer to the characteristic aspects of a group's everyday existence. In essence, culture can refer to highly regarded accomplishments as well as shared knowledge, beliefs, and behaviors that are applicable within a certain time and place and that are passed down through generations. A key component in understanding culture is that it is about "socially transmitted ways of thinking, believing, feeling, and acting within a group" which are taught to younger generations (Gollnick & Chinn, 2009, p. 405). Culture refers to potentially everything that influences our lives and shapes our identity (Bucher, 2010). As such, it is so vast and personal that we are unable to narrowly define or compartmentalize the concept of culture into a tidy descriptor. Teachers who are engaged in researcher-facilitated dialogues about how culture relates to their practice have realized that culture is "a complex construction that is contextually based in time, place, and experience" (Eberly, Joshi, & Konzal, 2007, p. 15). Essentially, culture is dynamic; it is created by people, and it changes over time and place. Listen to this **video** and consider how definitions of culture change over time.

Culture is meaningful on a larger societal level as well as on a personal level for the windows it provides into societal values as well as its influences on personal identity. Those widely shared beliefs, values, and behaviors that are shared by large groups are powerful forces in shaping societies. Even though culture is vast and conceptually complex, examining both levels of culture is an important part of professional practice. Understanding the two levels of culture (big "C" and small "c"—seen and unseen culture) and key theoretical frameworks helps us realize what culture means to individuals and how culture is perceived among groups.

IDENTITY AS A CULTURAL CONSTRUCT

Any discussion or exploration of culture needs to revolve around the concept of how culture significantly influences **identity**. "Humans develop through their changing participation in the sociocultural activities of their communities, which also change" (Rogoff, 2003, p. 11). Rogoff's perspective underscores the dynamic, bidirectional nature of children's development within families and societal groupings. Identity is so central to culture because our concept of who we are, what we believe, and how we behave is intimately connected to the messages and programming we are raised with as well as the choices we make. Sometimes identity manifests in beliefs and behaviors that run contrary to messages from upbringing or societal expectations.

In working with same-sex parents I have been moved by many of their powerful stories of coming out (revealing their homosexuality to others) and how family, religious leaders, and friends have disowned them in judgment of their relationship partner choices. Children who excitedly talk about family life with two daddies or two mommies may be met with awkward silence from teachers who are unprepared or unwilling to value same-sex parents as "a real family." When those same-sex parents come to their child's center or school for meetings or classroom activities, teachers' discomfort or disproval can be transferred to other children through lack of eye contact or quickly dismissive comments. This is a similar experience for children whose parent(s) are dual language learners. When we think about our own cultural identity as the "norm," we are prone to subjugating, marginalizing, and negatively judging people who act, live, speak, or look differently than we do. These beliefs and behaviors lead to a view that one cultural group is better than every other; this view is referred to as **ethnocentrism** (Gollnick & Chinn, 2009; Rogoff, 2003).

The personal stories throughout this book are intended to highlight one key point: that diversity of culture is present to greater or lesser degrees among everyone we have contact with. Cultural diversity is not about how people from another geographic area are different. As the shaper of our identity, cultural

In order to genuinely and inclusively welcome all children and families into early childhood settings, professionals need to know and appreciate the unique context of every child's family life.

Hidden Diversity

On a windy fall day, I stand in front of 22 first- and second-year early childhood college students and open up a conversation about diversity by asking them to think about how they might adapt their teaching to embrace diversity. After a short pause and several quizzical looks, one student says "Well, there's no diversity around this area, so that really doesn't apply to us, right?" This response, this unrealized misconception, has been a part of every semester for the 10 years I have been teaching college students. Change the date and the weather outside the classroom window, but the underlying idea that there is no diversity in this room of apparently White female students in a town that is seemingly largely Caucasian persists year after year. "Hmmm . . ." I say, eager for the experience we're about to embark on.

With a brief introduction to the complex concept of the hidden or unseen nature of human diversity and the complexity of the definition of diversity and self-identity, I ask students to make a list of personal responses to 10 aspects of their life and upbringing. A silence falls over the room as the class begins writing their lists, occasionally smiling or looking up reflectively as they remember things about their family life, their grandparents, travels, and childhood hometowns.

With individual lists complete, they set out in groups to interview each other and to list, graph, and map out the class's answers. Student groups make large posters of their findings. We hang them, step back, and fall silent again. And, just as it happens every year looking at those posters, my class and I are quietly awestruck by the roster of languages they have been exposed to (from Finnish to Cherokee, Italian to Korean), the map of places they have traveled to, and the similarities and differences in where our ancestors hailed from.

We look around the room again. The faces are the same, but those hidden diversities among us have just become more visible, and we realize a new respect for the vastness of the worlds we each bring to the classroom. This is always my favorite day at school. It is a moment in our semester that not only changes the way students think about each other, but that also changes the way they see and think about everyone they meet. As I listen to them excitedly talk about these cultural identifiers, connecting with others over shared histories and asking questions about differences, I feel a transformation beginning.

diversity exists across borders but also between neighbors, schoolmates, and even within families.

ETHNIC, ETHNICITY

What do you immediately think of when you hear the word *ethnic*? Many people will mention things like foreign food, or perhaps clothing that is not typical for Westerners, or other images that indicate things that are non-White-Western in nature. These images and ideas imply that ethnic things are in some way "other than" what is normal, typical, or familiar. The word **ethnicity** is defined as "membership based on one's national origin or the national origin of one's ancestors" (Gollnick & Chinn, 2009, p. 406). When we are among a group that identifies with the same national origin, we naturally feel a sense of belonging or a sense of "us."

We all have national origins and ancestors with national origins, and yet so many people think of something or someone different or exotic when using the word *ethnic*. Considering that each individual has a personal identity that reflects affiliation with the various characteristics that make up our sense of cultural identity, we each then are a part of an ethnic classification. We are all ethnic. We must become aware of the depth of the "us versus them" thinking that is so prevalent within us and widely perpetuated throughout society.

When I have had the pleasure of traveling and meeting with different students or workshop participants, I enjoy having time to talk casually after class or presentations. I am surprised by how many times I find myself being asked, "You're from New Jersey? Are you sure? You don't have an accent!" I can't help but wryly smile at the implication: everyone from New Jersey sounds a certain way, and it's not like we sound around here. The basic generalization is made for countless assumed ethnicities: "You're from Africa? But you're not Black." "You're a nurse? But you're a man." "You're his mother? But you're so old." "You're a skier? But you're in a wheelchair." The assumptions and personal biases in a generalized view can also sometimes lead to comments that imply a clear devaluing. I have also been the recipient of comments like "You talk weird" when I have presented in areas that have a regional dialect or accent that is different than how I speak. I've received confused stares when people address my husband as "Doctor," and he tells them that it is his wife, in fact, who holds the title. I can see the confusion on their faces: "She's the doctor? But you're the man."

CULTURAL COMPETENCE, CULTURAL INTELLIGENCE, CROSS-CULTURAL COMMUNICATION

Cultural competence encompasses these other distinct yet related concepts. Being a culturally competent educator is about being capable of interacting in reciprocal ways with all kinds of people. It starts with being sensitive to how differently people think and communicate and being able to foster open dialogues with families and children. One's values, experiences, socialization, and personal history influence all facets of interpersonal communication and can vary widely among people. While cultural competence begins with being sensitive to differences among people, successful interaction with people from different cultures requires specific knowledge and skills. It requires commitment to engaging in a process of ongoing personal reflection and professional development that heavily involves learning interpersonal and communication skills (Papadopoulous, Tilki, & Ayling, 2008). As one researcher writes: "Knowledge about cultures (facts and cultural traits) + awareness (of yourself and others) + specific skills (behaviors) = **cultural intelligence**" (Peterson, 2004, p. 13). You can gain knowledge through reading and studying, but awareness and adopting culturally intelligent behaviors require active, genuine participation on your part. Becoming culturally intelligent, like teaching, is not a spectator sport!

The most important step we need to take toward becoming culturally intelligent and culturally responsive educators is to hone strong interpersonal and **cross-cultural communication** skills. Cross-cultural communication involves recognizing specific behavioral differences between cultures, such as eye contact, smiling, personal space, physical contact, gender expectations, problem solving, directness of speaking, and more, and using a communication style that is appropriate for the audience (Gonzalez-Mena, 2008; Peterson, 2004). In addition, teachers need to recognize the many different ways children communicate ideas, and they must provide multiple opportunities for children to understand and represent their ideas. In this **video**, the teacher engages diverse learners in exploring a story through many different formats. Ultimately, being skilled in cross-cultural communication reduces misunderstandings and ensures that children's and families' needs are met (Olavarria, Beaulac, Belanger, Young, & Aubry, 2009). Developing your knowledge of the differences in communication behaviors and styles, along with the skills to adapt your own style to reflect your audience, are interrelated strengths of the culturally intelligent practitioner (Liang & Zhang, 2009).

EQUALITY AND EQUITY

At points along the journey toward education and a society that values all its diverse people and groups, emphasis has been placed on seeing people's sameness and avoiding their differences. For many, acknowledging differences felt risky and potentially insulting. However, to view all people as always being the same, with the same background, resources, and needs, can leave specific needs unmet and actually perpetuate imbalance. **Equality** basically means being equal or the same. In the context of education and society, it means promoting equal access to services and institutions—that all individuals must have access to schools, facilities, and services, regardless of their race, gender, ethnicity, or ability. Struggles for equality—equal access—by marginalized, oppressed groups, such as people of color, women, and individuals with diverse abilities, have been raging in the United States socially, politically, and legally for many decades. Access to education is codified in United States law through the Individuals with Disabilities Education Act, which seeks to ensure equality for all U.S. citizens (NICHCY, 2012), and Title IX, which bans sex discrimination in school activities (including extracurricular). However, in educational practice, equality does not necessarily mean that every environment is suitable for meeting every individual's needs. It is also important that we don't use ideas about equality to try to erase individual differences or only seek to treat each person as the same in all situations. Individual people are different and have different needs.

Equity, in comparison, is about fairness. Fairness in education or societal settings focuses on recognizing differences and disparities and structuring environments and services to meet diverse individual needs. Fairness is not about an everyone-gets-the-same perspective, but rather about distributing resources so that everyone gets what they need. While these concepts might be complex, at a basic level, even young children can relate to how something feels when it is fair or unfair. Children are also capable of understanding how it feels to have a need that goes unmet and how it feels to have a need met, even if others aren't getting the exact same response.

For example, rotating children in order from a list to determine who gets to sit on the teacher's lap for story time is a system of equality where everyone gets the same when their turn comes. However, if Keishann's mother has been away for a couple of days and he is feeling extra vulnerable and in need of extra cuddles, to meet his needs the teacher might take Keishann on her lap during story time and engage all the children in realizing the fairness in meeting his needs. The teacher might say something like, "Keishann is dealing with something that the rest of us are not. He needs a lap turn today." Or consider how you might deal with a child who always arrives after the start of the program day, seems unfocused and distracted, and repeats that he is hungry. Snack time is over and it's going to be 2.5 hours until lunch. If you give this child a snack from your teacher cabinet, you worry that all the other children will want one too.

In classrooms as in communities, fairness is about understanding that, at different times, people might be dealing with situations, challenges, or needs that others are not currently facing. It is about realizing other perspectives, considering how someone else is feeling, understanding someone else's needs and strengths, and taking action to provide resources for that person. Even very young children are well capable of understanding concepts of fairness and being guided to apply those concepts to the classroom community. Take a moment to think about how children might think about this statement: "Equal isn't always fair." Consider the following scenes and determine an equitable response that is based on validating and meeting children's needs and that reflects equity and cultural competence.

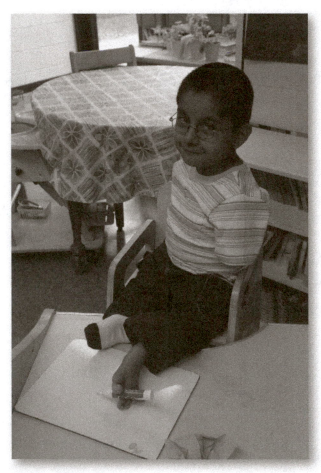

Children are well capable of understanding fairness and equity in their own ways and are particularly receptive to focused dialogues about fairness within the context of the classroom community.

ATTITUDE TO ACTION, BELIEF TO BEHAVIOR 1.2

Finding Fairness

Scene 1: Christos always has trouble sitting still at his desk during work time. He is fidgety and distracting. You realize that his body has extra energy he needs to get out, but you don't want him to be more of a distraction with a stress ball or yoga ball to sit on like your teaching colleague suggests.

Scene 2: James gravitates toward the basket of baby dolls and bottles every afternoon during choice time. He takes loving care of them—feeding, changing, and rocking. He sings them songs and sometimes reads books to them after he lays them in the crib. One day his older brother comes in to pick him up with his mom and teases him for being a sissy and playing with girls' toys. His mom tells you to encourage James to play with blocks or something more "appropriate" for him.

Scene 3: You and your two young children have just moved to a new town. Today is the children's first day of school (preschool and kindergarten). The bus picks up your older child, and you bring your preschooler to the center. When you walk in, you notice a large Christmas tree in the lobby, complete with elaborately wrapped gifts underneath. In the classroom are stockings with each child's name hanging along one wall and construction-paper Santa collages hung in the window. Your daughter looks confused and you feel your skin turn flushed. Your religious beliefs prohibit acknowledging any holidays. The teacher walks over and introduces himself and the class's Christmas theme for the week.

Scene 4: Xi-shu comes in to the classroom in the morning and appears to have bags under his eyes. At welcome center time he slumps on his carpet square, despite being asked to sit up like the other children. By the end of the circle time, he is laying down curled up on his square. He doesn't appear feverish or flushed, just very tired. It's almost time to go outside, but he just keeps asking for his cot and blanket.

SOCIAL JUSTICE (POWER, PRIVILEGE, PREJUDICE, OPPRESSION)

Social justice is also about fairness. It is a sociopolitical concept in democracy that relates to the equitable distribution of advantages, resources, and power (Gollnick & Chinn, 2009). Social justice acknowledges that a power and resource imbalance exists and requires that individuals actively strive to redistribute advantages to compensate for the imbalance. Implicit in the meaning of social justice is the expectation of developing multicultural knowledge and using that knowledge to create a more just world; it is about action (Banks, 2006). To understand social justice requires recognizing the breadth and depth of power and privilege as well as prejudice and oppression in the United States. **Prejudice** means having prejudgments about an individual from a particular cultural group that are not based on actual knowledge of the individual. Prejudice is usually negative opinions, assumptions, or feelings about a whole group of people based on incorrect generalizations, and it always has the potential to be hurtful. Theorists generally agree that negative prejudices are learned (Bergen, 2001). **Discrimination** occurs when prejudice drives negative action targeted at a particular group (Gollnick & Chinn, 2009).

It can be very difficult for individuals who have been raised within a culture of privilege to recognize their more powerful status and prejudiced beliefs. Being raised within the privileged dominant culture (middle-class, White, European, Christian, male), an individual then takes their culture for granted as the norm, and dominance is perpetuated for future generations. All cultural backgrounds that are not within the dominant culture are viewed with prejudice—as being inferior. **Oppression** occurs when prejudice and discrimination are encoded as institutionalized norms and used by a powerful group to dominate another (Sensoy & DiAngelo, 2009). Examples of oppression include different standards for acceptance into schools based on race, company policies which refuse benefits to certain families, different pay scales for men and women, or refusal to adjust school menus to include approved foods based on religious beliefs. Social justice is about actions people take—particularly people in the dominant culture—to reduce the disparities between privileged and oppressed people.

CULTURAL PLURALISM

From large urban cities through all kinds of suburbs to rolling hills and vast expanses of geographically dispersed rural communities, the population of the United States becomes increasingly diverse each year. For many communities and schools, numbers of non-White members are greater than White members, and researchers estimate that by the year 2050, the country's population will be equally "White alone, not Hispanic" and Black, Asian, Hispanic, and Other Races (non-White; U.S. Census Bureau, 2012). The term *minority* (meaning a percentage less than half), was once used freely to describe people of color. However, this no longer makes sense given the approaching numeric balance of White people and people of color in the United States. In a country founded as a democratic system and with such rich representation of diverse heritages, values, languages, histories, and lifestyles, the time has come to embrace cultural pluralism.

The word *plural* means multiple, or more than one. The definition of **pluralism** reflects this in its reference to multiple perspectives, cultures, or diverse people living within a shared social context yet retaining their uniqueness, identities, and diversity. More than simply coexisting though, cultural pluralism is really about a more equitable sharing of power and resources among all cultural groups without dominance, privilege, and superiority by one group (Gollnick & Chinn, 2009). A society that promotes cultural pluralism does not pressure individuals to give up personal cultural identity in order to obtain membership in a dominant culture (a process called **acculturation**; Banks, 2006). For example, distinct groups may form "communities within communities," where their unique ways of life (tradition, language, values) are preserved in contrast but in concert with different ways of life of the larger society. Neighborhoods like Little Italy, Chinatown, and some Indian nations are examples.

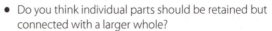

ATTITUDE TO ACTION, BELIEF TO BEHAVIOR 1.3

Metaphors of the United States

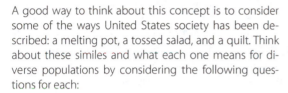

A good way to think about this concept is to consider some of the ways United States society has been described: a melting pot, a tossed salad, and a quilt. Think about these similes and what each one means for diverse populations by considering the following questions for each:

- Does each individual part (ingredient or piece) retain unique qualities while connecting with a larger whole?

- Do you think individual parts should be retained but connected with a larger whole?

- Do you believe that individuals should mesh seamlessly with larger society and blend into either one established way of life or blend together into a new version of the larger society (impacted and changed by the new members, a process called *assimilation*)?

- Create your own metaphor to describe the population of the United States.

MULTICULTURAL EDUCATION

"**Multicultural education** (ME) is an educational strategy in which students' cultures are used to develop effective classroom instruction and school environments. It supports and extends the concepts of culture, diversity, equity, social justice, and democracy into the school setting" (Gollnick & Chinn, 2009, p. 4). In essence, ME encompasses all of the core concepts summarized here. It is about recognizing differences, valuing them as strengths, and actively working to ensure all children are provided with equal, equitable, discrimination-free educational experiences. ME is about school reform and requires not just commitment from individual teachers but also curriculum, policies, and cohesive action across the span of educational institutions. ME must also engage all members of the school community (Banks, 2006).

Strategies to Build Cultural Competence

PART I: CROSS-CULTURAL COMMUNICATION SKILLS

Developing cross-cultural communication skills involves being aware of your initial reactions and becoming increasingly intentional in the ways you interact with children and families. To strengthen your cross-cultural communication skills, consider the following scenarios and quickly note what your initial response would be. It is so important to be honest in this initial response, even if it does not seem like the politically correct response. Being honest about your feelings, even if they are negative, is how you start to uncover biases that you can then choose to change in yourself. After noting your first reaction, consider an alternative way of responding to the situation. Think about taking on the other person's perspective or "walking in their shoes."

Scenario 1: Tyanna's mother approaches you at pick-up time and loudly complains that there is sand in Tyanna's hair. She demands to know how you could let this happen; she just got Tyanna's hair put in tiny braids the day before and it took hours. She raises her voice more as she points out that cleaning sand out of her daughter's braids and scalp is next to impossible and that sand is highly damaging to the hair.

Initial response	
Possible alternative	

Scenario 2: Ada's aunt is dropping her off today. Ada is out of diapers and wipes, and you have left a note for her parents on the sign-in/out book for three days. You stop the aunt at the classroom door to explain the diaper and wipe situation, but you quickly realize she does not speak English.

Initial response	
Possible alternative	

Scenario 3: Your principal stops by your room as you are tidying up and preparing for tomorrow. She tells you that a new student will be starting in your class next week. She says she doesn't know much about his school history, just that the mother and children are living in a shelter nearby. As she's leaving, she reminds you that state testing is in 2 months and she's expecting strong scores from all of your children.

Initial response	
Possible alternative	

Scenario 4: At your first open house of the school year, the father of twins Elianna and Jacob arrives. He is always the one who drops off and picks up, so you already know him. He mentions that his husband will be joining him soon but that he got stuck in traffic on the way from work. One of the other parents nearby looks up and stares when he overhears the comment.

Initial response	
Possible alternative	

Scenario 5: You have been preparing for a week to welcome a new child into your class. The child was born with severe club feet and, in addition to having endured a dozen surgeries, is currently in a cast and using a wheelchair. His doctors are not sure if he will walk normally, but his parents are optimistic. At circle time on his first day, you warmly introduce him to the class by saying "Class, we have a special new friend joining our class. Let's all welcome Justin!" To your surprise, Justin frowns, turns to you, and quietly says, "Please don't call me special."

Initial response	
Possible alternative	

Scenario 6: Parent conference night is beginning, and families are entering your room. You have planned some demonstrations of what classroom life is like for their 2nd graders and ask the families to sit in the children's seats, which have attached desks. Ishrat's father comes in after you have started your presentation and goes to Ishrat's seat/desk. He is a heavyset man and cannot fit into Ishrat's seat. He struggles for a moment, then pushes the desk a bit and loudly remarks "This is stupid! I'm not a kid anymore!" His face is flushed. Other families look at him and then at you.

Initial response	
Possible alternative	

PART II: TALKING THE TALK

Part of being a culturally responsive, respectful professional educator is to be thoughtful in the words you use to refer to people. The work we do as early childhood professionals, regardless of our title or capacity, is always about people first: the children and families with and for whom we work. The descriptions or labels that may be associated with them, legitimately or not, are secondary. To emphasize the person and validate our image of each person as valuable, we must adopt the use of *person-first* language that demonstrates valuing the individual as a human being first and using characteristics that describe them second (Gonzalez-Mena, 2008). In addition, I strongly advocate taking care to select the words we use to describe people from empowering options. For example, to call a child "a disabled girl" or "a special-needs boy" perpetuates a negative image both by assigning a label first but also by using a label indicating a deficiency. Using instead "a child with diverse abilities" focuses on a powerful image of this child and validates her strengths. Another example is to shift from referring to someone as "a low-income mother" or a "subsidy kid." Instead, we can use a phrase such as "family with limited income" or "family experiencing economic stress" when the family's income is an appropriate identifier, as in the case of qualification for certain programs.

Consider the following snapshots of classroom life during your first week of teaching, and discuss these scenarios with another student. Discuss the situations, being honest about your first reaction, biases, and what you think might be the challenges and opportunities of working with the children and families in these situations, taking on the role of co-teachers. Working together, discuss the people and situations and use positive, empowering, people-first descriptive language. Discuss what you think would happen next, both with staff and with children and families. Do not overlook the different characteristics of the people in these scenes, but rather focus on them in a way that values the diversity represented.

Scene 1: Eun Mi, 5, and her parents and maternal grandparents have just moved to Phoenix from South Korea. All of the family's English is slight, though Eun Mi's mother brings a family friend to translate for her when she comes in to talk. This afternoon at pick-up time, Eun Mi's mother came in to talk about Eun Mi's grandmother coming to the program with Eun Mi to support her transition to the center and new country.

Scene 2: Just after lunchtime in your toddler room, Rhadi becomes out of breath, hot, and nauseated. You are still learning the ropes of how to use his insulin pump-backpack system, so you call Rhadi's dad in to ensure that Rhadi is medicated properly and to test his insulin levels.

Scene 3: Kaitlyn comes in and hands you a note from her mother written on a piece of torn newspaper addressed to "K teachr." The note says, "No lunch today. got no food." You go to your director to talk about this, and he sighs and comments that this is one of the hard parts of accepting welfare-sponsored families. He tells you that he will work with the local food bank and also work on winter clothing in case Kaitlyn doesn't come in with a warm enough coat.

Scene 4: During group planning time, you ask the children what centers they want to play in. Karl says he wants to play at the water table. You mark him down on the chart. Karl wheels his walker over to the water table. Because he must stand behind the walker, he is unable to stretch over it and reach the water and cups. He looks down and goes over to the kitchen area instead.

Developing culturally sensitive ways of communicating is an essential aspect of being a professional educator. Choosing to talk about people carefully and thoughtfully is a start, but must be more than just lip service. The purpose is to let your words reflect your openness to human diversity and your commitment to viewing each person's uniqueness as a strength. It is much more than about trying to be politically correct; it is about a deeper commitment to actively try to empower each individual.

Summary

EXPLORING DIVERSITY

- Diversity is a complex concept that is defined in terms of individual and shared group characteristics.
- Diversity relates to how people are different from one another.
- Concepts of diversity are shaped by comparing others to our own cultural identity.

WHY STUDY DIVERSITY?

- Studying diversity is about exploring your own identity, sense of personal and family culture, values and beliefs, biases, and potential prejudices.
- The underlying purpose of becoming more knowledgeable about human diversity is to become skilled at communicating respectfully and effectively with people who are different than you in any number of ways.

BENEFITS OF STUDYING DIVERSITY

- Being open to and capable of working collaboratively with all kinds of people is essential in today's increasingly diverse world.
- Teacher education standards unanimously recognize the need for educators to have knowledge, skills, and dispositions that ensure their ability to work effectively with diverse families, children, and colleagues.
- Being more culturally competent increases the likelihood that teachers will have more positive influence and ensure more positive outcomes for all children.

DEFINING DIVERSITY AND IMPORTANT RELATED TERMS

- Diversity is about the many forms of differences between people, which include a long list of potential attributes and characteristics with which people may identify themselves or be identified by.
- Diversity is often connected to concepts of culture, which is about shared knowledge, beliefs, and behaviors that are passed along from one generation to the next.
- Culture can refer to everything in our daily lives and social environment that shapes our ideas about lifestyle, self, and group expectations.
- Cultural competence or cultural intelligence results from becoming knowledgeable about the variety of human cultures, being aware of your own and others' culture, and honing behaviors and skills which promote open communication.
- A key element of today's multicultural education practice is that it is about recognizing and valuing differences, actively working to promote equity and social justice, and is a curriculum- and school-wide effort.

STRATEGIES TO BUILD CULTURAL COMPETENCE

- Developing cross-cultural communication skills involves being aware of your initial reactions and becoming increasingly intentional in the ways you interact with children and families.
- Person-first language demonstrates valuing the individual as a human being first and secondarily uses characteristics to describe the individual.
- Culturally competent language is an important part of being a professional educator.

Chapter Learning Outcomes: Self-Assessment

Use this space to reflect on how well you have achieved the learning goals for this chapter in terms of evaluating your own competency in the topics below.

List three to five key concepts that you have learned from the chapter.

Explore the purpose of studying diversity.	
Identify key concepts in the study of diversity.	
Define *diversity* and related terms, including *culture, identity, ethnicity, cultural competence, equity, social justice,* and more.	
Practice strategies to build cultural competence through classroom scenario analysis.	

Chapter Activities

DISCUSSION QUESTIONS

1. Some people feel that creating inclusive, multicultural educational environments is a misuse of funds and requires too much time and effort that takes away from children's learning. How would you respond to this concern?

2. Many teachers wonder how to authentically integrate explorations of diversity into programs in which there is a seemingly overwhelming similarity among the children and their families. How would you explore this issue with colleagues?

SELF-REFLECTION

1. How are you feeling about your own abilities as a culturally intelligent professional? Imagine yourself in the various practical scenarios described in this chapter. Were there moments that you felt prepared or unprepared to face?

2. Assess your beliefs and practices using the self-inventories at the EdChange website (www.edchange.org), and complete the four self-assessment multicultural awareness quizzes

linked from the Projects tab. Bring a copy of your completed quizzes to discuss in class. These artifacts are a good addition to your teaching portfolio.

TEACHING DISPOSITION

Students are sometimes confused when it comes to identifying diversity. Many students only think about race or skin color as being representative of diverse cultures. It is important that students recognize and appreciate the many ways each individual brings diversity to the classroom, as well as the ways we share characteristics of diversity. Working individually, list the following aspects of your personal background:

- Three things you remember about family traditions in your home (daily or occasional traditions)
- The way holidays were/are celebrated in your family; which holidays were celebrated in your family
- The family members who were a part of your daily life (parents, siblings, stepfamilies, extended families, guardians)
- Where your parents, grandparents, and great-grandparents were born and raised (if they know)
- The places you have lived throughout your life
- The places you have visited or traveled to

- The languages you have been exposed to at home, school, on vacations, or at friends' houses
- Whether (yes or no) you have ever received a scholarship, grant, or funding assistance
- Three attributes you would use to describe yourself in broad terms (such as race or ethnicity)
- Three qualities you would use to describe yourself as a unique person (appearance, personality, family background, strengths, skills, hobbies)

In class: Divide into groups and discuss the items on your list that you are comfortable sharing. Talk about how your lives (your lists) are similar or different from one student to the next. Select three things that were different on your lists, and identify ways these differences enhance the classroom experience. Or form groups and select from the bulleted list a few items that are related. Then first interview each class member and gather their answers and create a visual representation of the class's answers. For example, create a large country or world map to plot out all the places classmates have lived and/or traveled to. Or create a pie chart of the percentage of students who have been recipients of funding assistance.

IN THE FIELD

Contact a local school district administrator and ask if you can interview one of the district's foreign language teachers. Or locate a foreign language teacher at an area college. Ask for her thoughts on and experiences with people who represent diverse cultures and languages. Ask her how she presents diverse cultures to her students and what suggestions she has for educators working with young children on promoting knowledge about diversity. Write a paper summarizing your interview, including an introduction paragraph where you describe the teacher's background, a section to paraphrase the interview responses, and a summary section where you reflect on the teacher's responses in terms of your own beliefs, experiences, and what you have read in this chapter.

Weblinks

EdChange: Professional development, research, and resources for diversity, multiculturalism, and cultural competence. *www.edchange.org*

National Association for the Education of Young Children: A professional association supporting early childhood professional policy and practice, including advocacy, professional development, frameworks for high-quality practice, and guiding publications. *www.naeyc.org*

Teaching Tolerance: According to the website: "A place to find thought-provoking news, conversation and support for those who care about diversity, equal opportunity and respect for differences in schools." *www.tolerance.org*

2

The Development *of* Cultural Identity

Understanding the definition of *culture* as any of the values, beliefs, and facets of identity that influence our lives is just the beginning. To be a skilled and successful culturally competent professional, you must understand the theoretical approaches researchers use to study culture, as well as theories about the development of individual and shared cultural identity.

Children's family and community members have a strong influence on their attitudes, beliefs, and cultural identity.

"Cultural identity is the feeling of 'belonging together' experienced by a group of people. It embodies the sentiments an individual feels of belonging to, or being influenced by, a group or culture" (Nsamenang, 2008, p. 18). Knowing the basic approaches to studying culture and having more knowledge of distinctive cultures themselves enables you to understand others' perspectives—to walk a mile in their shoes. To help you understand and respect diverse perspectives, it is helpful to understand how cultural identity develops in childhood and understand the forces that shape identity, bias, stereotyping, and prejudice throughout life. This exploration also engages you in critical, ongoing self-reflection of your own dynamic cultural identity and how it has been shaped and changed throughout your life. These are the essential tasks in the development of your "ability to work effectively across cultures in a way that acknowledges and respects the culture of the person being served"; in other words, the development of your cultural competence (Hanley, 1999, p. 9).

Frameworks and Illustrations for Understanding Culture

Anthropologists are social scientists who study humanity. **Ethnographic research** is an important process for understanding diverse perspectives, values, customs, traditions, and identities. It involves immersed observations (integrating into a group to make close, direct observations), direct interviews, and it can involve the researchers living within the community of individuals being studied. This form of research is intense and especially powerful for providing a window into the lives of indigenous people living in remote geographic areas, though it is also effective for studying other settings, such as organization culture and interactions.

In addition, key insights can be gleaned from survey research, which involves gathering and analyzing statistical data from target groups of people (Kottak & Kozaitis, 2008).

Sociologists, psychologists, and educators also work in people-oriented settings. Many of the key concepts that currently shape multicultural education theory and practice draw on the important work of these social scientists.

In the realm of current research, several models of culture can provide useful visual imagery to convey the dynamic scope of what *culture* means in a practical sense. Three useful and interrelated conceptual frameworks of culture include

- Big C and little c
- Culture as a tree
- Culture as an iceberg

- Explore the frameworks for illustrating cultural identity
- Identify experiences which have influenced the development of your personal cultural identity
- Explain the highlights of development
- Compare theories of how culture influences development
- Incorporate culturally inclusive strategies into practice

The key concept to understand through the exploration of these frameworks is that individuals and groups exist within cultural identities which tend to have obvious (easily seen) *and* hidden (under the surface) components. The emphasis on this dual layer perspective seeks to validate the complex and deeply rooted nature of cultural identities.

In all intercultural contacts (which is all human interaction, really) are characteristics of an individual's culture that you are aware of when you first meet someone. The characteristics you think you observe might include behavior, race, socioeconomic status, age, or gender, although often assumptions based on initial impressions are inaccurate. Regardless of what you observe, the majority of the factors influencing that person's way of thinking and communicating are not "written on her face." Most often these unobserved factors will have the biggest impact on that person's perception, communication, and understanding. In a learning environment this means that children's learning, development, and thinking will be most heavily influenced by nonobservable cultural factors. Culture involves the complex, socially created rules and ways of life that permeate groups of people, but it also involves the many beliefs, values, and attributes that shape individual identity and behavior. Operating within this complexity of culture are two themes that researchers have described as *big C culture* and *little c culture*.

BIG C AND LITTLE c CULTURE

In the description of big C and little c culture, a distinction is made between grand themes that are historical, political, or masterpieces of the arts (which tend to reflect historical sociopolitical currents) and minor themes that involve aspects of daily life and the ways people perceive and operate in their sociocultural contexts (Bennett, 2011; Petersen, 2004). Big C elements are considered "objective culture," and include architectural design, national-level politics, current legal trends, classical art works, and formal societal values. These elements are often widely recognized and accepted and are regarded with high esteem. Sometimes big C culture is considered highbrow or upper-class by people who think of museums, symphonies, classical literature, or other fine arts (Orlova, 2003). These works of fine art are part of the shared communication of societal values that are actively passed down to future generations in order to convey history and values. While big C culture provides important artifacts of humanity and a specific society's history, focusing on master works that are often defined by dominant or higher status members excludes all other members and overlooks the importance of more "common" aspects of daily life.

It is in these everyday moments that individual, family, and community norms, values, and expectations are revealed and shared. These cultural processes, the "personal" side of culture, are referred to as *little c culture*, in contrast to *big C culture* (Orlova, 2003, p. 180). Little c (or subjective) culture comprises more commonplace aspects such as norms of

ATTITUDE TO ACTION, BELIEF TO BEHAVIOR 2.1

Reflecting on Your Own Little c

Think about the implicit or nonverbal messages that your family life conveyed to you as you grew up and what little c messages you are currently living. Jot down some notes or lists of parenting expectations, peer norms, personal and family traditions, and customs that are part of everyday experiences. Use the following as a start, but feel free to add any other aspects of your daily life that come to mind.

When you have made notes on these more intimate aspects of your values, life goals, and preferences, share them with a classmate or colleague. Compare differences and similarities in your responses and take a moment to connect while sharing a part of your personal background.

What are your favorite meals?	
How do you spend free time?	
How you relax and "recharge"?	
What commitments do you balance? (Work? School? Children? Faith? Volunteering?)	
What personal and professional goals did your family have for you ?	
What personal and professional goals do you have for yourself?	
How do you define marriage both personally and legally?	
If you have children, what hopes do you have for them?	
What three core values do you live by?	
Other	

communication, popular opinion, casual clothing, typical foods and mealtime norms, dialects, and non-verbally conveyed assumptions (Bennett, 2011). Little c culture can be seen in the typical events in homes, such as dinner time routines and favorite food choices, in parenting expectations and behaviors, in popular fads and trends, or in messages within families, schools, and peer networks.

This terminology implies a hierarchy of importance that has been reflected in the value placed on the big C aspects of culture. However, in many practical settings such as schools and health care institutions, the little c aspects of individuals' and communities' lives are far more essential for professionals to understand and respect. A subtle but important distinction to recognize is that big C aspects are highly recognizable and overtly taught while little c aspects are more intimate and ingrained in daily life.

To focus on big C culture assumes that culture is something special to learn about—but not necessarily part of everyone's daily life (Edwards & Farghaly, 2006). It is essential for educators to be knowledgeable about the impact of big C culture but even more familiar with each family's little c culture—the norms of daily life—in order to sensitively and effectively create communities within classrooms and programs. Only when classrooms are more connected to children's familiar routines of daily life is it possible for teachers to facilitate authentic, meaningful learning. These commonplace habits and moments of life also provide the richest window for school–family integration.

CULTURE AS A TREE

Using the image of *culture as a tree* to explain that there are seen and unseen aspects of cultural identity can be useful because the tree is a universally recognizable image. This analogy uses the main parts of the tree to explain distinct aspects of cultural identity:

- Highly visible array of leaves
- Sturdy but flexible branches
- Strong and visible trunk at the center or core
- Unseen roots running deep and wide below the surface

The key ideas in the tree analogy are that there may be many different and distinct visible elements (above ground) that have varying degrees of importance for the individual, as well as the unseen root system which can be vast and highly influential. The concept that the unseen roots are extremely important to the strength of the whole tree is easily understood by most people (Peterson, 2004).

As individuals begin to explore and learn about culture, identity, biases, and the impact of prejudice, a simple tree outline is particularly useful to guide self-reflection. In the top third of the tree (the leafy canopy), write down the aspects of your own identity that are visible and obvious to people who either just meet you or don't know you too well. This might include skin color, sex, general age range, and primary language. In the trunk section, note the aspects of your cultural identity which become apparent to people who you interact with but might not be especially close to. These are important facets that you keep a bit more reserved, like economic status, education (which might also be part of your unseen root system), family makeup, religious beliefs, dialect or additional languages, relationship status, and gender identity. The roots of your image are those deeply held values, beliefs, ideals, goals, and hopes that are extremely important to you but that only people close to you really understand and know about you. Aspects in your root system might include gender expectations, spirituality, family values, life goals, satisfaction with career, beliefs about justice and fairness, moral code, and more. Consider varying the depth or width of your tree roots based on

IN MY FAMILY

Big C Culture

"One thing I always remember about my mother was that she was very worldly and insisted on exposing us to culture" begins Amanni one day as we discuss what culture means to us in an early childhood education class. Amanni stresses the word *culture* in her statement, indicating with her tone of voice that this was a word with a capital "C" and one that referred to important things. When asked what she meant by that, what kinds of experiences was she exposed to in the name of "Culture" with a big C, Amanni spends the next 15 minutes regaling the class with stories from her upbringing.

She lived with her family of four (mom, dad, brother, and herself) in a city suburb her whole young life until she went off to college. Her parents were both well-educated and professionals in the nearby city, self-employed as classical musicians. They were both moderately successful and instilled in the children a belief that "the classics" in the arts are highly valued. "My mom, especially, did not embrace so-called 'pop culture'" Amanni continues. "I remember many times that she scoffed at certain kinds of music, and definitely hated any sound of a dialect or non-standard English. I think to her it sounded uneducated. I definitely knew early on that education and refinement were norms to aspire to. We went to as many theaters, museums, and performances as we could afford. I guess for me classical arts—I mean, like masterpieces of arts—are what I was raised to think of when I hear [the word] Culture. I never thought of my peer group growing up and our 'uniform' of jeans and pocket-Ts with color-coded socks and penny loafers as culture. Nor did I ever think about Friday pizza, soda, and movie night as culture. I guess I'm realizing that there's more to it than dressing up nice and going to performances in the city. I drew my culture, like my influences, as a flower, but I also think there is a lot of who I am that would be in the roots under the ground." (See Figure 2.1.)

importance or influence in your life. Considering all of the levels within your personal tree graphic, imagine what a distorted view someone would have of you if they made assumptions based solely on your "leaves." Now think about times you have been the one making assumptions.

CULTURE AS AN ICEBERG

The view of culture as having highly visible aspects as well as a large unseen component is well illustrated using the metaphor of *culture as an iceberg* (Weaver, 1986). Most people understand that the tip of an iceberg represents only a small part of the actual total mass of the iceberg, and that the majority of the mass is not visible. You probably also recognize that the unseen section is a huge part of the overall mass and is an essential element in understanding the whole. This metaphor for imbalance, with its emphasis on the massive unseen parts of an iceberg, is an even better visualization for culture than the metaphor of the tree, where the roots are present but not as oversized compared to the visible elements. Weaver points out that people "are often concerned with mastering information about . . . external aspects when, in fact, the most important part of culture is internal and hidden. To this extent, culture is like an iceberg" (Weaver, 1986, p. 133).

FIGURE 2.1 *Amanni's Drawing of the Influences in Her Life*

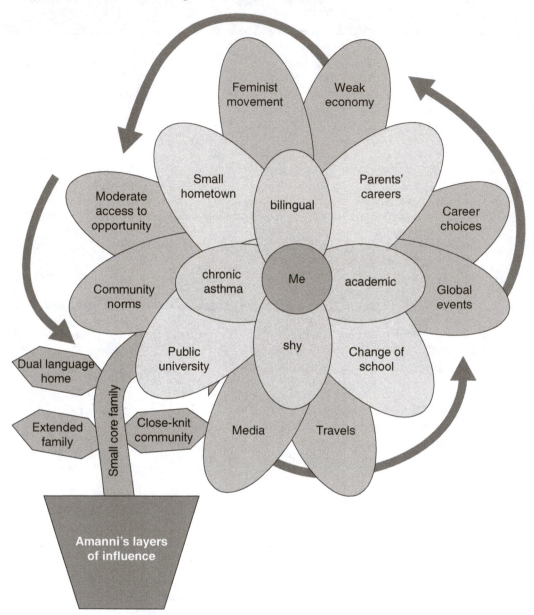

In the culture-as-iceberg diagram, external culture is described as encompassing behavior and objective knowledge. These are the norms that are explicitly taught and learned and are a part of spoken and written expectations and actions. As such, these elements are visible, overtly promoted as illustrations of certain groups; they also change through group action.

An example of this might be the expectation in a Jewish family that at 13 years old, boys and girls go through the coming-into-adulthood tradition of the Bar or Bat Mitzvah.

"But just as nine tenths of an iceberg is out of sight below the water, . . . nine tenths of a culture is also 'hidden' from view" (Hanley, 1999, p. 10). The elements under the surface, called internal or deep culture, include more personal beliefs, values, and thoughts. Because these are the norms that are learned implicitly and are not explicitly taught, it takes careful observation and real listening to learn them. Considering that "deep culture includes elements such

Visualizing an iceberg is useful when thinking about the relationship between seen and unseen aspects of a person's cultural identity and influences.

as the definition of sin, concept of justice, work ethic, eye behavior . . . approaches to problem solving . . . and approach to interpersonal relationships" (Hanley, 1999, p. 10), we can see how influential deep culture is. How parents interact with you, what they expect you to do with their children, and how children respond to you are all heavily influenced by that vast unseen culture of unspoken beliefs and values. Imagine a teacher of infants who warmly tells a parent at pick-up time about the lovely quiet time the baby and she shared as she rocked the infant to sleep and held him for a long time thereafter, singing softly. The teacher is caught off guard by the parent's anger and exasperated tone when the parent scolds her saying, "We're trying hard to teach Riley to be independent and sleep on his own and you're making things much harder for me!" The teacher feels upset because she believes autonomy develops in other ways in toddlerhood and she is distraught to think of leaving the infant alone to cry to sleep. The teacher and the parent have different views on the development of independence and the role of a caregiver. These views and beliefs are part of their deeper culture and values, the part of their culture that is only learned through building a more intimate relationship. Without this awareness of the under-the-surface culture, this parent and teacher are potentially headed for conflict.

A useful lesson that emerges from using the iceberg analogy is understanding the potential for a perilous crash that can result from not recognizing the importance of the unseen mass. Being able to understand a person's unseen culture is essential in navigating the sometimes tricky waters of intercultural collaborations. The key message of Weaver's research is that

ATTITUDE TO ACTION, BELIEF TO BEHAVIOR 2.2

Your Above and Below

Thinking about the similar aspects of the above–the-surface and below-the-surface frameworks of culture described previously, take a moment to map out your own layers of culture. How would you finish the statement: "Culture is like a _____"? Think about the aspects of your cultural identity that you feel are visible to people who meet you for the first time or who do not know you very well. Think about the aspects that are known only to people who know you better. Your lists aren't about what things you think are more or less important but about characteristics of yourself that you think are obvious and those that take getting to know. You may have to add reflective notes about things you think people will *assume* about you early on and those things they may learn more accurately by getting to know you. Consider the following, as well as any other aspects that you think of, and make notes about how these relate to the seen/unseen concept as it applies to you:

	Explicitly observable (seen)	Not directly observable (unseen)
Race		
Sex		
Gender identity		
Geographic origin		
Socioeconomic status		
Education		
Religious beliefs		
Parenting style		
Political beliefs		
Age		
Native language		
Extended family nationality		
Ambition		
Career goals and satisfaction		

Looking at these aspects of yourself, can you begin to trace the development of your cultural identity that has emerged over your lifetime? Which aspects are especially important to your personal cultural identity?

the necessary ingredient in being able to develop meaningful awareness of others begins with a focus on one's self. As with the "us–them" images many people conjure when reading the word *ethnic*, most people think of culture as belonging to other people. Our first task in becoming more culturally competent is to become more fully aware of our own culture and how it shapes our beliefs and behavior. This provides the essential platform for being able to recognize and value diversity.

Big Impact of Little c: Development of Self-Identity

"Developing positive identities touches on some fundamental questions facing every young child: 'Who am I?', 'Is it OK to be who I am?' and 'What is my place in this world?' Answering these questions is crucial to every child's well-being" (Vandenbroeck, 2008(a), p. 26). Children internalize the expectations and norms of their unique cultural context through a variety of messages. Families are a key part of children's learning process and are especially valuable partners for teachers, as this **video** explains.

Exploring how children's identities develop involves delving into sometimes uncomfortable concepts. Using terms like *power, prejudice, outcast,* and *exclusion* when talking about young children's behavior and attitudes can be difficult and feel at odds with the view of how a nurturing, loving adult sees children. A major goal of this book is to take you on an inward journey to better know yourself and an outward journey to better understand others. Moments in this exploration might be revealing, surprising, or uncomfortable, but above all, the overarching message is to realize the depth and incredible complexity of how cultural identity develops in childhood. We can't underestimate the subtlety or complexity of children's thinking, feelings, and behavior. Looking critically at how children develop prejudice and power hierarchies is a prime example of this surprising complexity and shows just how much more is really going on in children's sociocultural development than we might ever have thought. Think about what you believe or have learned about children's development, and make notes, with examples, on the following questions:

- When do children begin to understand differences in
  - boys and girls?
  - skin color?
  - physical attributes and diverse abilities?
  - family income level?
  - attractiveness?
- When do children start treating people differently based on perceived gender?
- How do children treat people differently based on perceived gender, skin color, attractiveness, or physical abilities?
- When do children demonstrate discriminatory behaviors?
- When do classroom cliques, social "power players," and outcasts emerge?

Theories of development provide a basis for beginning to answer these questions. While each child develops in his or her own particular time and in differing ways, basic trends of typical development contribute to children's emerging identity and culture. In addition to the meshing of universality and diversity, development is also impacted by the complement of biological drives and cultural influences (McDevitt & Ormrod, 2010).

A key element of cultural identity is that it is taught and learned (Kottak & Kozaitis, 2008), though it also reflects the emergence of innate traits. Biological processes that occur throughout infancy and childhood contribute to a child's knowledge of himself as well as his ideas about others. Paired with naturally unfolding cognitive and socioemotional development are the highly influential sociocultural, environmental cues that are present in each person's life. Early childhood professionals need to have a solid understanding of how typical developmental processes normally occur and are guided by interactions within a child's world. This section reviews normal stages of cognitive and socioemotional development, with emphasis on how identity, awareness of differences, and prejudices develop. Two key theoretical frameworks for the sociocultural influences shaping children's perceptions are also explored: Bronfenbrenner's bioecological model and Vygotsky's sociocultural theory.

Cognitive and Socioemotional Development

Sometimes messages about the values, beliefs, and behaviors that shape cultural identity are conveyed intentionally, but at other times messages are shared unintentionally. This is especially true when infants learn expectations and norms through observation. The process of learning one's culture, called **enculturation**, is internalized through social interactions and particularly by watching and mimicking the people in one's surroundings (Gollnick & Chin, 2009). This process begins in infancy.

HIGHLIGHTS OF INFANT DEVELOPMENT

From birth, infants are sensitive to the reactions and emotions of the caregiver adults in their lives. Before 12 months, infants engage in **social referencing**, where they will specifically look at a parent or caregiver for cues and direction on how to respond to unfamiliar situations (McDevitt & Ormrod, 2010). Infants are also already able to notice differences like skin tone and facial features that look familiar or unfamiliar and show preference for the familiar (York, 2003). So, when faced with someone who looks different than what she is familiar with, a baby will look at her parent's face and body language to "read" the parent's feeling about the new person. The infant's behavior will reflect what she has read in her parent's face, body, or voice. The parent's reaction can also ultimately become part of the infant's beliefs, values, and behavior. When parent reactions convey discomfort, disdain, or fear, infants internalize these feelings and values. Serving an important protective purpose in the case of real danger, social referencing can also instill prejudicial attitudes early in life.

Throughout the first year, an infant goes through a process of developing her sense of herself as an individual separate from her parent. With this beginning sense of individual identity, the older infant/young toddler begins to make decisions and realize her own wants, but she also feels strongly the need for belonging or identification with a group, community, or family (Derman-Sparks, 1989). This very basic need for belonging is a major driving force for ingraining family norms and expectations, which sets the stage for developing biases (identification with and preference for the familiar). This need for belonging is also what shapes later preschool classroom power hierarchies, cliques, and exclusivity. A child's need to feel a valued part of a group can prompt her to reject and exclude others to gain favor with peers she looks up to (Gallas, 1998). And the same drive in the excluded child can make that rejection especially painful. This need for belonging is a human need which continues throughout life.

HIGHLIGHTS OF TODDLER DEVELOPMENT

In their second year, young toddlers already notice differences in appearance (such as skin color, clothing, glasses), mobility, and speech/language, and they respond with curiosity or uncertainty (Derman-Sparks, 1989). They will point to people who look different and show preference for pictures, people, and dolls that look familiar. By later toddlerhood, children begin to ask questions like, "Why is that person's skin so dark?" or "How come that girl is in that funny chair?" or make comments like, "That man is so fat," or "You talk funny."

Once in a hotel breakfast room, I was at the counter getting my then 3-year-old some cereal. Behind me I heard him say "How come you only have one leg?" and turned to see him standing in front of a man with one leg and a crutch and looking up at the man with genuine interest and inquisitiveness. I barely had time to register the moment when the man answered openly and simply, "Because my leg was sick and the doctor removed it. Now I walk around with this [crutch]." My son paused, then said "Oh. I see," and went to our table to eat his cereal. I thanked the man for sharing and was about to apologize, but he quickly replied that he was always glad when kids just asked about it instead of shying away in fear or being shushed and pulled away by a parent. This kind stranger took advantage of a natural teaching moment for my son, who learned that differences, in this case physical differences, are a naturally occurring part of our lives and nothing to be feared or embarrassed about.

This is also the time when young children begin to show a preference for playing with dolls or pictures that are light-skinned when given a choice between light- and dark-skinned. Of particular concern is research evidence indicating that Black children show this preference for

Toy for a Girl or Boy?

A few months ago I was dropping my son (then 20 months old) off at his family child care provider's home for the afternoon, and the other small group of mixed-age children was already busily engaged in building a large town with blocks. My son has been smitten with horses for a long time (we lived among a ranching community at the time), and he was delighted with the little pink pony he had received with a fast food meal the day before. I did have to pause when I ordered his children's meal and the young man behind the counter asked me "For a girl or boy?" I looked at the options and replied "A horse please." The man looked mildly irritated and softly said "A *girl* toy then," to himself as he punched in our order.

Since my son wasn't in earshot to hear the presumptuous question, I didn't really think about it until this moment dropping him off at child care. As he ran into the emerging block village, he began to "gallop" his pink pony around. A 3-year-old boy he routinely plays with happily greeted my son but stopped abruptly upon seeing the pink pony. He looked at me, confused, and asked "Why does Greisan have that *girl's toy*? That's for *girls*!" He emphasized the word *girls* with genuine confusion, as though this moment was violating his understanding of the rules of toys. I replied that my son loves horses, all kinds of horses, and that a color didn't make it only for girls or boys. This little boy also liked to play with the more realistic brown, tan, and black horses, so I asked if he'd like to bring out a few more horses so they all could be corralled together. He was off and back to playing before I even finished my invitation. It was just a passing, quick exchange, the kind that could easily be overlooked by most adults. But it made me realize all too vividly how clearly and how early messages of stereotype, bias, and exclusivity are conveyed to children and from a variety of sources.

That day I realized two very overt sources of biased messages acting on my son's life: the fast food counter and his toddler friend. And the message of

A toddler's curiosity about the world emerges naturally and genuinely, but biases can develop quickly when children are exposed to stereotyping messages.

acceptable behavior for boys and girls was stated clearly and reinforced: pink ponies are for girls, and challenging this gender expectation is not appreciated. Messages like this can create insecurity and lead children to question their choices and preferences. What are the sources and messages of bias, social boundaries, expectations, or tolerance and intolerance that you notice in your community? What are the implications of these messages on children's development?

Source		Message
Implication		
Source		Message
Implication		
Source		Message
Implication		
Source		Message
Implication		

white-skinned dolls and choose white dolls when asked to select the "nice ones" or the "nice color ones" (Bergner, 2009). The preference for light skin is an internalized bias that comes from racist societal messages of preference, value, prejudice, and discrimination.

In addition, by this age toddlers show bias in expectations of gender behavior—things that are OK for boys to do but not girls, and things that are OK for girls to do but not boys. Many teachers report hearing children say things like, "Boys can't be the mommy to the doll," or "You can't wear the dress, you're a boy!" or "Only boys are allowed to be the fireman," or "Dolls are for sissies." In a more subtle way that most teachers don't often even acknowledge, young children are also becoming aware of and prejudiced against others who appear less wealthy. When asked why they might not be playing with a certain child, children have responded with comments like "Because his clothes are old and dirty," or "He smells bad." Can this be an indication of racism, classism, and sexism by 3 years old? Sadly, yes.

HIGHLIGHTS OF DEVELOPMENT IN PRESCHOOL THROUGH EARLY ELEMENTARY

In the preschool and early elementary years, 4- to 8-year-olds are astute at recognizing observable characteristics and will describe themselves in these terms as well. (Observable characteristics can include skin, hair, and eye color; sex; height and weight; clothing; and diverse abilities.) While this capacity to categorize helps children identify themselves as individuals and can be neutral observation, it can also lead to prejudice when combined with messages from the child's environment. If adults are not keenly tuned in to signs of children's thinking process about differences and prepared to address prejudice and guide children to valuing diversity, children's prejudice continues to grow. By the time children enter school, they have already internalized complex cultural views on themselves and others, which can be both strengthened and challenged in the school years.

Diverse values, beliefs, and traditions are explored through informal and formal experiences, like this class visit and discussion at a local American Indian museum.

Children are not necessarily able to clearly talk about their beliefs, values, and attitudes about diversity. It is up to the adults in their lives to learn how to observe carefully, listen intently, and engage children in experiences in order to guide reflection and discussion. Equally essential in children's lives is the importance of knowing our own values, beliefs, and behaviors about diversity. Our values, often deeply held, influence our behaviors, perceptions of certain children, expectations of children or families, and how we interact with children and families. This influence can exhibit in subtle ways, such as encouraging girls to be less physically active, disciplining Black boys for aggressive behavior more quickly than White children, or inviting non-English speaking families into the classroom less often than English speaking families.

Children internalize subtle cues more than many people realize and at an earlier age than many people think. But it doesn't all just come from parents. The following two sections highlight perspectives on the multiple influences in children's lives, with an emphasis on the cultural context of children's development.

Influences on Development

Most people readily recognize that caregiver parents typically have a great deal of influence on their infants and children through overt messages as well as subtle cues and messages (things children observe parents doing or saying). But many different sources of influence act in dynamic, bidirectional, and fluid ways. Understanding the nature of these systems of influences and the ways they interact in children's and families' lives will help you better meet the needs of diverse children.

BIOECOLOGICAL MODEL

Urie Bronfenbrenner is known for developing the **bioecological model** of human development. The innovative elements of his view include an expanded perspective of the many "layers of influences" in children's lives beyond the immediate family and his view of the bidirectional nature of influences (Bronfenbrenner, 1979). His was one of the first theoretical frameworks to recognize that children themselves have an influence on their environment and the people in it—not just that they are being influenced. By positioning children in an active and influential role, Bronfenbrenner envisioned a perspective that empowers and validates children's role within the family and society.

The following is an example I use to illustrate the concept that children have an impact on their world: Think about one of the common concerns for families who are house-hunting. Many families will ask for information about area schools, or select certain communities based on school district reports, area recreation opportunities for families, or how many other families live in the area. In essence, having children guides many parents when choosing an area to live. Having children or planning to have children also guides many adults when choosing a job. Family-friendly policies such as health care benefits, family leave, flexible scheduling, and more liberal personal leave can factor heavily into a parent's or prospective parent's job search.

Another important part of Bronfenbrenner's theory is that he described detailed structure within the systems, organizing influential/influenced forces into an immediate **microsystem** and an extended **macrosystem**. The child's microsystem, or inside layers, includes the stronger and closer relationships that have a greater degree of influence—and that are more influenced by children—such as immediate family, child care, friends, faith settings, and schools. In these settings children learn and share the majority of the values, expectations, socially acceptable or taboo norms, and early perspectives on their world; this is the unique cultural context of their early life. Moving outward from the core are other influential/influenced aspects such as media, health care, extended family, and family friends. The outer macrosystem encompasses the more ancillary layers in the child's world, including political structures (local, regional, national), parental workplace policies, and social and welfare services (Bronfenbrenner, 1992). Another example of the way in which children influence even these ancillary layers is to consider the legislation and political involvement around educational issues and expectations. Issues related to the health and welfare of children remain at the forefront of presidential and legislative debates and demonstrate the growing influence children hold in society. In turn, the results of these political agendas influence children's welfare and status within society.

SOCIOCULTURAL THEORY

The sociocultural theory of development, shaped by the work of the Russian psychologist Lev Vygotsky, has become increasingly influential in early childhood settings for its emphasis on the interrelationships of children and the cultures they are raised in. Vygotsky recognized that human cognitive development is more than just a biological process that unfolds in a routine manner.

Rather, sociocultural theory states that children who are raised in different societies or environments with different human influences will develop differently. Vygotsky wrote prolifically about the ways that a child's development is initially influenced by the relationships between close people in his life in an external process. As a child observes and imitates adult models, his behavior and beliefs are shaped and reinforced by his interactions with the people around him. Within these interrelationships, adults (including teachers and parents) shape the child's learning through mediated exchanges and guidance, which Vygotsky called **scaffolding**. This same process is used by teachers in formal learning settings. Later, the older child's developmental process becomes an internal one, revisiting socially shaped beliefs through his inner reflections (Kozulin, Gindis, Ageyev, & Miller, 2003).

Vygotsky's writings on the relationship between cognitive development and language are particularly relevant to understanding how cultural identity develops. Two key concepts emerge here: First, as a young child's concept formation moves toward abstraction, she becomes able to categorize things in her world based on attributes (characteristics). Second, "once a child has associated a word with an object, he readily applies it to a new object that impresses him as similar in some way to the first" (Vygotsky, 1962, p. 78). So even as toddlers, young children notice and think about specific differences of attributes and make generalizations about how all things with similar attributes will be the same. This is the same kind of thinking process that can lead to over-generalizations or stereotypes: for example, thinking that all furry animals are doggies because the child has a puppy at home, or people who drive taxis don't speak English because the child has taken a few rides with nonnative English-speaking drivers. Sociocultural perspectives emphasize the depth and complexities in children's cultural development.

An interesting implication of these developmental perspectives is to recognize that no child is "raised in a vacuum," meaning that development unfolds on many diverse paths, based on the child and environment. Knowledge about differences in development based on parenting and socialization in diverse communities is relatively new. It is essential to realize that the older foundations of early childhood education, which have been the basis for developmentally based practice, have roots in White, Western, dominant norms of child-rearing

Positive everyday experiences with friends and families promote development of positive beliefs and values.

and socialization. The work of early developmental theorists (Piaget, Gesell, Hall) primarily emerged out of Europe and the United States and was based on observations of middle-class White children. So while we have learned a great deal from these theorists, the landscape of today's communities requires that we embrace more global perspectives. As our classrooms, families, and communities continue to become more diverse, we must broaden our theory base to include a larger knowledge base that is more reflective of all our children.

CLASSROOM STORY CORNER

Kaoru's Dried Fish Snacks

In my first year of teaching kindergarten, I was so excited to have a Japanese child in my class. Her father had moved the family to our town for a new job. Mom and the little girl didn't speak very much English. I was fortunate to have learned some Japanese from my own grandparents, who still lived in Japan. The little girl's name was Kaoru and she was understandably shy at first, but observant and interested in learning all about how things worked in our classroom. She quickly picked up new words and I was so pleased with how involved her parents were with me.

One afternoon the children were sitting in their table groups eating lunch while I was at my desk preparing for an afternoon project. I heard some giggling and low talking from one table but that wasn't unusual for our social lunchtimes. Then I overheard one child say, "Eww, gross! You're so weird!" followed by laughing and other children repeating "Eww!" I immediately looked up and saw Kaoru looking down at her table, face flushed and red. I quickly came over, knelt down, and asked the children what was going on. Kaoru abruptly got up and went to the bathroom down the hall. Several children sitting next to Kaoru pointed to the little bag of tiny, dried, whole silvery fish she had brought with her lunch and remarked that, "She eats the grossest things." Kaoru's mom delighted in packing beautiful, traditional foods for Kaoru's lunch, including fish, rice, meats, and vegetables which were not recognizable to other children in the class. Kaoru was a master with her chopsticks too, which the children thought was actually pretty neat.

Today, however, these children had really hurt Kaoru's feelings and had demonstrated for me how little I had done to create a classroom community that recognized and valued differences. That moment really stays with me. That tiny bag of dried fish snacks sparked an ongoing change in my class and my teaching. I thought I was pretty open to family diversity, but I realized I had not done enough to engender respect and support for differences among my children. In essence, I had focused only on my attitudes and behaviors towards diversity, but had not done my job as far as the children's attitudes, knowledge, and behavior went. I had grossly underestimated how much children notice differences and how negative their reactions can be.

Over the coming months we spent a lot of time exploring our own differences and similarities, finding many things that, at first, the children found strange about each other. We gradually replaced words like *weird* and *strange* with comments like "Oh, that's new to me," and "I've never tried that." I saw my children become eager to find things about themselves, their families, and each other that were different and to really celebrate those things. I loved seeing them take pride in the characteristics of their family traditions that brought something new to our group. They just beamed when their show-and-tell items generated comments like, "Ooh! That's new!" from the other children. I learned a lot that year about how capable young children are at understanding concepts of fairness, cultural appreciation, and social justice. As adults we just have to be willing to validate their capabilities and engage them in the journey. It has to extend beyond just ourselves!

THE DEVELOPMENT OF PREJUDICE OR APPRECIATION

Understanding how young children learn culture is an important start to recognizing the processes through which bias and prejudiced attitudes develop. Processes of normal cognitive development are part of the picture. Beginning within the first few months of life, infants start to develop mental categories, such as gender and skin tone, based on attributes of people. Throughout the earliest years, children develop the ability to categorize people using a growing array of attributes that they associate closely with their own attributes (Bergen, 2001). As children recognize visible differences, they also compare what they notice in others to what they know about themselves, or their identity conception. This recognition turns into children's concept of "people like me" and "people different than me." While simply acknowledging difference can be a neutral cognitive action through the learned messages that surround children, this recognition can quickly become a negative comparison. In other words, noticing that, "Ooh, that person's face looks different than my mama's," can turn into, "Why is that person's skin so dark (or pale)?" or "Eww, that person's skin looks funny (or ugly)." As we know from theories of development, especially those of constructivist theorists like Piaget and Vygotsky, children actively build their concepts, ideas, beliefs, and values through direct experiences that they act on with their own internal cognitive process.

However, as sociocultural theories affirm, maturing cognitive development is one influence, though not the primary contributor to how a child's prejudiced attitudes form. The majority of children's values, biases, and identity conception develops through observation and modeling of everyday experiences of the adults in the child's life (Ball & Simpkins, 2004). Essentially, children have the *capacity* to recognize difference, but adults and society are teaching children negative beliefs, attitudes, and behaviors or not teaching them how to overcome these messages and become culturally competent individuals. And these lessons are happening often without adults even realizing it. Think about how messages are conveyed to children as you listen to this **video**.

Valuing Culture in the Classroom

For many teachers, the goal of integrating multiple cultural elements into the classroom is a high priority. While their intentions may be well meant, many teachers also struggle with identifying appropriate and useful strategies for creating a respectful and culturally responsive learning environment and experience. One of the obstacles even the most well-meaning teachers might face is a lack of knowledge about different cultures, which might make teachers feel insecure about including diversity in the environment and curriculum (York, 2003). A common place for teachers to start is with what is called "the one-shot traveler approach," which focuses on celebrating heroes (famous people) and holidays in a "celebratory subject approach to diversity" (Hyun, 2007, p. 262). In this approach, teachers use culture-specific celebrations like Cinco de Mayo or Chinese New Year to introduce the concept of nationality diversity to children. Teachers may also spotlight racial diversity by highlighting single historic figures like Dr. Martin Luther King, Jr. to represent all Black Americans, or targeting certain months or planned lesson units to focus on Women's History or Native Americans.

On the surface these efforts might seem like a way to introduce children to diverse people and traditions. However, spotlighting either a certain group or a specific celebratory holiday can actually send a message of "other-ness" which can further distance children instead of develop their understanding and appreciation. In addition,

> tokenism . . . involves treating the 'culture' of a child's home life as fixed and static. In practice this means that special, yet stereotypical, events or displays are set up for children and families (such as festival celebrating Iraqi New Year with traditional clothing and food). Such activities risk being both patronizing and stigmatizing, in that they overlook the complexities of children's personal histories and family cultures and ignore socioeconomic and other differences. (Vandenbroeck, 2008(b), p. 28)

The focus is on the big C, or above the surface facets of human experiences, without acknowledging the more vast and personally relevant little c or hidden culture. A tourist approach to exploring diversity rests on the surface, also not delving deeper into the more complex, sometimes unsettling classroom issues of power, prejudice, or disdain. Nor does it emphasize the dual, entwined elements of sameness and differences that are a part of the true human experience.

CREATING PLURALISTIC CLASSROOM COMMUNITIES: STRATEGIES

So what can teachers do to create a more pluralistic, culturally relevant classroom community? "An important way to avoid these pitfalls is to build real and symbolic bridges between the public culture of the early childhood centre and the private cultures of families, by negotiating all practices with the families involved" (Vandenbroeck, 2008(b), p. 28). Think about the imagery of building a bridge: in order for it to

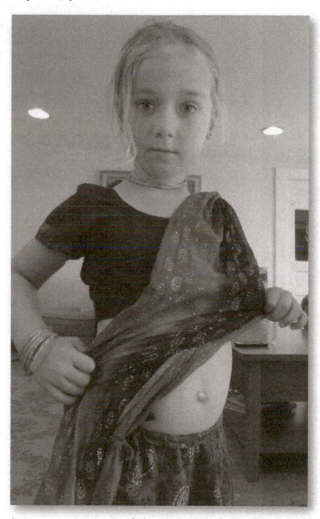

Incorporate a variety of play materials that reflect diversity for children to explore and enjoy.

be functional and strong, a bridge requires a strong foundation on either side of the span. One foundation is you or the classroom, and the other is the child's family and home life. They need to be equally balanced, represented, and present in the relationship in order for the bridge to span the distance and support travel. The beginning of the journey starts with you and the work you are doing in this book to raise your awareness of your own culture and the diversity among the people around you.

Environment and Materials

Environmental design has a powerful impact on all of us, but the messages that environments convey have greatest impact on young children who are not as adept at processing their surroundings in critical ways. Culturally sensitive practice can include simple accommodations such as intentional seating arrangement or calling on children in specific order, as described in this **video** about Dual Language Learners. When professionals commit to culturally competent practice, they take time to know each child and family and carefully plan environments and interactions which support all children's strengths and needs.

Because of this sensitivity, intentionally and respectfully designed spaces have the potential to emphasize that cultural pluralism is valued. Teachers should integrate visual images and authentic artifacts which reflect the diversity of the children in relevant ways. An important starting point is with the rich and varied lives of the children in the class, which, in turn, requires getting to know their home and family life. Focus on the *little c* aspects of children's daily lives by engaging children and families in an exploration of:

- The ways they spend their time
- Who their family members are
- What their neighborhood looks, sounds, and feels like
- Who their friends are and what they do together
- Places they go around town
- Things they like to eat at home
- Music, stories, and the ways family and friends play

Consider including materials that focus on daily life, such as photos, artwork, weavings, tools, and literature; add these materials in integrated ways, with authenticity and not insulting caricatures:

- Add a sari and dhoti into the dramatic play area, with photos of Sasha's Indian relatives wearing the clothing and engaging in everyday activities; integrate with discussions, stories, and visits from individuals familiar with India and Indian lifestyles.
- Use a simple tortilla press in the dough/art center along with rolling pins, a pasta press, and bread pans with colorful recipe cards made from photos found online. Explore with children the unique ways that bread-like foods are prepared in homes around the community and

world. Focus on the message: "We all eat bread-like food, it just looks different in different people's homes." Bring in Ada, the teacher from down the hall, so that she can demonstrate how her mother taught her to make tortillas.

- Add authentic, diverse, empty food containers with print in multiple languages, such as packages of Udon noodles, beans, kosher crackers, and the like.

- Fill a basket with different textiles, including Alpaca wool—popular in Peruvian clothing; silk—from an Indian Sari; cotton; boiled wool—used in many European countries; hand-tanned leather; beadwork found in both Native American traditions and African nations; weavings; fur; quilts; and more. Research with children the reasons for the different types of materials, how the materials are used, their historical and traditional importance; re-focus children on the materials/textiles used in their own homes and lives (clothing, bedding, tableware, etc.).

- Create a display of assistive devices used by people with diverse communication abilities: for example sign language cards, Braille books, type and speak machine, amplifiers or hearing aids, and picture boards. Invite a local speech language pathologist to share experiences and facilitate children's exploration of the resources.

Differences in family life	Implications for environmental design
Young children are held more of the time.	Provide baby carriers, ensure that space for napping is not separate.
Children have roles in caretaking and housekeeping.	Provide opportunities for children to visit siblings during the day; provide home-like centers with simple authentic tasks of home life.
Some children live with one parent, a guardian, two same-sex parents, in foster care, in a shelter, or with extended family.	Replace labels like "parent board" and "parent night" with a more inclusive "family" label; begin letters with "Dear Families," and so on.
Interdependence is stressed as a family value or goal for child.	Consider family-style meals with children grouped to eat together; centers for slightly larger groups; mediated conflict resolution center.
Self-sufficiency and independence are stressed as a family value or goal for the child.	Create more independent small group centers; make materials accessible for self-serve; add a conflict resolution table; encourage child to eat and use the bathroom more independently.
Child care is preparation for school.	Arrange space as one large open room; take a more prominent role in directing activities; focus activities on learning goals.
Child care is an extension of home, or is a "home away from home."	Arrange space in smaller, intimate nooks and areas; focus activities on tasks of daily life; ensure children socialize together.

In your environmental design, consider changing more than just materials or displays. Think about the cultural differences in how children are raised and the implications for how space, materials, and interactions can be designed to reflect family differences.

Children's Play

Children's social play is not only their primary venue for their learning but also an ideal setting for exploring beliefs they have internalized about roles, social rules, processing internal conflicts, and practicing expression of self-identity. "Shared pretend play is an important resource for developing emotional and moral qualities of friendship and allows children to experiment with a range of social roles and identities. As children participate in role-play they acquire a sense of themselves as future adults and future citizens, as well as experiencing an enhanced sense of their identity as children" (Danby, 2008, p. 36). There is no more powerful tool to assess children's development concepts than observing children at play.

In children's social play, particularly sociodramatic play, careful observers will find an open window into children's identity development and growing prejudices and biases. It is here that adults can hear revealing comments such as "That's a toy for boys," or "A family can't have two daddies," or "You can't be one of the horses because you can't walk," or "All Mexicans wash dishes, so you have to be the dishwasher in our restaurant." These are prime moments for teachers to calmly integrate into children's play and guide the scenes towards a more open-minded framework. These are opportunities to:

- Engage children in new play which can replace prejudiced or exclusionary language (for example, "you can't . . ." or "all Mexicans . . .") with more respectful and reciprocal dialogues ("In real restaurants all kinds of people have each job. How about if we each take a turn being the chef, the customer, the server, and the kitchen staff?").

- Provide support for more empowering self-identity concepts ("I brought in this magazine about people who build buildings, called contractors. There are pictures and articles about men and women who do this work and use these tools. See how these aren't just tools for boys?").

- Offer suggestions for new ways to value and integrate each other's unique culture into play ("Katie's dad is a caterer and he showed Katie how to make fresh bread last weekend. Katie's going to show us how they kneaded and shaped it when we get the clay out today.").

- Expand children's play scenarios with prompts, cues, questions, or specific ideas ("What kinds of things could Rhakim and Samuel (the two daddies) do in our dinnertime play?" "What if Sienna (in a wheelchair) is the lead horse and we follow her in two lines like a sled team?").

- Take on a role in children's play scenarios instead of observing from afar; use cues and prompts to guide children's play in more inclusive directions.

Summary

FRAMEWORKS AND ILLUSTRATIONS FOR UNDERSTANDING CULTURE

- Social scientists use research methods that are people-oriented, such as surveys and ethnographic research.
- There are observable and unseen aspects of human culture, both of which influence personal identity, bias, and prejudice.

BIG C AND LITTLE c CULTURE

- Big C culture refers to formal or grand themes that are historical, political, or master works of art.
- Little c culture refers to the minor themes that involve aspects of daily life.
- Little c aspects are the most influential on a person's thinking and behavior.
- Examples of little c culture include typical events in homes such as dinner routines and favorite foods; parenting expectations; popular fads; messages within families; schools; and communities.

CULTURE AS A TREE

- The leafy canopy can represent the most visible components of individual identity, such as skin color, sex, or primary language.
- The trunk represents visible but slightly more intimate elements such as economic status, family style, relationship status, or religious beliefs.
- The unseen root system contains the most intimate values and norms that are not apparent at first sight, but rather take time to discover; these include spirituality, morality, or gender expectations.

CULTURE AS AN ICEBERG

- While we can learn about someone from noting observable characteristics, the most important elements are hidden from view and require formation of a deeper relationship.
- Failing to carefully consider the deep culture can lead to conflict and prevent reciprocal relationships and interactions.

COGNITIVE AND SOCIOEMOTIONAL DEVELOPMENT

- Cultural identity is taught and learned; it is also impacted by unfolding maturation and development.
- Enculturation is the process through which culture is learned and internalized, impacted especially by watching and mimicking people in our environment.
- Within the first few months, infants are already capable of noticing differences in physical features.
- Throughout toddlerhood and the preschool years, as children's awareness of their own features and attributes emerges, they will notice and ask questions about differences, initially with neutral curiosity.
- Bias and prejudices develop when a child learns from overt or subtle messages in her environment to dislike or be fearful of differences.
- It is important for adults to address children's questions and prejudices with honest answers and the clear message that differences are important and valued.

INFLUENCES ON DEVELOPMENT

- Bronfenbrenner theorized that children are influenced by the many aspects of the environment within which they are raised and that they also influence family life, community structures, and political systems.
- Vygotsky contributed to the growing research base within the larger constructivist theory framework, which focused on the unique

cultural aspects in children's lives and the impact that different cultural environments have on different children.

- Children's early capacity to notice differences, then to categorize attributes based on comparisons to their self-identity (*like me* and *different than me*), can lead to negative attitudes towards people who are different.
- Adults might teach negative beliefs and not be aware of the negative attitudes and prejudices developing in children.
- Teachers must become sensitive, careful observers of and listeners to children and families in order to identify negative attitudes early.

power and prejudice and develop positive attitudes towards diversity.

- Teachers should avoid tourist-style subject spotlights in favor of explorations which focus on commonalities and differences in everyday life experiences.
- Explorations of diversity should begin with the lives of the children in the class and integrate authentic elements of the surrounding community.
- Teachers must become knowledgeable about and sensitive to negative stereotypes or token efforts and instead explore the rich and complex layers of children's and families' lives.

VALUING CULTURE IN THE CLASSROOM

- Many teachers lack the knowledge and confidence to appropriately and meaningfully create learning experiences that address

Chapter Learning Outcomes: Self-Assessment

Use this space to reflect on how well you have achieved the learning goals for this chapter by evaluating your own competency in the topics below. List three to five things that describe key concepts you have learned from the chapter.

Explore frameworks for illustrating cultural identity.	
Identify experiences that have influenced the development of your personal cultural identity.	
Explain the highlights of development.	
Compare theories of how culture influences development.	
Incorporate culturally inclusive strategies into practice.	

Chapter Activities

DISCUSSION QUESTIONS

1. Collect a wide variety of popular magazines or access their pages online. What biases do you notice in the images? For example, among different magazines do you notice over- or underrepresentation of women, people of color, individuals with diverse abilities, families in economic stress, or multiple languages? What messages might be perceived through the examples of overrepresentation or underrepresentation that you noticed?

2. Map out the systems of influence in your life using Bronfenbrenner's bioecological model as a guide. Consider the complexities of the

sociocultural context of your life. Share your influences, and discuss differences and similarities within a small group.

SELF-REFLECTION

Using the prompts throughout this chapter, create your own analogy of what you think culture is like and draw a corresponding model. Create your own visual illustration of what your culture means to you and how you want people to get to know the seen and unseen aspects of your personal culture.

TEACHING DISPOSITION

Go to the NAEYC website, to the resources/position statements link, and download the statement entitled "Responding to Linguistic and Cultural Diversity" Using this and any other relevant resources you have access to, create a card file or personal book of at least 20

specific strategies for learning about and integrating all children's little c experiences into the classroom throughout the day, throughout the year. Also create 10 ideas of how to integrate your own everyday life experiences. Your personal culture is important in the classroom too! This artifact is a good addition to your teaching portfolio.

IN THE FIELD

Go to your school or local library and collect at least three magazines, including a travel or adventure-related source (such as *National Geographic*); a parenting magazine; and a fashion magazine. Browse the images and article titles for content which reflects human diversity. Make a note of the frequency (Prevalent? A fair amount? Scarce?) of the following characteristics and reflect on the appropriateness of the content (authentic, stereotypical, big C or little c):

Characteristic of Diversity	Frequency	Appropriateness (What is the content/message? Is it empowering?)
Skin tone		
Body type		
Sex		
Gender		
Diverse abilities		
Nationality		

Weblinks

Anti-Defamation League: The Anti-Defamation League (ADL) fights anti-Semitism and all forms of bigotry in the United States and abroad through information, education, legislation, and advocacy. *www.adl.org*

Bernard van Leer Foundation: Grant-making programs support innovative ways to improve

opportunities for young children from families with limited resources. Free publications for practitioners and policy makers shape the debate about early childhood. *www.bernardvanleer.org*

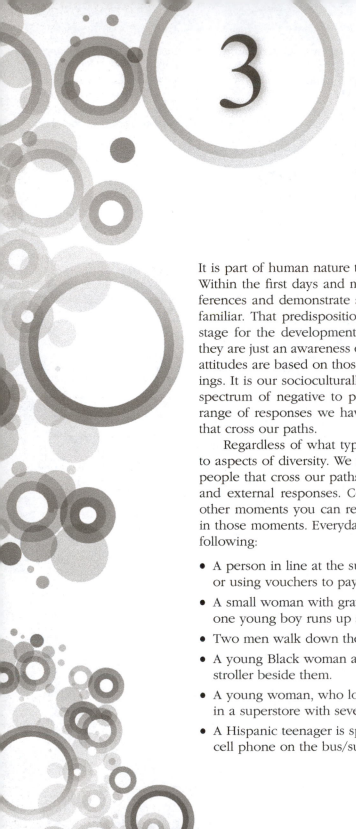

3

The Spectrum *of* Responses *to* Diversity

It is part of human nature to become acclimated to things that are familiar. Within the first days and months of life, infants are able to determine differences and demonstrate awareness of and preference for things that are familiar. That predisposition to prefer things that we are used to sets the stage for the development of biases. Biases are not necessarily negative, they are just an awareness of and comfort with the familiar. Our actions and attitudes are based on those biases and are shaped by our social surroundings. It is our socioculturally shaped actions that can fall within a range or spectrum of negative to positive responses. "The spectrum" refers to the range of responses we have to various experiences with human diversity that cross our paths.

Regardless of what type of community we live in, we all are exposed to aspects of diversity. We may not always recognize the differences in the people that cross our paths nor are we always really aware of our internal and external responses. Consider the following scenarios as well as any other moments you can recall from your week and the reactions you had in those moments. Everyday experiences with diversity might look like the following:

- A person in line at the supermarket is counting out a big bag of change or using vouchers to pay for groceries.
- A small woman with gray hair is watching children at the park slide and one young boy runs up and says "Mommy, can I have a drink?"
- Two men walk down the street holding hands.
- A young Black woman and a Cambodian man sit on a bench with a stroller beside them.
- A young woman, who looks like she's barely past her teens, is shopping in a superstore with seven children.
- A Hispanic teenager is speaking Spanish and laughing loudly on her cell phone on the bus/subway seat next to you.

- A long-haired woman with tattoos across her neck and on her hands is maneuvering down the sidewalk in a wheelchair, with an infant in a sling carrier cradled in her lap.

- You place your order at a fast food speaker box, and the voice giving you your total speaks with a foreign accent—you aren't sure you understood how much you owe.

- As you settle into your seat on the crowded bus (or airplane), you notice a very heavyset person coming down the aisle towards the open seat next to you.

- It's your two-year-old toddler's first day of child care, and as you bring her into her new room, you are greeted by a tall, older man who introduces himself as her teacher.

- A woman in a draping dress and a head scarf that covers her face walks just behind a tawny-skinned bearded man.

- Looking up from your menu at a popular area restaurant, you abruptly notice that your waiter has a large scar on his face, a misshapen upper lip, and unusual tooth alignment (a repaired cleft palate).

Imagine yourself in these scenarios and make an honest assessment of your internal response. Consider the following questions and use them to prompt genuine self-reflection and discussion among colleagues.

- What was the first thing you thought of? What thoughts popped immediately into your head as you read the scenarios?

- As you imagine yourself in these scenes, what would you be doing?

- Have you had similar or other experiences?

- What did you think in the moment of those other experiences?

- What did you do?

What is the Spectrum? The Ugly, the Bad, and the Good

Reponses may be internal and appear as subconscious reactions or overt beliefs and values that are part of our thinking process. Internal responses are the thoughts that immediately pop into our heads when we become aware of something in our space. The trigger for our responses can be many things. It might be a face-to-face encounter, such as those listed above—a strong smell when passing by a restaurant, an advertisement, a movie, a comment made in conversation, or something we read. This internal response can drive our actions even if we don't realize it. Many times our responses are positive: a smile, perking up with interest, or feeling drawn to

LEARNING OUTCOMES
....

- Identify ways people tend to respond to diversity

- Trace the spectrum of positive and negative responses to diversity

- Reflect on personal values, biases, and potential for prejudice

- Explore teaching strategies to promote positive responses to diversity

Engaging with people from different backgrounds creates the opportunity to embrace differences and value diversity.

a person or experience. A semi-subconscious negative response might be a frown or an expression of disgust; a slight turn away; a roll of your eyes; a tensing of your body; or locking your car door. Many people do these things almost instinctually, and without even realizing it, when faced with something they feel is unpleasant or unfamiliar. These responses are a way either to avoid that unpleasant something or to communicate dislike.

External responses include behaviors that usually reflect our values and beliefs. Our external responses are not necessarily accurate reflections of our internal responses—but they can be. Many people are not fully aware of their responses to obvious diversity and are thus not always aware of their behaviors. A response might seem slight, like those mentioned above, or it might be more obvious and purposeful, such as making a negative or derogatory comment, stating an opinion like "That's not right!" or even committing aggressive or violent acts. An action that is prompted by prejudice is called *discrimination* and is designed to degrade, hurt, humiliate, or exert power over others. Discrimination (including name-calling, exclusion, or hate crimes) falls at the extreme negative end of the spectrum of responses. While the majority of responses might not necessarily be intentionally negative, the resulting impact on individuals can still be hurtful. Consider the personal reactions of Mariana as she describes being treated as less important because of her cultural background in this **video**.

At the opposite end are positive, inclusive actions that are prompted by genuine appreciation and valuing of human differences and an effort to promote equity for all people. The entire spectrum is represented below from most negative to most positive (Figure 3.1). A variety of teaching strategies for responding in affirmative ways and fostering positive responses in children are presented in the section following the spectrum definitions.

FIGURE 3.1

Summary of the Spectrum of Responses to Diversity

Discrimina-tion	Ethnocen-trism	Prejudice	Colorblind-ness or Mini-malization	Awareness	Acceptance	Valuing
Actions, poli-cies, or prac-tices which negatively impact cer-tain people or groups; stemming from negative attitudes.	Believing that one's own race or cul-tural group is superior to all others.	Assumptions about a cer-tain group; negative atti-tudes or feel-ings towards a certain group.	Ignoring differences among peo-ple; focusing on "we're all the same" and avoiding ways people differ.	Recognition of differences in appear-ance, values, economic status, or power, which may or may not prompt discomfort.	Recognizing differences and respond-ing neutrally to engaging together.	Seeking out individu-als who are different; believing differences enhance life. Taking action to demonstrate appreciation for human differences, minimize marginaliza-tion, and pro-mote social justice.

DISCRIMINATION

When extremely negative attitudes or feelings incite a person to take action against individuals who are assumed to belong to a certain group, those actions or negative practices/policies rise to the level of **discrimination**. The degree of negative action can certainly vary, but the impact remains degrading and hurtful and is intended to exert power over and subordinate others. Discrimination can range in form from verbal to physical. Verbal discrimination can include talking about target groups, avoidance, or name calling. Physical responses can take the form of rejecting others, destroy-ing property, battery, or even killing and large-scale genocide (York, 2003). Examples of violent discrimination stemming from racial and cultural supremacy values include:

- Ethnic slurs ("dirty Jew," "sand nigger," "dot head," "Jesus freak," "ghetto rat," "trailer trash," etc.)

- Policies or laws which exclude people based on presumed group affiliation (for example, limiting acceptance based on race or gender; refusing to offer benefits to same-gender spouse/partner; forced kidnapping and slavery of Africans)
- The Nazi Holocaust in Europe from 1938–1945 (the killing of 6 million Jewish people with intent to exterminate all Jews)
- The genocide in Rwanda, Africa, in 1994 (mass killing of a reported 800,000 members of the Tutsi tribe by the ethnic majority Hutu tribe)
- Policies and practices, from the 1500s through the 1900s, to remove indigenous people/Native Americans (by mass killing, forced relocations, and abducting children to indoctrinate them into White European culture)

Discrimination can be perpetuated by individuals and also by groups in organized government or group-sanctioned programs. The underlying motivation remains the same and is based on negative attitudes and assumptions based on group classification.

ETHNOCENTRISM

Individuals engaging in **ethnocentrism** believe that their own race, nationality, or heritage is superior to that of others (Koppelman, 2011). There is a perhaps subtle difference between ethnocentrism and prejudice: ethnocentric-focused people do not necessarily hold strongly negative feelings towards a specific target group. Rather, their perspective is negative or dismissive of all groups that differ from their own—rather like having tunnel vision. The ethnocentric person can be highly unaware or ignorant of others' lifestyles or cultures, sometimes by choice—refusing to acknowledge any other culture and ascribing higher status and power to their own group. Their focus is solely on themself and the group with whom they identify; their feeling is that "our way is the right way, the only way!"

Ethnocentrism is about power and oppression, and gaining or maintaining power and supremacy and using it to hold all "outsiders" or "others" in a lower status. Sometimes individuals with a robust sense of patriotism can tread into exclusion and dominance in the name of "love of country." No doubt many of us have heard an individual proclaim loudly and proudly that "This is America! This is how we do things here. If you don't like it, get out!" Such a challenge is often used to assert English as the only language, or when objections are made to pledging allegiance to the flag. But ethnocentrism can also include many other customs or traditions. Knowledge and appreciation of United States history, customs, and traditions is an important part of life here, but dismissal and exclusion of individuals from foreign nations or of United States citizens with diverse family customs and traditions promotes supremacy and violates individual rights. This behavior is not the same as minimizing differences in an effort to focus on sameness or connectedness.

PREJUDICE AND BIGOTRY

Individuals responding at this level have developed assumptions, which are not based on accurate information, about people who they perceive as belonging to a certain group or groups. **Prejudice** involves categorizing a person into a certain group, based on observed characteristics or inaccurate assumptions. These assumptions provide an excuse for not actually learning about the person and provide a perceived rationale for negative attitudes. Prejudice is closely connected to *bigotry*, which is a more extreme negative attitude or hatred of people in a certain group (Koppelman, 2011). Because of their extremely negative feelings for and classification of "those people" (regardless of any knowledge of the specific person they are referring to), bigoted people are at risk of engaging in negative actions (discrimination). An individual might, however, be prejudiced or bigoted and not express those feelings with outward action. Identifying prejudice in children can sometimes be hard for teachers. Adults working with children and families must take time to explore children's underlying beliefs and attitudes when children express negative thoughts about others, even if those attitudes might not seem based on group categorization at first.

COLORBLINDNESS OR MINIMALIZATION

In a potentially well-meaning effort, people sometimes choose to focus entirely on the universality of humanness and to minimize the differences among people (Koppelman, 2011). Choosing **colorblindness** often comes from a desire to appear unbiased and unprejudiced (Apfelbaum, Sommers, & Norton, 2008). An important point, however, is that *choosing* to ignore skin color and cultural diversity can, in turn, lead to ignoring the differential experiences of people with diverse cultural backgrounds (Gordon, 2005). On the surface this can seem like a way to form connections among diverse people. You might have heard comments such as "we are all the same on the inside" or "I don't notice skin color"—all offered in an effort to focus on connectedness and to minimize divisive attitudes about differences. Sometimes people choose to take a colorblind perspective because it feels safer, either politically, socially, or intellectually. It might also feel like an easier way to address a sensitive topic that might be laden with guilt. By taking a colorblind stance, we might feel as though we can sweep aside the history of oppression which looms across our past in the optimistic (albeit oversimplified) belief that the racist past is not perpetuated in current reality (Gordon, 2005).

Certainly validating similarities among people can foster a sense of connection and community and is an important aspect of inclusive multicultural education (Gomez, 1991). But a focus solely on similarities serves to devalue individual and diverse group culture (de Freitas & McAuley, 2008) and denies both the obvious differences among people and the different realities lived by people of color (Derman-Sparks & Ramsey, 2006). The simple truth is that, though all people share similarities, we are not all the same.

Scratching Out Color

I finally made it—my own class! Well, for seven weeks anyway, for my student teaching. I felt like I was totally ready for my first-grade placement. The school was a small, rural school and well-known for being the best in the area. But on Thursday of my first week I had a moment that left me at a loss and sent me right back to my professor's office.

I had just handed out worksheets that my cooperating teacher had left for me and was circulating around the room to observe how the kids were doing. I stopped over one boy's desk and watched him for a couple of moments. Around the edge of the page there were cartoon-type drawings of kids of different skin shades. I noticed he was scratching out the kids' faces with his pencil—just scribbling back and forth over the faces really intently. But when I looked more closely I saw that he was only scratching out the faces that were shaded, not the white ones. He was very deliberately scribbling over any face that wasn't white. I was caught off guard and thought to myself that he couldn't realize what he was doing or be doing it deliberately. Could there be racism in first grade?

I knelt down next to him and asked him what he was doing. He paused, looking down at his paper, and said "I don't know." I felt like there was more to this than just an 'I don't know'; he was clearly deliberate in which faces he scratched out. I asked him why he had just scratched out some faces and not the others. This time he didn't reply, just looked at his paper without showing any emotions. I let the issue go for the moment. But as soon as school was out I went to my professor and asked for advice.

We talked about the demographics of the class and how there was only one child who was non-White in the class. My professor told me that prejudice and bias could certainly be ingrained by first grade—sooner even—and that I might very well be seeing manifestations of racist attitudes. But she did encourage me to observe more

closely over the coming week and to use these observations as a starting point for building in antibias learning experiences into the curriculum.

Over the coming days I observed more carefully, and I can't believe how much I was missing before. I had always just assumed that prejudice and racism were

Sharing a common experience (such as losing a tooth) with the class for show-and-tell helped all the children see common connections instead of just differences.

"adult" attitudes, but I started to see clear indications that these children were already adopting ideas and values that were exclusionary and hurtful. For example, the only child of color, an American Indian/Native American whose family recently moved off the nearby reservation, was less involved in the class activities than the rest of the children. She was almost never invited to join others and was sometimes outright ignored when she initiated participation. I heard comments like "You're dark; you don't fit in this play," and "You're not allowed here," accompanied by a physical blocking of her from an area of the classroom. I also noticed children saying "You're not from around here" and "You don't belong here" on other occasions to other children. This is a pretty conservative rural area where we live, and I know a lot of locals don't like people visiting or moving here from other places. By watching more closely, I realized that children were learning those messages and acting on them just as aggressively as adults were.

At first I felt powerless, overwhelmed, and unsure where to start to address the discrimination and begin building a community with these children. My professor and I went back to a video we had seen in one of our classes. In it, a kindergarten class had done a study of skin tones by mixing paint colors together in various combinations to create a spectrum of shades of brown. Through the talking, mixing, and blending of a drop of this color and a squirt of that color the children had discovered that no one was White, no one was Black, and that everyone was just a little bit of a different shade of browns and peaches. I borrowed two books on colors of skin (*The Colors of Us* by Karen Katz and *All the Colors of the Earth* by Sheila Hamanaka), a bunch of paints (I chose the multicultural skin tone set), and brought a bunch of little mixing cups and brushes to class. I partnered with the art teacher and math teacher at school to integrate learning about color blending and proportions. As a team we were able to weave the learning unit across the curriculum and spend more time with the children on exploring their feelings about self, differences, inclusion, fairness, and community.

I was only a student teacher and there for a short time, so I can't exactly say that I made this huge impact on the kids. But I know from the questions we talked about and the feelings that were shared that we were able to make the children more aware of their own feelings and how discrimination feels to others. And all of us as teachers learned something about just how quiet but present negative attitudes and actions can be in children. To me that was an important start!

When we deny individual or group culture or race, we deny a major part of who we are as individuals or members of a self-identified group. This purposeful denial risks sending the message to people of color that "who you are, what you look like, or how you are unique isn't OK here" or that differences are a bad thing. The impact of this message can erode children's sense of self and identity and can undermine pride in and connectedness with family (Gordon, 2005). Numerous studies of schools and communities that tout a colorblind philosophy and practice have actually revealed that, beneath the veil of colorblindness, beliefs and practices influence vastly different treatment and expectations of children based on race classification, with significantly negative effects on academic, social, and emotional development of children of color (Atwater, 2008). Acknowledging differences represents the next step along the spectrum.

AWARENESS

Unto itself, **awareness** is a neutral state of simply noticing how people are different; it is neither depreciating nor appreciating those differences. Acknowledging differences is natural. From an infant's first months, he is capable of noticing differences, and he responds initially with neutral awareness. Preference develops early, especially in relation to an infant's anxiety when met with strangers (Bergen, 2001). In the early years, awareness and preferences are based on attachments (for care givers and comfort items, for example), but this time is the also the beginning of potential prejudices, when children internalize messages from people and society around them who ascribe higher status or power to certain groups (Kowalski, 2003; York, 2003). Young children tend to focus on external attributes (qualities they can see, like body shape, skin tone, or features) and make group associations based on those visible attributes. Throughout their early years, children become cognitively capable of identifying attributes and classifying items based on similarities and differences. These cognitive skills are applied to materials and objects but also apply to their early concepts and feelings about differences in people.

As cognitive skills develop, children become capable of recognizing that people or items can possess multiple attributes. "Mastering multiple classification allows them to make finer differentiations among people and to understand the complex notion that people can be both 'the same' and 'different'" (Powlishta, Serbin, Doyle, & White, 1994, p. 527). When a neutral attitude is maintained in the face of awareness of differences, individuals are able to remain at this level of response and not deteriorate into negative attitudes. Neutral awareness manifests in children's natural curiosity about and interest in differences; it is a healthy, natural part of the social nature of human beings. Children may make comments or ask questions about differences they notice in others, often in public, sometimes leaving the adults with them embarrassed and unsure how to respond. Among families I have worked with, many parents echoed the same discomfort when their children publicly made comments like these:

- Why is that lady's skin so dark?
- Why is that man so big?
- Why does that boy have only one leg?
- Why doesn't that girl have a daddy?
- Why does that boy's mommy look different than him?
- That lady is too old to be his mommy.
- Papa, why does that person smell so bad?

Adults are often uncomfortable with the onset of this awareness when it is paired with the child's realization of the inequities present in the differential experiences of in-groups or out-groups. When children ask "Why is that man dirty and sitting on the ground? And what does his paper say?" adults often respond by looking away and making some kind of dismissive comment like "He's just resting." We might feel unprepared to discuss homelessness and socioeconomic status with young children, or worry that the person will hear us and be offended by our focus. Or we might wish that being blind to economic differences will somehow keep children from

Teachers need to be tuned in to the subtle and overt ways children may be marginalizing or excluding peers and facilitate development of appreciative attitudes and social skills.

noticing. But without active, sensitive guidance about how to consider the realities of differences, children's awareness and wondering is left open to misconceptions. Our discomfort is perceived by children and can lead them to internalize associations of shame, fear, or disdain.

Teaching with neutral awareness of diversity does not undermine individual or group culture per se, but it also does not strengthen confidence in one's identity. Neutral awareness also does not help children develop skills and attitudes to collaboratively navigate a complex, diverse world and their feelings and responses to differences. Adults can help to move children's neutral awareness towards tolerance, understanding, and positive valuing by actively exploring differences, power, and privilege and by integrating positive, honest messages about human and social differences.

ACCEPTANCE OR TOLERANCE

Acceptance or **tolerance** of human differences is a more positive response to diversity, though the terms retain a somewhat passive connotation. Common definitions of both terms imply a sense of "putting up with" something or someone. These terms similarly evoke the idea of allowing something or someone to exist, but not necessarily of having positive feelings about it. Individuals at this level might recognize the fact that people are different in many ways, but their responses to these differences might remain neutral acknowledgement or might include acceptance. Sometimes people responding at this level may make remarks like "That's just the way things are. We just have to put up with it," or "I guess it's fine with me if he joins our group, I don't really care either way."

When individuals resent the inclusion of certain people (a negative response) but don't protest or react, their response remains at this neutral level. For individuals who represent a nondominant culture or group, the idea of being tolerated can still feel quite negative and unpleasant. For example, I don't want a child with a visual impairment to be accepted as "that child with the IEP we make accommodations for" or "that boy with that extra thing on his glasses" (extra optical lens). Rather, he should be appreciated for the important ways that he understands and participates in our classroom. It might be satisfactory for some people to tolerate differences, and this is certainly preferable to negative responses. However, as early childhood professionals we must hold ourselves to a higher standard and commit to truly positive, active responses to diversity. Recognizing the growing research that demonstrates how prejudice develops in children through social learning, it is our job to model and explicitly teach an attitude of valuing differences and appreciating each other that our children can learn from (Kowalski, 2003).

APPRECIATION AND VALUING

Appreciation involves valuing, rating highly, and admiring. The United Nations Educational, Scientific, and Cultural Organization (UNESCO), a leading advocate for international peace and equity, includes *appreciation* in their published definition of tolerance. "Tolerance is respect, acceptance and appreciation of the rich diversity of our world's cultures, our forms of expression and ways of being human. It is fostered by knowledge, openness, communication, and freedom of thought, conscience and belief" (UNESCO, 1995, p. 76). The key element of this framework and this level of response is the attitude of holding another person in high esteem and respecting them because of who they are. This respect might be because of their unique characteristics, special talents, or the cultural group they affiliate with. The added element of *acting with respect* is the signature of this positive, active level of valuing response.

An individual who is demonstrating *appreciation* seeks opportunities to meaningfully engage with others who represent different ideas, values, background, language, ability, and more, *because* of their differences, not in spite of them. (In contrast, someone may tolerate or accept another person in spite of their differences, but not hold them in high regard because of their differences.) Individuals who value diversity will seek to learn more about other languages, cultures, foods, traditions, resources, and ways of life, because they feel these new experiences enrich our world. In essence, this individual feels that together we are stronger, better, and richer than we are individually, where *individually* may refer to one's self or cultural group.

An individual who appreciates human diversity is more apt to respond by asking another person to share her experiences, values, and traditions, and to enjoy listening to the human stories we all have to share. Whereas rejection, dismissal, or just "putting up with" others serves to shut down relationships and connections, reaching out and listening appreciatively serves to strengthen bonds between people and groups and forms a sense of community and connectedness. Research from cultural anthropologists has revealed that in some communities, cultural values promote embracing newcomers and responding to foreigners with genuine interest and creatively adopting new ideas learned from them. These communities have proven successful, adaptive, and able to evolve over time—to really thrive—whereas those that are less welcoming of new ideas and people tend to not thrive as well (Rogoff, 2003). The people in communities like the ones Rogoff writes about view ideas or ways of life that contrast to and challenge their own as an opportunity to grown stronger, and they see diverse people as a resource. "The diversity of ways that different communities handle life provide humanity with a reservoir of ideas and resources for the uncertainties of the future" (Rogoff, 2003, p. 362). Culturally competent teachers embody this spirit by encouraging varied ways of interacting within classroom communities, as described in this **video**.

Threat of Negative Responses: Small Assumptions Have Big Implications

Cultural concepts have been explained using the iceberg analogy to illustrate the visible and unseen nature of personal identity and culture. Unseen attributes and personal experiences are the bulk of one's cultural identity, and this analogy demonstrates how important it is to consider the unseen elements of an individual's culture. It is this vast unseen component which strongly shapes behavior, identity, and understanding. When assumptions are made about a person based on what he looks or sounds like, the true nature of the person is missed or misunderstood. And when behaviors and responses are shaped by these assumptions, the error can be far more devastating than we ever realized. Compelling research indicates that assumptions people may make based on observable elements in another person can have profound impacts on that person's health, education, employment, and quality of life.

Any one of the observable factors (i.e. race/ethnicity, age, gender, disability and attractiveness) is among the first things that people notice about a person, which may trigger differential responses. Research evidence suggests that race plays a central role in predicting poor or limited outcomes—in the case of

Opportunities to develop genuine friendships and reciprocal relationships with individuals from different backgrounds through informal or semistructured activities helps develop children's ability to appreciate differences and interact with a variety of individuals.

minority groups—for employment, education, rehabilitation and/or health outcomes, particularly when associated with other factors like low-socioeconomic status, limited levels of education and/or immigration status. (Balcazar, Suarez-Balcazar, & Taylor-Ritzler, 2009, p. 1155)

There are two key parts to understand in this research. One is that there is a fundamental inequality of outcomes in a wide array of important quality-of-life indicators based on cultural group identity factors. Second is that *other people's perception* of a person's cultural group (including attractiveness) and their resulting behaviors can negatively impact that person's outcomes. In other words, people are treated differently and have different access to opportunities because of prejudgments based on how they look and negative assumptions about groups (Baca Zinn, Eitzen, & Wells, 2008). This is a clear illustration of prejudicial beliefs and the resulting discriminatory actions or responses. Research-based evidence like this might feel upsetting and unfair, but it is important that we not ignore unpleasant data because it is hard to face. The deeply ingrained patterns of inequality in our society will only be mitigated when we all face the differences in power, privilege, and opportunity, and our roles within unequal systems. And as early childhood professionals, we are called upon by professional ethics and integrity to serve our children and families well in an effort to mitigate the effects of negative responses to diversity.

TEACHERS AS AGENTS OF CHANGE

Just as the most negative end of the spectrum involves hurtful actions prompted by negative beliefs about differences, valuing involves feelings of respect and appreciation towards differences but also social actions stemming from those beliefs. We are communicating appreciation and creating a welcoming place for each person to be valued for who they are when we actively reach out and say things like:

- "I really like the drape and pattern of your dress; I haven't seen that before."

- "There's room at my table, wheel your chair near and eat lunch with me."

- "When your grandfather walked you to school today I heard him use some words that sounded new to me when you said 'good-bye.' Can you teach me those words too?"

- "I see all your tiny braids! It looks like someone spent a lot of time on them."

- "Your dads sound like a lot of fun! Tell me more about what your family did this weekend."

- "I noticed you wanted to play with the children on the swings, but they said you couldn't because you talk funny. Would you like me to help you talk to them about why that is not fair?"

In the face of prejudiced messages children hear from other sources, it is essential that children spend time with adults who very clearly give messages of appreciation, valuing, and welcoming everyone. Moving yourself to the positive end of the spectrum is important personal work. In our professional role, our ethical responsibility pushes us even farther to speak and act out to promote social justice in our classrooms and communities (Derman-Sparks & Ramsey, 2006). The impact of negative responses is widespread and affects all members of the classroom:

- Anxiety and fear of exclusion is created in almost all children, even those who were not directly targeted.

- Tensions among children prompt arguments or aggression, even when not targeted towards group identity.

- Children's confidence and ability to recognize and embrace their own identity is eroded.

- Negative feelings and actions towards others, family members, or one's self are bred.

- Family connections are undermined.

Because of the virulent nature of negative responses—but also the contagious nature of promoting equity—teachers must commit to making classrooms places of action, reflection, and even accountability for social justice. The following sections give ideas for responding to comments and actions related to differences, and outline strategies for our efforts towards social justice.

"You're in America. Speak English!!"

I have been in the United States for 22 years now. I've raised two children here, both now in college. My husband and I have always been committed to maintaining our bicultural heritage, and raised our children to be bilingual. We see this as an asset. You know, like "two languages are better than one." It hasn't always been easy though. I can vividly recall the numerous times that I have been glared at or heard an irritated "Yuck" when we have been out and people overheard us speaking Vietnamese.

Once I was in a small clothing shop in the one-street downtown where I live and saw someone I knew from my child's school. She was one of the three Vietnamese parents in the school. She was having trouble understanding the store clerk because she was still learning English. I spoke to her in Vietnamese about the question she had for the clerk and after she finished paying we just started talking about life in general. I hadn't noticed this other woman near us until she came over in a huff, pointed her finger in our faces, and said "You know, you're what's going wrong with this country today. You're in America for Christ's sake. Speak English! You people come here illegally and think that we should have to accommodate for you all over the place and you don't even bother to try to fit in." She paused to catch her breath and I slowly raised my hand and calmly and slowly said *in English* "Ma'am, hold on. I do speak English

fluently, and can read and write as well, in fact. I also am fluent in other languages and am proud to be. My friend here is also working on being fluent in English as well as her home language. And to clarify, I have been a legal United States citizen for over 10 years. I pay taxes. I have a college degree. I'm as American as anyone else and have made a great effort to fit in here."

She stopped her rant then, and while her face wasn't as pinched with anger as it had been, the look in her eyes told me that she wasn't quite ready to accept us as fellow community members. She simply made a sound like "Hmmph" and walked away. I replay that scene a lot in my head, knowing that I could have handled that woman a bunch of different ways. I was proud of myself for being so calm and articulate, even though inside I was hurt, embarrassed, and angry. I feel like I am sort of like a model for bicultural people somehow. Like I want to conduct myself with grace and intelligence so that I can improve the reputation of immigrants and hope that people like the "Speak English!" woman will be the ones embarrassed of how they think and act. Pretty much everyone in America has roots from somewhere else, you know? I laugh now at that woman's comment about being in America so we should speak English. For goodness sake! Even the English language comes from somewhere else!

Teaching Towards Social Justice: Strategies and Considerations

Early childhood professionals are in a uniquely influential and supportive position in children's and families' lives. Because of this position of influence, it is imperative that we strive to embody, model, and promote only sincerely and meaningfully inclusive attitudes and practices. However, modeling is not enough. To effect real change in attitudes and actions about differences, we must facilitate children's personal inward and outward journey, exploring beliefs, values, and behaviors about human diversity. A key strategy is to use negative comments and actions as an opportunity to engage children (or adults around us as well) in recognizing the impact of those words and actions. It is in these *teachable moments* that we must reinforce the message that negative responses are hurtful, and emphasize that fairness, equity, and feelings of self-worth are rights of everyone. Calling attention to and labeling negative words and actions and emphasizing basic concepts of fairness and human rights shines a light into the shadows of injustice. These efforts are just the beginning, however. The work continues with deep self-reflection about your own beliefs and your role in an unequal society, as well as similarly meaningful engagement of children in reflecting on beliefs and choosing to act on behalf of equity.

WHERE AM I AS A TEACHER ON THE SPECTRUM?

This question can be a very difficult one to delve into. Certainly most early childhood professionals care about the impact they have on children; often we care very deeply about "our children" and the work we do with families. Even in the face of our complex and challenging work, in general we teachers feel quite protective of our children and can hesitate to see them as strategic players in a hierarchy of power and oppression. Many providers struggle to see children as anything other than innocent and genuine. However, we are doing them a disservice when we do not recognize that young children are keen observers of the people and messages in their world. Children will mimic people around them and repeat messages they hear. They are capable of complex thought processing from a young age and can internalize ideas and values from their world with or without fully understanding them. Think about how you would meaningfully engage with families like those described in this **video** who may have different views on education and success.

An essential first step in being able to both model social justice values and prompt reflection and action in others is to be prepared. Be prepared to notice racism, classism, sexism, ableism, harassment, prejudice, discrimination, oppression, and stereotyping. Then be prepared to identify it—to shine the light and reinforce fairness and equity. A powerful tool in this preparation is the use of a **script**, either one that you adopt or make up on your own. A script is a quote or specific response that you can use when you are in a moment that might normally leave you shocked and speechless. Consider the response scripts in Figure 3.2 as a place to start, but also practice finding your own words to suit your particular settings. When you have a well-practiced and planned response, you can let your rehearsed script take over when your mind would otherwise go blank or you would prefer to ignore the situation. I have used scripts to feel prepared and confident when navigating interpersonal conflicts at work or in my personal life, as well as to strengthen my commitment to speaking out against discrimination. A script can be an incredibly empowering tool to avoid being tongue-tied in uncomfortable or stressful situations.

As early childhood professionals we need to recognize that certain groups are faced with obstacles that others might not face or of which others are not

Teachers can use small group instruction times to reinforce positive relationships and facilitate interpersonal conflict resolution through focused discussion and social skill building.

fully aware. Wherever we find common shared experiences of prejudice, there can be strength in talking about those experiences. Valuing diversity is more than just recognizing that people look, think, feel, and act differently. It is also about recognizing the deeper roots of differences in power that are less visible but that profoundly impact life outcomes. Teaching for social justice is about acknowledging how people differ, recognizing the variety of responses to human differences, and committing to prompting and promoting social justice in ourselves and our communities. As lofty and complex as these goals might sound, our children are capable of making this journey with us, and the quality of their self-identity and success in society are impacted by our ability and willingness to engage them in this necessary exploration.

FIGURE 3.2

Ideas and Scripts to Redirect and Reengage Negative Responses

When you are faced with a negative response at work or in personal situations, you can use one of these ways of advocating for social justice (Derman-Sparks, 1989). Consider these a starting place to help you feel prepared to act for social injustices.

Discrimination	• "I noticed some terms in the benefits section of my contract that I'm wondering about. Does 'family member' include civil union partners?" Requesting clarification on the source of definitions like "family members" can reveal outdated or inappropriate sources of information and prompt revisions of policies.

	• "It looks like nearly all of the children being referred for behavioral intervention in our grade cohort are children of color. I'm wondering if there is something unexpected going on in the referral process or assessment instrument." Neutrally calling attention to obvious discrepancies and seeking clarification for such discrepancies positions you and colleagues as a team reflecting on your practices and is less likely to spark defensive responses. • "That comment would hurt (name someone or say 'my friend's') feelings and is insulting. Please don't use words that hurt. I wouldn't let someone say something insulting about you either." When ethnicity is used as an insult, as in a verbal slur or 'joke', call attention to it in a calm, firm tone with a simple message, and relate it back to individual rights.
Ethnocentrism	• Observation: Children in the pretend play area are putting baby dolls to bed. A new child enters the area to join the play. She goes to get a baby doll, but says with great disappointment "I can't play with those dolls! White ones are the only best ones." Response: "Corrine, I heard you say that only the white dolls are good ones. I do see three other dolls on the shelf. What makes the white ones the only good ones?" Initiating conversation with an open-ended question allows children and teachers to use negative comments as a learning opportunity. • "I don't want to sit with nobody else but my boys. My dad says none of them (pointing at a group of children in the class with different skin tone) is worth being with." Response: "Sean, I heard you say that you would rather sit with your friends and I can understand that. But I wonder what you think about what your dad said about your classmates who have different skin color than you. I know you know a lot about those children because we are all in the same class here and sometimes you have had fun playing with them. I believe you are worth being with and I believe they are worth being with too. What do you think about these different feelings?" • Invite children to clarify their words, encourage them to keep talking by remaining calm and not scolding or dismissing. Only by engaging in conversation can we clarify; we can also prompt children to think more deeply about their words and beliefs. The initial comment is just the window into the deeper belief and values, and that is really what we need to explore.
Prejudice	• Comments: "I don't like people like her" or "I don't like his kind"; pointing at or referring to attributes like skin color, dress, physical features, and language. Response: "Do you mean people who look/sound a certain way? What makes you say you don't like that part of them? Do you know people who look/sound like that?" A goal of responding to prejudiced remarks is to encourage the speaker both to think more about her beliefs and to call attention to what she is actually saying. Sometimes people make comments without realizing the impact of their words. It is important to help the speaker not feel attacked and shut down, but rather to open dialogue with reflective questions. Focus on and ask for clarification of words or terms the speaker used. • Comment: "I wish she wasn't in our group. She don't even talk like us (or walk, or hear, etc.)" or "He dresses poor (or ghetto, or gay, etc.). He shouldn't be here." Response: "Sam, I hear you using words that hurt and exclude someone. That isn't fair, and in our classroom (company, school, family, community, etc.) I know we value treating people like we want to be treated. She (or he) has many ways to contribute to the group even if some ways might be different than ways that you might contribute. I can help you figure out some ways to work together."

(Continued)

The Spectrum of Responses to Diversity **71**

FIGURE 3.2 *(Continued)*

Awareness	
(When children recognize and comment on how someone looks different than they do, often beginning around 2 to 3 years.)	• "Why is that lady's skin so dark?" Response: "Everyone's skin shade is different. Sometimes shades are similar and sometimes they're different. Let's look at yours and mine next to each other. Do you notice any differences?" Or "Our skin tones are determined by a chemical inside our bodies as well as things like sun rays or even makeup. People are born with certain skin tone, which usually stays pretty much the same throughout their life. Hmm. Look at the skin on my hand next to yours. How could we describe how our tones are different or similar?" • "Why is that man so big (or fat, or short, or tall, etc.)?" Response: "Bodies are different shapes and sizes, and they change, just like your body changes as you're growing up." Or "People's bodies are all different shapes and sizes. Many things can make people's body size and shape look the way they do. People's bodies change as they get older, just like you are taller now than you were last year and bigger than when you were a baby. The food we eat and activities we do can also change our bodies. Sometimes people's bodies change from illness. If you keep looking around, do you see lots of different body shapes?" • "Why does that boy have only one leg?" Response: "I don't know that boy, so I don't know why exactly. But sometimes people are born without a leg, and sometimes people have had an accident or illness that meant that the doctors at the hospital had to remove the leg. That boy has learned how to use crutches (or a chair or new leg) to help him get around. He uses them really well! People who move around differently still do the same things as you do, like playing games with your friends." • "Why does that boy's mommy look different than him?" Response: "We don't know that boy, so we don't know for sure. But how we look is made up from different things likes special codes we inherit from our parents, which sometimes make us have hair, eye, or skin tone just like them. Sometimes the codes we get from them make us look different though. And sometimes babies and parents are brought together after the baby is born when parents adopt a baby from someone who can't take care of him. Sometimes parents and children blend together in a new family when adults meet and join together. There sure are a lot of ways to become a family, aren't there?" • "Isn't that lady too old to be his mommy?" Response: "People have babies at all different times in their lives—sometimes when they are younger and sometimes when they are older. We don't know that mommy, so we can't really know how old she is. What makes you think she is too old?" (Consider possible responses about appearance.) • It is helpful to briefly address the child's remark or question so as not to dismiss it, but especially important to ask a question that gets the child talking more about what prompted their question. Sometimes children see a person they don't know, but they are reminded about someone they knew or heard about and they make a false association or assumption.

Your Examples	Reflecting on your own practice or experiences, list a few examples of situations or comments from children about human differences and create a response which promotes appreciation and also engages in deeper discussion:
	1. Child Comment: _____
	Response: _____
	_____
	_____
	2. Child Comment: _____
	Response: _____
	_____
	_____
	3. Child Comment: _____
	Response: _____
	_____
	_____

Summary

THE SPECTRUM OF RESPONSES TO DIVERSITY

- From infancy, humans are wired to notice our surroundings, especially other people, and have a predisposition to favor familiar things. This early awareness and bias is a part of the development of our beliefs and responses to things that are different.
- Responses to difference or diversity fall along a spectrum. The *spectrum* refers to the range of responses we have to various experiences with human diversity.

WHAT IS THE SPECTRUM? THE UGLY, THE BAD, AND THE GOOD

- Internal responses are the thoughts that immediately pop into our heads when we

become aware of something in our space; these responses can drive our actions even if we don't realize it.

- External responses include behaviors that usually reflect our values and beliefs.
- When an action is prompted by prejudicial feelings, it is called *discrimination* and is designed to degrade, hurt, humiliate, or exert power over others.
- Responses fall along a spectrum, from negative responses like discrimination, prejudice, and ethnocentrism; to neutral responses like colorblindness and awareness; to more positive and inclusive responses like acceptance and valuing.

THREAT OF NEGATIVE RESPONSES: SMALL ASSUMPTIONS HAVE BIG IMPLICATIONS

- The vast unseen components of culture strongly shape behavior, identity, and understanding.
- Compelling new research indicates that assumptions people make based on observable elements in another person can have profound impacts on the observed person's health, education, employment, and quality of life.
- As early childhood professionals, we need to recognize that certain groups are faced with obstacles that others might not be face or of which they are not fully aware.
- Valuing diversity is more than just recognizing that people look, think, feel, and act differently; it is also about recognizing the deeper roots of differences in power that are less visible but that profoundly impact life outcomes.

TEACHERS AS AGENTS OF CHANGE

- In the face of prejudiced messages children hear from other sources, it is essential that children spend time with adults who very clearly give messages of appreciation, valuing, and welcome to everyone.
- Because of the virulent nature of negative responses—but also the contagious nature of promoting equity—teachers must commit to making classrooms places of action, reflection, and even accountability for social justice.
- In this way, teaching becomes a work of advocacy: teachers advocate for equality and fairness.

TEACHING TOWARDS SOCIAL JUSTICE: STRATEGIES AND CONSIDERATIONS

- To effect real change in attitudes and actions about differences, early childhood professionals must facilitate children's personal inward and outward journey, exploring beliefs, values, and behaviors about human diversity.
- A key strategy is to use negative comments and actions as an opportunity to engage children (or adults around us as well) in recognizing the impact of those words and actions, reinforcing the message that negative responses are hurtful, and emphasizing that fairness, equity, and feelings of self-worth are the rights of everyone.
- A powerful tool to help teachers be prepared to turn negative responses into teachable moments is a script or planned response—to help respond appropriately and engage children further when they express negative ideas about diversity.

Chapter Learning Outcomes: Self-Assessment

Use this space to reflect on how well you have achieved the learning goals for this chapter in terms of evaluating your own competency in the topics below. List three to five key concepts that you have learned from the chapter.

Identify ways people tend to respond to diversity.	
Explain the spectrum of positive and negative responses to diversity.	
Reflect on personal values, biases, and potential for prejudice.	
Explore teaching strategies to promote positive responses to diversity.	

Chapter Activities

DISCUSSION QUESTIONS

1. Consider your responses to the scenarios presented in the beginning of the chapter. How do you feel your responses align with the spectrum?

2. What contributing factors can you identify in your life that have impacted and influenced your actions in response to diversity?

3. What concrete, specific planned scripts can you create to prepare yourself to turn a negative response into a teachable moment?

SELF-REFLECTION

Go to the Understanding Prejudice website and use the links to take the "Test yourself for hidden biases" online surveys. Make a note of your results and think about the tests, the questions, the process of taking the surveys, how you were feeling during the surveys, and your results. How do you feel about the results and the category that the tests revealed in terms of your beliefs?

TEACHING DISPOSITION

Go to the Teaching Tolerance website and locate the *Speak Up!* handbook. Download and print this resource. Practice some of the scripts for responding to and speaking out against bigotry in public and at home. Create a strategy card file of scripts that you found particularly useful and those that you created on your own. Keep these available to practice or review when you are faced with an example of "everyday" bigotry. Consider the pledge and campaign ideas in the appendices of the handbook.

IN THE FIELD

Observe teachers in classroom settings in your community or through online clips (such as on YouTube or the HighScope website). Listen for responses or interactions which reflect attitudes and behaviors about diversity. Identify and classify the individuals' (teachers', family members' or children's) level of response based on the spectrum. If this was your classroom, how could you respond to promote social justice values?

Weblinks

Understanding Prejudice: A website for students, teachers, and others who are interested in the causes and consequences of prejudice. *www.understandingprejudice.org*

Teaching Tolerance: A website for students, parents, and professionals that is dedicated to promoting and supporting the work for social justice. Free resources for parents and teachers are available both to engage personal reflection and action and engage children in exploring what social justice means. *www.teachingtolerance.org*

4

Race *and* Ethnicity

This chapter is about more than race, skin color, or categories and labels. Race is an incredibly complex issue both in our own individual conceptions as well as in the sociopolitical and historical context. It is also a topic that people approach sensitively and that sometimes leads to anxiety in teachers who seek to integrate issues about race into their classroom and curriculum. Prevailing unease might result from a variety of factors, including a shared history riddled with oppression and exclusion, existing socioeconomic disparities based on race, or lack of awareness about useful teaching strategies and appropriate content coverage with young children. This chapter

Aspects of external appearance, such as skin tone or facial features, are often used to presume an individual's race. As the number of multiracial families grows, such presumptions are problematic and often unnecessary.

outlines acknowledged definitions of race used by different agencies, current disparate realities of experience that might be attributed to race, and effective strategies and topics for early childhood professionals to consider when working with all children and families in any setting. To spark your thinking about creating an inclusive and shared sense of history and place, watch this **video** about multiple perspectives.

What Does *Race* Really Mean?

The term *race* generally makes us think of words like Asian, Black, or White, among others, and conjures images of individuals with different shades of skin tone and different facial features such as eye shape or bone structure. Definitions and labels have been created and modified throughout history to attempt to classify diversity among humans. Often ideas about race also suggest geographic origin or nationality, such as Hispanic. The process of racial classification has been informed by biology, sociology, and politics as justifications for category criteria. Early racial classifications and labels were understood primarily in biological terms (Lee, 2001).

IS THERE A BIOLOGICAL BASIS FOR RACE LABELS?

From the 1700s to the earlier 1900s, research abounded purporting that there was a scientific basis for racial classification of Whites of Western-European descent and people of color, or those descendant from other parts of the world (O'Flaherty & Shapiro, 2002). This early research even claimed that innate differences existed in abilities (intellectual and other) based on biological differences between defined races, with claims of White superiority. These findings were used to justify discriminatory, racist laws and practices, even to the extent of embedding in the U.S. Constitution language which counted Black slaves as only three-fifths of a person. However, for well over 50 years these early, highly flawed research and pseudoscientific findings have been widely discredited and rejected (O'Flaherty & Shapiro, 2002; Derman-Sparks & Ramsey, 2006).

Currently, stronger research evidence indicates that there are actually more variations *among* groups within racial categories than across categories (Derman-Sparks & Ramsey, 2006). So without the discriminatory agenda of generating evidence to support a false claim of racial superiority, researchers are finding no scientific basis for laws, policies, or practices which position any race over another. It might not be surprising that racist practices are based solely on an agenda of sociopolitical domination and have no legitimacy. This can lead to the question, "Why classify people based on racial categories at all?"

LEARNING OUTCOMES
....

- Identify definitions and conceptions of *race* from sociopolitical and historical perspectives

- Explore current statistics on racial disparities in the United States

- Examine children's ideas about differences in skin color, power, and privilege

- Create curricular connections to explore skin color and promote racial equality

- Practice teaching strategies to meaningfully engage families

SOCIOPOLITICALLY DEFINED CONCEPTS: WHAT AND WHY

Since 1790 the U.S. government has conducted population census reports every 10 years to obtain and disseminate information about children and adults living in the United States. From this early date, the statistics have revealed, and continue to reveal, disparate outcomes for people, based on self-identification with a racial category. The statistics were and are used to inform policies and practices in both government and nongovernment agencies that are designed to reduce differences in socioeconomic status, opportunities, and treatment of people. The census is conducted every 10 years and "almost every census for the past 200 years has collected racial data differently than the one before it" (Lee, 2001, p. 1). A major change beginning in the 2000 census was the ability to self-identify with multiple racial categories instead of just a single category. This change finally recognizes the millions of people from multiracial backgrounds who identify with more than one racial/ethnic identity. In the 2010 census, multiracial respondents increased by over 32% from the 2000 report, with multiracial children comprising the largest number of respondents (Humes, Jones, & Ramirez, 2011).

Definitions of Race on the 2010 Census

The 2010 census report clearly states that "race categories in the census questionnaire generally reflect a social definition of race recognized in this country and are not an attempt to define race biologically, anthropologically, or genetically" (Humes, Jones, & Ramirez, 2011, p. 2). This notation reflects society's broader understanding of race as a sociopolitical construct not rooted in a genetic basis. The report also includes a section for all respondents to indicate Hispanic origin status, which is defined differently than race. *Hispanic* or *Not of Hispanic Origin* comes before the question about race, with an explanatory note that the Hispanic Origin categories do not relate to race. In other words, a person can identify as Hispanic in origin and also identify with any of the six race categories. So Hispanic origins are thus recognized in the census framework as an ethnic category, not as a race. Table 4.1 outlines the current census definitions of race and the breakdown of individual self-identification on the six race categories (Humes, Jones, & Ramirez, 2011). In earlier census questionnaires, the following terms were selected as preferred terms by individuals who self-identify as being from a particular background: *American Indian* (preferred by over 50%, though a significant percentage preferred the term *Native American*), *Black* (with *African American,* selected by the second largest group, although *Black* can include individuals with heritage roots in countries other than African), *Hispanic*, and *multiracial* (Tucker, Kojetin, & Harrison, 1995).

While the majority of the U.S. population identified as White (including Hispanic), there were major increases in populations of people of color and multiple race categories and also in the Hispanic ethnic category. These increases in populations reveal the continuing and rapidly growing racial

TABLE 4.1 *Results from the 2010 Census*

Race (specific terms used by the census)	Definition of Race Category	Percentage of population	Increase from 2000 census
White	"Origins in any of the original peoples of Europe, the Middle East, or North Africa" (p. 3)	72.4%	5.7%
Black or African American	"Origins in any of the Black racial groups of Africa" (p. 3)	12.6%	12.3%
American Indian and Alaska Native	"Origins in any of the original peoples of North and South American (including Central American and who maintain tribal affiliation or community attachment" (p. 3)	0.9%	18.4%
Asian	"Origins in any of the original peoples of the Far East, Southeast Asia, or the Indian subcontinent" (p. 3)	4.8%	43.3%
Native Hawaiian or Other Pacific Islander	"Origins in any of the original peoples of Hawaii, Guam, Samoa, or other Pacific Islands" (p. 3)	0.2%	35.4%
Some other race alone	Includes responses not listed above, and written-in responses such as "multiracial, mixed, interracial, or a Hispanic or Latino group (for example Mexican, Puerto Rican, Cuban, or Spanish)" (p. 3)	6.2%	24.4%
Two or more races	Used for individuals who self-identify with more than one of the above categories, which are written into the census form by the respondent	2.9%	32%

and ethnic diversity of the U.S. Data from the 2010 report reveal that the growth of the Hispanic origin population accounted for the over half of the total population growth in the U.S. (with most Hispanic origin respondents identifying their race as White). Additionally, the Asian population increased more than any other racial category between the 2000 and 2010 report (Humes, Jones, & Ramirez, 2011). Recognizing this continued diversification of the U.S. population is essential for early childhood professionals, especially with disproportionately more White teachers than teachers with racial and ethnic backgrounds which reflect this diversity.

Children with diverse backgrounds benefit from teachers and curricula that recognize, understand, and meaningfully integrate their racial and ethnic diversity throughout their early experiences. In particular, as multiracial and multiethnic families continue to grow and are more freely able to acknowledge their own diverse backgrounds, early childhood professionals and curricula must robustly recognize and support the development of children's self-identity and multiple group association. Some researchers even suggest that it is time to shift away from racial classification frameworks in favor of

The continuing increase in the number of multiracial families contributes to the increase in the number of individuals self-identifying with more than one racial category.

a focus on exploring similarities and differences which make each person unique (Fitzgerald, Mann, Cabrera, Sarche, & Qin, 2009). The call to view each child as a uniquely developing individual within a larger complex cultural context has also been at the forefront of advocacy efforts of NAEYC, especially since the 1997 revision of the *Developmentally Appropriate Practice* manual and emphasized in the latest revision (Bredekamp & Copple, 1997; Copple & Bredekamp, 2009). To accomplish this shift, early childhood professionals need to understand broad sociocultural contexts as well as each child and family.

Relationship Between Race and (Unearned) Privilege: Whiteness in America

"Membership in racial categories...shapes the social status and experiences of individuals, from childhood to old age" (Lee, 2001, p. 2). Overwhelming evidence indicates a continued gap in access to opportunities and the outcomes for children of color. Despite some progress to close the gaps through landmark legal and sociopolitical actions, there remains in the United States a value system that positions middle- and upper-class Whites in a privileged status. Sometimes this status, or "racialized power," is unseen or ignored by White teachers (and people in general) who equate racism with individual acts of discrimination or prejudice (Vaught & Castagno, 2008, p. 100) or who try to minimize race by considering themselves color-blind to differences of skin color. There is more to the context of present-day racial disparities than individual acts of racism, however. Regardless of the context of their family, school, or immediate community, children are living within the context of the broader racist society. Exploring and developing some understanding of the context of race and racism in our lives is an important part of children's early identity development and thus a key part of our work with children.

PERSISTENT RACISM

While overtly racist policies like legal segregation of schools and public facilities have been ruled illegal by U.S. courts, racist practices and beliefs remain a part of present-day experience. Unequal opportunities and overtly or subtly unfair assumptions translate to preferential treatment for individuals who appear White. Even when individuals do not hold racist views or promote racist values, failing to take action to equalize opportunities and promote equality in systems and policies serves to perpetuate racial inequality, a phenomenon referred to as **institutional racism** (Derman-Sparks & Ramsey, 2006; Vaught & Castagno, 2008). The results of institutionalized racism can be seen in a variety of disparate outcomes for people of color, in spite of antidiscrimination laws. Examples of grossly unequal experiences based on race include:

- Infant mortality rate for Black/African American infants is 12.6%, and 8.1% for American Indian infants, compared to an average across races of 6.6% in 2008 (Kids Count, 2008).

- The percentage of children living in single-parent households in 2010 was nearly double the average (34%) for Black/African Americans (66%) and 1.5 times the average for American Indians (52%; Kids Count, 2010).

- At the end of 2010, Black non-Hispanic men were almost seven times more likely than White non-Hispanic men to be incarcerated, and Black non-Hispanic women were three times more likely to be incarcerated than White non-Hispanic women (Guerino, Harrison, & Sabol, 2010).

- Families of Hispanic, American Indian, and Black/African American children are 2.5 times more likely to live in poverty than White non-Hispanic families (Kids Count, 2010).

- American Indian and Alaskan Native teenagers are over three times more likely than non-Hispanic Whites to not complete or graduate from high school, and Black/African American and Hispanic/Latino teens are twice as likely to not graduate from high school (Kids Count, 2010).

CRITICAL EXPLORATION OF RACE DATA

More important than just a compelling list of statistics is a critical examination of the potential roots of and contributing factors to racist implications. Recent research reveals that health care professionals are more likely to provide a reduced level of care to people of color than to White counterparts (Lee, 2001), and health care in economically limited communities might be less available. With greater numbers of people of color living in poverty and without health care insurance, reduced access and quality of prenatal health care negatively impacts their infants' health. So when viewed in a larger context, infant mortality rates are connected to disparate health care access for families of color and not due to an infant's being biologically prone to poorer health due to skin color.

Likewise, statistics on single family status can potentially be misleading and prompt misinterpretations about relationship commitment among people of color. Grossly inequitable incarceration rates lead to a different perspective on the frequency of single-parent status. Furthermore, exploring the statistics above requires caution so that we refrain from simple causal misconceptions such as assuming that more people of color commit crimes. The statistics actually convey that more people of color are sentenced to prison, but they do not necessarily reveal information on commission of crime, arrests, investigation, and sentencing patterns, and how these may be discrepant based on race. When we pair the higher concentration of people of color living in communities (with limited employment prospects and economic resources) with potential law enforcement strategies that might take current incarceration rates by race into account (*profiling*), we see that the risk factors contributing to the socioeconomic and health wellbeing of people of color produces a far more complex and interrelated picture. This complexity requires that we not negatively stereotype and make narrow assumptions about the character of people of color compared to people identified as White.

Critical examination of statistics on academic and scholastic achievement gaps between races is particularly important for early childhood professionals. Instead of inaccurate assumptions about the capability of students of color, a more critical stance requires that we consider the disconnect between school culture, content, and teacher practices that position students of color at a disadvantage. When schools, curriculum, and teacher perception and practice are centered around a White, Western/European dominant perspective, children who do not "fit the mold" are marginalized and unrecognized, and underperform as a result. The key consideration is for early childhood professionals to delve into how schools are failing children, not how children are failing schools. Then it falls to each of us to take deliberate action individually and systemically to work towards high expectations with appropriate support to ensure success for all children.

Why Discuss Race and Racism With Children?

From the earliest years, children notice and think about different skin colors. Children are also as capable of understanding the subtleties of fairness intellectually and emotionally as they are of developing cognitive capacities to understand even distribution of items in a mathematical sense. This conceptual knowledge of numeric equality allows children to connect to sociological concepts of equality or treating people equally. Considering children's natural curiosity about differences in skin tone and their capacity to understand both fairness and equality, early childhood is the prime time to engage children in forthright discussions about race and racism.

Attempting either to avoid or dismiss their curiosity, questions, and feelings about these concepts and realities can leave children feeling confused, shameful, or disconnected from you. A child who is shushed when asking about someone with a different skin color is left wondering why the question is bad or wrong and what is strange or scary about the person. But the prospect of opening up discussions or explorations of racial inequality can leave many teachers wondering how to begin. As a start, prepare yourself for children's questions or comments so that when they initiate the topic, you are able to acknowledge their comments and engage in more conversation as needed. In this **video**, listen to the teaching strategies offered for presenting similarities and differences in a cohesive approach to multicultural education, and consider the complexities in the ideas presented.

When children make comments or ask questions about differences in skin color, it is important to validate their curiosity and interest in new people, particularly if their comments reveal a potential misconception or assumptions. Letting three-year-olds in the prolific "why?" phase share their ideas or answers before you provide your own can be helpful. For example:

CHILD: *Why does Jessi's dad have dark skin like that?*

ADULT: *Hmm. I'm thinking about that question. Why do you think that might be?*

IN MY FAMILY

An Uncomfortable Topic

I grew up in a pretty segregated neighborhood, a White, middle-upper-class outskirt suburb of New York City. My parents both worked in the city and both were immigrants to the U.S. They had their share of experiences as "outsiders," but by the time my brother and I came along, they both spoke English and held professional positions. As young children, we were sheltered from any feelings of exclusion and from their beliefs about differences. I have one vivid memory from preschool age, though—one of very, very few memories from those years. It was so confusing, though, that I guess it sticks out in my memory.

Driving home from dropping my brother off at kindergarten, I said something to my dad about "negroes." At that time (over three decades ago), there were memorable ads on television for the United Negro College Fund, and I assumed this was an appropriate term for people with dark skin. My father stopped me immediately, speaking firmly and said "You don't use that word. They don't like that." I felt upset that I had said a "bad word," and corrected myself by saying "colored people." He further clarified that he didn't think this was an acceptable term either. I was embarrassed and upset that I was potentially insulting and asked what I should call them. He said he didn't really know. I sat quietly in the back seat then. We didn't talk about it again. I never really understood the seemingly positive use of the term "negro" on TV, but that it was insulting from me. I was left just wondering, since race or race relations weren't topics my parents discussed with us. This was a confusing moment which left me feeling ignorant about how to respectfully think or talk about race, but also feeling like my dad didn't really have any better idea either. This is the kind of teachable moment that parents and adults working with young children need to make the most of to develop antibias awareness and behaviors in children.

This strategy of referring the question back to the child might be met with their own idea about why, or with a genuine "I don't know. You tell me." If the child shares her own ideas, this can give you an opportunity to learn more about her thinking as well as to engage in a longer dialogue about differences. If she asks you again, you will have had a bit more time to craft an answer with additional prompts to encourage the child's reflection about her world. The bottom line is that children notice differences and wonder about them. Our role has to be to balance encouraging children's natural awareness of their world, prompting for more dialogue, and providing information and appropriate messages about valuing differences.

Curricular Connections

Look for materials that accurately and appropriately reflect the racial and ethnic background and identity of all children in your classroom; this is especially important for self-portrait activities where children need access to many choices for skin tone and hair color/texture.

As a well-meaning first step towards adding images of racial diversity in the classroom, many teachers begin by adding items to the shelves that represent differences. These might include dolls with different skin tones and facial features, a handful of books featuring people of color, or posters with children of color and White children represented. These efforts are a start, but when they are not part of a much richer integration across the curriculum, they can actually perpetuate a belief that reflecting images of skin tone variety is enough (Cross, 2003). The risk here is that if adults don't take up the deeper, more meaningful work of activism for social justice, then children will not truly develop the cognitive and socioemotional skills necessary for a lifetime of sustained efforts towards equality for people of all skin tones. This deeper work is about exploring the sociopolitical implications of racial categories and skin tone as well as taking a closer look at how social dynamics (interpersonal and across larger social contexts) are impacted by a person's skin color. The early childhood years are the prime time for children to internalize the ideals, goals, and behaviors for promoting equality and antibias. The following sections outline a variety of efforts teachers can integrate into their environments and curriculum to promote antiracist attitudes, beliefs, and behaviors. Materials are a familiar place to start.

MATERIALS

Ensure that a wide range of shades of skin tones and facial features is represented in the classroom and school. Carefully select books or posters that represent people with various skin tones engaged in genuine everyday experiences of family and community life. Take special care to include images of multiracial families and individuals (Wardle, 1998). An important consideration is to avoid stereotypical images of holiday or celebratory dress (Native Americans in feathered headdresses as opposed to everyday clothes like jeans, chinos, and t-shirts or sweaters; Japanese women in kimonos eating sushi; white man in a business suit) and to focus instead on typical everyday experiences. Photographs by themselves can also serve as conversation starters and can be collaged into small books or posters. Be careful to gather photos that represent people of all skin colors in America. While photos from foreign countries can be beautiful, they can also perpetuate an impression that diversity means things foreign or found only in "other places." Focusing on children's local communities as well as on people in settings across the country provides authentic representation of the diversity around them. Foods, dress, and customs may certainly vary, but ample representation of people with all shades of skin engaging in simple, relatable daily experiences are important for children to see.

Encourage families and children to share drawings, pictures, stories, or empty boxes from the typical foods they eat at home. Starting within your group's own diversity allows children to make personal connections to different norms and connect similarities and differences in personally relevant ways. Allow children and families to contrast everyday types of meals and foods with special occasion foods from their own family traditions. Children can even compare and contrast how similar foods are prepared differently, such as pasta, rice, and bread, and whether some families eat meat or not. An added benefit is that this exploration will likely also highlight family style and religious and economic diversity.

Perhaps the most important materials are items that show people in varied shades of skin tone. For children to explore labels like *Black* and *White*, (which are not accurate color descriptions of actual skin tones), as well as the true shade of their own skin, they need materials that can reflect this. Crayons and pencils in shades of peaches, tans, and browns are important; these media do not blend as easily as paints. If budgets are too limited to purchase pre-mixed skin tone paint, creativity can come to the rescue. With more standard colors of paint, we can mix and blend brown, orange, yellow, red, black and white, like scientists, to find many shades of human skin color—and our own unique shade.

Children's literature also provides an opportunity for stories about racism, and about individuals or groups who have worked hard to promote equal rights. Look for simple but direct stories that:

- Include contextualized definitions
- Provide appropriate levels of details

- Omit graphic brutality
- Do not overdramatize violence
- Do not position people of color as helpless victims
- Include information on how both people of color and Whites work for racial equality
- Consider nonfiction (informational) books as well as fiction

The purpose of using these stories is not to vilify Whites or sanctify or pity people of color, but rather to reflect realities of historical inequality and emphasize the ongoing efforts to promote social justice. Sharing stories that define racism and engage children in thinking about what is fair or unfair might at first feel uncomfortable to some professionals working with young children. However it is essential that adults not underestimate children's observations and sensitivity to messages around them nor their capacity to meaningfully engage in thinking and talking about fairness, equity, and the hurt that negative beliefs about skin tones inflicts. Children notice differences in skin tone and internalize messages of differential value and expectations based on skin color/racial classification. It is our ethical and professional responsibility to support and guide their concept development and to encourage antiracist values and behaviors.

CLASSROOM STORY CORNER

Preparing Families

Dimitri had been teaching kindergarten for a few years, but his school had just adopted an antibias curriculum approach. This new approach included integrating books exploring racism in overt terms. He was excited with the goals of the new initiative, and after inspiring professional development training, was eager to get started and explore how his students were thinking about skin color. "The very morning after the PD session, I came into the classroom armed with some of the book titles the presenter had shared and some discussion prompts I might try if my kids didn't have much to say on their own. I shared the first story with them and they had a lot of questions and interesting comments. None of the students appeared shocked or upset, but rather intrigued by the new topic, and they seemed willing and able to investigate this new exploration of fairness and equality. It was a good start that morning. But by that evening things felt different.

I received three phone calls from families: two fathers and a custodial grandmother. One parent was out-rightly angry that his daughter was being exposed to concepts and history of racism. The other two family members expressed more surprise about the new terms their children came home talking about (racism and segregation). I realized that I had been so inspired by the importance of taking up this work with the children that I had not paused long enough to share the journey with families and invite their feedback and input. I know better than that! Parental buy-in is essential, even when the topics aren't so emotionally charged as this one, but exploring definitions, history, and current evidence of racism with their five- and six-year-olds? I needed to bring parents in on that first. I quickly backed up and provided the families with information, goals, and plans that eased their minds and actually generated great support. It sure was an important reminder though."

ENVIRONMENT

Overt exploration of different skin colors can be supported by some minor adjustments to the classroom space in addition to the careful selection and integration of key materials. Consider three suggestions:

- Add more space for dramatic play
- Create a self-portrait exploration area
- Designate space for family photos, stories, and artifacts

Adding more space for dramatic play provides a natural support for children's emerging explorations, questions, and the "trying-on" of social conventions. When given space, time, and open-ended materials, children are able to construct scenes and original dramas that allow them to wrestle with ideas, feelings, and experiences that might be too complex for them to discuss or process alone. Pretend or dramatic play is a safe place that allows children to feel more confident and empowered, which in turn allows for expanded dialogues and social negotiations. In their play, children are able to sort through confusing concepts and experiences by role playing, reexperiencing, and trying out different responses to those experiences. In their play, unlike in so many other areas of their lives, children are in control of what they experience and are able to choose to accept or reject roles.

This empowerment and confidence can, however, also reveal negative stereotypes and racist messages that children are exposed to from community or media sources. For children who have had negative experiences based on physical attributes associated with racial categories, their dramatic play might be a time when they relive hurtful memories. Or the pain associated with an experience might be refreshed by something another child does or says as they work through prejudiced beliefs. Because there is so much value in supporting children as they work through these experiences in their play, teachers should not shy away from situations in which these things might arise. It becomes even more important for early childhood professionals to listen to and observe carefully what children's play reveals about what they are thinking and feeling, and to be prepared to step in to guide expressions or prompt children to delve deeper into their beliefs when necessary.

To spark play explorations centered on skin colors, begin by stocking the dramatic play area with items that represent the norms and traditions of the children's close families. Even if all of the children in a group appear to be of the same racial category, simple everyday experiences are a safe, logical, and concrete place to begin exploring. As items and routines are shared from children's home and close family, additional information can then be sought on extended family members, customs, and routines. This chaining of children's family life from immediate to extended usually reveals a wider coverage of cultural traditions and customs. For example, a group of fair-skinned children who appear to be "all the same" will find that their extended family members' daily lives vary a great deal from one another.

Life experiences of family members who emigrated from other countries or who lived in various parts of the United States will shape their unique backgrounds and family heritage. There is great value in this kind of natural realization that rich variation resides among members of the same race category. Focus on items or activities that are used in or represent aspects of everyday activities, such as:

- Clothing
- Personal care
- Hair care
- Utensils
- Job tools
- Food items
- Related and varied environmental printed materials (such as menus, lists, labels, and signs)

Later, expand the variety of items in the space to integrate a wider range of racial/cultural artifacts, though still maintaining the emphasis on everyday routines. Be especially careful to avoid overused and inaccurate stereotypes, such as feathered head-dresses to represent Native American people or sombreros to represent Hispanic people. By focusing on universal aspects of everyday routines instead of on special occasions or holidays, you are keeping the connection close and concrete between children's own family experiences and the lived experience of individuals who are different from them. A learning goal here is for children to be able to clearly internalize that there are big or small differences between families but also common threads connecting us all.

From the toddler years, young children keenly attend to things that are the same and different. When you cultivate a climate in which children feel welcomed and supported to acknowledge what they are noticing, you will hear toddlers remarking with curious delight about similarities and differences. In my work I often hear the young toddlers noticing "same-same" or "not same-same," and they regularly make such assessments in relation to lunch items packed from home, clothing, girls' and boys' body parts, physical features, and toys. Often they will take the item being compared and hold it near the comparison piece, while exclaiming "Look! Same-same!" with quite a sense of accomplishment. This is the early cognitive categorization process which will prompt them to notice and comment on how skin colors or facial features are different or the same.

As children become keen observers of attributes in the people around them, facilitating an accompanying focus on their own features through self-portraits is a natural companion activity. Providing several small hand-held or larger wall-mounted mirrors is a useful strategy to support thought processes related to the comparing, categorizing, and matching of skin color. Select simple framed hand mirrors or empty makeup compact containers so that children can look at their reflections, but also provide larger mirror space where children can stand next to each other to make comparisons. Creating a small area that is in a quieter part of the room allows children to spend time focusing on their own features. Guiding children to learn to really look closely at their own and others' face encourages their aesthetic sense (their "artists' eye") and emphasizes the importance of seeing each person as a unique individual.

Young children can attend to physical features like hair texture and color, eye and nose shape, and skin shade—when adults take time to guide keen observation of themselves and each other. To support this attention, adults need to be comfortable noticing these differences and feel confident that looking at physical features through the artist's eye is about validating the inherent beauty in all human features. Cognitively, the ability to identify several attributes that are used to categorize people will expand children's thinking about labels and categories. When children are able to recognize that individuals retain several attributes that cross categories, they are building a cognitive flexibility that reduces the likelihood of rigid racial profiling and of categorizing people based solely on skin color.

Give children materials that enhance their ability to look closely and notice similarities and differences, and guide them in appreciating both.

Once children are making observations about their own and others' physical features it is important for adults to provide opportunities for varied forms of representation of what children are noticing and thinking. Beginning with an integrated project exploration of each child's own unique skin shade and continuing through their specific features encourages more awareness of similarities and differences among classmates. Using a plate as a palette, or small cups, have children keep track of dabs and drops of colors to literally blend and create their own personal shade, sort of like a makeup technician would do; mixing and testing a dab on the back of a hand. Discovering that I'm a toasted almond-gingerbread-peach while a friend is cinnamon-gingerbread-ivory is a new way to look at skin color and race labels. It is a new framework which is far more accurate to true human skin tones than *Black* or *White*. When children have created their personal paint shade, they then can paint self-portraits that more honestly represent what they look like.

Providing materials to color, paint, collage, sculpt, and draw representations of themselves helps children connect and represent in a variety of ways what they think about their own and others' skin tone and physical features. The artwork and stories the children create also provides teachers with valuable sources of assessment and evidence to understand children's internal processing of these complex concepts. Displaying children's real self-portraits with brief notes describing the process and purpose of mixing their own skin shades provides richly colorful documentation and establishes the group's intentionality in regard to studying race and skin color. This documentation is valuable evidence for families to share in children's process, and helps contribute meaningfully to children's explorations.

INTERACTIONS WITH CHILDREN

As you introduce racially diverse materials to children, engage them in discussions about what they see and think about the materials. If children have been around adults who have been uncomfortable with comments and questions about skin color differences, children might already be accustomed to holding back from verbalizing their thoughts. Start off with a simple statement about how the purpose of the richly diverse materials and experiences is to value and reflect the many ways that we are each different and similar to one another. Then invite children to explore and share their ideas, validating that ideas change through interactions but also that each person in the class has rights to a safe, respectful place here. Let children know that it is OK to ask questions and share opinions but that they also need to be open to listening to how their comments make other people feel. Just as with some of the antibias or antiracist books you may select to share with children do, these messages may feel unusually explicit and direct. However, it is important to outline clear goals, expectations, and ground rules to support children's feeling of psychological safety in the face of sensitive topics as well as to promote more meaningful and personal engagement with dialogues and activities.

As the explorations begin, observe children's play and interactions carefully to note value judgments or biases. Prepare yourself to use these moments to explore ideas of racism, racial equality, and curiosity about differences by listening and guiding conversations and play scenarios about skin color and fairness. Consider practicing scripts, which are prepared responses to things children might say. For example, what will you say if children ask why another child's skin is so dark or if they call it "dirty"? Take a few moments and write down a specific, short response that calmly acknowledges the child's comments and prompts further discussion. Creating a few simple scripts for any situation or comment that would typically leave you speechless is a valuable preparation tool that allows you to make the most of these teachable moments.

Newly hired preschool teacher Mei-Lin anticipated that her new class of children might wonder or ask questions about her heritage since she is the only Asian teacher in the small district. She wanted to be able to maintain a calm and open demeanor in the face of any sort of comment, so she planned responses and even role-played scenarios in her head. "I was new to the school and also the town, but I had enough experience there to know that I would appear unfamiliar to many of the children. I needed to be able to project an attitude that welcomed their curiosity but I also wanted to help them learn about personal respect and boundaries.

"I worked on planned replies to help me not get tongue-tied. Most started off with acknowledgement and an invitation to talk more, like 'I hear you asking me about my accent (or my eyes, hair, skin). I sound (or look) different than you because my family is from a different place. I am Chinese American; my family is from a country called China, but I was born in the United States. Do you know some things about China?' I wanted to appear confident to my children and families both in my own background as well as with their questions. I hoped this would open up more dialogue about anything they are wondering about."

INTERACTIONS AMONG CHILDREN

Opening up the path for children to explore their ideas and attitudes about racism and skin color can lead to increases in dramatic play scenarios as children use their play as a natural place to work through confusion. Observation and careful attention to children's dialogue is always a key element of quality teaching, but when engaging around social justice issues, it becomes even more important that teachers listen and observe vigilantly to capture children's dialogues and support their efforts to process and think through these new ideas. Children's internal conflicts, misconceptions, or emerging values become evident through their play, even when they are not evident during other activities. Children will repeat new terms and phrases, use or misuse new information, and wrestle with reconciling new ideas with existing internalized ideas and feelings. Wrestling with internal cognitive conflicts (new ideas that challenge existing ideas) and negotiating social conflict as concepts are challenged by others—these are essential elements of the learning process. This conflict is a natural and important part of all learning, but when children engage in dialogues about skin color and their thoughts and feelings about it, discriminatory or exclusionary values might emerge. The inflammatory or hurtful nature of racial comments or stereotypes that emerge from children's developing ideas about skin color differences can make many teachers nervous. Preservice teachers in my classes often comment that they shy away from books which explicitly talk about racism, such as Pat Thomas's *The Skin I'm In: A First Look at Racism.* The term and the topic cause anxiety, revealing a lack of confidence in knowing how to guide children's discussions about provocative topics that the teachers worry might involve hurtful interactions.

When we hear and note negative or hurtful interactions, we are obligated to respond, albeit sensitively and carefully. We must balance children's need and their right to express their developing ideas against children's rights to a safe setting, free from disparaging or degrading comments. Further, we must also support children who are treated unfairly while still providing them with space to assert themselves and develop conflict-management skills. In short, we have to carefully decide when to step in and when to give children room to grow.

Shantay's experience with a group of three boys in her kindergarten reveals this dilemma:

> Jamal, Andre, and Cole were in the kitchen area during a free play time last week, playing at cooking and eating in a café. I heard their voices get raised and Jamal saying "Yeah, you do!" I quietly moved closer but did not directly enter their area so that I could observe and listen better, but I didn't rush in too quickly. As I listened I heard the following dialogue, which I wrote down in my notebook.

> **ANDRE:** *Sitting at the table with dishes.* No, not me again.

> **JAMAL:** Yeah, you gotta.

> **ANDRE:** No way, man. It's not my turn today. I'm still eating. Cole, you gotta get the dishes.

> **COLE:** I'm on my way to work now. *Pretending to pay his bill.*

> **ANDRE:** *Softly.* Not me.

> **JAMAL:** *With a push at Andre's chair.* Oh yeah? You gotta because you're a wetback and alls your kind does is dishes! *[With the racial slur I begin to come over. The boys continued as I entered the play space.]*

> **ANDRE:** *In a louder tone with a flushed face.* We don't!

> **JAMAL:** *Lowering his voice.* Oh yeah? If you don't I gonna call and get your ma deported, wetback!

> At this point Andre became visibly upset and I stepped in. I put my arm around Andre's shoulder and a hand on Jamal's chair. I needed to stand up for Andre and let Jamal know this kind of racist insult isn't OK, but I also had to let Andre take a role in standing up to it appropriately. I started by reflecting what I heard and saw. "Jamal, I heard you use a really hurtful word to Andre and say something untrue, hurtful, and threatening about his family. I see that Andre doesn't like this, and this kind of talk hurts me too. I can't let people in this room hurt each other." Honestly, I was kind of taken aback by the intentionality in Jamal's statements and not totally sure what to do, but I continued to engage both boys to try to use this as a learning moment. "Andre, it sounds like Jamal's words upset you and they upset me too. It's not fair to use hurtful words like that and when someone says something hurtful about you or your family you have a right to say *stop that.*"

In our community, I know there is a lot of tension between racial groups, and children here are exposed to a lot of openly racist messages, so it's not too surprising that Jamal knows how to deliver a racial slur. I don't think he fully gets what he is saying, but he knows it's hurtful and who to use that language with (Andre's family immigrated to our city from Honduras, though I happen to know they have actually become legal citizens). I knew I needed to get Jamal talking more about his ideas and the things he is repeating, not shut him down. If I shut him down he will still hear and take in those messages but will just become more skillful at hiding it from me. I wrapped up the moment with the two boys by saying that we are all going to talk more about things we have heard around our community or on TV about race as a class. Some days it's so hard to juggle the realities of our children's lives with the learning goals I have for them from a teacher perspective. But I really believe the kids need me to guide them through all of these things, and I can't leave them alone to figure out those hard lessons.

As a seasoned teacher in urban schools, Shantay's experience gives her a foundation for making decisions about when and how to handle children's conceptions about skin color and racism. She has also lived in her community for a long time, and the children respond to her with an unspoken sense that she understands the context of their lives. For teachers who are newer to their school communities, getting to know children's family and neighborhood lives can be a tremendously helpful step in bridging personal culture gaps and creating bonds. This work of building relationships through learning about one another is essential work of all newly gathered groups and is a rich starting place at the beginning of a school year. Children's trust and feelings of physical and psychological safety need to be addressed in these early days, so that children and families feel comfortable opening up. Successful and meaningful antiracist, antibias education depends upon group members' ability to reflect and share among each other. And being able to do that requires building trust and a sense of community early on.

Building trusting relationships takes time and intentional effort, including experiences, groupings, choices of materials, and promoting open dialogues about similarities and differences.

LEARNING EXPERIENCES: PROMOTING POSITIVE RACIAL IDENTITY AND ANTIRACIST BELIEFS

Meaningfully exploring skin colors with children involves an intentional, integrated curriculum approach in which adults guide children to look inward and outward: inward in terms of their own appearance and beliefs about different skin tones, and outward in relation to how others are similar and different from themselves. The learning will deepen self-awareness as well as strengthen relationships among the group. Because of the personal and reflective nature of the study, building trust and forming good relationships is a building block into the study of skin tone. Teachers should begin with overarching learning goals and map out progressive, related experiences which will support progress towards the goals. Consider the following sequenced chain of experiences as well as those in Table 4.2:

TABLE 4.2 *Learning Experiences*

Sequenced Learning Experience Goals and Age-Related Considerations

Learning Experience	Infant–Toddler	Preschool Age	Kindergarten–1st Grade	2nd–3rd Grade
My Favorite Things: Lists and Stories Goals: • Encourage children to share things about themselves. • Engage in creating multiple representations of self.	• Use observation notes and photographs to create favorites lists. • Create photo albums of pictures of favorite items. • Prompt toddlers to talk about favorites with prompts like: What do you like best (to do at home, to eat for dinner, to play at school, to do with friends, etc.)? Write down their answers.	• Create lists with drawings, photos, and dictated stories. • Share picture books with "What I like about…" messages. • Create "What I like best about…" books or collages. • Play guessing games around favorites; identify several descriptive attributes and have your class guess what it could be by using attribute clues.	• Organize lists into themes (self, family, friends, neighborhood). • Create mini-books from children's lists. • Connect to children's literature. • Identify favorite attributes of self and create a story where this is amplified; talk about the "superstar me."	• Create daily "favorites"—reflection journals with children's reflective writing about their favorite part of school today. • Create poems from favorites lists using different formats. • Celebrate each other with "10 best things about you" notes (Each child has a page with 10 lines taped to their back, class has 10 minutes to run from person to person filling in one line.).

Learning Experience	Infant–Toddler	Preschool Age	Kindergarten–1st Grade	2nd–3rd Grade
Who I Am: Words, and Pictures to Describe Me Goals: • Identify attributes of self. • Categorize attributes as internal and external. • Create representations of self.	• Prompt awareness of external image with mirrors and dress up items. • Describe caring behavior and how friends act toward each other. • Use child's name and attributes in rhymes.	• Play guessing games using attributes to guess child's name. • Make "All about me" books. • Write "Who am I?" riddles. • Read books that use predicting and guessing prompts about attributes.	• Trace the child's body; have the child write and draw aspects of himself inside (around edge for external and in center for internal); post these around room or halls, and have others guess who outline is. • Create "I am…" and fill-in-the-blank poems.	• Create more intricate external/internal descriptions and representations of how children see themselves. • Expand vocabulary with synonym strings.
Self-Portrait Images: Painting Goals: • See physical appearance from an artist's eye. • Identify unique elements of physical appearance. • Create and compare unique skin tone to others.	• Consider using more photos of children as a start. • Prompt children's dialogues about their physical characteristics. • Match similarities and differences among children. • Mix and blend paint as a prelude to mixing skin shades.	• Mix and blend with a variety of materials. • Explore paint chips from a hardware or paint store to see the spectrum of shades in related colors. • Use mirrors to look closely at specific features.	• Create stories and poems about own skin shade and the process to create it. • Make equations about how much of each paint color was used to mix (for example, 1 drop tan + 3 drops nutmeg). • Use a magnifying glass to look closely at skin and hair textures.	• Keep graphs and tally charts of skin-shade mixing. • Create comparative charts or Venn diagrams of similarities and differences. • Explore stories and literature with overt discussion of skin color and multiracial and multiethnic people.
Exploring Our Rainbow: Shades of Skin Tones and Labels Goals: • Encourage children to share things about themselves. • Engage in creating multiple representations of self.	• Blend and mix paints of similar colors to make subtle shades. • Include paint chips in color families to focus on subtle differences.	• Display all the unique shades. • Count and recognize all the differences and similarities. • Discuss how we are the same and different. • Emphasize the beauty of the "rainbow of us."	• Make patterns and mosaics from all the shades. • Identify items in nature that also have a range of shades (tree bark, grasses, stones, etc.). • Discuss connections to naturally occurring shade variations.	• Mix skin tone shades for family members, compare to class's. • Sort and chart other found materials with naturally occurring shade variations. • Explore up close with microscopes or magnifying glasses. • Identify other similarities and differences among us.

(Continued)

TABLE 4.2 *(Continued)*

Learning Experience	Infant–Toddler	Preschool Age	Kindergarten–1st Grade	2nd–3rd Grade
Equality Means Respect for Everyone Goals: • Encourage children to share things about themselves. • Engage in creating multiple representations of self.	• Integrate key vocabulary like *fair, needs, equal, value,* and *caring*. • Comment when children demonstrate care-taking actions and acts of fairness. • Connect feelings with actions about fairness and caring.	• Focus on feelings related to acts of caring and kindness. • Demonstrate how we stand up (for ourselves or others) when things are unfair. • Share stories about how we feel when things are fair or unfair.	• Read stories about people who have advocated for fairness and equality. • Identify laws that are written to provide for equality. • Explore how rights and needs are different. • Connect to equality and equity.	• Engage with community guests or family members who are part of advocacy groups or efforts to promote equality and equity. • Identify ways children can take on advocacy work in their community (letter writing, resources drives). • Read stories about people who have worked for social justice.

My Favorite Things: Lists and Stories. This is a comfortable place to start along the path of building relationships and focusing children on sharing reflections of themselves. Encourage children to share things they love or appreciate about their personalities, skills, families, and neighborhoods. As they generate their lists, prompt them to talk about specifics and why each item has made their favorites list. Numerous products can be created from the lists to capture children's thinking and also prompt continued reflection. Prompt children to expand on *why* they consider something their favorite thing they love.

Who I Am: Words and Pictures to Describe Me. Building on the favorites lists, the children's focus will begin to narrow in on themselves as they delve more deeply into physical characteristics, family style, and personality attributes that they can use to understand and describe themselves. Children's words and images should include both external and internal attributes, and artifacts can be categorized to emphasize internal and external features. Consider lists, stories, poems, and photo collages to represent children's thinking about how they respond to "who I am." This segment sets the stage for being able to recognize others' similarities and differences in comparison to self. The dual external/internal emphasis also lays a conceptual foundation for recognizing that people's identities are made up of a variety of attributes, that appearance is just one type and internal aspects are a big part of who we are. Early, albeit rudimentary, awareness of appearance attributes (like skin color) in the larger context of the whole person is an important part of reducing the likelihood of adopting prejudiced beliefs. ("People are defined by more than just the color of their skin.")

Self-Portrait Images: Painting. This project begins to focus children's attention specifically on skin color and on comparing their unique shade to other children's. As children begin with either basic paint colors or a set of skin-tone-shaded paints, they will embark on a mixing project to make, test, remake, retest, and discover their very own personal color. Using small paint cups, add drops of color and mix, keeping track of colors and quantities. Dab a dot on the back of their hands to test it against their own skin shade. Children will discover that their shade comprises starting colors similar to other children's, with some different colors and different end results. One major advantage to this exploration is that it will yield different shades even among a group of children who all identify with one race category (all White, all Hispanic, etc.). When children have blended their own personal shade, they can then paint self-portraits using mirrors and pictures of themselves as reference. When the final portraits are displayed, a rainbow of shades of brown and peach will span the classroom walls. This is truly an inquiry process as children engage in a "prediction-test-observation-conclusion-discovery" exploration of self and others. Engage children with ample open-ended questions, such as:

- Which shades do you think will mix and be closest to your own skin tone?
- What can you do to make it darker/lighter?
- Did you think there would be so many shades that would blend to make your own color?
- How is your color different from other children's?

Exploring Our Rainbow: Shades of Skin Tones and Labels. Once children have created their unique skin tones, they have personal data to use to compare their unique shade to others in the group. As children examine similarities and differences in the colors and quantities used to blend shades, they are able to make connections about how we share certain attributes and are different in others. A key concept that is revealed through this comparative exploration is the variety among all of us—that human skin color is different than the color categories used and misused to describe races such as white, black, red, and yellow.

For older children, conversations can more explicitly explore how, when, and why such labels were created and their use. Children can be guided carefully and sensitively through some of the historical context, including derogatory uses of certain labels like "yellow" or "red" in reference to skin color. For younger children, comparisons of their own skin shades is a concrete experience through which to recognize that there is a difference between color labels like those above and actual skin tone(s). Children are also given a concrete framework for recognizing that, within each category, great variety exists and that we can fit into a category label like White or Black, but our skin tone is actually *not* that color. When children's investigations reflect the variety of shades of skin tone and show the connections and similarities among us all, they can more readily internalize the message that sameness exists alongside difference. This is a strong foundation for the next step: an explicit exploration of equality and respect for everyone.

Equality Means Respect for Everyone. When they are aware of the natural variety among all shades of human skin, children can more easily make their own connections towards valuing all people equally. When they have had the concrete experience of blending and seeing the connections among each of us, the focus is then on our shared humanness, and the differences among us are secondary. It is important for children to have this foundation so that they can learn to see and counteract racism and systemic racism. As children develop a relationship to their own self-image and ethnic, racial, and cultural self-identity, they are able to do so through a lens of equality. Activities that focus children on identifying the rights of all people, through the framework of rights they wish for themselves, provide language and values they can readily internalize. Consider beginning with discussions about rights with, and writing down children's responses to, questions like the following:

- What does it mean to have a right to something?
- What do you believe every one of us has a right to?
- How are rights and needs alike or different?
- Do all people everywhere have the same rights or the same needs?
- What does it feel like when our rights are taken away?
- What kinds of things can people do to make sure our rights or needs are met?

As children demonstrate understanding of concepts and terms like *rights*, *needs*, *equality*, and *equity*, they can then create their own so-called Bill of

Rights, either focusing on rights for all children or for all people, depending on their interest. The Internet includes several examples of adult- and child-created documents as a resource. When the document is complete, host a signing event at school or in your community to publicize the document and the children's explorations.

Family Partnerships

Meaningfully involving families in young children's school life and programs is an essential component of professional practice. Families are rich resources on children's interests, habits, and experiences, in and out of early childhood settings. In this **video**, listen to these professionals describe the valuable "funds of knowledge" that family life provides for children, and consider the important place of this knowledge base in children's school lives. Consider also how you can tap into this knowledge base.

WELCOME LETTER

Taking up social justice work with children is intense and not what most families are expecting from children's early education experiences. In your first communications with families it is important to outline your values and beliefs, and some of the ways the children may be exploring these topics and issues together. Emphasize the child-centered nature of your goals and the overarching purpose of providing children with a safe place to discuss their thoughts and feelings about these issues. You can share with families that this is a naturally occurring part of children's ongoing identity development and that providing ways for children to explore and represent their thinking about it is valuable to healthy identity development.

ASK FOR STORIES AND SUPPORT

Another way to involve families in the self-exploration is to designate shelf, table, or wall space specifically for family items. Families can be encouraged to share artifacts, photos, and stories about life in their home, special customs or traditions that are shared, and members of the family network. Ask families to share everyday traditions, routines, or major family happenings as they feel comfortable with the emphasis on valuing and celebrating each child's home and family life. Reserving space can sometimes be hard to manage, with early childhood spaces needing to serve so many purposes throughout the day. But setting aside a prominent place and helping families take care in the design of displays conveys a message that families are as important here as in children's lives. Consider attaching large frames with plastic "glass" to cabinet doors in sink cabinets and storage or changing areas; use these to create family photo and story collages. Children will be comforted by feeling their family present during their day but will also have ready access to a window into others' family members and home traditions.

INVITE TO HONOR FAMILIES

At least a few times during the year, engage children in creating ways to value and honor their family members and home traditions. Children all need to feel their families are a valuable part of their care and education settings, and families need to feel connected and integral too. Focus on children's everyday home lives and the daily routines that are a part of their lives. This is a comfortable, emotionally safe way to ensure that families feel a sense of supportive connection among each other, as opposed to focusing on type of home, parent jobs, or holidays. These may be important parts of children's lives certainly, but be aware of families who may be homeless or in temporary housing, of foster children, or of parents who are not employed outside the home.

INVITE TO CELEBRATE LEARNING

As children's explorations cycle and their representations emerge, take time along the way to share your reflections, notes, and samples of children's work with families. Information can be sent home, back-and-forth journals can be created, and families can be invited in to share documentation panels, slide shows, and movies of children engaging in this work. As children share their investigations and explorations with family and people important in their lives, their messages of awareness and appreciation are being emphasized. As with all family communication, creating opportunities for two-way communication is essential. Be sure to convey information in ways (language and format) that families can understand. When inviting family members to the program, be sensitive to work or home schedules and considerations such as child care and transportation. Asking families to share reflections ahead of time on the topics children will be learning about can generate interest and give you a "heads up" on any unforeseen concerns that you will want to address.

Summary

WHAT DOES *RACE* REALLY MEAN?

- Major flaws and inaccuracies in early research have since discredited any claims of scientific basis for racial superiority or difference.
- Research now recognizes more differences among groups than between groups.
- There is some use for collecting data on people based on racial categories, as with the U.S. census, when this information is used to drive policies, laws, and practice designed to reduce disparate outcomes based on race.
- Census data reveal a continuing trend of rapid growth in Hispanic groups and other groups of people of color.
- Recent decades have seen major growth in multiracial and multiethnic populations, especially among children.

RELATIONSHIP BETWEEN RACE AND (UNEARNED) PRIVILEGE: WHITENESS IN AMERICA

- Despite some progress to close the gaps through landmark legal and sociopolitical actions, there remains in the U.S. a clear value system that positions middle- and upper-class Whites in a privileged status.
- Even when individuals do not hold racist views or promote racist values, when they fail to take action to equalize opportunities and promote equality in systems and policies, their inaction serves to perpetuate racial inequality.
- Professionals need to critically examine the compelling and overwhelming evidence of disparate access to opportunity and outcomes for people based on race, especially in terms of academic and scholastic achievement.

WHY DISCUSS RACE AND RACISM WITH CHILDREN?

- Young children notice and think about different skin colors and are intellectually and emotionally capable of relating to being treated fairly or unfairly, and having needs met or unmet.
- Considering children's natural curiosity about differences in skin tone and their capacity to understand both fairness and equality, early childhood is the prime time to engage children in forthright discussions about race and racism.

CURRICULAR CONNECTIONS

- Curricular planning for engaging children in exploring race and facets of ethnicity requires deliberate, careful planning and widespread integration.
- Early childhood professionals should consider all materials, interactions, and guided experiences when planning instruction and learning goals that include a focus on race, ethnicity, equality, and equity.
- Materials and experiences should focus on children's own lives: their own skin color, their families, simple everyday routines and the ways these are similar and different from each other.

FAMILY PARTNERSHIPS

- When classroom topics include investigations of race and racism, beginning with open communication with families is especially important.
- Include families in the investigations as well as in celebrations of children's progress and learning.
- Invite families as valued partners into the classroom through visits, stories, artifacts, or photos, to promote a feeling of valuing and connectedness for children.

Chapter Learning Outcomes: Self-Assessment

Use this space to reflect on how well you have achieved the learning goals for this chapter in terms of evaluating your own competency in the topics below. List three to five key concepts that you have learned from the chapter.

Identify definitions and conceptions of *race* from sociopolitical and historical perspectives.	
Explore current statistics on racial disparities in the United States.	
Examine children's ideas about differences in skin color, power, and privilege.	
Create curricular connections to explore skin color and promote racial equality.	
Practice teaching strategies to meaningfully engage families.	

Chapter Activities

DISCUSSION QUESTIONS

1. How does the current research and thinking about race labels impact how you think about and define race, skin color differences, and racism?

2. Identify examples of institutional racism. Discuss the implications of institutional racism on children's development, on family functioning, and on society in general.

SELF-REFLECTION

1. Have you ever felt treated differently based on the color of your skin, or do you know someone close to you who has? Describe the situation and how this felt. What did you (they) do? How did you—or could you—regain a sense of equity and fairness?

TEACHING DISPOSITION

What three things do you feel will challenge you the most about teaching antiracist, antibias perspectives to young children? Create your list and elaborate on why you feel these will be challenges. For each one, brainstorm two resources you will use for support in working through the challenges.

Challenges to teaching antiracist perspectives	Why these are challenging for me	What supports will help me work through the challenge

IN THE FIELD

Watch the documentary film *A Class Divided* about one teacher's experiment with young children and bigotry, online from *Frontline* through PBS.org. Consider the classroom and individual implications of messages (both implicit and explicit) that promote racism and how early childhood professionals can reduce these impacts. Identify strategies that could work to reduce racist messages in current early childhood settings. http://www.pbs.org/wgbh/pages/frontline/shows/divided/etc/view.html

Weblinks

Race: An online project of the American Anthropological Association that provides research-based resources and information about race and differences among humans and skin color and includes historical information about racism in the U.S. *www.Understandingrace.org*

The Children's Bill of Rights: An online document that was created by children from seven countries and is a useful advocacy tool in support of equal rights for all children. *http://www.newciv.org/ncn/cbor.html*

The Annie E. Casey Foundation (AECF) is a private charitable organization that focuses on building better futures for disadvantaged children throughout the United States. The foundation website includes a wealth of statistical data and reports, as well as resources for teaching about race and antiracism. Search for AECF.org.

5

Language *and* Nationality

Of all the ways that humans differ from one another, linguistic communication is one of the most likely to present itself in early childhood classrooms. The population of school-age children living in homes where English is not the primary language continues to increase, reaching over 11 million, or 21% of school age children (U.S. Department of Education, 2010). In some areas, the vast majority of non-English speaking children and families share a common language. In other areas, a regional dialect or nonstandard form of English is spoken in homes and communities. Some of our language differences are due to regional pronunciations, immigration from other countries, and family culture. Nationally, our linguistic diversity creates a symphony of distinct voices. Yet this is sharply in contrast to a largely English-only monolingual teaching force that does not reflect the growing cultural and linguistic diversity of the student population (Robinson & Clardy, 2011). This mismatch of cultures can lead to a discord between children's background and teachers' background, causing challenges for communication and mutually respectful, highly interactive partnerships.

Early childhood professionals are uniquely positioned to validate the complex context of communication and linguistic differences and to support all children in becoming successful, literate communicators. The influence we have on children's early school experiences leaves a lasting and vivid impression on children and families and absolutely lays the foundation for later emotional and intellectual success. Unfortunately, in many schools and classrooms communicating in languages other than Standard English is rejected and viewed as inferior or unacceptable. It is imperative that early childhood professionals recognize the rich context of language as more than just a communication tool and value bi- and multilingual family culture as a resource in children's and schools' lives. This chapter explores the larger context of language in terms of communication and culture, as well as strategies for embracing and enhancing linguistic diversity while supporting children's process of learning English.

Integrating children's home language into early childhood settings through bilingual communication (whenever possible), materials, and labels, is an important way to make connections to children's family life.

LEARNING
OUTCOMES
. . . .

- Define characteristics of linguistic diversity including different languages, dialects, and accents

- Identify successful approaches to supporting linguistically diverse children

- Explain the purpose and complex contexts of language

- Practice teaching strategies to support linguistically diverse children

- Create partnerships to support linguistically diverse children and families

Understanding and Valuing Linguistic Differences

Children from linguistically diverse backgrounds may have little or no proficiency in English and may be in varying stages of learning English, but some children may be proficient speakers and literate in English even if family members are not. And yet other families may be fully fluent in English while using another language as the primary family language. Communication differences include formats other than verbal language, such as with sign language, but these will be explored in a separate chapter. While there is an overidentification of children learning English who are referred for special education services (though these are often not required), linguistic diversity is not a classified "special need."

Recent research also points to the benefits of growing up bilingual because of the positive outcomes that follow from the challenge of having to work harder to interpret nonverbal cues to make sense of interactions with individuals speaking a new language (Yow & Markman, 2011). As children are faced with communication which is unfamiliar, they are challenged to use more cognitive strategies and social cues (such as speaker eye gaze). But researchers have also found that bilingual children tend to be more sensitive to the communication partner's perspectives and cues. Bilingual children tend to both interpret ambiguous situations more readily but also provide more information to the listener. Research such as this underscores the perspective that growing up bi- or multilingual can be a strong resource for children's linguistic, cognitive, and social development. However, effectively and confidently teaching linguistically diverse children can be intimidating for teachers.

There are a number of reasons a teacher might feel challenged when it comes to effectively working with linguistically diverse children and families. Part of the picture relates to the heavy emphasis schools place on verbal communication skills, and part of it relates to socialized values which regard **Standard English** more highly than other languages. A final aspect that can challenge teachers is feeling unprepared or lacking confidence in the skills needed to successfully bridge linguistic gaps with children and families. Ideally, teacher preparation programs include focused study on diversity issues as well as a clear integration throughout courses (Robinson & Clardy, 2011). So for example, a program might include a course on diversity in early childhood or multicultural education, and also integrate strategies for supporting multiple languages in bilingual children in a Language Arts course. In a family systems course, the program might also identify resources and tools for communicating with families whose language is not English.

This kind of focused and widely integrated approach is important for strengthening the skills and dispositions teachers need to confidently apply the principles advocated by researchers and the National Association for the Education of Young Children. A key overarching message that you must recognize throughout your professional preparation is the overwhelming evidence (from both research and personal stories) that learning more than one language is a developmental and social strength. And while successfully teaching and caring for linguistically diverse children does not require that all teachers become fluent in many languages, success does begin with valuing multilingualism as an asset to the classroom and children's lives. Mounting research evidence validates that modifications to instruction designed to support children learning English actually benefit all children academically (Hernandez, Denton, & Macartney, 2008).

DUAL LANGUAGE LEARNERS

Over the past few decades several terms have been used to describe children who are learning multiple languages. These terms include *bilingual, limited English proficient,* and *English language learner.* The more recent term, *dual language learner,* is used as a way to validate the continued development of the child's home language while also learning English (as opposed to an emphasis only on learning English in a term such as English language learner; Fuentes, 2011). **Dual language learners** (DLL) comprises a highly diverse group. These individuals can enter centers and schools with prior formal care and learning experience ranging from nothing to highly organized and structured academic schooling. Their prior experiences will influence how quickly they adjust to the new setting and achieve program expectations. Nationally, Spanish-speakers represent over 77% of the DLL population, and Spanish is the top language spoken by DLL children in 43 states. However, in some parts of the United States the number of different languages spoken in communities and schools is counted in the dozens and more. For example, 80 different languages are spoken in the Bellevue, Washington, school district (bsd405.org, 2012). Distinct Asian languages (Chinese, Vietnamese, Korean, Hmong) are among the most frequently spoken languages after Spanish, representing nearly 10% of the DLL population (Batalova & McHugh, 2010).

However, regional patterns of immigration and resettlement of refugees vary across the United States and impact the concentration and distribution of non-English speakers. As population patterns and language concentrations continue to increase and fluctuate, it becomes even more imperative that early childhood professionals develop skills and dispositions to ensure linguistic, academic, and social success for DLL children. In addition to understanding language diversity, professionals need to be aware of the unique adjustments that recently immigrated or refugee families are making. Consider the experience of the teachers in this **video** as they experience children's concerns about undocumented immigrant family members.

STANDARD ENGLISH AND DIALECTS

Standard English is the written and spoken form of English that is sociopolitically considered the norm or standard. It is defined as "standard" by groups in positions of power. In general, Standard English is the basis for the format and structure of English used in education settings and grammar books, though there is no official single dialect (or pronunciation style) that is ideal. Some nonnative English speakers who might be fluent in English might still speak with an accent. Individuals who live in the some geographic areas of the United States are often identified with that region by dialect. A dialect can involve alternative pronunciation as well as changes in grammatical structure, compared to Standard English. The dialect of the southern United States is the largest regional dialect, and African American or Black English is the best-known (Gollnick & Chinn, 2009). While it is controversial, there is educational value in using dialect language in schools, both to validate children's home/community identity and to connect instruction to their familiar or predominant form of language and thinking. Dialects are grammatically complex, culturally rich speech pattern systems, and are not "slang" or watered down versions of English.

There are many dialects across the United States, and all are valid and should all be viewed as equally legitimate. Unfortunately, negative and inappropriate assumptions are often made about an individual's intellectual prowess or social class based on accent or dialect, with some dialects being held in higher esteem than others. This kind of bias has a negative impact on children's linguistic, academic, and social development, as Christine's story illustrates.

My Dialect Made Me "Disabled"

When I was in kindergarten my mom left my dad and we moved from Georgia to Wyoming. When I first started school, I remember my teachers were constantly correcting my pronunciation. Looking back I can understand the goal of having me acclimate to the speech patterns of the area, but I still remember how embarrassed I felt by the public and sharp corrections. It really felt more like being shamed in front of the other children. The teachers became so frustrated with how I spoke that they made me leave the classroom three times a week for special education services.

I hated being labeled as "special ed" and disabled. I mean, I talked like my mom and sister and like all the other people did around me where I was from. Why was that "disabled"? The teachers didn't try to hide their disdain for me and I felt picked on about how I talked. The other children started to correct me like the teachers did, which made me talk less and less. I fell behind in class activities because I became so quiet. These early years of school were just torture, painful torture.

NAEYC Position Statements

RESPONDING TO LINGUISTIC AND CULTURAL DIVERSITY

The National Association for the Education of Young Children (NAEYC) has a longstanding history of promoting teacher practices which support and value children from diverse backgrounds. In addition to frequent specially themed editions of the journal *Young Children* and regular articles on innovative practices in multicultural and antibias education, NAEYC has also drafted focused statements to guide professional practice. The 1996 revision of the *Developmentally Appropriate Practice* position statement included a newly strengthened emphasis on understanding the unique cultural context of children's lives, also emphasized in the most recent 2009 revision (Bredekamp & Copple, 1997; Copple & Bredekamp, 2009) and was supported by the pivotal statement on linguistic diversity drafted the year before. The 1995 position statement, specifically and solely focused on linguistic and cultural diversity, was created to (NAEYC, 1995):

- Clarify terms
- Identify challenges for professionals and linguistically diverse children in early childhood programs
- Outline recommendations for best practices when working with linguistically and culturally diverse children

The statement on Responding to Linguistic and Cultural Diversity (NAEYC, 1995) remains a guiding framework for professionals. It emphasizes language as a key connection to children's family culture and traditions and calls for professionals to support families in preserving the continued acquisition and use of home language while English is acquired. Drafted in response to increasing enrollment in early childhood programs of children whose home language is other than English, now nearly 20 years later, the enrollment trend continues even more robustly and the need for skilled practice is even greater. The 1995 statement presented research evidence that supports professionals' realization—that "knowing more than one language is a cognitive asset" (NAEYC, 1995, p. 2), and that supporting children's development of multiple languages enhances overall development. The statement emphasizes practice which is child-centered and uses a "non-deficit approach," meaning that children's unique strengths are focused on and maximized, as opposed to the focus being on what children are lacking (NAEYC, 1995, p. 4). For example, children should be valued as language learning or emerging bilingual, as opposed to being labeled as lacking proficiency in English (or

as *limited English proficient*, an earlier term used in research that positions children as deficient). In the years that have passed since the statement, the research evidence supporting these views has only increased. The core recommendations for practice remain valid and useful for professionals and are summarized in Figure 5.1. Use this chart to also reflect on specific practices or ideas for strategies you can use in your own work with linguistically diverse children and families.

SCREENING AND ASSESSMENT OF YOUNG DUAL LANGUAGE LEARNERS

NAEYC's newest statement relating to DLL children is a joint effort in collaboration with the National Association of Early Childhood Specialists in State Departments of Education. Released in 2005, *Screening and Assessment of Young English-Language Learners* focuses on goals and strategies for evaluating linguistically diverse children (NAEYC, 2005). The statement was specifically drafted in response to several challenges:

- Growing numbers of English language learners in early childhood classrooms
- Widespread mislabeling of English language learners for special education services
- "Scarcity of appropriate assessments to use with English language learners" (p. 2)
- Lack of adequately trained staff to provide assessment and evaluation recommendations

Including the families of dual language learning children can help support teacher efforts to meaningfully integrate children's home language in the early childhood setting.

FIGURE 5.1

NAEYC Linguistic and Cultural Diversity Statement Summary

Stakeholders	Recommendations	Key Practices	Your Examples: What Do You Do to Support English Language Learners?
Children	• Recognize that language-learning is complex and heavily reliant on context; connect literacy skills to broader conceptual contexts. • Encourage children to share and build knowledge in a variety of ways. • Support development and instruction of English skills through the child's home language for several years as proficiency develops. • Understand that children's conceptual knowledge (what they think and know) might lag behind their skills (what they can do or express in English).	• Make connections among content areas such as by using a thematic or project approach so children can more readily see conceptual relationships. • Look closely at children's expressions in art, dramatic play, block building, gesturing, and problem solving to see existing knowledge, skills, and complex or abstract thoughts being expressed as well as opportunities for growth. • Use bilingual materials, provide instructions in child's native language, assess progress using bilingual instruments. • Model appropriate English. • Accept children's attempts at English use, even if incorrect, and expand or adjust their attempts by rephrasing or repeating their ideas back to them.	
Families	• Validate families as the child's first and primary teachers. • Recognize that all learning happens in and is supported by the context of children's home life. • Forge active and reciprocal relationships with families. • Articulate to families the intellectual benefits and cultural importance of continuing to foster development in the home language as children (and families, in some cases) learn English.	• Visit children's home community and interact with family and community members to be able to make connections to the context of children's lives. • Invite families to share who they are and who their child is in the larger frame of their lives outside of school. • Welcome families to share important parts of their home and community life with the class through stories, songs, art, routines, and customs. • Share information about the child's life at school in formats that the family can understand (native language for non-English speaking families, appropriate language level).	

Professional Preparation	• Teacher education should include specific education and training in diversity studies (approaches and skills), multicultural education, cross-cultural communication, and family diversity. • Support the ongoing development of a diverse teacher force. • Recruit and support bi- or multilingual teachers.	• Promote courses, conferences, and workshops that cover topics related to working with diverse children and families. • Provide teacher education and training in a variety of formats and community-centered venues to make professional preparation programs accessible. • Support bilingual teachers as a resource and advocate for children and families but do not overwhelm or over burden them (for example, by using them as school-wide translators, giving them extra tasks, or continually pulling them out of the classroom to serve other rooms).
Programs and Practice	• Support and value home language use as an asset to children's learning. • Maintain high expectations for all children in both linguistic and overall development. • Develop reciprocal relationships with families.	• Integrate children's home language(s) throughout the classroom and curriculum (using labels, schedules, materials, bulletin boards, and more). • Identify ways children develop and express complex ideas, especially nonverbally, to ensure that language learners are expressing knowledge and being recognized as having complex ideas. • Model appropriate English language skills while welcoming and encouraging children's attempts at English use. • Convene parent-staff committees or working groups to design and evaluate multi-cultural programs.

The statement outlines seven overarching recommendations and describes several specific indicators for each to guide practice. Many of the guidelines for assessment and follow-up of all children, regardless of language, apply to all DLL children with some unique considerations.

Universally, all children benefit from systematic, ongoing assessment using a variety of tools based on developmental theories, methods which connect to the context of children's lives and yield results that are used to understand and support meaningful learning and appropriate development. The choice of assessment tool and implementation method should always be intentional and driven by the purpose of the assessment and the child's developmental level. We begin with the question "What am I trying to learn about, measure, or assess?" From there, we select the method, format, and instrument that is most appropriate.

For example, to better understand a toddler's cognitive processing of cause-and-effect, a teacher might provide a variety of familiar button, switch, and lever toys and ask the child to manipulate them. Then the teacher would observe and record the child's use of the material through video, notes, and/or photos. From the notes, or "raw data," teachers make interpretations that inform knowledge about how the child is developing; these notes also guide planning for next experiences for the child. Such planning could include new materials, new words or terms, and extension activities. For another example, a first grade teacher might ask children to create a new version of a familiar story to determine the children's understanding of literary forms like character, plot, and setting. Or children might be instructed to design a flag for their own made-up place, with a description of the colors and images used as a way to assess knowledge of symbolism and use of aesthetic choices.

Determining the progress of DLL children in the developmental domain, in content knowledge, and in skills requires careful individual assessment.

Take a moment now to consider how each of those scenarios might pose challenges for children who do not speak English. If instructions or directions are given verbally or in writing only in English, how can the teacher know if the child's performance accurately and fully reflects his cognitive ability, or if he was limited by language barriers? Without ensuring that children clearly understand directions and the purpose of the assessment, we run the risk of misinterpreting errors in performance as developmental delays or deficiencies (Schulz, 2009). Children whose thinking is on one level but whose English communication skills are at a lower level are often incorrectly assessed as being not as intelligent or capable as their peers. This discrepancy reflects a major error in assessment practice and is a disservice to bilingual children. When their development is incorrectly assessed at a lower level, teachers plan and implement an inappropriate program which neither supports their needs nor challenges them adequately. This lack of challenge can lead to chronic underachievement and unrealized potential. Think about the connections between academic success and children's self-confidence as you watch the following **video**.

To help early childhood professionals understand the unique characteristics of working with English language learners, NAEYC recommends that carefully designed, culturally relevant assessments be used intentionally to appropriately document children's progress and to plan next steps. Recommendations include the following (NAEYC, 2005):

- Be purposeful in the timing, selection, and implementation of assessments.
  - Results can only be accurately interpreted when the assessment method/tool is used to assess the behaviors or skills it was designed to measure.
- Use culturally appropriate instruments, including observation guides and standardized formal assessments when appropriate.
  - For assessment instruments to be considered "culturally relevant," specific tools or materials must be created and verified by reliable sources to ensure accuracy in terms of language, style, and translations.
- Teams who are involved in conducting and evaluating assessments should have cultural and linguistic competence and knowledge of the children being assessed in order to most accurately interpret results.
  - Assessors should speak the child's native language and have some understanding of conventions of communication of child's native culture.
- Families must be involved in the assessment, interpretation, and planning process in appropriate ways.
  - Family members are the most knowledgeable about the context of children's lives and have particular goals for children, but should not be used as translators or assessors since they are not trained professionals and not likely to be able to remain unbiased in data collection.

Instruction begins with appropriate assessments such as observations, notes, work samples, and formal tests to determine children's strengths and needs and to spark individualized learning plans. Dual language learners also will benefit from highly interactive, carefully scaffolded (with tailored structure and cues) experiences where teachers closely model the process and progressive steps in literacy skills (Schulz, 2009). Care must be taken to engage children in building literacy skills while also capturing and promoting growth in existing content knowledge and skills. Teachers can use oral or visual cues from children to determine their comprehension of story reading or the ideas they are sharing in their writing, for example. Consider self-assessment checklists and rubrics which outline key steps or content and which may include bilingual and picture cues. An important consideration to keep in mind when working with English language learners is that competence with English is about literacy functions as well as the more complex context and deeper meaning of communication.

The Complex Context of Language

An important first step in supporting linguistically diverse children is to understand that language involves both a functional aspect as well as a host of deeper, more personal meaning connections. For many families, language is closely connected to national origins, family history and roots, regional affiliation, and even racial/ethnic identity—as in the case of Black English dialect (Gollnick & Chin, 2009; Robinson & Clardy, 2011). Children who are surrounded by one form of language at home or in their community but by a different language form at school face a discord that leaves them disconnected from either or both environments. When teachers convey messages of valuing Standard English over other languages, children can also internalize a discord between themselves and their own families.

Kieren's experience is echoed by many dual language learner children, as the acquisition of English results in the loss of their home language. This "subtractive" approach to English language learning can cause deep erosion in children's identity and in their connection with family culture. Language is inexorably tied to identity, both personal and family, and this context cannot be splintered apart in schools. A far more appropriate and successful approach is an "additive" one in which English is added to the child's communication repertoire, while the home language is simultaneously supported and enhanced. This approach aligns with a pluralistic philosophy

IN MY FAMILY

English Was More Important

Kieren's family immigrated to the United States from Egypt when he was in the first grade, with only his father speaking a modest amount of English. Years later, Kieren is able to reflect on his early immigrant experiences:

As the only Egyptian kid in the class, I didn't have the option to have parallel classes in my language. Being immersed in an English-speaking environment all day I had the benefit of many models and opportunities to learn English quickly. I was pleased with myself to earn my teachers' approval, which they showed strongly when I used English more and more. At first my family was pleased with my progress as well. But things started to change as I became more involved with my classmates and school culture, and less involved with my family and Egyptian community. As a child, I knew that America and English were important and highly valued—by my family as well as the kids around me. I don't know exactly when it started, but I became annoyed that my parents didn't learn English as well as me and even embarrassed of them in front of school friends.

As I grew older, my American friends became more important to me and I withdrew from my family heritage and language. As my Egyptian [language] became eclipsed by my English and my parents' English learning lagged, I became distant from them and our relationship suffered. It really never recovered. As I look back, I feel such deep pain because it seemed like they had to sacrifice me—our relationship—in order to make a life in America. I hate my early years here for that. I will never feel like a real family with them and I do feel like my early language experience is a big reason for that. It's a loss I will never get over.

and also has a strong supporting research base. For children who possess a strong degree of proficiency in their home language, these skills serve to enhance and hasten English acquisition when professionals learn to use home language to build on English proficiency.

LANGUAGE DEVELOPS FOR COMMUNICATION

Certainly a primary consideration with respect to language is that it is a main source of communication between people. Human beings are primed to seek out interactions with other humans, and from early infancy these interactions take on a vocal and verbal quality. Through listening, mimicking, and shaping by others, our formal and recognizable language develops rapidly in the first years. Children quickly master the forms and structures of the language(s) that they are exposed to on a regular basis. As children are exposed to talking, singing, and nonverbal cues like touch, eye contact, and gesture, they make meanings associated with the sounds, words, and cues. In particular, the following are modifications to speech that are helpful in language learning:

- Slowing down
- Using more melodic voice cadence and intonation
- Focusing on concrete objects
- Using shorter phrases and sentences
- Using gestures and simple hand signs

Children are capable of mastering several languages simultaneously or in sequence. Their level of mastery will depend on the context of their learning (how much they are exposed to and how much they use the language), as well as their mastery of their native language. Children are also highly skilled at recognizing the context in which language is used—in different settings or with different people. Bi- or multilingual children are able to switch language, depending on the place and person they are communicating with. This ability to switch languages is called **code switching**. In the early stages of acquiring the additional language, children go through a phase in which they may mix or blend words or strings of words among the different languages, but this does not indicate that adding a new language is detrimental or competes with either the first or additional language. The blending is a natural process that the language learner will move through as competence increases in the new language.

Speech modification and focused listening are important strategies to encourage DLL children's conversational communication skills. However, academic literacy and English proficiency require more focused content learning, as it does for all children. **Academic language** refers to linguistic styles and vocabulary that are part of content area knowledge (math, science, social studies, and so on) but that differ from conversational language (Gollnick & Chinn, 2009). Much of the school day engages children in academic language, which also involves higher level cognitive processing skills. Children who are new to English must first develop proficiency in conversational skills in order to be able to then develop proficiency in academic English. It is important to continue challenging content area learning while also continuing to support the development of academic English throughout the school years. Professionals must recognize the multiple facets and purposes for which we use language to communicate, both orally and academically, in order to develop strategic plans to support DLL children's communication and academic competence.

LANGUAGE AS CULTURAL AND FAMILY SOCIALIZATION

In addition to recognizing the communication purposes of language, we also need to recognize the socioemotional and cultural elements of language. As children participate in social interactions in the course of daily life, they internalize norms of language use (form and function). Children are also keenly picking up on subtle and overt messages of values and expectations, and the identity of their specific cultural community. Through this social exposure, which is rooted in the context of the child's life, language is closely tied to family and community culture and cohesiveness. It is this close tie between language and culture that can pose transition challenges for children who are new to English or new to the United States (immigrant families). Nonverbal communication rules—eye contact, physical touch, how close people stand, and so on—vary greatly from one culture to another. Recent immigrants might not yet be familiar with these norms and conventions of U.S. English communication and might have quite different cultural expectations of nonverbal communication. Consider the complexities of cultural differences in communication and implications on behaviors as you watch this **video**.

Some of these norms are tied to measures of respect, status, and power. Making eye contact with adults is expected as a sign of respect in some families and cultures, while in others it is a sign of defiance and disrespect. Physical closeness and touching is also a practice which varies greatly in meaning and interpretation. In order to support effective verbal and nonverbal communication skills, professionals must be aware that there are differences in general, and they must be open to learning about the norms and customs DLL children or children from immigrant families are used to.

Being a dual language learner often also involves learning new expectations for nonverbal communication such as eye contact, physical closeness, or gestures.

CLASSROOM STORY CORNER

Little Lapin Saved the Day

Jen was pleased to be hired as a preschool teacher in a midsized early learning center in New Jersey shortly after it opened. She settled into the daily routine with her small group of children, and slowly new children joined as enrollment grew. Their first DLL child demonstrated an important lesson for the teacher:

One Thursday afternoon, my director came in and discussed a new girl who would be starting on Monday; she spoke only French. I spoke only English. I was nervous about how I would communicate with Chantal. How would I know what she needed? How would I be able to teach her all the things my other children were learning? I didn't have much time to figure it out, but I guess that meant I also didn't have much time to get too worried either. Monday came quickly. Chantal's parents had just transferred to the area for her dad's job, and Mom was not currently working. Chantal's mom spoke some English and came in with her for the first week, but the family was clear that they wanted Chantal to adjust quickly and learn English. They were supportive of how smoothly children can learn to speak English by playing with peers and the activities of a preschool classroom.

The first week went OK, for the most part. Chantal was very quiet and stayed very close to her mom, holding a stuffed bunny all the time. I would hear them speaking softly in French, but I was so busy with the other children that I didn't really get a chance to learn any of their words myself. Looking back, I wish we had been able to manage our staffing so that I could have learned more from Mom during that week. When the next week came, Chantal was quite upset and cried quite a bit at not having her mom there. It was just heartbreaking. Monday afternoon we went outside on the playground for our regular outside time. As soon as we left the classroom, Chantal became more upset than usual. My director heard her sobbing from the office and came out. I explained that I wasn't sure what was upsetting her more than usual and I was near tears myself. I hadn't wanted to tell the director about what a hard time I was having comforting Chantal, but finally I couldn't help it.

Immediately my director knelt down, and with an arm around Chantal, spoke softly to her in French! Chantal's body relaxed and she spoke back just a few words. "*Ah! Alors! Allons-nous chercher le lapin!*" said my director with her hands around her eyes like pretend binoculars. Chantal smiled brightly and put her hands up too. My director stood up and told me that Chantal had been crying for her stuffed bunny—her *lapin* in French. She said she only knew a little bit of French from high school, but that was a word she knew. I felt so awful that I hadn't been able to help Chantal with such an important, but small, request that I started crying myself. My director put an arm around me too, apologized and said she would work out some staffing schedules to provide extra support in my room so I could work with Chantal's family to learn key words and phrases to talk with Chantal. Then they went off inside together and retrieved little Lapin. When they came out Chantal was smiling, holding Lapin tightly. I smiled and said "Yes, here is Lapin!" to let her know that I would help her keep him close when she needed him. She moved closer to me and held my hand for the rest of the outdoor time. I felt so relieved but also overwhelmed I just wanted to cry. Instead I stood with Chantal and held her hand.

It sure was a hard lesson that day, but it really turned things around for us. Well, it didn't exactly change immediately and I still sometimes felt kind of lost with Chantal. But little by little I learned some new words and phrases in French, just as Chantal did in English. I never became fluent, but that wasn't really the point. I labeled the room and used a lot of picture symbols to associate content and meaning. I learned to read Chantal's cues more closely, like her pointing and gesturing, her drawings, and in her playing. I feel like I was reading her face more . . . you know? And almost every day after school I had a chance to visit with her mom and we were able to share a lot about Chantal's routines and things she liked. That helped me be able to respond to Chantal better, and her mom became a frequent visitor in the classroom. She would share songs with puppets for all the children and she became a highlight of our week. After a few months other parents even commented about how great they thought our new "languages program" was! This was my first experience with a non-English speaking child and I realized that there was a lot I could do to connect with her both by learning specific words in her familiar language but also by really listening and observing more closely. I didn't realize before that experience just how much communication happened apart from specific words!

Curricular Connections

MATERIALS

Selecting materials in different language(s) or that represent different cultural norms and traditions must be done carefully and with guidance. Sometimes translated materials, such as English books written in Spanish, may not be translated accurately or appropriately, and some images might even be negative, stereotypical, or offensive. Seek out resources in your community for review of materials or find suggested materials lists from reliable sources online. When carefully selected, the following are highly valuable resources:

- Books
- Posters
- Videotapes/audiotapes
- Labels
- Games
- Software
- Printed materials in the environment—everyday materials such as labels, logos, menus, brochures, maps, directories

Provide ample dramatic play materials that are open-ended and reflective of all of the children's home lives. This will require taking some time to get to know as much as you can about children's home lives. Consider using brief surveys, checklists, and letters home, as well as talking to family members (in their native language, with assistance if needed) or sending home disposable cameras for families to capture images of their home settings and routines. Be especially intentional about selecting appropriate, authentic materials. It can be quite appealing to simply purchase a "multicultural food set," but including an egg roll, taco, pizza, or croissant does not respectfully nor meaningfully reflect accurate examples of diverse home life. Similarly, adding a sombrero, feathered headdress, or kimono to the dress-up clothing is equally stereotypical and insulting. This kind of token expression can do more to alienate and segregate children and families from diverse backgrounds and should be avoided. Instead, ask families and community members for authentic items that are a part of everyday life and routine, items that represent a realistic example of home and community life. Families might share or suggest items that are similar or different from other children's. Items that can enhance dramatic play opportunities, include:

- Kitchen utensils
- Clothing/shoes
- Toys
- Books
- Artwork
- Labels

- Food containers
- Tools from specific work or professional activities

Dramatic play provides a variety of roles and ways of being that are important to the play group and that do not necessarily need language proficiency. These roles can be good initial entrance opportunities for children who lack skill in English and who might otherwise be marginalized by other children.

ENVIRONMENT

Using pictures and symbol cues, along with words in the languages spoken, to label materials and different areas of the classroom, and in daily schedules, helps language learners make associations between new words and meaning. Labeling also helps all children develop autonomy and make sense of their surroundings and routines because they can more easily understand classroom organization, anticipate transitions, and be productive in locating and replacing materials.

When space allows, add a quiet space with soft materials where children who need a few moments of "down time"—apart from the bustle of the room—can take a break and regroup. The constant work of thinking in one language and translating into another can tire DLL children and add an extra burden to their day. A small, quiet space with defined purpose and rules for use can serve as a place where children can remove themselves when they are feeling overwhelmed with interactions. Consider adding picture books in the child's home language, noise-reducing headphones, and perhaps a pillow or small blanket for comfort.

For center-based classrooms, organize at least two individual or two-person centers, including a literacy center. This allows for more intimate interactions and also provides professionals with a chance to work more closely with individual DLL children. In dyads, DLL children can focus on communications with just one partner, as opposed to trying to keep up with a bigger group of English-speaking children who may inadvertently leave out the DLL child.

INTERACTIONS WITH CHILDREN

Children entering care and/or educational settings with little or no English language proficiency may need additional time to adjust socially and to routines, and to acclimate to educational norms and expectations. Professionals can ease transition stress by learning about and validating families' home language and cultural practices and developing partnerships with family members (Sims & Hutchins, 2001). Always keep in mind that children (and humans in general) have basic needs for nourishment (food and hydration), access to hygienic toileting, social acceptance, and some sense of predictability in order for stress to be manageable enough not to completely shut down higher level brain functioning. For DLL children or children who are entering a new environment, stress levels are already high and children's cues and communication about their needs might be harder to read or interpret. Many anecdotal stories are shared by DLL children who experienced deeply hurtful, embarrassing moments in classrooms where teachers did not make an effort to understand when that child conveyed needs like going to the toilet or being thirsty or hungry. These early painful experiences are especially damaging to children's newly developing identity in a bilingual world and to their confidence as effective communicators.

Conversely, positive stories also abound from teachers who model nurturing and valuing of DLL children's unique skills and attributes, thereby elevating the DLL children's status to that of a child with valuable assets to contribute to the classroom (Ghiso, 2013; Gillanders, 2007). When teachers listen with focus, patience, and genuine interest, DLL children share more complex ideas, speak more and freely, and are able to think about what they are sharing. Teachers must resist the urge to:

- Finish sentences for children
- Talk over them
- Assume they know what children are going to say next
- Fill in pauses with their own comments

This "tsunami of words" silences DLL children and erodes their confidence as communicators (Keat, Strickland, & Marinak, 2009, p. 19). To reduce stress and support social and linguistic adjustment, consider the following suggestions:

- With children and families, create picture books or boards that reference key routines such as bathroom practices, eating and drinking, and different daily activities; include classroom, outdoor areas, special rooms, and the children's homes, so that even children with no English background can communicate needs and be prepared for transitions.
- Take time and be patient with DLL children's English communication. Give children time to speak or write, understanding that they are thinking in their native language and then translating into the new language. In essence, they are going through an entire extra process and should not be rushed or cut off.
- Accept efforts to use English but also validate *code switching*, in which children blend words or grammatical rules from both languages. This is a normal part of the process of acquiring additional language(s) and is a sign of children's efforts to make sense and meaning.
- When children communicate, validate their meaning by listening carefully and paraphrasing back what you have heard and understood. Expand on their verbalizations with extension phrases and sentences. For example: when Victor says "I go bus with Abuela," teachers can respond with acknowledgement and extension by modeling correct speech and possibly prompting for additional related information "Oh, Victor, you go on the bus with your grandmother, your Abuela. (Pause, and if the child appears interested in talking further, make a prompt.) Where does the bus take you?"

- Attempt to learn at least a few important words and phrases in the child's home language. The goal is not necessarily to become fluent, but rather to demonstrate willingness to become a language learner yourself, to show the DLL child(ren) that you value their language, and to show English-speaking children that in communities (social classroom groups), we make caring efforts to include everyone.

- Try to schedule one-on-one time each day to visit with DLL children about things they would like to share or their experiences of the day. This can give both of you an opportunity to meet privately and be able to focus on building a strong relationship.

INTERACTIONS AMONG CHILDREN

Modeling caring, patient, nurturing communications is the best way to start engendering positive communications among children. Let children see you attempting to learn and use words in the child's home language and carefully listening to DLL children. Do not be afraid to openly acknowledge that some children speak differently than others, or that some children may come from other places. When English-speaking children understand that there are others in the group who speak a different language and are coached on some strategies for supporting communications, they are very often willing to make an effort to apply these techniques. The following are some ideas for engaging children in building community with DLL children:

- Talk openly during circle or meeting times about the different languages that people use to communicate and how the *ways* we use languages and the *purpose* of our language are much the same around the world and around our communities. The formats might be different—English, Spanish, Japanese, Bosnian, and so on—but the messages and reasons that we speak to each other are the same. People speak to each other to share ideas, convey needs, and connect intellectually and emotionally.

- Talk with all children about some of the "big ideas" that are important to being a successful communicator, including the roles of listener and speaker:

  - Active listening: focus on the speaker, let her pause and finish her own sentences, reflect back the points you understood, and check for approval or correction.

  - Speaking clearly: especially with DLL children, speak intentionally (not overly slowly or loudly, but purposefully).

  - Taking turns: share your ideas (and validate or correct) but also let the other person share. While he is speaking, listen to him rather than thinking about what you are going to say next.

- Point out a few simple words and phrases that the English-speaking children use frequently, such as how to for ask for items, permission to use the bathroom, how to ask for a drink, how to seek attention

("Excuse me," "May I have a turn?" and so on), and learn translations together. Pair the new phrases with a common gesture that all children can learn and use, such as these used in American Sign Language: to ask for a drink, mimic holding a cup to your mouth; to ask to use the bathroom, make a fist with thumb between index and middle finger, and shake or twist the hand. Pair the action with the word in English or the child's home language to facilitate language learning. Make charts of words in multiple languages and images and post it where children can refer back to it.

- Meet regularly as a group to invite sharing and dialogue. During these times, model and prompt collaborative communication skills among all children. Ensure that DLL children are encouraged to share as well, both to practice English and bilingual skills but also to share what they are thinking. Research validates the important role that oral language plays in organizing our thinking and retention of content; in essence writing and speaking are the primary tools for making meaning in our world (Huerta & Jackson, 2010; Vygotsky, 1962/1986).

Representing multiple languages in the environment supports dual language learning children's autonomy and sense of belonging in the classroom and promotes awareness and appreciation for linguistic differences among all children.

- Validate and value the different interaction styles that children use, both verbal and especially nonverbal. Some children are used to being very physical and using a lot of contact during play times, which might feel invasive to other children. Discuss with children the different norms and expectations of families and cultures in regard to their communication styles. For a child who is used to frequent close physical contact, a classroom climate which resists or punishes this behavior can be confusing and feel like a rejection of the child (Onchwari, Onchwari, & Keengwe, 2008). It can be appropriate, in time, to guide children to recognize social norms and expectations in the school community, even when these differ from those at home. Children are capable of recognizing that there might be different sets of expectations for different settings in their lives, but it is essential that professionals guide this acclimation sensitively and with continued respect for how the home culture might be different. Encourage children to talk about experiences that they liked or didn't like so that you can facilitate and guide respectful, reciprocal dialogue and problem-solving.

LEARNING EXPERIENCES

Photo Stories

Invite children to use disposable cameras to create photo journals and photo stories. These are series of images that tell a story, convey personal meaning for the child, and serve as a window into their thinking and their life. Disposable cameras are useful because they are relatively affordable and fairly simple to use—two key considerations when working with families who might not be familiar with technological tools or who are anxious about being responsible for equipment. Take time to explicitly guide children on how to use the camera, and instruct them to be deliberate and intentional about what they are taking pictures of. The novelty and excitement of the camera can prompt random snapping, so remind children that their images are limited! Give children a meaningful topic such as "Things that are important to me," or facilitate a group dialogue about what their topic should be. When they have taken their pictures, you can either print an index page and have children select a handful for their book, or print all of their pictures and let them choose which to use. If you have access to a computer and movie maker or slide maker programs, you might also be able to have the children's pictures scanned to a disc that you can then download. Then the children could create slideshows on the computer. Have them collect and organize their images into a sequence that shares their ideas about the topic. As children are able, they can write reflections and notes to accompany their photos. This is an engaging activity for all children, but it certainly provides a rich way for DLL children to capture and share meaningful parts of their world that they might not yet be able to talk or write about.

Story of My Name

Our names are intimately tied to our identity, and for many families, naming children also involves family values, heritage, and history. Not every family will have naming rituals or customs and not every child's name carries positive family connections, but children can explore meanings for parts of their name and create their own story behind their name. Since children have a name, inviting them to seek or create the story of their name builds shared community and validates individual and family identity. Children can begin by sharing how they got their name, if they know the story. Or they can create a list of questions to use to interview parents or family members in order to gather information about their names. Children who are adopted or living with appointed guardians might have different questions, so be sensitive to diverse family backgrounds. Other families might not have particular meanings behind naming. Read stories about names and naming and about having an unusual name and a more popular name. Ask children to gather information about their own name from their families, reference books, or Internet sites, and also invite them to create a story about how they were given their names. Children can write or dictate "I am . . ." poems to further explore, share, and celebrate their unique identities. These poems are particularly useful with DLL children because they can be created with the insertion of a single descriptive word after the "I am . . ." prompt and can be meaningful even when they are just a few lines long.

Family Partnerships

COMMUNICATING WITH FAMILIES

Children's academic success is also strengthened when parents are involved in connecting learning at school to learning at home through teacher outreach, when families are welcomed into schools, through family literacy activities, and by communicating effectively about children's school experiences and developmental progress (Harper & Pelletier, 2010). Family communication must be viewed as a mutually beneficial, reciprocal relationship, not as a one-way communication where teachers inform families about their child. For families who do not speak English, it is incumbent upon professionals to seek resources to bridge language barriers so that both sides can communicate accurately and effectively together. Explore additional suggestions for welcoming all families in this **video**. Send invitations in the home language to meet families, or have families come in to the center or school and locate a translator to be present when the family members come in. Consider locating some of the following resources:

- Online translation services (take care to locate reputable sources)
- Telephone translation services
- Computer translation software
- Dictionaries
- Community members with language and cultural proficiency who may be from:
  - Houses of worship
  - Area schools (high school language teachers)
  - Older students
  - Local businesses
- Center or school staff with proficiency in the home language

ENCOURAGE FAMILIES TO SUPPORT CHILDREN'S DEVELOPMENT IN THE HOME LANGUAGE

Children's competence in learning English is strengthened and supported when families engage children by using their home language in everyday activities, and in talking, reading, and singing (Hernandez, Denton, & Macartney, 2008). Families can also record themselves reading stories or singing songs; these recordings can then be brought to school and integrated into the school day.

Recordable story books can be sent home and recorded in the child's home language with the English print read aloud at school for a bilingual story time.

VALUE FAMILIES' UNIQUE GOALS FOR THEIR CHILDREN

Families from different linguistic and cultural backgrounds may have varied goals in the education of their children. It is important to find ways to seek feedback from them about what is important within their family context. Some families may have strong opinions about when and how their children learn and use English, as well as other culturally determined communication styles. It is important to work collaboratively with families towards shared goals for DLL children. Begin by learning some general customs and norms for the child's family heritage, but be sure to sensitively seek specific information from families themselves. Consider creating a parent survey in English and in the home language or conducting short interviews or home visits, with a translator if needed, to ask families to tell you about the goals they have for their child's linguistic and academic development. There is so much you can learn about how to promote optimal outcomes for children from understanding the family and community context of children's lives.

Summary

UNDERSTANDING AND VALUING LINGUISTIC DIFFERENCES

- The terms *linguistic diversity* and *dual language learner* refer to children who are from homes in which the primary language is something other than English or who speak a distinct regional English dialect.
- Children and family members from linguistically diverse backgrounds can have varying levels of English proficiency—from no fluency to fluent.
- Growing up bilingual can have benefits in terms of stronger general communication skills and more cultural competence.
- Spanish is the most predominant language spoken by DLL children; however, language differences vary by region of the country.
- Standard English is connected to sociopolitical power structures, though dialects are as complex and valid a form of communication and should not be viewed as less valuable.

NAEYC POSITION STATEMENTS

- Two pivotal statements on developmentally appropriate practice and working with culturally and linguistically diverse children and families serve as guidance and a framework for overcoming barriers to successful support of all DLL children in the classroom, and address attitudes, practices, and professional preparation.
- Specific guidelines for practice (especially assessment and instruction) include making clear that linguistic diversity is valued; validating children's attempts at using English even if it is not perfect; and awareness about selection of bilingual materials.

- Emphasis is placed on family connections and the importance of developing reciprocal relationships with DLL families.
- Selection and implementation of assessment and screening instruments and practices are particularly important to identify strengths and needs in DLL children, with special attention to inappropriate materials and practices that can undermine children's success in programs and schools.

LANGUAGE IS MORE THAN WORDS

- Foundational to developing appreciation for linguistic diversity as a family strength is the awareness that language develops for functional purposes of communication but is also highly embedded in family and community culture.
- Language develops through interactions with family and community members, often with important modifications such as slower pace, simpler vocabulary, and shorter phrasing.
- Language is intimately tied to family culture and there is often powerful and intense connection between language and family heritage.
- Verbal and nonverbal communication rules vary widely between languages and even among dialects, and nonverbal cues in particular can convey important cultural norms.

CURRICULAR CONNECTIONS

- Select materials in different languages, taking care to make accurate and quality selections.
- Encourage dramatic play opportunities that allow for use of materials that provide nonverbal cues and allow meaning to be conveyed without strong English skills.
- Use picture cues paired with simple words to support language learning.
- Use active, sensitive listening with DLL children and encourage these skills in all children.
- Encourage all children to learn key words in different languages spoken in the class.

FAMILY PARTNERSHIPS

- Seek out reliable resources in the community or online to assist with translating for families with limited English proficiency to ensure that important program and school messages are understood.
- Welcome families and validate the importance of maintaining home language while encouraging their use of English as well.
- Understand that different language backgrounds are interrelated with different family culture and varied family goals for their children.

Chapter Learning Outcomes: Self-Assessment

Use this space to reflect on how well you have achieved the learning goals for this chapter in terms of evaluating your own competency in the topics below.

List three to five key concepts that you have learned from the chapter.

Define characteristics of linguistic diversity including different languages, dialects, and accents.	
Identify successful approaches to supporting linguistically diverse children.	
Explain the purpose and complex contexts of language.	
Practice teaching strategies to support linguistically diverse children.	
Create partnerships to support linguistically diverse children and families.	

Chapter Activities

DISCUSSION QUESTIONS

1. Consider the potential problems that can arise in family relationships when young children attend English or bilingual schools and their parents do not have English skills, nor access to English instruction. Discuss the emotional impact on the parent(s) when children develop proficiency that they themselves do not have.

2. Discuss the potential benefits to all students that can emerge when teachers implement a variety of instructional strategies designed to support DLL students.

SELF-REFLECTION

Recall any personal experiences you have had either with learning a new language yourself or with other DLL students you have known. If you have taken foreign language classes, you have a modest experience of what it feels like to tackle the task, although being in the language minority or the only one speaking your native language can be especially emotionally daunting. Reflect on how it felt to try to understand someone speaking to you in a foreign language; describe any frustrations or insecurity you felt. If you have known a DLL student, can you recall their feelings and emotions during their early years learning English?

TEACHING DISPOSITION

It is important for teachers to be knowledgeable and resourceful, with a robust "toolkit" of skills. This is a two-part search and identification of resources: one online and one at your local library. Begin by visiting your local library and seeking out resources for English language learners and adult learners. Identify what kinds of materials and classes are available. Ask resource librarians for their advice on teaching language learners. Next, review online translation sources, including software and online services. Be sure to verify accuracy and reliability. Create a list of resources to add to your "toolkit."

IN THE FIELD

Locate your local school district's website and search for a recent student demographics report. Find out the linguistic and nationality backgrounds of the students attending school in your area. Identify the top three languages spoken by students/families and create a list of the ten most common words (such as greetings, terms used to convey basic needs, and so on) in English and the other language.

Weblinks

National Clearinghouse for English Language Acquisition and Language Instruction Education Programs. *http://www.ncela.gwu.edu/*

State of New Jersey Department of Education Bilingual Education Resources. *http://www.state.nj.us/education/bilingual/resources/*

California Department of Education English Learners Resources. *http://www.cde.ca.gov/sp/el/*

6

Socioeconomic Factors

Exploring topics of family financial and social resources involves a larger exploration of issues of social justice, including power, privilege, classism, and gross inequalities in society and schools. This exploration is about individual children and families but is also about the larger systems and structures that perpetuate poverty and classism over generations. There are often strongly held beliefs and values about what it takes to become successful in the United States, beliefs that are deeply rooted in our history. In a country known as *the land of opportunity*, where the "American dream" refers to the potential for anyone to find financial stability through hard work and

Families experience economic stress across the United States, in cities, suburbs, small towns, and rural areas.

perseverance, poverty and lower social status are often viewed as evidence of individuals' lack of effort to better themselves.

This perspective is an oversimplification of highly complex circumstances that exert pressure and influence across generations and often tend to cycle and perpetuate ongoing stratification of classes. Our society is built on a stratified class model with upper, middle, and lower classes defined by wealth and income, access to social capital (social networks with productive benefits), and educational and intellectual achievement (to a lesser degree). In order to understand the needs and strengths of children living in families with limited income and limited resources, it is essential to recognize the larger systems and structures of social class and status. This chapter provides a background on socioeconomic factors and their impact on children's development and education and prompts you to more deeply consider the sociopolitical context of classism.

What Do Family Economics and Socioeconomic Status Mean?

The term **socioeconomic status** *(SES)* is widely used as a gauge of family financial stability. But the term also includes related aspects in the context of the child's life outside of the immediate family and home, including neighborhood and social resources. The factors specifically considered in determining a family's socioeconomic status include:

- Parent employment status (employed, unemployed, seasonally employed, temporarily employed, migrant worker)
- Type of employment (professional, service, labor, self-employed, etc.)
- Family income level
- Poverty levels around the family's neighborhood/community
- Parent education level

Family income is typically a key determinant of access to resources for meeting children's basic needs like nutrition, health care, housing, and education. But living with limited financial resources can also impact children's social experience and status among peers, and it increases the potential for access to negative role models and relationships. Risks associated with limited financial resources can be compounded when caretakers (parents or care-taking adults) work more than one job or long hours and are less available as a support for children, leaving open the potential for negative external influences.

Frameworks for understanding the many interrelated facets that impact quality of life include recognition of the role that psychological skills, emotional support systems, physical health, and community/cultural awareness play in influencing quality of life and impacting development

- Define *socioeconomic status* (SES) and related measures

- Identify the potential for challenges and resiliency connected to SES

- Discuss the myths and realities of SES

- Describe strategies for supporting resiliency in children

- Practice teaching strategies to support children from lower SES backgrounds

- Create partnerships with families from lower SES backgrounds

(Payne, 2009). Recognizing that there are broader contexts to family status well-being than just income aligns with Bronfenbrenner's *ecological systems theory* perspective. This perspective acknowledges that there are many layers of bidirectional influence within children's lives and these impact developmental outcomes to greater and lesser degrees. In essence, this is a "bigger picture" approach to thinking about the quality of children's lives within the scope of family well-being. This approach emerges from decades of research that has demonstrated that a number of closely related factors are often present and interrelated, such as parent education and income level (Bronfenbrenner & Morris, 1998). Family socioeconomic status may be higher or lower, depending on the factors listed above; SES is not specifically negative. Much attention has been paid in the research base to the impacts on children of living in lower SES homes, but it is important to note that SES is not synonymous with living in poverty. Poverty is a specifically defined income threshold.

FEDERAL POVERTY GUIDELINES

The U.S. Department of Health and Human Services publishes an annual measure of poverty guidelines which define the income threshold based on number of persons in the household. The dollar threshold generally is calculated to include costs for basic necessities such as food and shelter; however some researchers point out that actual costs to sustain a family above poverty are greater than the federal guidelines (Wood, 2003). Researchers estimate that it costs roughly twice the poverty threshold to cover actual basic expenses adequately, so the term *low income* is used to refer to the threshold from the poverty line up to 200% of that figure (Addy & Wright, 2012). The guidelines include alternative figures for Alaska and Hawaii; figures for these states are slightly higher than the threshold for the lower 48 states, again based on cost of living estimates. The 2013 HHS Poverty Guidelines for the contiguous states are summarized in Table 6.1 (USDHHS, 2013).

TABLE 6.1   *2013 Federal Poverty Guidelines (Partial) and Corresponding Low-income Threshold*

Persons in family/ household	Poverty guideline (income threshold)	Low-income threshold (200% of poverty guideline)
1	$11,490	$22,980
2	$15,510	$31,020
3	$19,530	$39,060
4	$23,550	$47,100
5	$27,570	$55,140

The federal poverty guidelines are used in a number of ways. For example, some social service agencies use the figures to determine family eligibility for welfare programs and researchers use the guidelines to gather data about children and families living in different income brackets to compare quality of life and health and welfare outcomes. A robust and growing body of research has connected a number of lifestyle conditions to income level and developmental outcomes. Family income is related to access to health care and health insurance, nutrition, cognitively stimulating interactions and experiences, and parenting quality (connected to maternal depression; Wood, 2003). When family resources are severely limited, children's development and school success are significantly impacted, often due to impoverished and underresourced neighborhood and school conditions. Due to the kaleidoscope of these related quality-of-life factors, living in a family whose income is at or under the poverty level is a major risk factor for negative developmental outcomes in children.

SCOPE OF POVERTY IN THE UNITED STATES

The U.S. Census Bureau conducts periodic surveys of U.S. households to obtain and compare data on the socioeconomic status of American families. A report entitled *Income, Poverty, and Health Insurance Coverage in the United States: 2011* revealed a decline in median family income and a consistent poverty rate from the previous year, with the number of people living in poverty remaining at a 50-year high (over 46 million people; U.S. Census Bureau, 2012). Specifically, 22% of all children in the United States live at or below the poverty line, and 44% are living in low-income homes (Addy & Wright, 2012). There are significant differences in the incidence of poverty based on race. The poverty rate broken down by race/Hispanic origin in the Census Bureau 2011 report reflects a deep and persistent racial disparity. Poverty rates for Black and Hispanic people were more than double that of Asians or Whites (U.S. Census Bureau, 2012). Table 6.2 lists the percentages of poverty across racial and ethnic groups.

TABLE 6.2 *Percentage of Children in Poverty by Race*

Race	Poverty Rate
Black	27%
Hispanic Origin	25%
Asian	12%
White (non-Hispanic)	10%

Connections Between Family Resources and Development

Understanding the nature and scope of socioeconomic status in general, and in the context of families living with limited resources in particular, is especially important for early childhood professionals. The early years, specifically from prebirth through age 8, are the most crucial years in development as structures and processes are formed and strengthened. In essence, it is in these early years that the building blocks of development are formed that become the foundation impacting all later school and life experiences. Adequate maternal nutrition, supplements, and rest, coupled with reduced stress, anxiety, and exposure to potentially harmful environmental hazards are important for developing healthy babies. These continue to be important components of physical health throughout childhood. These goals are threatened when family resources are significantly limited, living conditions are inadequate, and community supports are strained. A comprehensive review of early development is outside of the scope of this text, but brief key highlights are warranted, given the interrelation of adequate resources and support for development during these early years.

BRAIN DEVELOPMENT AND COGNITION: MILESTONES AND SUPPORTS

Brain structures are formed and are regulating body functions within the first two months after conception. Many neural connections are also formed and begin to develop before birth (Kail, 2007). Adequate maternal nutrition (including supplemental vitamins) and prenatal health care are important supports for this crucial fetal work, beginning at conception (even before pregnancy tests reveal positive results). Throughout the early years of life, new brain connections are formed, and existing connections are strengthened through rich interactive experiences. Previously formed connections that are not used will atrophy and die away through a process called *synaptic pruning*. This is an important cleanup process that allows essential connections in the child's life to become strengthened. Synaptic pruning is a key part of making brain processing faster and more efficient and is highly dependent on the context of our daily lives. Brain development can be summed up in one phrase: Use it or lose it!

Chronic understimulation in the early years can lead to underdeveloped neural connections that can negatively impact children's later cognitive abilities. This is especially true of the early need for ample stimulation in interactive language experiences. Language development as social communication and also as a foundation for later literacy is largely formed in the earliest years through rich interactions with caregivers. Consider how family literacy programs, described in this **video**, can support language development in all family members. Additionally, early inadequate nutrition (not having balanced nutrition or enough food) has been linked to ongoing inattention, distraction, and difficulty in school or in interactions with parents. If chronic undernourishment leads children to attend and engage less with caregivers because the children lack body energy, their responses can be misunderstood and labeled as lack of interest (in dialogue, sharing books, active play, and so on) and might lead to fewer attempted interactions with the child, thereby leading to a downward cycle (Kail, 2007). Nutrition plays a big part in supporting neurological and cognitive development, as well as in the interrelated social interactions that are an important part of family and community life.

Living in poverty increases the likelihood of living in unsafe housing conditions and of parental psychological distress (such as depression and anxiety), which in turn increase children's stress levels (Wood, 2003). The chronic stress that emerges from fear for safety or from parental depression prompts psychoemotional as well as physical reactions in the child's body. These reactions include the release of stress hormones, which diminish the brain's ability to engage in higher level functions like problem solving and emotional regulation (Ansell, Rando, Tuit, Guarnaccia, & Sinha, 2012; Arnsten, Masure, & Rajita, 2012). In essence, living with chronic stress serves to effectively switch off the kinds of functions that are expected during the school day and triggers lower level, fight-or-flight brain functions. Until children's basic needs are met and stresses about food, shelter, and safety are reduced, engaging higher level cognitive functions is a significant challenge. Figure 6.1 maps out the impact of chronic stress on brain functions.

FIGURE 6.1   *This is Your Brain on Stress: A Simplified Model—Stress Chemicals Push Brain Function Away from Higher Level Functions*

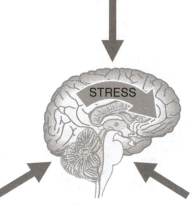

Mid Brain: Occipital and Temporal Lobes
Visual tasks, language comprehension, and information processing are controlled by these middle areas of the brain.

STRESS

Front Brain: Frontal and Parietal Lobes
Higher level functions like problem solving, emotional selfregulation, talking, and academic functions are controlled by these areas of the brain.

Hind Brain: Cerebellum and Brain Stem
Balance, coordination, and basic body regulatory systems like breathing and heart rate are controlled by these areas.

PHYSICAL HEALTH DEVELOPMENT: MILESTONES AND SUPPORT

Physical systems and structures also develop rapidly in utero and require adequate nutrition and health care to promote healthy development. Maternal exposure to alcohol, nicotine, aspirin, and illegal drugs poses serious risks to fetal development and can result in physical malformations, motor control problems, and cognitive impairments. Chronic and extreme stress, cigarette smoking, and undernourishment can lead to low birth weight, which puts a child at risk for sudden infant death syndrome, delayed cognitive development, and behavioral problems. In infancy, nutrition is especially important because physical growth is at its most rapid. During the elementary school years, ample and adequate nutrition is again essential as another burst of physical development and children's active lifestyle demands nutritional support (Kail, 2007). For example, adequate calcium consumption during childhood supports bone development during the time of life when nearly all bone mass is acquired. At a very basic level, imagine how persistent hunger would erode a child's ability and interest in academic or social activities; how could the child focus on anything with an aching stomach, sleepiness, and gross lack of physical energy?

In addition to the risk of nutrition deficiencies, living in poverty or at the low-income level increases the likelihood that a child will be living in unsafe, inadequate housing. Risks include unsafe structures and lead paint; these are associated with older homes and central city location (Eamon, 2001). Children from households falling under the low income threshold are more likely to suffer from chronic illness and have more hospitalizations than children from wealthier households (Wood, 2003). Programs that provide school breakfast and lunch subsidies, as well as the Temporary Assistance for Needy Families (TANF) programs, have provided support for meeting these basic needs for disadvantaged children (Kail, 2007). Early childhood professionals must be knowledgeable about these and other federal and local supportive programs to be able to assist families in gaining access to these services.

Access to adequate high-quality nutrition is a key concern for children in families experiencing economic stress; early nutrition is an essential foundation for healthy development and is a component of early intervention programming.

CLASSROOM STORY CORNER

"It's Much Different than I Expected."

I can't even explain how excited I was when I finally got my first teaching job! I graduated three years before and I was really starting to worry about bills and loans and if I was ever going to get a job. I knew I had to be flexible and I was willing to take anything that came my way. So when the district in an area of Philadelphia that wasn't too far from my home [in the suburbs] called, I took the job immediately. I was actually hired just a few weeks before school started, so I didn't have much time to freak out about how different things might be.

But once I started and met my third grade class, it hit me like a tidal wave just how different we were and how little preparation I had to handle that difference. My first weeks were rocky, to say the least. But I started where all teachers have to start—by getting to know my children individually. I knew I needed to know who they were, what they knew, what they liked, and important things about their home and families. That's a huge task right there, and then I had to be sure to address district curriculum content too! I was exhausted at first. And I was scared, to be honest. Most of my children and families were Black or Hispanic, some didn't speak English, several were on IEPs; I quickly realized that a few could not read yet or complete basic computations, and nearly all of them were qualified for programs based on poverty or low-income guidelines. I would lay awake every night the first week wondering how these kids and families could look at this young White woman from the suburbs and feel any sense of connection or willingness to trust me. Talk about anxiety!

I was sure I wanted this: this career, this job, this class…all of it. I knew my life had some different dynamics from my students' but I also knew that I could find ways to connect with them. So I worked really hard to be personally present with the children. I asked the children a lot of questions about their experiences and what they were thinking about. Not even about school stuff, though, but more about what they were thinking about life things. I had to make a lot of notes during those conversations so that I would be able to refer to the things they talked about later on. I watched them and listened very closely. I made mental note of how they looked when they arrived in the morning. I wanted to be aware of who might not have enough food to eat, who might not have clean or weather-appropriate clothes, [and of] possible visible health conditions. I asked about the children from their teacher from last year and I read up on any files that were available. I knew that I couldn't ask them to do hard academic and social work with me if they were chronically hungry, ill, or stressed. I felt like an investigator those first few weeks.

There were definitely some children and families who needed extra services and support, and that is something that is an on-going part of my teaching even years later. But for the start of that first year the biggest thing I learned was that I had to start by showing them I cared enough to really get to know them. As soon as I started making a personal connection to myself or one of them in the school work we were doing I felt like we built a relationship more and more. I talked about things they liked and places they went when they were outside of school. On weekends I sometimes went to their areas of the city to see the shops and homes around the areas so that when I talked about their home lives I could feel more authentic. These were little things, I know. But they were my way of showing the children that I wanted to know them and their lives and that I wanted to be a part of it in some way. I am sure that those little efforts helped me make connections with them. And knowing more and more about them allowed me to connect supports where they could help the family and find ways to help them "click" with curriculum content.

Over the years the "building relationships" part of my teaching has come more and more quickly in the beginning of the year, but I still do lots of little things to know who my children and families are, what resources they have, and what gaps or supports I might be able to help locate. Teaching in a struggling city classroom is much different from what I expected, but even with opportunities to move out to schools in the suburbs I wouldn't change a thing. This is where I am at my best!

Impact of Socioeconomic Status: Misconceptions and Research Evidence

The relationship between a family's socioeconomic status and children's developmental and academic outcomes can be hard to clearly define due to interrelationships with race and other factors (Pungello, Iruka, Dotterer, Mills-Koonce, & Reznick, 2009). However, a robust and growing body of research provides evidence that living in lower-SES conditions is an increased risk factor for the development of challenges that can negatively impact socioemotional and cognitive (including academic) development (Evans & Rosenbaum, 2008; Huaqing Qi & Kaiser, 2003). In light of the compelling messages emerging from this research, it is vitally important to carefully and critically analyze the highly complex interrelationships between potential risk factors—and to not jump to narrow and inappropriate conclusions. Some prevailing stereotypical and over-generalized misconceptions negatively impact children's school outcomes.

MISCONCEPTIONS ABOUT A "CULTURE OF POVERTY"

Among social groups that do not fall within the lower SES category, there exist internalized ideas that contribute to broad assumptions about "poor people," including the idea that there are vast similarities among those living in poverty. Overgeneralized images of what life is like for individuals and families living with limited resources are pervasive in the media, popular culture, and within individuals' conceptions, and these images seem to be accepted as fact. Myths and misconceptions about the values, habits, and beliefs of those living in poverty have sparked a large body of research, with many divergent outcomes, "but on this they all agree: *there is no such thing as a culture of poverty*" (Gorski, 2008, p. 33). What this means is that there are as wide variations in individual values, habits, and beliefs among individuals and families categorized as lower SES as there are between socioeconomic groups. Table 6.3 summarizes common misconceptions and presents research-based realities (Gorski, 2008). As with many prejudicial stereotypes, each of these myths is not only false but the widespread belief of them is damaging to children's development and academic progress. When preservice and in-service education professionals internalize these myths, whether they themselves realize it or not, they are prone to hold lower expectations of those children and families. And reduced teacher expectation, in turn, reduces children's successful outcomes.

A key consideration in analyzing these myths and realities is to become aware of the deeper, more complex biases and prejudices that can be involved in the perpetuation of such myths. As you read the myths presented in Table 6.3, do you find yourself agreeing or perhaps saying to

TABLE 6.3 *Myths and Realities about Poverty*

Myth	Reality
People living in poverty: are lazy and have no work ethic; are using "the system" to avoid having to work.	The large majority of adults living in poverty or in low-income status are working—often multiple jobs or long hours. Research evidence reveals that the "working poor" actually spend more hours per week at work than do wealthier counterparts. Access to adequately paying jobs is limited by education or skill level, availability, child care arrangements, transportation, and more.
are not involved in their children's lives; do not value education.	Working multiple jobs or long hours impacts parents' ability to spend time with children at leisure or supporting school work and can make physical presence at school events extremely difficult. Inability to afford transportation and child care can also make attendance at school functions impossible. And yet, many teachers lament the lack of parental involvement, often citing this as a reason that children are not performing well in school. This negative, punitive perspective can further shut down family communication and involvement, especially if efforts to reach families in ways and schedules that work for them are not attempted.
do not have good language skills (often speaking in dialects).	While there is an association between lower education level and lower SES, speaking an English dialect or with an accent is not an indication of language deficiency. Dialects involve similar structural and grammatical complexities and are equally viable forms of communication.
are more likely to abuse drugs or alcohol.	Research actually shows that alcohol use is significantly higher among the middle and upper classes, and prevalence of drug use equally distributed among the classes. Visibility or arrest rates may be higher for lower SES neighborhoods or individuals, but a critical perspective requires that we consider ways these statistics reflect far more complex patterns of arrest and sentencing and visibility than actual rate of occurrence.

yourself "I've known people like that," or "I've heard stories about people who are like that." All the myths outlined above involve either an overt or a more subtle judgment and blame: at their core is the belief that people are poor due to their own action or inaction. There is a comfort in this belief. It removes responsibility from each of us and from society in general for the inequities of a classist system. This perspective allows us to not have to acknowledge or address the structures and systems of power and privilege that provide benefits to dominant individuals and groups and maintain subordinate groups. Teaching for social justice demands that we be willing to explore our own potential biases just as we explore societal biases, and then be willing to make individual and systemic efforts to change classist structures, routines, and systems. Teaching for social justice begins with our own values and beliefs but it has to extend to our practice with children and families. Failure to take this reflective stance in our work contributes to the realities of disparate negative outcomes that continue to plague education and damage children from lower SES backgrounds.

RESEARCH: IMPACT ON ACADEMIC OUTCOMES

Evidence gathered for the past 40 years has clearly documented an achievement gap in academic performance in which middle- and upper-SES White students consistently score higher than Black and Hispanic-origin, lower-SES students on tests of reading and math skills (Hemphill, Vanneman, & Rahman, 2011; Vanneman, Hamilton, Baldwin Anderson, & Rahman, 2009). While some progress has been made within those decades of research to close that gap, disparities persist. However, we cannot attribute these gaps to children's lack of intellectual or academic potential, or dismiss children from lower SES backgrounds as less smart because they come from disadvantaged homes. There is more to the big picture than such a deficit perspective considers.

Remember that SES involves measures of parent income and education level but also includes community contextual factors such as percentage of other households at the poverty or low-income level. Access and limits to resources extends beyond just the home and family and is also often a problem in neighborhood schools. Children living in poverty or lower SES homes and communities are often faced with impoverished schools with far more underqualified teachers than more affluent schools (Haycock, 2001). Without adequate supports, underqualified or underprepared teachers are strapped and tend to see less potential and expect less of lower SES children. When basic needs for stable shelter, adequate nutrition, health care, and safety are not being met, professionals and children alike may have a hard time viewing educational achievement as realistic. However, targeted, focused efforts across the country have demonstrated success in school performance and life outcomes for children from significantly disadvantaged backgrounds.

Successful Early Intervention

Developed in the 1960s, Head Start is the nation's largest, federally and locally funded program designed specifically for children from low income families. Head

Teachers who support all children's learning through individualized instruction and promoting high expectations help increase achievement in children from families experiencing economic stress.

Start (and the newer Early Head Start program for infants to three-year-olds) promotes school readiness for preschool children from low income homes through a comprehensive approach that includes family involvement; nutritional, medical, dental, and mental health support; and school programming. Services and programming are designed to address the child within the family and community context and are focused on supporting all areas of children's development (USDHHS, n.d.). Head Start has strengthened early childhood education professionalism through initiatives like focusing on preschool curriculum and requiring bachelor's degrees for teachers. Ongoing results of the widespread research into Head Start and Early Head Start interventions continue to demonstrate positive outcomes in:

- Increased parent warmth, involvement, emotional engagement, and language stimulation in interactions with children (Love, Kisker, Ross, Raikes, Constantine, Boller et al., 2005)
- Increased maternal contribution to children's education, both in the classroom and at home (Bruckman & Blanton, 2003)
- Stronger family support with lasting gains extending beyond just the child's academic outcomes (McAllister & Thomas, 2007)

With an even stronger emphasis on research-based curriculum and ongoing data collection over the past 50 years, the HighScope Curriculum and Perry Preschool Study are landmark interventions that are informing early childhood practice for children from low income backgrounds, as well as informing the field in general. "The **HighScope Perry Preschool Study** is a long-term research study of 123 African American children from low income homes, 58 of whom were randomly assigned to a high quality preschool program at ages 3 and 4 between 1962 and 1967. Data were subsequently collected over the course of the participants' lifetimes, with the latest data at age 40 (Schweinhart, Montie, Xiang, Barnett, Belfield, & Nores, 2005). The study involves collecting data on various academic, developmental, and lifestyle outcomes from program participants and parents annually during childhood and periodically through middle adulthood (with 95% continued participation).

One of the most compelling outcomes of the current reports is the cost-benefit analysis: the actual dollar amount of return on the public investment in this early intervention program. For every dollar spent on the intervention program, the public saw a return of over $16. Investment return is calculated by analyzing the cost savings through program impact on participant school performance measures (less special education services, higher graduation rates) and lifestyle indicators (higher employment status and better paying jobs, reduced arrest rates, increased home ownership). General conclusions of the study indicate that there are positive lifetime effects of high-quality early intervention preschool programming for children of families living in poverty. Furthermore, these lasting effects impact school performance, economic welfare, and social functioning into middle adulthood and result in a larger public savings than originally expected (Schweinhart, Montie, Xiang, Barnett, Belfield, & Nores, 2005).

Learn more about the comprehensive intervention aspects of Head Start (and the HighScope Curriculum) in the following **video** and consider the importance of an approach that takes the larger context of the child's life and family needs into account. The message from this research is clear: children from low income backgrounds are capable of long-term life success when they are engaged in high-quality early intervention programming as preschoolers.

Supporting Resiliency

Families living with limited resources or who in poverty tend to be generally defined by not having adequate resources, or by what they do not have. However, all families and individuals have strengths, and a key to supporting children's success comes in being able to recognize these strengths and use them as resiliency factors. **Resiliency** refers to a family or individual's ability to "bounce back," "rise above," or compensate for challenges and risk factors in their lives and to create positive outcomes in spite of those challenges. Viewing children and families as resilient, or with great resiliency potential, is an important value to bring to teaching and operates in concert with a realistic awareness of what are sometimes tremendous emotional, financial, social, or physical challenges and setbacks. The two views are not mutually exclusive; it is not about ignoring realities just as it is not about focusing solely on them. An honest but optimistic perspective is an important asset for working with children from across the socioeconomic spectrum.

Early care and education settings are especially robust resources of positive, supportive adult role models and are especially powerful for children whose home or community lives may be lacking strong models and relationships. Having a strong, positive, long-term relationship with an early childhood professional can have a tremendous, long-lasting impact on a child's school and developmental outcomes, and this impact is even more heightened for children living in less advantaged situations. The support system that a caring professional can provide extends beyond school support or access to social service programs; it also can provide exactly the kind of socioemotional supports and self-confidence that equip children with the inner resources that are necessary to succeed in school and life (Payne, 2009). In addition, supportive relationships with caring adults actually serve to protect our brains from the negative impact of chronic high stress, which can be associated with living with great economic stress (Schwartz-Henderson, 2013).

With compelling research evidence showing that foundations of resilience (as with all other areas of development) begin early in a child's life, it is essential for early childhood professionals to understand how to strengthen children's resilience factors as a means to supporting the effort to move out of lower SES circumstances (Nesheiwat & Brandwein, 2011). A key research finding is that self-concept is a valuable attribute of resiliency. The good news in this finding is that self-concept can be shaped and that high-quality early childhood professionals and programs are uniquely suited to the task of bolstering and improving children's self-concept. The message is clear: a key task for early childhood professionals is to strengthen self-concept of children from lower SES backgrounds. This can be addressed by:

- Developing long-term supportive, trusting relationships
- Acknowledging and encouraging children's strengths, talents, skills, and positive behaviors
- Setting high expectations and goals with the clear message that you believe children are capable; ensuring that supports are in place to promote achievement
- Recognizing children's accomplishments
- Engaging children in self-reflective activities that help them acknowledge and appreciate their own strengths

Think about risk and resilience as you watch this **video** and listen to how this child sees her neighborhood's strengths and discusses areas she would change. How can you relate this to perspectives of risk and resilience?

IN MY FAMILY

What Really Mattered

Growing up poor was a constant stress. We weren't homeless, like some of the kids I knew about, but we lived in a really run-down place and didn't have money to pay bills or buy food all the time. My mom worked three jobs so I don't remember her being around much. But she always did what she could to make sure we did good in school and didn't get into trouble. My grandmother lived with us and she took care of us a lot since she worked nights after we were in bed. Sometimes it was so hard to not have clothes that weren't worn through and really old and in the winter we didn't have coats so we layered as many shirts as we could get on. Sometimes I remember getting picked on at school for how I dressed or for not having school stuff like other kids. But mostly I remember how my family and my few close friends made me feel accepted and kept me focused on school as the way to a better life. And I remember when school all changed for me.

It was in second grade, because of my second grade teacher. He was always neat and dressed teacherly, but he was also really cool and easy to talk to. He was the first one who made me feel like he was really listening to me, like he actually wanted to know how I thought about things in school and around my neighborhood. I was kind of invisible before that. I'm sure he wasn't poor like me, but I never felt like he was looking down at me or like he even noticed my raggy clothes. Like when he saw that I didn't have anything to write with, even though there was a note sent home at the beginning of the year with a list of supplies to come with, he started setting out a can with extra pencils and pens on the table by the door so I could grab one when I came in. I did it kind of sneaky so no one would see. It was a little thing, but it let me feel like a normal kid to have a pencil in my hand when we started writing. He let our desks be in small groups instead of facing the front, too. I got to be friends with my table group that year, and they are still my best friends now. It was just a lot of little things like that. He really made school feel like someplace . . . possible. Like I could actually do this; like we all could. Before I didn't really like school, but from then on it was all different.

Curricular Connections

MATERIALS

As with all components of diversity, it is important for professionals to be vigilant about negative stereotypes that might be present in books, posters, and other materials, as well as omission of the variety of economic circumstances that reflect children's lives. Poverty and low SES backgrounds are reflected less than other forms of diversity (such as nationality or race, for example). Our society generally holds negative views of poverty, and images and messages tend to position families with limited resources as victims or as people to be pitied. We need to watch for these connotations and work to reflect the various realities of family life in positive ways—not reinforce messages of "those poor kids" who need saving or pity. Some families might certainly need more support at different times in their lives, but we all have strengths and areas of need to contend with. So, for example, seek out books that show a variety of types of work (people who work outside of home, homemakers, job seekers) as well as the variety of homes and shelters in which families live.

Since some children might not have prior experience with materials that seem more commonplace, such as blocks, books, or drawing materials, it is important to provide guided instruction on how materials can be used. Open-ended materials are especially important for all children and allow for maximum freedom of use in creative ways. However, it is still acceptable to discuss with children some basic guidelines for how materials can be used, and ways they should not use things. For example, you might have old newspapers, magazines, or scrap paper for children to tear and cut so that they can practice fine motor skills or make collages. However, books appear similar with their paper pages—but they are not for cutting. Make these basic rules clear for children.

All young children are hands-on, sensory learners. Early childhood teachers maximize on this natural inclination to touch and explore through engaging, sensory activities. Sometimes teachers rely on food because it provides touch, taste, and smell cues that seem engaging for children in a variety of ways. However, this can be confusing for many children—and especially problematic for children who do not have enough to eat. Food is used to nourish our bodies, and many families also teach their children to not play with their food. To use food as a source of play (noodle necklaces), drawing (pudding paint), building (cracker houses), in sensory bins (beans or rice), or as math manipulatives, is insensitive to children who are chronically hungry. It is also potentially disrespectful of foods that are an important part of family cultures. Instead, consider using recyclables and found materials. Items collected in nature, such as sand, bark, small stones, leaves, or pinecones, can be used for sensory tables and for counting, seriating, making patterns, and more. Many area businesses (offices or restaurants) are usually willing to donate boxes, packing materials, jars, bottles, or other items that would be trash for the business but that can be cleaned and used in all areas of the curriculum. Reusing items is an important lesson for all children: it demonstrates resourcefulness and hones an ability to see the value and new purpose in things that might

TABLE 6.4 *Alternatives to Using Food as Play or Learning Materials*

Item	Learning Goal	New Alternative	Where can I find it?
Noodles for necklaces	• *Fine motor: stringing* • *Sequencing patterns*	*Colored plastic straws cut to different lengths*	*Convenience store donation*
Pudding for painting	• Touch discrimination •		
Beans or rice (on a table or in shakers)	• Sound discrimination • Exploration of how different sizes and shapes scoop and flow differently		
Cereal or candy manipulatives	• Counting correspondence • Color recognition • Sorting, sequencing		
	• •		
	• •		

be considered waste by others. While the use of some food items might be so common or familiar to teachers that finding an alternative seems frustrating, being highly intentional in your work is an essential element of quality teaching. Start by asking yourself: "What is the learning goal or what is the curricular purpose in this activity?" Your answer will make it easier to see an alternative material or activity that can still support goals and purpose. Use Table 6.4 to brainstorm found or repurposed alternatives to the items listed.

ENVIRONMENT

Children who are from backgrounds with limited resources may feel overwhelmed by rooms that are overstocked with materials. All children benefit from organized spaces that are intentionally designed for a clear purpose. For example, some spaces are for quiet, individual activities and some spaces are used for more active kinds of work. Carefully organize items on shelves to allow for easy access, use, and cleanup so that children can be as autonomous in their space as possible. Using word labels and simple picture cues helps children who are developing literacy skills to identify organizational structure and provides a concrete image to pair with the associated word. When possible, plan spaces to provide small group, team, and individual activities. This will provide an opportunity for children and teachers to develop closer relationships than would develop through mostly whole-group activities. Small class sizes have also demonstrated lasting positive outcomes for learning gains in math and literacy for children from lower SES backgrounds (Nye, Hedges, Konstantopoulos, 2004).

INTERACTIONS WITH CHILDREN

Developing strong, nurturing, caring relationships which support children but also prompt them to reach higher than they may have believed they could must be the first order of business for early childhood professionals. With the establishment of positive relationships, children build self-confidence and see themselves as worthy of investment and capable of achievement. Strong relationships also allow children to be comfortable in striving to meet the high expectations teachers should convey. Communicating high expectations comes from a belief, built on strong research, which recognizes how capable children from lower SES homes are of achieving success in school. Teacher expectation is a strong predictor of students' outcomes, so it is essential that early childhood professionals communicate reasonably high expectations of all students (Stronge, 2002). Use these strategies for setting and communicating reasonably high expectations:

- Understand developmental goals and milestones for the children you work with; know what they are typically capable of and ready to do.

- Assess your children to understand their individual levels, strengths, and areas of need; use observations, family reports, review of previous files, developmental checklists, and so on.

- Understand and share school, district, state, and national learning standards with children and families in clear language with specific examples; make benchmarks clear to all participants so that they can strive towards those benchmarks.

- When appropriate, identify goals and design steps or objectives along the path to goal achievement together with children; this makes the goal more meaningful and attainable.

- Use visual aids such as checklists, charts, graphic organizers, posters, and maps to identify and clarify goals, to organize effort towards attainment, and to serve as reminders.

- Revisit both the big picture and details: continually refer to the overarching purpose of the goals as well as the small steps being taken to reach it so children can see the value of what they are doing.
  - How will this help them succeed in school and life?
  - What will they get out of achieving this goal?
  - Why will this skill, knowledge, or disposition support their success?
  - When will they use this skill, knowledge, or disposition in their present or future life?

- Acknowledge successes in achieving goals as well as objectives or steps towards the goals/expectations.

An important aspect of meeting school expectations is being able to understand the expectations. Many children and families living with limited resources are more accustomed to a direct communication style focused on

TABLE 6.5 *What is My Communication Style?*

Phrase	Sounds like me	Does not sound like me
It sounds like it's getting noisy in here. (I)		
You need to quiet your voices now. (D)		
I wonder if anyone can tell me what this means? (I)		
Janelle, can you tell me what this means? (D)		
I see students pushing each other in the line. (I)		
You need to stand quietly with your hands holding your elbows before we can leave the classroom. (D)		
Is that how we use that material/ask for a turn/get my attention? (I)		
The blocks are for building, not throwing. You need to use the words "May I have a turn next, please?" when you want a turn. I need you to raise your hand to get my attention. (D)		
Add your examples here:		

controlling behavior, with less room for child directedness. Many educators from higher SES backgrounds are more familiar with an implicit or indirect communication style that promotes and expects more child directedness (Hoff, Laursen, & Tardiff, 2002). If children are not accustomed to the teacher's communication style and related expectations, children's resulting confusion about directions or requests can be misinterpreted as a lower capacity for thinking, decision-making, or academic success. As a part of forming strong relationships, professionals can listen, observe, and learn about family communication styles and family expectations of children (Quietly obey authority or assertively question rules? Follow directions or make decisions?), and can explore ideas children have about their

Helping children develop positive interpersonal and social skills aids them in developing stronger peer relationships and increases acceptance—two important resiliency factors.

own role in schools and centers. Knowing what ideas and beliefs children have about who they are supposed to be inside and outside of the home allows professionals to better support children's success in education settings. Professionals can also become more aware of their own styles of communication and, if more direct or indirect, consider balancing how they phrase communications. Start with a self-analysis chart like the one in Table 6.5, or look for communication style self-assessments online. If you find that you tend to use much more indirect (I) or direct (D) phrasing, consider balancing them both to be better understood by children who are used to one or the other way, and to encourage children to become familiar with both styles.

INTERACTIONS AMONG CHILDREN

Young children from families living at or below the low income threshold might tend to have behavior problems more prevalently than children from higher SES backgrounds (Huaqing Qi & Kaiser, 2003). Negative behaviors, which are more likely to be used by children from low SES backgrounds, include physical aggression, negative verbal outbursts, and lack of self-regulation (waiting, turn taking, delaying gratification; Evans & Rosenbaum, 2008). If these antisocial behaviors are coupled with lack of material resources such as adequate clothing or hygiene routines, children are far more likely to be rejected by peers. Peer networks are particularly powerful for children and serve as a resilience factor for children from low SES backgrounds. When children from low SES homes were asked directly, they reported that being part of a circle of friends was one of the three most important elements of their lives (Percy, 2003). For children in district schools and programs, peers may be a more long-term constant in their lives than teachers who tend to change from year to year. Thus, supporting the cultivation of friendships is a way to help build long term support networks for children. To foster collaborative relationship building among children, consider:

- Shared, collaborative work in teams
- Group efforts that require unique contributions from all members
- Reduced emphasis on competition
- Identifying what qualities about oneself and others are most valued
- Initiating partners for transitions (like a "buddy system")
- Sharing circles as a whole group and as partners
- An "Ask three then me" policy: when children have questions they ask three peers before the teacher

LEARNING EXPERIENCES

Early assessments of children's academic abilities should accompany initial getting-to-know-you activities such as sharing personal stories, parent questionnaires, share-and-listen circle times, and community connection activities. Children who have lived with limited resources might potentially have literacy and math skills that are not on level with children from more advantaged backgrounds, although this should not be automatically assumed. In the early days of meeting children, teachers should frequently observe children's use of language and materials in the classroom. Consider performance assessments using materials that are familiar to children, taking care not to assess just children's performance using items which might be new and unfamiliar to them. In dialogues with children, be sensitive to different communication styles that may be a part of family culture, even if not part of typical school culture. Use assessments to guide planning for instruction and to tailor materials and instruction to meet individual children's needs. For example, individual assessments will drive choices for:

- Specific book titles and levels
- Types of pattern blocks and prompts with unit blocks
- Types of manipulatives to use in math problem solving
- Same-sound item collections, tracing materials (sand, stencils), letter cards, word cards, rhyming word card matching games

Providing a strong language base is especially important for children from backgrounds with limited resources (Espinosa, 2005; Payne, 2009). Integrate frequent and varied language experiences that are both informal (frequent casual dialogues throughout the day, impromptu story sharing, teacher modeling) and formal (recognizing story structure; phonemic awareness activities; vocabulary development; playing with language through rhymes, songs, word games). Encourage children's efforts and attempts, even when unexpected or below age or grade-level expectations. Select story books carefully to integrate varied home life experiences and contexts, taking special care not to inadvertently promote middle- or upper-class values exclusively. Frame story comprehension and recall prompts in concrete ways that children can relate to so they are able to make connections between home and school experiences. Scaffold connections between verbal expression and written representations to prompt and support ties between oral language and literacy. These efforts should be used early in the academic year to promote strong relationships and help children feel comfortable developing relationships; they can lead to instruction in more formal language and literacy formats. Formal language and literacy skills are important for school success and the ability to navigate various social settings. Providing children with a strong foundation in these skills is also a key part of current national scholastic academic policies.

Formal language and literacy includes teaching children differences between casual spoken language and formal discourse patterns, and Standard English and dialects. Encourage children to tell their stories in both informal and formal languages so as to develop both skill and awareness of the differences (Payne, 2009). Using personal stories and experiences to explore literacy elements and narrative writing is a strong hook to engage all learners. Stories also serve as a connecting thread throughout content areas and can provide a vivid way to reinforce concepts in math, social studies, science, and the arts, or as a vehicle to convey rules about behavior.

Family Partnerships

Most early childhood professionals are comfortable creating short newsletters and updates to send home at pick-up time or through email. Others create welcoming family bulletin boards to post important notices. These are important features of early childhood program updates, but are just a start. Additional recommendations for opening up communications with families include exploring alternatives to relying solely on written notices and newsletters. Some schools have found success with creating short video clips of teachers and staff highlighting center and school procedures and expectations, and providing an overview of the school experience (Payne, 2009). Some early childhood professionals lament the lack of attendance at school functions and feel this reflects a general lack of concern by parents about their children's education. However, family outreach is also about building a relationship and demonstrating sensitive caring about the family, not just concern for the child's education. Try a variety of communication methods (email, video, photos, written notes, calling, parent conferences, informal dialogues, home visits if possible) and invite families to share in ways they can arrange and feel good about. Some families might want to share stories, traditions, or expertise, but others might be hesitant or lack communication skills. Reciprocal partnerships are built on a relationship developed over time and on positive interactions.

SUPPORTING LEARNING EXPERIENCES AT HOME

Research has demonstrated that children living in lower SES families are at risk of experiencing less cognitive stimulation and learning experiences at home. Additional research has also demonstrated the further value of boosting learning experiences at home and at child care or school and coordinating to improve children's learning outcomes, with benefits lasting throughout elementary school. Importantly, the most significant academic gains were noted when home environments were cognitively stimulating and paired with similar stimulation in either child care/preschool or kindergarten (Crosnoe, Leventhal, Wirth, Pierce, & Pianta, 2010). So while classroom learning engagement is important, learning engagement at home is a more powerful intervention to support learning in children from lower SES backgrounds. This research should shape the ways that early childhood professionals implement family partnership practices, including emphasizing the value of supporting cognitive stimulation at home.

Ideas for extending supports for in-home learning experiences should be simple, clearly defined, easy to follow, meaningful, and reflective of family culture, values, and resources. Consider the purpose and implementation of a welcoming home visit as well as potential challenges as you watch the

CLASSROOM STORY CORNER

Infants and Sports Drinks

"I love being a teacher in the infant center, but sometimes I'm just left speechless. Even after 15 years!" With that and a sigh, Kathy sat down in the chair next to me in the teachers' room at our center. As one of our most experienced and certainly most professional staff, Kathy also served as our assistant director and was a source of support and guidance for all of the teachers. She had worked in a number of different settings, including 10 years at a Head Start. "Evan's mom came in today with sports drink in his baby bottle. He's three months old! My first thought was just 'Are you kidding?!' Gosh. Sometimes I just don't know....."

I shared her concern and asked her what she did and if she needed my help. I have to admit that my mind immediately jumped to definitions of neglect and if I should call my contact at the state licensing board for advice. But Kathy smiled and continued: "I'm glad I was here at drop off time, so I could ask her about it. She said that he likes it at home, so she's been giving him that in his bottles. I asked her about formula, though, for nutrition. She said she still was giving him formula sometimes but that he seemed to like the sports drink better. I had to work hard to stay calm, but I know from experience that if I let her know I was upset she might not talk to me about Evan as much. And I may be the only knowledgeable contact she has! So I just started talking to her about him, about some of the ways I give him bottles, and asked her more about what eating habits are like at home. Luckily, she and I have a good relationship and I try hard not to make her feel judged. She is so young and I know I can do more to help her and Evan by being kind and patient. I am glad, too, that I had some pamphlets from the free clinic about nutrition in my room. I got some and read her a couple of parts. I made a couple of little jokes but also focused on how important the ingredients in formula are to help Evan stay healthy. I mentioned a couple of stories about families I had worked with who didn't have decent nutrition and some of the long-term health problems the kids had—and the related doctor bills. I could tell that got her thinking. I also gave her coupons for free formula and a place where she could get help with more. She said she knew the address and could stop there after work. I offered to stay 15 minutes later than normal so she could go there today. After all these years, I still have moments which remind me just how complicated and overwhelming life can be sometimes!"

That day, and so many others, I was really impressed with Kathy and glad that our children and families have teachers like her. She really demonstrated a depth of care and professionalism in her approach to working with children and families by recognizing the larger context of Evan's life. The sports drink bottles were just one piece of the puzzle of this child's family life. Kathy could have responded very differently, and perhaps prompted even less appropriate parenting and made things worse for him. But by realizing that Evan's mom needed some support and guidance, and that with kind, nonjudgmental outreach his mother could be given skills and resources to become a better parent, Kathy made a lot more progress towards improving Evan's life. That deliberate approach to her practice always made Kathy stand out as an exemplary teacher. She taught us all a lot about building bridges with families!

home visit clips in this **video**. The following are some potential ideas for supporting at-home learning experiences that are coordinated with center and school experiences.

"Words in our World" (Environmental Print) I Spy game

Share with families the importance of literacy and how much we use it in our daily lives. In our homes and around the community are signs, labels, directions, logos, and other kinds of print. Often there are related colors, shapes, and fonts that make the print recognizable and associate it with particular products or uses. For example, popular restaurants, names of cereals, milk cartons, and food wrappers all often contain highly recognizable print. Pointing these out to children is a way to connect the purpose of literacy and to extend reading beyond just books. Even if literacy skills are not yet fully developed, the associated fonts and images help us "read" these titles, names, and labels, even if we aren't formally reading the words. Consider creating simple scavenger hunt or *I Spy* cards that ask families to find common labels or words together.

Simple Games

Encourage families of infants and toddlers to engage in interactive activities that build relationships and encourage exploration. Encourage families to focus on observation, identifying objects, naming items, people, and emotions, and exploring how everyday items work. Prompt children and families to notice similarities and differences. Some simple games to make and play with infants and toddlers are:

- Shape-matching cards
- *I Spy* cards with common everyday items or photo images from around the community
- Simple picture books with and without words, which can prompt observation (talk about what you see in the picture) and encourage families to make up stories

Take-home Book Packs

A book pack is a collection of materials and a couple of children's books that relate to a familiar topic of interest to children. Materials are chosen to support understanding of the story and spark interest in the story topic or message. Consider downloadable online books, request book donations from families and businesses, or find low-cost used books at library sales, donation-supported stores (Goodwill, Salvation Army), and yard sales. Be sure to include books at different reading levels and bilingual books (if families' home language is not English or for family members with limited literacy skill). You can even create a simple book with photographs and make stapled photocopies. Materials should be simple items that are made or found and allow families to engage in simple related activities together. An example of a book pack on weather could include:

- Books about weather changes, including nonfiction and fiction stories
- Simple weather-tracking picture charts or checklist, including pencil or pen
- Matching games with weather symbols or pictures
- Images from the book, cut out and glued to sticks to make simple puppets
- Parts of the book recreated on cards that can be used for sequencing games

Summary

WHAT DO FAMILY ECONOMICS AND SOCIOECONOMIC STATUS MEAN?

- The term *socioeconomic status* is used to categorize the stability of family resources and includes parent employment status and income, parent education level, and economic conditions in the family's neighborhood.
- Socioeconomic status can impact access to and quality of health care and education, nutrition, materials to stimulate learning, and other important contributors to children's development.
- Poverty guidelines are determined by the federal government and are used to gauge economic stability and govern access to welfare support programs.
- In the United States, 20% of children live in poverty and 44% live at or below 200% of the poverty line (considered the low income threshold).

CONNECTIONS BETWEEN FAMILY RESOURCES AND DEVELOPMENT

- The early years, specifically from prebirth through age 8, are the most crucial years in development as structures and processes are formed and strengthened.
- Adequate maternal nutrition, supplements, and rest coupled with reduced stress, anxiety, and exposure to potentially harmful environmental hazards are important for developing healthy babies—and continue to be important components of physical health throughout childhood.
- Nutrition, health care, and engaging experiences play a big part in supporting all areas of development in childhood, as well as the interrelated social interactions that are an important part of family and community life.
- Development is potentially jeopardized when adequate resources are not available to support these important functions.

IMPACT OF SES: MISCONCEPTIONS AND RESEARCH EVIDENCE

- Overgeneralized images of what life is like for individuals and families living with limited resources are pervasive in the media, popular culture, and within individuals' conceptions—and they seem to be accepted as fact.
- Misconceptions about families living within the low income threshold include judgments about work ethic, language skills, involvement in children's lives and education, and substance use.
- When preservice and inservice education professionals internalize these myths, whether they themselves realize it or not, they are prone to hold lower expectations of those children and families. Reduced teacher expectation, in turn, reduces children's successful outcomes.
- Strong evidence gathered for the past 40 years has clearly documented an achievement gap in academic performance in which middle- and upper-SES White students consistently score higher than Black and Hispanic lower-SES students on tests of reading and math skills.
- Factors contributing to this discrepancy in academic achievement include underresourced schools, lack of access to materials and engaging experiences, and unmet health and nutrition needs.

SUPPORTING RESILIENCY

- High-quality early intervention programs, which are designed to address these contributing factors, have demonstrated significant improvements in outcomes for children from low income backgrounds.
- Resiliency refers to a family or individual's ability to "bounce back," "rise above," or compensate for challenges and risk factors in their lives, and create positive outcomes in spite of those challenges.

- Having a strong, positive, long-term relationship with an early childhood professional can have tremendous, long-lasting impact on a child's school and developmental outcomes, and this impact is heightened for children living in less advantaged situations.
- Self-concept is a valuable attribute of resiliency.

CURRICULAR CONNECTIONS

- Teachers can support high learning and development outcomes for children from low income backgrounds by setting high expectations for all children and providing individualized support as needed.
- Teacher expectation is a strong predictor of students' outcomes, so it is essential that early childhood professionals communicate reasonably high expectations of all students.

- Intentionality is key when selecting and using materials; take the time to ensure that all types of family backgrounds are reflected in positive ways and that classroom materials demonstrate resourcefulness.
- Support small group interactions and foster prosocial skills to reduce likelihood of behavior problems.
- Ensure that learning activities focus on supporting and strengthening literacy and mathematics development.

FAMILY PARTNERSHIPS

- Be sensitive to family schedules and constraints, and provide multiple ways for family members to be involved in children's program or school life.
- Utilize multiple modes of communication to share important program or school information.

Chapter Learning Outcomes: Self-Assessment

Use this space to reflect on how well you have achieved the learning goals for this chapter by evaluating your own competency in the topics below. List three to five key concepts you have learned from the chapter.

Define socioeconomic status (SES) and related measures.	
Identify the potential for challenges and resiliency connected to SES.	
Discuss myths and realities related to SES.	
Describe strategies for supporting resiliency in children.	
Practice teaching strategies to support children from lower SES backgrounds.	
Create partnerships with families from lower SES backgrounds.	

Chapter Activities

DISCUSSION QUESTIONS

1. Describe the messages that media (television, movies, magazines, newspapers, Internet) convey about people living with limited incomes or within the poverty threshold. Identify at least five specific examples which demonstrate those messages.

2. Some researchers describe families living in poverty as a "hidden population." Discuss why they would choose this term and whether you agree or disagree.

SELF-REFLECTION

Children living in low income families or in poverty describe feelings of rejection and exclusion due to lack of resources such as name-brand clothing or shoes, and popular material goods like music and media devices or electronics. Recall a time in your own life when you felt rejected by peers, made fun of, or wished you had more material wealth or goods compared with other children (or describe the experience of someone close to you). Consider these feelings in light of developmental norms of seeking to belong and of friendship acceptance at this age, and discuss the potential impact on children's development of being socially rejected. What impact did that experience have on you (or your friends)?

TEACHER DISPOSITION

Imagine you are teaching and you overhear a group of your children making disparaging comments to another child for "being dirty and having lame clothes," or being "trailer-trash" or "ghetto," and excluding that child from engaging in activity with the group. Create a script (exact words) for how you would respond; set the goal of responding to the group and the child, and addressing bias with the whole class.

IN THE FIELD

As early childhood professionals we must be familiar with social service and welfare resources within our communities to be able to refer families in need to support. Using the Internet, phone books, or your local library, identify contacts for families in need of support with food, shelter, clothing, school supplies, and transportation.

Weblinks

"The Children's Defense Fund (CDF) is A non-profit child advocacy organization that has worked relentlessly for nearly 40 years to ensure a level playing field for all children. We champion policies and programs that lift children out of poverty; protect them from abuse and neglect; and ensure their access to health care, quality education and a moral and spiritual foundation." *www.childrensdefense.org*

National Center for Children in Poverty: Mailman School of Public Health, Columbia University. *http://www.nccp.org/*

7 Religion

For many people, religious beliefs and practices are intensely important to daily life and are a cornerstone of family culture. For many others, aversion to structured religious practice and doctrines shape family culture. And for many more still, core values and beliefs align with broad concepts found across religions but are attributed more to personal spirituality than to organized religion—and these beliefs are essential family values as well.

Regardless of where you place yourself on the spectrum of beliefs, or what type of beliefs you hold, it is incumbent on you, as an early childhood professional, to be familiar with major religions, understand the concept of spirituality, and recognize the choice to not ascribe to religious tenets or spirituality. The role of early care and education with

For many families, religious education and traditions are intimately connected to family culture and community identity.

regard to religion is a delicate and often hotly debated one, especially publicly funded or supported programs and schools. In the face of so much potential for conflict as well as the connectedness shared religion brings to people, the educators' task is to foster opportunities for intellectual and academic exploration of religious pluralism, for ourselves and the children and families we work with. Building awareness of religious beliefs held and practiced by people across the United States, while also appreciating each child's and family's personal convictions, is part of the essential body of knowledge and disposition that marks a high quality professional practice. This call to action involves exploring several important aspects integral to understanding the context of religious diversity in the United States:

- Examining the scope of religious practices in this country
- Understanding important terms and concepts
- Recognizing similarities and differences among major religions practiced in the United States
- Acknowledging the legal and ethical challenges that silence so many educators
- Uncovering the biases that serve to marginalize religious minorities

This chapter provides brief overviews of major religions practiced across the United States and strategies for early childhood professionals to appropriately and legally respond to and guide explorations about religious diversity and pluralism.

Why Study Religious Diversity?

An essential overarching point here is that "pluralism takes the reality of difference as its starting point. The challenge of pluralism is . . . to discover ways of living, connecting, relating, arguing, and disagreeing in a society of differences" (Eck, 2007, p. 745). Religious beliefs—or not practicing any religion—are included within the scope of human cultural diversity, and as such, must be a part of our lives with the children and families we work with. Avoiding knowledge or explorations of different religions and faith practices is an incomplete education, marginalizes important parts of children and families' lives, and does not serve our overarching goal of preparing children to be successful in a diverse world.

Children are naturally curious and notice differences among peers and among people around them. It is also natural and appropriate for children to share with teachers and classmates questions or ideas they have learned from others in their life. Early childhood professionals are often unsure how to respond to direct questions or comments about religious content, and thus often respond dismissively or inappropriately (even unconstitutionally).

- Explain the purpose of exploring religious diversity

- Discuss the context of religions and spirituality within families, schools, and across the United States

- Describe important ideals and values of the five most popular religions in the United States

- Practice teaching strategies to explore and appreciate religious diversity

- Create connections with families from different religious backgrounds

Messages and activities that are interpreted as promoting or discriminating against specific religions are potentially illegal, exclusionary, and problematic for many reasons. However, since "religion cannot be abstracted from the everyday lives of the people who embrace it," we cannot dismiss or marginalize what might be a highly influential aspect of a child's or family's life (Corrigan, Denny, Eire, & Jaffee, 1998, p. xvi). Your role in children's and families' lives is to understand the family context, to value each individual child and family, to orchestrate learning, and to support children's healthy development. This role includes the development of moral dispositions that validate the rights of each human to think and believe freely. Guiding and supporting young children's growth into and as creators of a pluralistic world requires that we provide them with broad knowledge about even the more passionate ways that people differ.

For so many of us, the highly publicized, passionate legal and sociopolitical battles over integrating religious topics into schools leave us insecure about both the content of diverse religious practices and the methods for appropriately protecting religious freedom while learning about religious differences. But as educators we do not have the luxury of simply avoiding religious diversity lest we fall short of providing our children with the breadth and scope of knowledge and dispositional development they need to be successful in the larger world outside of the program or school walls. To allay concerns about the "whether to" and "how to" of religious study in any school setting, several useful resources designed for educators provide clear guidelines. *A Teacher's Guide to Religion in the Public Schools* (Haynes, 2008), for example, is freely available online and provides 18 clear question-and-answer segments outlining content and instructional strategies for teachers and schools to meaningfully engage children in appropriate study of different religious practice.

Another extensive publication freely available online is *Religion in the Public Schools*, which has been used by individual states in responding to religious diversity, as well as in crafting religious studies curriculum standards (Lofaso, 2009). A prominent theme in these (and many other) instructional guidelines is for programs and schools to begin with an academic approach to studying various religions, with a focus on developing basic awareness of religious diversity. Programs and schools, in collaboration with families and communities, work together to design appropriate curricular expectations for comparative religious studies, with particular care for the sociopolitical and historical context within which the academic exploration of religion rests.

In our own practice, however, we might feel left alone to handle impromptu questions, discussions, or even disagreements among children about religious differences. And we might often be left wondering what is appropriate practice when it comes to integrating symbols, celebrations, or personal religious or faith information into our work. Content knowledge about religion does not need to be hushed or dismissed in programs and schools, as long as the information is neutral, has a clear academic purpose, and does not promote or denigrate any other beliefs. Preparing ourselves to navigate such sensitive content starts with an exploration of core beliefs and values of the five different religions with the most followers in the United States, premised on a platform of appreciation for family differences. Understanding the basic history, beliefs, and traditions of these five most popular religions provides professionals with some background content to better understand the family context. To be able to keep conversations about religion focused on neutral content and serve secular (not religion-promoting) purposes, professionals need to be knowledgeable about the context and basic ideologies of religions.

Context of Religious Diversity in the United States

The terms *religion* and *spirituality* are sometimes used interchangeably and certainly are concepts and terms that intermingle in a study of human life and the beliefs that shape individuals and societies. Understanding religious diversity and the context of family values calls for understanding the connections and differences between these key terms.

KEY TERMS: RELIGION AND SPIRITUALITY

Religion, in a broad sense, is so deeply entrenched in history, so complex, and so widely varied in its definition and meaning that it is a great challenge—even counterproductive—to try to distill this vast area into one short description (Corrigan, Denny, Eire, & Jaffee, 1998). We need to start somewhere with a shared meaning, but doing so should be considered only a start.

Religions provide belief systems and common practices. Religion is a connecting agent that binds people together; it is also invoked in practices that divide people. Religion is internalized differently by different people and groups, but at its basis, it offers and perpetuates ideas about the meaning of life, death, and beyond, and often involves belief in a higher power. Religions can "provide adherents with an interpretation of their universe and a direction for living" (Shibley, 2011, p. 186). They provide structure and organization, both conceptually and logistically, to belief in the existence of a higher power. It is the structural nature of religions that allows for its longevity across time—for people to pass down information, intact, across centuries (Bowker, 2006). This passing down of doctrine or codes for living religiously usually takes the form of a holy text, though some religions maintain an oral retelling tradition. Religion, then, can be considered an organized framework and system for understanding concepts and interrelationships of divinity and humanity.

While some people equate or relate spirituality with religion, many others find room under the scope of spirituality to contemplate and discuss meanings in life, death, and especially self-understanding, with no integration of specific religious belief or belief in a deity (Cook, Powell, Sims, & Eagger, 2011; Gall, Malette, & Guirguis-Younger, 2011). Among religious scholars and individuals alike there seems to be awareness that two contrasting kinds of spirituality exist: one that is defined relationally to religion and one that is not embedded in religion of any kind (Earl, 2001; Gall, Malette, & Guirguis-Younger, 2011).

Spirituality can exist beyond and outside of religion (independently within individuals), but it can also involve groups. Whereas religion might be an organized, externally located set of beliefs, spirituality is an internal self-identification process in which we wrestle with what it means to be human and with the mysteries of the world. Spirituality is used by many people as an important identifier or qualifier for personal beliefs and may be an individual or shared framework for understanding self, humanity, and society (McSherry, Cash, & Ross, 2004). *Spirituality* is a life perspective for many people,—meaning that it is an important component of how individuals not only see themselves but also how they relate to others, especially in terms of being kind or doing good. This connection between spirituality and relationships with others also includes relationships among all living, dynamic things in the universe (Gall, Malette, & Guirguis-Younger, 2011). Within this universal perspective, though, there also reside earth-based spiritualities that are considered formal religion by those who practice them, complete with sacred rituals and organizing frameworks (as with more traditional religion; Shibley, 2011).

DEMOGRAPHICS OF RELIGIOUS AFFILIATES IN THE UNITED STATES

The ways in which different religions emerged and developed over the past several centuries is historically rooted in geographic regions of the world. Looking at maps of religious concentrations, it would appear that people in the United States are majority adherents of some form of Christianity (of which there are literally thousands of denominations including Catholic, Protestant, Orthodox, and so on). Christianity is typically categorized in public survey reports in a broad and inclusive way and includes Mormon, Jehovah's Witness, historically Black churches, Orthodox, evangelical, Protestant, and Catholic groups. Surveys of U.S. households estimate the population of Christian adherents to be around 76% (Kosmin & Keysar, 2009) to 78.5% (Pew Research Center, 2008), though surveyors have acknowledged that some groups may be underrepresented due to limits of poll-taking (Griffith, 2008). Of the total surveyed U.S. population, 83% report some religious affiliation (Pew Research Center, 2008).

But the religious landscape in America is rapidly changing. In today's more mobile world, religious diversity is spread around the globe, and the United States is considered one of the most religiously diverse countries in the world. This past century, and particularly the past 50 years, have seen a tremendous increase in the population of non-Christian religions (Buddhism, Hinduism, or Islam, for example). Liberalization of immigration laws in the mid-1960s paved the way for an ongoing influx of people from Asia, Africa, the Middle East, and Latin America, countries which previously had not had such robust representation in the United States (Griffith, 2008; Halim, 2006). Equally significant is the doubling in the past 20 years of the number of Americans who self-report as having no affiliation with organized religion or as being atheist or agnostic—currently at 15 to 16% of the surveyed population (Hout & Fischer, 2002; Kosmin & Keysar, 2009; Pew Research Center, 2008). Snapshots of the U.S.'s religious diversity show that (Hamm & Banks, 2008; Pew Research Center, 2008):

- Black Americans are the most religiously active and affiliated racial or ethnic group in the United States (87% of Black Americans are religious), with 78% being Protestant (including Baptist, Methodist, Pentecostal).

- 85% of Latinos in the United States report religious affiliation, with 68% identifying as Roman Catholic and 15% as evangelical Protestant.

- 45% of Buddhists in the United States live in the western half of the country; one third of U.S. Buddhists are of Asian descent.

- 41% of Jews live in the Northeast; 95% are White.

- The Muslim population is relatively evenly distributed around the United States; 37% are White, 24% are Black, and 20% are Asian.

- The Hindu population is relatively evenly distributed in the northeast, west, and south (lower population in the Midwest); 88% of Hindus are Asian.

For some families, holiday traditions take on more social meaning and are a time to gather with friends and family for social activities (such as participating in an Easter egg hunt). For other families, holiday traditions are deeply connected to religious meaning and may be a time for solemn and joyful affirmation of faith.

While the overall population of non-Christian religions and nonreligious people grows, these groups still comprise a small percentage of the total U.S. population (about 5% non-Christians [Pew Research Center, 2008], and 15 to 16% nonreligious). But even as the non-Christian U.S. population increases, public opinion polls indicate that the belief that one must be Christian in order to be "truly American" is growing stronger (Smith, 2002). In essence, an increasing number of people in the United States view non-Christian religions as unpatriotic, different, and outside the normal (Subedi, 2006). Religious intolerance has a long history, with roots in violence and oppression across the globe, as with the history of the United States. Listen to the historical perspective shared in this **video** as you think about the impact of history and religion on individuals and communities. Religious divisiveness stems from a lack of awareness or experience with differing belief systems and is perpetuated even today by the fact that "most Americans . . . tend to deal with religious diversity by simply avoiding it" (Merino, 2010, p. 233). Yet other opinion polls indicate that roughly 80% of respondents believe religious diversity has a positive effect on America. These seemingly conflicting results certainly point to an inner struggle among many people in the United States about the status of religion, nonreligion, and religious differences, particularly in relation to national identity. When we consider the compelling evidence that indicates that personal experience with people of different religions promotes tolerance for religious diversity even among highly devout individuals (Campbell & Putnam, 2012; Merino, 2010), it is clear that we need to be providing opportunities for interreligious exploration and education.

Major Religions of the United States

The following five distinct religions are considered the most popular due to the number of followers as self-reported in the American Religious Identification Survey (ARIS). The 2008 survey included over 54,000 respondents and was conducted in English and Spanish (Kosmin & Keysar, 2009). The results from the ARIS report are similar to the Pew Research Center's slightly smaller-scale religion survey report from 2008. While the following list is in order of number of adherents, the second largest category group (ranked directly below Christianity in terms of number of followers) remains those who indicate no religious affiliation (nonreligious, agnostic, and atheist combined). This data serves as a reminder to avoid assuming that everyone is religious, just as we must not assume that everyone who is religious is Christian, believes in God, or goes to church. Religious diversity also includes individuals who reject all religious beliefs.

A premise is warranted for this section: clearly vast volumes of texts and teachings exist on each of these (and more) religions, an in-depth review of which is far beyond the scope of this book. The purpose of this extremely brief, broad overview of each religion is to provide basic awareness of core beliefs, practices, and traditions of each. Individual families, as well as individual places of worship or meditation, will undoubtedly practice in slightly or vastly different ways. For example, Buddhist practices vary among country or geographic locale, and within the broad heading of Christianity are literally thousands of differing types or denominations. The following sections serve as a brief primer to open your academic awareness to some of the religious diversity around us in this country (though it is by no means an exhaustive list).

CHRISTIANITY (76% OF U.S. ADULTS)

Christianity is a **monotheistic** religion based on the belief that there is one omnipotent God who sent a mortal embodiment of his word in the form of Jesus Christ to spread his word of love to all people. Christianity is an outgrowth of Judaism and shares some common history, beliefs, and texts. The life, crucifixion, and resurrection of Jesus and the belief that he is the savior of humanity sent by God is a uniquely Christian belief (Corrigan, Denny, Eire, & Jaffee, 1998). From the early years of Christianity, water baptism, as Jesus commanded of his disciples, became a ritual requirement of being Christian, replacing the Jewish ritual of circumcision. With the shift of weekly holy day from Saturday to Sunday, Christianity further distanced itself from Judaism.

Christianity emerged in the first century CE, when Jesus, born a Jewish man, lived and traveled as a wandering teacher and healer throughout the Roman Empire lands of the present-day Israeli–Palestinian region. In his life, Jesus preached God's word, performed miracles to make evident God's power, and though his mortal body was ultimately crucified, he is said to have been resurrected after death and later ascended to God in final evidence of God's salvation. His life, death, resurrection, and ascension are the cornerstones of the Christian faith. Roughly 35% of the world's population today claims adherence to some form of Christian denomination (Bowker, 2006).

The primary holy text in Christianity is the Holy Bible, comprising the Hebrew Bible, also known as the Old Testament, and the New Testament which chronicles the story of Jesus's life and teachings. The New Testament is made up of gospels, letters, and early writings. Followers look to examples from Jesus's life for guidance on what pious living should be. Core values in Christianity include:

- Being closer to God through prayer and pious living, bringing the reward of an afterlife in heaven
- Charity for those less fortunate and taking care of one's neighbor (defined as *fellow people*, not necessarily those living in proximity)
- Treating others as you want to be treated, which is the "Golden Rule" for Christian living

Prayer and worship are central to Christian life. Christians worship in churches, where religious authorities who are generically called *clergy*, guide religious sessions. (In different denominations, title of religious authority varies—for example, *priest, pastor, reverend,* or *minister*). Above all, Christians are called upon to pray often, whether at home or in gatherings. Charity and commitment to those in poverty are important methods of carrying out Jesus's message of love in the name of God (Bowker, 2006).

In the 16th century, a major split known as the Reformation occurred in Christianity. As a result of this split, modern day Christianity encompasses two main branches, Catholic and Protestant. While Catholic churches tend to have less variation of practice due to more centralized authority, many thousands of denominations exist among Protestants, each with varied beliefs and practices. See Figure 7.1 for a diagram of divisions within Christianity.

Two practices shared by all Christians and central to the religion are summarized in Table 7.1 (Corrigan, Denny, Eire, & Jaffee, 1998; E. Krajewski, personal communication, January 25, 2013).

FIGURE 7.1 *Major Branches of Christianity*

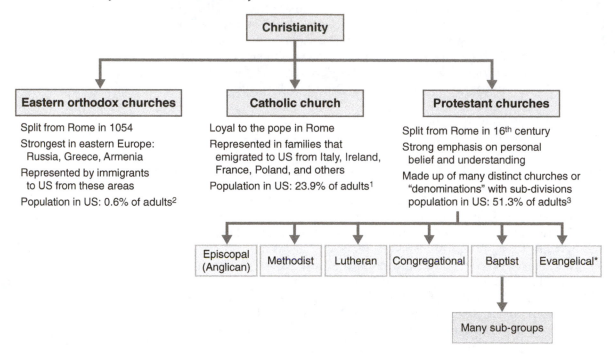

* The term "evangelical" has taken on a range of connotations in recent decades. While it originally indicated the notion that the teachings of Jesus Christ represented "good news," it has recently been appropriated by some Christian groups who use the term to indicate their commitment to spreading that "good news" to others via active proselytizing. Others use the term to indicate a socially conservative viewpoint which they attribute to Christian teaching.

[1]Pew forum on religion and public life, accessed on january 23, 2013.
[2]Pew forum on religion and public life, accessed on january 23, 2013.
[3]Pew forum; number obtained by adding the following: Mainline protestant, evangelical protestant, and historically black churches.

Holy days and celebrations in the Christian calendar are centered on Jesus's life, death, resurrection, and ascension, with the addition of days commemorating certain saints. Certain annual holy days are especially important, including (Breuilly, O'Brien, & Palmer, 1997; Corrigan, Denny, Eire, & Jaffee, 1998):

- Christmas: celebration of the birth of Jesus on December 25

- Easter: celebration of Jesus's resurrection (some families may also observe related holy days)

  - Ash Wednesday, the beginning of Lent preparation for Easter; church-goers are often marked on the forehead with ashes

  - Lent: 40-day fast or sacrifice in preparation for Easter

  - Palm Sunday: one week before Easter Sunday, marking Jesus's entrance into Jerusalem

  - Good Friday: commemorating the day of Jesus's crucifixion

TABLE 7.1 *Essential Practices of Christianity*

	Catholic	Protestant
Baptism	• Washing clean of Original Sin • Done to infants as early as possible • Necessary to enter heaven after death • Usually a large celebration with extended family • Adults designated as "Godparents" and commit to supporting religious upbringing	• Rite of initiation into local congregation • Done to adolescents or adults who freely declare belief in Jesus Christ and desire to join the church • Celebration primarily focused on individual and church community, less on extended family • Church members may act as "sponsors" rather than Godparents
Communion	• Also called Holy Eucharist, Lord's Supper, or Holy Sacrifice of the Mass • Bread and wine blessed and converted into Body and Blood of Jesus Christ • Priest or bishop can perform blessing and give bread and wine to people in congregation • Normal mode of worship on Sundays, also for weddings and funerals	• Bread and wine or grape juice considered symbols of Jesus's self-sacrifice at his death • Less strictly reserved to the clergy; members of the congregation share the elements with the people • Not necessarily the norm for Sunday worship; many denominations do this once a month
	In addition to these two rituals, Catholics recognize five others: Confession, Confirmation, Matrimony (marriage), Ordination (anointing of clergy), Anointing of the Sick (also known as Last Rites). All seven are called *sacraments* and to be considered efficacious, require ritual actions on the part of a priest.	Within the range of Protestant churches are many variations in understanding and practice of these seven rituals, sometimes called *ordinances*. This is due to the inherent tendency of Protestant Christianity to seek a more individualistic relationship between the believer and God, in contrast with the Catholic tradition in which all authority is centralized and localized in the office of the pope.

JUDAISM (1.2% OF U.S. ADULTS)

According to the Hebrew Bible, Judaism began when Abraham (who was believed to have lived around 1900 BCE [Before the Common Era]) heeded God's call to leave his home and set forth for a new land, to create a new nation that would be blessed by God. The land of Israel in the eastern Mediterranean was, and remains, of vital importance to Jewish history and identity (Bowker, 2006). In essence, Judaism is a religion rooted in the history of Abraham's pious obedience to God, and this remains the thrust of life for Jews. Judaism is a monotheistic religion recognizing one God and belief in his Commandments, as handed down to his prophet Moses at Mt. Sinai in the 1500s BCE.

The Jewish religion and tradition are preserved in the Hebrew Bible, comprising three parts: the Torah, the Nevi'im, and the Ketuvim. Together these sacred texts tell the story of the origin, rise, fall, and repentance of Israel, as outlined below (Corrigan, Denny, Eire, & Jaffee, 1998):

- *The Torah:* "The Torah describes the origins of the world and the history of the Israelite nation from its beginnings with Abraham to the death of its great leader, Moses" (p. 8). It recounts the promises made by God to Abraham and his descendants of a rich homeland and protection

Jewish religious ceremonies are often a time for remembrance and closeness with family and community.

from enemies. The Torah is considered guidance on what it means to be holy and live with obedience to God.

- *The Nevi'im:* The history of the chosen land, the kingdoms of Judah and Israel and how the chosen land was lost to invaders as a result of Israel's violation of obedience to God.

- *The Ketuvim:* The restoration and resettlement of the chosen land through Israel's repentance and recommitment to uphold the tenets of the covenant with God.

The Ten Commandments are arguably the most important laws of Jewish religious life, with the first commandment being the heart of Jewish belief. Table 7.2 outlines the Ten Commandments (which are also foundational to Christianity; Breuilly, O'Brien, & Palmer, 1997, p. 29).

The synagogue is the center of worship, gatherings, and study for Jewish people. Traditional Jewish practice includes prayer at the beginning and ending of each day, and a weekly day of rest to commemorate the Creator's day of rest, called the *Sabbath*. The Sabbath day of rest and worship begins at sundown on Friday and ends at sundown on Saturday. Prayer involves praising God and affirming the covenants of Israel as recounted

TABLE 7.2 *The Ten Commandments, Handed from God Directly to the Prophet Moses*

1. You shall have no other gods before me.	6. You shall not kill.
2. You shall not make for yourself graven images, nor serve them.	7. Neither shall you commit adultery.
3. You shall not take the name of the Lord in vain.	8. Neither shall you steal.
4. Observe the Sabbath (seventh day) as a day of rest.	9. Neither shall you lie against your neighbor.
5. Honor your father and mother.	10. Neither shall you covet your neighbor's wife or property.

in the Hebrew Bible (Bowker, 2006). The history of Judaism, both early and modern, involves tremendous religious persecution, the overcoming of which is a source of strength and solidarity for many Jews. Judaism, like most religions, has evolved over the centuries and modern practice now includes a more active role for women (historically excluded from synagogue worship or clergy roles; Corrigan, Denny, Eire, & Jaffee, 1998). At synagogue and at home, education of children in the Jewish religion and ways of life was especially important for Jewish parents. Reading of the Torah and the Talmud, the Jewish law book, as well as understanding various interpretations of the holy texts, is an important goal for Jewish children. Other important rites of passage include ritual circumcision of infant boys and the blessing of girls, and a coming of age ceremony for boys (and girls in some practices) at age thirteen which marks the entrance into adult Jewish life.

In Judaism, religious laws governing the slaughter, preparation, and consumption of foods are extensive and extremely important, impacting Jews at home and in public (at school, for example). Pork products and rabbit are forbidden (among other non-cloven hoof meats), as well as shellfish. Ritual slaughter of meats is essential, and birds and meats must be drained of blood before being prepared or consumed. Meat and dairy products are kept separate in preparation as well as in consumption (that is, not together at the same meal). There are wide variations in the observance of exact food laws among groups of Jews; permitted foods are always called *kosher*. It is always important to discuss dietary needs with families for program and school-day meals and snacks.

In addition to food laws, daily rituals, and the Sabbath, there are annual festival days which commemorate important events in the history of Israel and are highly important to Jewish life. The most notable holy days are:

- Passover, in spring: celebrating the mass exodus of Israelites from slavery in Egypt, making their way to the promised land of Israel

- Rosh Hashanah, in autumn: marks the Jewish New Year and is a time for reflection and renewal

- Yom Kippur, in autumn: a solemn day of confession of sins to God, prayers for forgiveness, and atonement

- Chanukah, in winter: known as the Festival of Lights, commemorating the reclaiming of the Temple in Jerusalem and the miracle of one day's oil lasting for eight days as the temple was restored; currently stands as a symbol of the perseverance of the Jewish faith in the face of adversity

ISLAM (0.6% OF U.S. ADULTS)

In Indonesia and in countries in central Asia, the Middle East, and northern Africa, Islam is considered the national religion, with a nearly total majority of followers (Bowker, 2006). It is also considered the fastest-growing world religion. In the United States, Muslims (those who follow the religion of Islam), represent the third most popular religion, and across the globe Islam is the second most popular religion. Evidence of Muslim presence in the United States dates back to explorers before Columbus, with a strong influx of Muslims from various countries in the latter half of the 1900s. While backlash in the form of violence and discrimination against Muslim Americans grew in the wake of the September 11, 2001, attacks, the Muslim American population continues to grow and maintain its intrareligious diversity (Halim, 2006). Many Muslims continue "to feel the pain of being decent people stereotyped by some as coming from a religion of terrorists," an egregious misunderstanding of Islam stemming from lack of knowledge of Muslim people (Reyton & Jalongo, 2008, p. 301). Similar to Christianity and Judaism, Islam is a monotheistic religion that recognizes Allah as the one true God, though there are diversities among Muslims just as there are among other religions (Halim, 2006).

The Qur'an is the major religious text for Muslims, and it serves as a guide and source of joyful inspiration in all matters of life. The Qur'an is considered to be the direct word of God as revealed to Muhammad (there are many variations in the spelling of the prophet's name across different languages and alphabets), the last prophet sent by God to bring his final word to the people between 610 and 632 CE (Common Era). The Qur'an clearly tells Muslims that there is only one God and no other divine beings (prophets, including Jesus, are solely mortal). Muslims believe that the life and actions of Muhammad, called *Sunna*, are a perfect example of allegiance and worship of God (Corrigan, Denny, Eire, & Jaffee, 1998). Thus, *Sunna* is the example by which Muslims live their lives. This is a conviction so deeply felt that many Muslims feel devoted to faith every moment of their day—they fit their life into their religion and not the other way around (Marks, 2004). In Islam, God is considered a constant presence, and Muslims are especially close to God during prayer (Bowker, 2006).

At the time of Muhammad's death in 632 CE, a split among Muslims arose over the selection of a successor, and the Sunni Muslim and Shi'a Muslim branches emerged. Today roughly 80% of Muslims are Sunni. Both subcommunities follow the same religious doctrine and worship practices and engage in ritual duties together. However, it is on political, not religious, grounds that differences have provoked significant conflict (Corrigan, Denny, Eire, & Jaffee, 1998).

The required devotional acts outlined in the Qur'an that are incumbent upon all Muslims are called the *Five Pillars of Islam*. These provide structure to everyday life for Muslims. By age 7, children begin to practice the Five Pillars, under careful guidance from parents (fathers especially; Callaway, 2010). The pillars include acknowledgement of God and the messenger Muhammad, specific procedures for worship five times per day, giving to the poor, daytime fasting for one month, and the pilgrimage to Mecca (Corrigan, Denny, Eire, & Jaffee, 1998). Table 7.3 outlines the Five Pillars of Islam.

While the Five Pillars serve as the primary structure for worship, ritual purification of the body is an even more important and inextricably entwined aspect of Muslim life. Impurities are cleansed through ritual washings, the procedures for which are determined by the degree of impurity. Through the process of

TABLE 7.3 *The Five Pillars of Islam*

Pillar 1: *Shahada* Declaration of Faith	Pillar 2: *Salat* Prayer	Pillar 3: *Sawm* Fasting	Pillar 4: *Zakat* Welfare Tax	Pillar 5: *Hajj* Pilgrimage
Witnessing the unity of God, Muslims recite the following: "There is no god but God, and Muhammad is the messenger of God"	The set of prayers which Muslims perform five times each day (facing the direction of the sacred shrine in Mecca)	Fasting during daylight hours during the entire month of Ramadan	Charitable donation to the poor or charitable causes, often equaling one fortieth of one's annual income	A pilgrimage to the holy city of Mecca in the 12th Islamic month at least once in a lifetime, provided one is physically and financially able

washing away impurities from the body prior to engaging in *Salat* (prayer), Muslims maintain a focus on discipline and devotion to God. The ritual purification is considered a way of Muslim life and is another way that Muslims demonstrate their complete surrender to God (Corrigan, Denny, Eire, & Jaffee, 1998). Most Muslim prayer happens at home, work, at the mosque, or in other community areas since Muslims worship throughout each day. But many often gather on Fridays, the Day of Assembly, in a mosque (Bowker, 2006).

Of special consideration are the dietary restrictions of practicing Muslims. In particular, meat products must be processed in accordance with religious law, and the Qur'an strictly forbids consuming any pork products whatsoever. This includes derivatives and by-products such as anything containing lard or gelatin (Breuilly, O'Brien, & Palmer, 1997). Muslim practice forbids the consumption of alcohol, which is commonly found in high percentage in vanilla extract. Given that families might practice strict dietary restrictions, always discuss with families the food that will be served at school in order to explore the possibility of modifying school menus or having families provide acceptable foods if they prefer.

Ramadan is the most sacred time for Muslims, commemorating when the Qur'an was revealed. Ramadan occurs in the

In Islamic religion, traditions of prayer and dietary restrictions are especially important.

ninth month of the Islamic calendar and its dates change each year. All months in the Islamic calendar contain 28 days. (Corrigan, Denny, Eire, & Jaffee, 1998). For example, in 2014 it begins on June 24; in 2015 it begins on June 18. While only healthy adults or older children are required to maintain the daily fast (abstaining from food, drink, and sexual intercourse), some children choose to engage in the ritual fasting along with their families as a dedication to their faith and closeness with God. This is of particular importance for early childhood professionals to be aware of as it may require extra attention to fasting children's energy levels and hydration and might require changes to scheduling high-energy activities. Eid al-Fitr is the three-day celebration following the Ramadan month of fasting. Muslim families gather for feast, prayer, and gift-giving. In Muslim countries all three days are national holidays.

BUDDHISM (0.5% OF U.S. ADULTS)

The origins of Buddhism, (*Buddha* meaning *enlightened one*) are linked with Hinduism, which began in northern India and focuses on personal responsibility and spiritual development as opposed to relationships between God(s) and humanity. Buddhism addresses both knowledge and practice (action) in daily life and is viewed as a teaching guide in striving for clarity. Buddhists do not worship God(s) as other religions do, but rather believe that deliverance from suffering can be gained through the cause and effect of one's own efforts (Mahathera, 1982). Today Buddhism (in different forms) is the predominant religion across Mongolia, China, Southeast Asian countries, and Japan (Breuilly, O'Brien, & Palmer, 1997).

Buddhism emerged in the fifth or sixth century BCE (Before the Common Era) from the teachings of Siddhartha Gautama, a man who is said to have attained enlightenment, nirvana, or freedom from the rebirth cycle in his mortal form through years of self-sacrifice and meditation. He was compelled by the Hindu god Brahma to share what he learned in his attainment of enlightenment. His visions are documented as the Four Noble Truths and the Eightfold Path, which are the foundation of Buddhism. These teachings are based on the principle of *karma*, or moral law of action and consequence which includes belief in reincarnation. While most Buddhists believe that there have been many and will be more Buddhas, the original writings still serve as the foundation of Buddhist thought and practice. The teachings of Buddha have been passed down through oral retelling traditions as opposed to through a written book.

The Four Noble Truths are:

- Suffering: all existence is filled with suffering.
- Its cause: suffering emerges from clinging and attachment to impermanent things; everything is impermanent.
- Its end: ending suffering is possible (achieving *nirvana* or freedom from suffering).
- The Middle Way: the way to end suffering is to live by The Eightfold Path, the steps to self-improvement and freedom from rebirth.

TABLE 7.4 *The Eightfold Path, the Middle Way, to Achieve Nirvana*

Right Understanding	Right Thoughts	Right Speech	Right Actions	Right Livelihood	Right Effort	Right Mindfulness	Right Concentration
Knowledge of the Four Noble Truths; to understand things as they are and not as they appear to be	Selflessness, kindness, compassion	Speak truth	No killing, stealing, or sexual misconduct	Avoid trading in humans, arms, controlled substances, animals for slaughter	Vanquish evil and promote good	Be always conscious of self and feelings	Meditative absorption

The Eightfold Path includes guidance on developing essential knowledge, ethical actions, and mental dispositions that combine into the only way to be delivered from the suffering that is a requisite of life on earth (Bowker, 2006). Table 7.4 summarizes the Eightfold Path (Mahathera, 1982).

From this early Buddhist philosophy, two forms of Buddhism emerged that are now practiced across different parts of Asia: Theravada Buddhism, which closely follows the original teachings, and Mahayana Buddhism, which extends the teachings of Buddha. Communities of monks or nuns (those who have dedicated their lives to the study of Buddhism), the Buddha, and his teaching are revered as The Three Jewels of Buddhism. The Buddhist place of worship is called a temple and most are recognizable by their bell-shaped roofline or towers. Monasteries and shrines are also plentiful in countries with a strong Buddhist population and are an active part of daily life and festival days. Sand and stone gardens may also be used for meditation and chanting, which are primary forms of Buddhist worship and practice to bring one closer to enlightenment (Breuilly, O'Brien, & Palmer, 1997).

Celebrations and festival days vary in different countries but usually include temple fairs or offerings at shrines (Breuilly, O'Brien, & Palmer, 1997). Festivals are joyful celebrations, marking the New Year (dates vary by ethnic background) and important days in the Buddha's life. *Vesak*, the birth of Buddha and his passing into nirvana, is widely celebrated with festivals, rituals, and offerings, usually during the first full moon in May.

HINDUISM (0.4% OF U.S. ADULTS)

Hinduism originated in the river valley region of what now covers parts of northern India, Pakistan, and Afghanistan, and the traditions of the Indus people from around 2500 BCE to 1500 BCE. The title *Hinduism* was first used by outsiders to describe religious practices in India, and Hindu people use the term *Sanatana Dharma* (or *eternal truth*) to refer to their religion. Hinduism is based on a belief that the "eternal soul . . . is reborn millions of times and in many forms, from the heavens to the hells, according to the moral law [of cause and effect], or *karma*, that prevails in the

Making offerings and prayers to deities is an important part of Hindu traditions that young children take part in from infancy alongside their families.

universe" (Bowker, 2006, p. 20). Reincarnation will continue as the soul's path towards release to be with God eternally (*Moksha*). Life situations are viewed in the context of this eternal goal of being released from the cycle of reincarnation in earthly lives. *Karma* refers to both one's actions and the resulting consequences. Thus, negative life situations (such as living in a lower class, or caste), is considered a necessary step for the eternal soul to earn its way through the cycle towards a higher status incarnation and ultimate release from mortality. And one's actions have direct consequences for the rebirth cycle; living righteously or appropriately will ensure more positive life circumstances in the next life. "For Hindus it is a religious responsibility to carry out the duties that are associated with each stage of life and with the family and part of society into which they are born" (Breuilly, O'Brien, & Palmer, 1997, p. 89).

Hinduism is a **polytheistic** religion, in that there are many gods and goddesses who appear in the texts of eternal truths, or *Vedas*. The trinity includes the three principle Gods of Hinduism:

- *Brahma*, the creator
- *Vishnu,* the preserver
- *Shiva,* the destroyer

Worship is extremely important to Hindu life and is more of an individual than group activity, with followers using prayer (*mantras)*, rituals, chants, and sacrifices to worship at home and at temple. Offerings to the deity are an important part of worship and can include gifts of coconuts, fruits, sweets, or money. Lighting incense is a common practice as the fire God, Agni, is the primary vehicle for bringing offerings to the heavens. There are many different deities which Hindus may devote themselves to, including important feminine forms of deities. In Hinduism, the divine is approachable and may manifest in many earthly forms, particularly in forms of nature such as animals, flowers, and trees. Stemming from foundational beliefs in karma and divine manifestation in animals, most Hindus are vegetarians and none eat beef; a practice which requires that programs and schools discuss dietary restrictions and daily menus with families to ensure acceptable alternatives as necessary.

There are many Hindu festivals that are based on a 12-month lunar calendar and are closely tied to seasonal changes and weather patterns in

India (Breuilly, O'Brien, & Palmer, 1997). The three primary festivals are Holi, Diwali, and Dussehra (Bowker, 2006).

- *Holi:* A celebration of spring and the New Year held in March that includes an evening bonfire symbolizing the end of the old year, followed by playful games, noisemaking, and pranks on the day of Holi.
- *Diwali:* A harvest festival and national holiday in late October and mid-November in which small lamps are lit to celebrate the inner light of the eternal soul within each person and offerings are made to the goddess of wealth and prosperity in hopes of a prosperous coming year.
- *Dussehra:* A national holiday and nine-day long celebration in September to October which honors the triumph of good over evil and involves prayer, feasts, and fire sacrifices.

OTHER RELIGIONS NOT SPECIFICALLY MENTIONED

The preceding five religions are by no means exhaustive nor are they representative of all of the children and families with whom you will work. Across the United States there is widespread religious diversity, but there are also high concentrations or groups of people who participate in a shared religion. The following are just a few examples (Pew Research Center, 2008):

- The southeastern quarter of the United States hosts a thriving concentration of active Baptist Christians.
- Coastal New Jersey to Massachusetts and southern Florida host a strong Jewish population.
- Utah and Idaho contain active and growing Mormon groups.
- California, Arizona, New Mexico, and Oklahoma are home to the largest population of American Indians or Native Americans, with different nations practicing different traditional faiths and religions.

All early childhood professionals should take the time to explore the variety of religions and denominations that are a part of the community and families' lives, including a basic understanding of historical context. You can begin by reviewing religious centers or places of worship or mediation listed in an area phone book, and then learn about those faiths through a variety of means (visits, reputable online sources, colleagues, family members, books, and more). Think of this as a mini-research project and approach the task academically, possibly charting the following information as we have done for the religions above:

- Type of house of worship or meditation (ashram, mosque, temple, church, etc.)
- Name of or contact for officiate (pastor, rabbi, pujari, etc.)
- Primary religious holy text or source
- Summary of most important beliefs

"She Said My Mom was Wrong about God and was Going to be Punished."

When she was five, Najya's family moved to the United States from Indonesia. As Muslims, her family maintained a close connection to the Qur'an and continually reaffirmed for Najya family rules as outlined by their faith. Najya wore a headscarf like her mother and maintained the ritual cleansing and prayer throughout the day. These practices were very important to her family, and she was diligent about living up to her family's expectation even though she was one of only a few Muslims in her school.

In second grade, Najya's class started a study of world religions. Her tablemate and friend, Janessa, was beginning to outline the chart that was assigned for the children to complete as a comparison of beliefs. "I started the chart with Christianity, because that was the one I knew the best from going to church on Sundays," Janessa said. "When I had a few boxes filled in, I mentioned to Najya that I started with things my mom had told me about God. She got a stern look on her face and told me that my mom was wrong about

God and not to listen to her or else I'd face the same 'painful punishment' that my mom was sure to face. She said she felt sorry for my mom. I didn't know what to do, I remember feeling mad and embarrassed at the same time. I just started crying and didn't say anything until the teacher came over. He told me my mom wasn't wrong and that we were 'good Catholics', and he told Najya not to say hurtful things again. We went back to our study and Najya and I completed separate charts. We weren't really friends as much after that.

"It's been many years since that moment, but I still remember it and how awful it was so hear someone talk about my family's faith like that. Over the course of the religions study, we all learned more about different religious beliefs and also similarities. I guess it helped some, but Najya and I never talked about that comment. I didn't know how to and I think my teacher didn't really either. I wonder if our friendship could have gone differently if we had been able to talk about it more."

- Essential practices (prayer, gatherings, rituals)
- Important holidays or holy days and their meaning (celebration, fasting, prayer)

Curricular Connections

While most non-faith-based programs and schools are considered secular (nonreligious), it is important to explore the ways that the European influence on care and education in the United States includes a *Christian normalcy*. **Christian normalcy** refers to ways in which White, European-influenced, Christian values and practices are so historically and deeply ingrained that many people don't even realize the bias (Joshim, 2007). Consider program and school schedules, craft activities, and wall decorations or displays which include vestiges, icons, or characters. Most school and program schedules are arranged in such a way that the major Christian-based holidays are during school closings (winter recess, spring break, for example), but holidays of other religions are not deliberately encompassed within these breaks (though sometimes they may fall within them). Children who practice other holy days must often choose between unexcused absence or family religious commitment, a position not in line with pluralistic values (Peyton & Jalongo, 2008). Likewise, themed décor and displays often represent characters or images which stem from Christian history or festivals. We often justify this pervasive inclusion of Christian-based imagery on the grounds that it reflects the home life of the majority of children in our programs and schools. In essence, it affirms the lived experience for these children. But for children who do not practice family traditions related to these holidays, such school activities can create a major conflict in terms of a sense of belonging at program or school, as well as conflict with self-identity.

Seasonally themed projects such as gingerbread houses, snowman crafts, and springtime scavenger hunts are sometimes substituted for more overtly religious-themed projects, but teachers must be careful and intentional about potential connotations to specific religions.

The conflict deepens for students of color, who are exposed to a vast media of Christian-related images which predominantly convey people associated with Christianity as White, even when retelling Biblical stories that originate in Africa and the Middle East (Subedi, 2006). Consider for a moment your own exposure to religion-related images. What images pop into your mind when you think of "religious icons" (however you define that)? What books, posters, movies, or television shows are a part of your memory of "religion"? (Even if formal religious practices are not a part of your everyday life now or weren't when you were growing up, you undoubtedly have some imagery stored in your memory related to religion.) As you hold these images in your mind, can you notice any racial and religious bias? The revealing look into your own background and existing bias (naturally emerging from your own lived experience) is an essential first step for being able to shed old familiar knowledge in place of a new more pluralistic knowledge and framework. From this self-revelation you can then move your focus on to your practice with a much more deliberate and aware perspective on the learning experiences you want to create for the children you work with.

MATERIALS

A number of children's books explore topics of religious diversity (including nonreligion) in ways that are informational, interesting, and supportive of diversity. Zeece (1998) presents an overview of eight children's books that explore basic beliefs of major world religions in developmentally appropriate levels. Other books validate some of the questions children have about religion, God, and faith. Peyton and Jalongo (2008) present an extensive list of books to engage children in stories of religions (history and practices) with both fiction and nonfiction sources. Books include stories of growing up in families with dual or multiple religions practiced, an increasingly popular choice as rates of interfaith marriage increase. Local libraries and websites also host free book sources for children (such as Buddhanet.net), and Religioustolerance.org offers online review of many books comparing religions and stories promoting religious pluralism.

Work to explore and integrate a rich variety of images and authentic stories of daily life from families, those practicing all forms of religion as well as nonreligious families. Be especially careful to avoid simply sharing one or a few images, items, or stories, and keep in mind that "too few images of a group oversimplifies the variety within the group" and can lead to narrow or inaccurate views of differing groups (Derman-Sparks, 1993, p. 70). In essence, you are working to avoid a "tourist" approach that reduces groups to a few highlights or special occasions. There is a balance here, certainly, between appropriate generalizations or summaries and stereotypes and overgeneralizations. Remember that families' practices vary widely even within the same religious group (intrareligious diversity). Exploring summaries and basic religious frameworks is a starting point. The next step is to delve deeper into authentic, meaningful practices and rituals that are practiced by families in your class or program group and community. Focus explorations on items and routines of daily life. Here children will find as many similarities as differences, and this realization is the heart of understanding diversity among people.

ENVIRONMENT

Considerations regarding how you design your environment are especially relevant to certain holidays with widespread celebrations, such as St. Patrick's Day or Valentine's Day. There is always a tension between program and classroom décor and activities which subtly or overtly promote these holidays versus acknowledging the relevance of related activities in children's lives. Children will naturally come in to your setting talking about holiday events or displays they have noticed around the community or in the media. While professionals in non-faith-based programs can and should refrain from exclusive promotion through single-holiday decorations, crafts, or lessons, even with groups who appear to celebrate the same holiday, it is also important to validate important family traditions and practices.

So a general rule to consider is that when children initiate conversations, you should be prepared to support discussion of things that are important to them. If you choose to introduce information about religious practices or events, be sure to make a practice of equally integrating information about a variety of religions, holidays, and traditions. Consider pen pals; or video conferences with classrooms in other areas, community religious leaders, and families as resources to guide a group exploration of variations in religious and holiday practices. The key is to be balanced and neutral to ensure that you are not excluding or promoting one form of religion or holiday at the expense of another in your classroom displays and activities. Be especially cognizant of families whose beliefs do not allow the acknowledgement of certain holidays or celebrations. Work out a plan for appropriate alternative programming and space for families who refrain from celebrations so that children do not feel singled out and excluded from their group.

For children whose religion emphasizes modesty, provide separate bathroom facilities for boys and girls when possible. If open or unisex bathrooms are used, consider procedures to ensure privacy, such as a curtain or divider and an indicator to show when the bathroom is in use (red or green, free or busy, or open or closed signs).

For children who practice prayers during the day or rituals before meals, provide some quiet space and a short interval of time to complete these tasks (Hoot, Szecsi, & Moosa, 2003). It is acceptable for children to remain with the group or in the room during these sessions, but take time to educate all of the children about the activities, and guide respectful responses to them. It is natural for children to be curious or even to want to imitate the children who are practicing a ritual—and this might or might not be appropriate or acceptable. Prayers or blessings of meals are important and solemn activities in which praying children should have space to focus.

For young children choosing to fast with their family for Ramadan (not required of young children, but many children and families choose participation), consider alternative activities or areas of the building when other children are eating. Limit strenuous physical activity in the afternoon; watch for signs of physical distress (exhaustion or dehydration; Hoot, Szecsi, & Moosa, 2003).

INTERACTIONS WITH CHILDREN

Many children are excited to share their family religious or spiritual practices and traditions, and encouraging them can be easy. Others might not be as comfortable. Many children say they feel burdened or singled out by teachers who ask them many questions about their religion as a means to inform the group. Being from a Muslim family, for example, does not necessarily make the child a representative or spokesperson for the entire religion. Gauge children's interest in sharing, and offer opportunities—but don't push them. Be deliberate in cultivating a climate that welcomes sharing and validates each child and family's own way of experiencing religion, spirituality, and ideas about being human. Seek people within your community who can act as resources, and invite them to share their ideas and experiences with your children.

Children are naturally inclined to talk about family religious celebrations, and this sharing should be encouraged. Intervene only when children express negative views of others. Validate that it is natural and exciting that different families have different beliefs.

As children find a place at program or school to discuss religion, it is likely that they will ask you about your beliefs and values. They might even ask you to resolve conflicts between differing views or definitions of God, for example. Prepare your response for when children ask for your beliefs about religion and God, remembering your position of influence and your responsibility not to promote one religion over another (if in a non-faith-based program). Your role is to be a facilitator of dialogue, focusing on inclusion of ideas. An inclusive dialogue is one in which you share your own ideas, but those ideas should be premised in your genuine belief that each person has other ideas which are as valid (Shady, & Larson, 2010). So you may briefly share ideas and practices from your life while also inviting children to share theirs as equal dialogue partners. The key rule of thumb is to be careful not to cross the line into promoting or denigrating other beliefs. If this delicate balance feels intimidating, it is possible to craft a response that validates the question but does not necessarily answer it outright. While you might feel it necessary to redirect the child's question away from your own beliefs, it is important to your relationship with children to not be dismissive. For example, a response might be: "Ali, I believe that people should do good and be kind to each other and that people can find help with that through many sources. What do you think about it?"

INTERACTIONS AMONG CHILDREN

An unfortunate reality echoed by many religious minority children is the experience of overt bullying, shaming, and exclusion by religious majority children (Abo-Zena, 2012). While some children are valued and sought after for the ways their religion is different from the majority of the class, many more children share stories of feeling marginalized and made fun of because of foods, dress, prayers, or modesty values which set them apart from other children. Programs and schools must have clear policies and practices for reducing bullying in all forms, and professionals must model and enforce practices that value differences. They must unconditionally refuse to tolerate violence and discrimination. While professionals should be clear on such policies and practices, it is also important to discuss them specifically with children. Sharing stories of children's experiences from research articles and professional magazines can help to make a personal impact on children. Tell children that discrimination is never acceptable, and be vigilant about stopping exclusionary words or actions when you see them. Guide children to be advocates for themselves and their classmates and to make violations known to teachers or parents. Discrimination often lurks in shadows, and children and adults alike can be pivotal in shining the light of social justice to stop it.

Support candid and respectful conversations among children that allow sharing questions, ideas, misconceptions, and experiences about religion and religious diversity. Many children might repeat messages they have heard; these messages might be positive or negative and might reveal misconceptions that should not be dismissed or ignored. We are here to guide our children in exploring the vast and varied knowledge and experiences of the world and to encourage them to think about these. Questions or ideas that emerge out of religious experiences are often abstract and can be approached in many, many ways. These kinds of topics are sometimes scary for professionals, especially if you feel that your role is to provide answers. I encourage you to think of yourself as a facilitator of questions, not always an answer giver. Our goal is to support children's development as thinking, feeling, acting humans living in a diverse world. We accomplish this by allowing ourselves to, at times, lead our children, but at many other times to follow and journey alongside our children. As young children wrestle with abstract concepts (challenging for them given their level of cognitive development), it is healthy to encourage their cognitive conflict and intellectual struggle. These are not simple topics, but they are also a part of children's lives.

- Let children ask questions; facilitate or mediate as needed if hurtful stereotypes emerge.

- Encourage group research and exploration ("Aryeh, that's a great question. Let's find out more about that together!")

- Validate that there might be conflicting ideas that promote a "right way," and emphasize that the "right way" can be different for different people.

- Help children understand that sometimes big questions linger and we have to keep thinking about them over time; they do not need a final answer on some questions.

- Keep families' role present in conversations, reminding children that they can ask their families for additional information. Consider taking notes on big questions to be able to update families on discussion topics at school, to encourage their participation at home.

- Explain up front to families (in a welcome letter or initial conversation) your approach to supporting children's thinking about complex topics such as religious differences (also important for questions about where babies come from, death, and more) so that when topics naturally emerge from children's questions they are not surprised to hear their children have been talking about "sensitive" topics. Explain that the role of the family is always reaffirmed but that silencing questions harms children's thinking, socialization, and identity development.

LEARNING EXPERIENCES

Exploring religion in schools and programs is about building important knowledge about humanity and the human experience. It is as much a part of a comprehensive curriculum as any other topic—such as our bodies, community professions, plants, animals and insects, seasons, motion and vehicles, and so on, and it naturally aligns with exploration of our families. As a group community-building experience, beginning a year with a project on "my family life" can easily include information about important values, beliefs, and special practices or traditions that can be both religious and nonreligious. For families who participate in religious practices or affiliate with a religion, this sharing within the context of daily family life is a natural way to validate this part of their life. For those who are nonreligious, there are all of the other aspects of daily family life to share, so there is not a great emphasis on religion, which might feel exclusionary to those who do not practice.

From this initial, personal data collection (having children share, ask family members, and so on), invite children to share photos, items, and stories from their family's religious or spiritual life. These can then be a starting place for introducing similar content and artifacts from other religions not expressed by the families in your program or class. Introducing unfamiliar religions is an important part of expanding children's thinking beyond themselves and integrating multicultural education through a personal frame.

Related to the exploration of family religions is the potential for a more personal identification of values, morals, and beliefs upheld in society. There is a clear distinction between religion and moral character, often considered "character education." Teachers should guide children's learning about "the personal and civic virtues widely held in our society, such as honesty, caring, fairness, and integrity. They must do so without either invoking religious authority or denigrating the religious or philosophical commitments of students and parents" (Haynes, 2008, p. 6). These sound like lofty topics, and indeed they are, but they are not beyond the scope of even our youngest children in varying forms and to varying degrees. The following are key considerations which may be involved in exploring character, ethics, morals, and values:

- They are a part of the human experience and rooted in a cultural context.
  - They are shaped by individuals, family, community, and society.
- They are part of a set of shared goals and expectations for behavior within general society.
  - Values of "good character" are applied to all people, regardless of religious affiliation or lack of religious beliefs.
- They might be deeply entrenched in clearly conveyed family culture.
  - They can include dress, faith practices, routines, community events, and traditions.

- They may change with time, maturity, and experiences.
- They may reflect both intellectual and emotional components.

From infancy and toddlerhood, young children internalize messages about the values and related behaviors that are promoted by the community around them. We often coach even our youngest children to share, be a good friend, be gentle, listen to one another, and take turns. These are the beginnings and foundations of how we develop the kinds of character traits that children will need to successfully thrive within a particular society. Consider engaging your professional group or the children you work with in a dialogue about what values they believe are most important and what behaviors demonstrate those values. These discussions might evolve into a form of class rules or might grow into a more lofty discussion about living peacefully within a group. By preschool age, children can understand concepts of character, integrity, community, and civic engagement when they are guided in exploring and learning about them.

IN MY FAMILY

Being Vegetarians is for Our Religion, Not Just about Food

As a Hindu family, we take our faith very seriously and our religion is a lifestyle, not just something that we do on weekends. Maintaining a strict vegetarian diet is a big part of religion and our lifestyle. When we had our children, it was never a question that we would extend these important practices and choices to their lives. We never really had a problem with it until we moved to a conservative, more rural area for my work.

I enrolled our young children in a child care program located where I worked, and I was excited that my girls would be close to me during the day. When I noticed on the center's website that their food service program included meat nearly every day, I told their teachers that we were vegetarians and asked if there was an alternate menu option. The teachers and director said they couldn't really manage that and to be sure to meet the girls' nutritional needs, that their menu was created and approved by a nutritionist. They did let me pack lunches for my girls and things seemed fine.

But a few months in, my younger daughter's teacher started leaving notes on her daily report saying she didn't know if my daughter was getting enough nutrition.

She reminded me that a nutritionist had made the center menu and that she worried that I wasn't giving my daughter enough protein. I ignored it a few times, but then I decided to talk to her about it in person. When I told her that vegetarianism is an important part of our religion and that we include plenty of non-meat protein in our diets, she actually said to me "I can't believe you would jeopardize your children's health for *some crazy religion.*" I was so stunned I didn't even know how to respond for a moment.

I finally took a breath and told her that Hinduism isn't a "crazy religion," [and] about our faith and its origins, and about the reason for vegetarianism. I also told her plenty about the health benefits and all the ways my children were getting enough complete nutrition. I had a lot to say, both on our religion and the science of vegetarian nutrition, and I am glad that her teacher was quiet and listened. She didn't look too pleased with me, but she said "I see. I'm sorry about what I said. I won't bring it up again." I remember feeling personally attacked but also being so irritated at such ignorance. People call it religious illiteracy, and it should really be viewed as a deficit, not the norm.

Family Partnerships

The first rule of early childhood practice—know your children—is especially important when considering a family's religious background. Some religions have very strict rules about food preparation and foods that are unacceptable to eat, rules governing modesty and contact between genders, and rules about holy day practices. When professionals do not take the time to learn about families' religious beliefs and practices, we run the risk of violating religious rules in the course of what might seem like normal program expectations. For families who practice strict religious observances, these violations are serious insults, though we certainly might not have intended such. This kind of insult is made more common by our general lack of knowledge about different religions and by professionals' hesitance to engage in conversations about religious topics with families and children. We do not need to feel insecure or that religion is "taboo" in our work with children and families. With 85% of the U.S. population reporting some form of religious affiliation, we actually cannot afford to dismiss the important role that religion (or nonreligion, for that matter) plays in family life. So what are appropriate strategies for learning about and involving family faiths and religious beliefs in our work? Begin with this **video** which emphasizes the importance of being sensitive to working with diverse families.

First and foremost, maintain a perspective of neutral information-gathering. Your role is neither to validate nor repudiate family beliefs, but rather to seek more information to better understand each individual child within the context of his or her family. You might have strongly held beliefs of your own, which contribute to the richness of your life and positively impact your work. However, as a professional, your role is not to interject your own religious beliefs, even if doing so is to connect with other adherents of your religion. Yes, your religion may be a valued part of who you are. But if your professional setting is not overtly faith-based, then your religious beliefs should remain in the background to your profession.

- Consider creating a short questionnaire or interview for families to ask about meaningful practices, rituals, and celebrations that are likely to either be a part of the child's day at school or program or are likely to be things that he or she will talk about.
- Review answers. For practices that are not familiar, seek more background knowledge from reliable sources (the Internet, community, books). Clarify your understanding with follow up conversations with family members.
- Make notes or charts about important restrictions or practices that require adjustments in the program or school day. This might only occur on holy days, but some restrictions or practices might be daily activities.
- Discuss with program or school administration how to handle absences or waivers for certain activities due to religious reasons. Consider the consequences of policy decisions, and be sure to share policies with families ahead of time.

The vast majority of families are eager and willing to share more information about their religious life and practices when they feel a genuine interest and appreciation. Make clear efforts to welcome families to share this part of their lives, honoring the importance it has in children's lives and the interrelated nature of program or school and home.

Summary

WHY STUDY RELIGIOUS DIVERSITY?

- Religion can be considered an organized framework and system for understanding concepts and interrelationships of divinity and humanity.
- *Faith* is a person's deeply held set of beliefs about humanity, life, and death and may or may not be framed within a religious structure.
- *Spirituality* is a life perspective for many people and is often closely tied to self-identity and one's role within humanity.
- Like faith, spirituality may or may not be entwined with religious affiliation.

CONTEXT OF RELIGIOUS DIVERSITY IN THE UNITED STATES

- The religious demographics of the United States continue to change and diversify, particularly over the past 50 years.
- The majority of U.S. religious adherents are some form of Christian, though the number of nonreligious and non-Christian adherents continues to grow rapidly.

MAJOR RELIGIONS OF THE UNITED STATES

	Summary of Beliefs	Primary Text	Primary Holidays	Common Practices
Christianity	• Monotheistic belief that there is one God, attended by messenger angels • Jesus was the son of God, sent to spread his word • Through belief in Jesus and living by the model of Jesus and religious law set forth in the Bible, one can achieve salvation after death	• Old and New Testaments	• Easter in March or April • Christmas on December 25	• Worship at home and more formally in churches • Includes important rites of passage performed by clergy, including baptism, communion, marriage • Frequent rituals also performed by clergy include confession and Eucharist • Prayer and charity are cornerstones of Christian life

(Continued)

	Summary of Beliefs	Primary Text	Primary Holidays	Common Practices
Judaism	• Monotheistic belief in one God, with prophets bringing God's word to the people • God sent Abraham to the promised land of Israel • God sent the Ten Commandments to Moses as the laws for living by God's word	• The Hebrew Bible • The Torah is of particular importance	• Passover in spring • Rosh Hashanah in autumn • Yom Kippur in autumn • Chanukah in winter	• Worship at synagogue and home • Important rites of passage at birth and when becoming an adult • Food preparation is extremely important (kosher) • Pork products are forbidden • Meat and dairy are kept separate
Islam	• Monotheistic religion recognizing Allah as the one true God • The Five Pillars of Islam guide daily life and are the primary structure of worship	• The Qur'an	• Ramadan • Eid al-Fitr occurs at end of Ramadan	• Living by Sunna, or the perfect example of living by God's plan • Ritual prayer five times per day • No pork products consumed; meat products must be processed according to religious law • Worship at home and at mosque
Buddhism	• Enlightenment is possible for all people through appropriate living and meditation • Reincarnation: the soul undergoes many births and deaths and exists across many lifetimes • Moral law of karma: there is a cause and effect of all of one's actions, and positive or negative life circumstances relate to reincarnation • The Four Noble Truths acknowledge the suffering of humankind and the path to end the suffering • The Eightfold Path is the way to end suffering and reach nirvana • Path to nirvana might take many lifetimes to achieve or might be attainable within current lifetime	• Oral tradition	• Vesak in May • Festivals and celebrations vary by culture and country	• Buddhists worship at home and at temples • Individual meditation is an important part of Buddhist life • Offerings at in-home or community shrines
Hinduism	• Polytheistic; many gods and goddess • Reincarnation • Karma • Ultimate goal is release from mortal life	• Collection of Vedas	• Holi in March • Diwali in October–November • Dussehra in September–October	• Worship, most often at home, includes prayers, chants, and offerings to the deity (sweets, money, fruit) • Shrines in homes may be simple or elaborate, with photos, statues, incense, and an altar

CURRICULAR CONNECTIONS

- From legal and instructional perspectives, religion has a place in classrooms, especially recognizing that religion can be an important part of family life.
- The key considerations are to ensure that discussions or study of religions maintains an academic and informational approach and does not promote or denigrate any particular religion or lack of religion (atheism).
- If religious-based activities or displays are included in the program or school day, professionals should ensure that a variety of religious are equally included.
- Carefully chosen specific materials such as children's books, dolls, and artifacts can be helpful tools to explore family beliefs and practices.

- Knowledge about family religious practices that impact children's program or school day is essential to be able to support those practices.
- Sensitive responses should be prepared to answer children's questions about religion and religious diversity with appropriate information and resources.

FAMILY PARTNERSHIPS

- Studying different religious or nonreligious beliefs is a part of learning about self and family.
- Sensitively and appreciatively ask families about their beliefs and religion; knowing as much as possible about the family context is the most important part of our work.

Chapter Learning Outcomes: Self-Assessment

Use this space to reflect on how well you have achieved the learning goals for this chapter by evaluating your own competency in the topics below. List three to five items that describe key concepts you have learned from the chapter.

Explain the purpose of exploring religious diversity.	
Discuss the context of religions and spirituality within families, schools, and across the United States.	
Describe important ideals and values of the five most popular religions in the United States.	
Practice teaching strategies to explore and appreciate religious diversity.	
Create connections with families from different religious backgrounds.	

Chapter Activities

DISCUSSION QUESTIONS

1. Think about the conflicts that arise from religious differences. If we seek to recognize and validate differing views, how do we reconcile validating major theological and philosophical differences while also promoting connection? Can you identify necessary "rules" for how we can disagree passionately and still get along?

2. Identify five barriers to including discussion or study of religion in programs or schools that are commonly cited. Next, identify at least two solutions to reduce the barriers.

Barriers to including religion in programs and schools, and solutions.	
	• •
	• •
	• •
	• •
	• •

SELF-REFLECTION

What positive and negative experiences do you personally have with individuals whose religious beliefs are different from yours? Describe friends whose religious beliefs differ. How many different religions have you had personal contact with through friends or acquaintances? What qualities did you like about these people?

TEACHING DISPOSITION

Reflecting back on the people you have crossed paths with who have had different religious beliefs than you, make a list of "personal stories of pluralism" in which you briefly describe at least five specific moments or memories of these people. Think about ways you can use these personal stories to help children see personal connections with people who are different. The purpose of this activity is to reinforce your own experiences with diversity and identify a personal connection to people with diverse religious beliefs. Recognize that your personal experiences can positively shape and impact your teaching.

IN THE FIELD

This activity prompts you to consider the typical academic calendar and overlay a lens of religious diversity to explore potential bias in favor of Christianity, even among non-faith-based programs. First, go online and print out or mark a calendar with your local school district's academic calendar (start and end dates) and school closings. Next, overlay the three most important holidays in all five of the most popular religions in the United States, using online sources if necessary. Finally, note how many holy days also coincide with school closings for each religion.

- Were there specific religions which had many holy days out of school and others with holy days in which school was in session?
- What impact could this have on the instructional progress of children whose holy days are school days? (Will they miss school? How would this be handled?)
- What inadvertent or overt messages might this send about preference?
- What messages does this convey to families about family religious practices?
- What ethical considerations are there if scheduling indicates a religious bias?

Weblinks

The Pluralism Project: "In 1991, the Pluralism Project at Harvard University began a pioneering study of America's changing religious landscape. Through an expanding network of affiliates, we document the contours of our multi-religious society, explore new forms of interfaith engagement, study the impact of religious diversity in civic life, and contextualize these findings within a global framework." *www.pluralism.org*

Religious Tolerance: Background information on world religions, definitions of terms related to religious pluralism, and books and resources for explorations of religions. *www.religioustolerance.org*

Facts on World Religions: Providing basic information on 40 religions practiced around the world. *www.religionfacts.com*

8   Families

In early childhood education the most important resource in our children's lives, and thus in our work, is families. Families are widely validated as children's first teachers, as a source of support and socialization, and as partners in children's education. In general we are quick to appreciate the essential role families play in children's development, but at times, teachers are also prone to negative views of family lifestyles and structures that are not a part of a now-outdated picture of two-parent family units. Membership in the family is very deeply connected to children's sense of themselves and their roots. Families have a tremendous potential for positive impact on children, and it is essential that early childhood professionals develop sensitivity to and appreciation for the variety and complexities of modern family structures. This chapter explores the diversity in family structures and membership in the United States today and prompts you to examine unique considerations when working with children from all types of family structures.

Defining *Family* in Modern Terms

A few decades ago defining *family* was approached as a simpler process and included a narrow view of a married mother, father, and biological children living in the same household (married, cohabitating). This was termed the **nuclear family**. And while some families that did not fit this standard picture, at that time the great majority of U.S. families were composed of this membership, and there was a clear privilege afforded to this configuration. Today, however, defining *family* recognizes the more complex and changing nature of how we live, considers individual variations in experience, and may take into account legal, emotional, financial, religious, political, functional, and structural aspects of what it means to be a family.

LEARNING
OUTCOMES
· · · · · · · · · · · · · · · · · · · ·

- Describe the complexities in definitions of family

- Explain demographic contexts and trends in family structures

- Compare characteristics of diverse family structures

- Practice strategies for promoting appreciation of diverse families with children

- Create partnerships with diverse families

The nuclear family was once the only accepted or typical family structure; however today's families come in all sizes and configurations and form through a variety of life events.

First, to get a sense of the challenge, take a few minutes to write a short definition of what makes a "family." Think critically about this, trying to be comprehensive and to encompass the elements that you feel are essential parts of "family" (for example, is the presence of a child necessary, or are childless couples family?).

My definition of *family*:

Think about the impact of defining family as well. Think about the implications of the definition of family as it could be used for access to and exclusion from services in the following contexts:

- Legal services (for example, in family law/custody, immigration, school access, taxation, and so on)
- Social services
- School services and communications
- Employee health benefits
- Financial support programs
- Acceptance in religious organizations
- Social status and acceptance
- Emotional support, caretaking, feelings of connectedness
- Genetic history, heritage roots

Perhaps at first, generating your definition of family seems like a straightforward task. Most of us draw on our own family background and experiences as a natural bias or starting point. But as you begin to consider the many different settings and purposes in which a definition of family would be used—and the implications of it—the task becomes much more complicated and debatable. When given this task, some of my students begin with a more legal approach, including terms of marriage or biology. Others chime in with an emotional component in an attempt to be more inclusive, with a comment like "a family is a group of people who love each other." Invariably not everyone agrees with this. And then the group spends a great deal of time trying to wrestle with defined structures and relationships and the variations and exceptions to try to create a broadly inclusive but clearly defined frame. It is not an easy task, and while we usually end up with a working definition which necessarily includes some compromises, a companion purpose of the activity is to realize that there is as much variation as there is similarity among U.S. families. Simply stated: defining families today is complicated. In personal and professional settings alike, individuals and scholars find significant problems with attempting a bounded definition. A seemingly small but significant shift in thinking about *defining the* family is to consider who families are—a shift in language that acknowledges variety and plurality (Powell, Bolzendahl, Geist, & Steelman, 2010).

DIFFERENT PERSPECTIVES ON DEFINITIONS OF FAMILY

College students aren't the only ones who find the task of defining family tricky, and even young children recognize that there are emotional and structural aspects to consider. When young children from a variety of family structures were asked to describe what family means to them, younger children tended to consider marriage and frequency of contact, along with having children, as key criteria for being a family. Older children tended to focus on the quality of the relationships and affective factors among adults and children as important criteria (Rigg & Pryor, 2007). This change reflects children's developmental differences, with young children naturally forming more concrete and less elaborate concepts than older children. However, researchers noted that emotional connections were present to some degree in definitions of family for young and older children alike.

Definitions also may shift based on whose perspective is used as the starting point. For example, the definition family from a child's perspective tends to focus on functional and operational qualities, while adults looking at families (intimate relationship and/or having children or not) may focus more on affective relationships and feelings of connectedness (Powell, Bolzendahl, Geist, & Steelman, 2010). Much of the research on families includes a shared residence component: "A family consists of two or more people who live together and are related by such enduring factors as birth, marriage, adoption, or long-term mutual commitment" (McDevitt & Ormrod, 2010, p. 64). While this definition is more inclusive than others, adding the cohabitating criteria can serve to exclude nonresident family members (such as a parent who lives in a different house after a separation) and it does not acknowledge nonparent extended family.

Extended family generally means relatives other than parents and siblings and can include grandparents, aunts and uncles, cousins, and more. Often these extended family members have a strong role in children's daily lives, though as immigration and family mobility has changed over the past many decades, more families are living at a distance from extended family. Think about how the Frisellas describe their family and support of extended family in this **video**.

With so much variation and individuality among families, and given the challenge in formulating a clear identity of families, we might wonder why we bother trying to define it. The reality is that who makes up a family does indeed matter both in general public opinion as well as in official forums. This is especially true when we consider that legal systems tend to adopt or modify practices in response to shifts in public opinion. "At the private level, these definitions affect who is and who is not considered a family in day-to-day interaction. At the broader, more public

IN MY FAMILY

My Atypical Family was Just My Normal

Growing up since as long back as I can remember it was just my mom and me. I didn't ever remember thinking that we were unusual or "disadvantaged"; that was just how our family was. It wasn't until later on in college classes that I read about how badly I supposedly had it for being raised by a single mom. I don't remember finances being so hard or my mom being depressed. She worked and I went to an after school program till she got home at 6 and we lived simply, now that I look back, but we always had enough and I always knew she was there for me. In the evenings she did homework with me or we played games and talked. We lived in a close neighborhood and it seemed like families around there were friends together, not just the kids. I never saw my grandparents, and my uncle lived pretty far away, but I also don't remember feeling isolated or alone somehow. My mom had a group of close friends who we spent a lot of time with and I think they acted like a kind of extended family for us. I know them now as mostly gay and lesbian couples, but until about the middle of high school I didn't notice any of that.

I always felt normal somehow, though of course now I realize that my mom was gay. My family may have been "atypical" according to those books I read, but my atypical family was just my normal. She never actually talked about her own sexual orientation with me, but she definitely raised me to think broadly and accept each person's decisions. Sometimes I wonder about what it meant to her to have to hide that part of herself. I think maybe she did that to make me feel as normal as possible growing up. I guess it worked though, right? She died when I was in college, so I didn't really get to know her adult-to-adult. But if we had the chance, I hope that we would have been able to talk about all parts of ourselves and our lives. She was the most supportive, loving, dedicated mom and no part of her being lesbian would have made her less of a mom to me. If anything, that close (gay) community was a big family support for both of us.

level, they have consequences for who is and who is not treated as a family in the legal systems, with all the rights and obligations that are legitimated by these definitions" (Powell, Bolzendahl, Geist, & Steelman, 2010, p. 34). At the very least, in generating your own conception of families, and when you engage children in exploring their ideas and definitions, it is important to carefully and deliberately emphasize that there are many kinds of families and that individual variation, both in concept and lived experience, is equally valued (Nieto & Bode, 2012).

One overarching concept that permeates literature and experience is the changing nature of families on an individual family basis as well as across society. Families change in membership and dynamics as members mature, but they also might change through member transitions or life circumstances (births, death, divorce, new relationships, incarceration, moving, etc.). Likewise, the types of families have changed over decades. The next section provides a snapshot of current family structure demographics in the United States as well as descriptions of seven different types of family structures.

Family Structures in the United States

So, we might still be wrestling with how to define or even conceptualize *family*. For the purposes of this text, we will use the perspective of the child and explore family structures related to children's lives. A key component is to become aware of the most commonly framed family structures, beginning with a snapshot of the percentages of children living within these kinds of families. Some are not mutually exclusive; for example a single parent household might also be an adoptive family, or a two parent household might also have gay or lesbian parents. The following descriptions are not meant to exclusively define families or categorize children you work with, but rather are to provide a broader background for understanding dynamic and diverse characteristics of today's modern families. Of vital importance as you explore different family structures is to bear in mind that some research demonstrates that there are slight but not major differences for children's outcomes or achievement based solely on family structure (Gennetian, 2005), though others point to evidence of more negative outcomes after a family transition. For example, while there might be evidence of higher rates of emotional or academic difficulty for children in blended families (Strohschein, Roos, & Brownell, 2009), critical examination of data reveals that some of these difficulties were apparent prior to marital dissolution. And while most researchers acknowledge evidence that stressful family transitions can pose challenges, there are also many factors involved in family transitions, in addition to a divorce or a change in relationship with one parent, that impact children's development (Cherlin, 2010).

Increasing numbers of children are growing up in blended families than can include stepfamily members and half-siblings; this blending might involve sharing time between family households.

In particular, a key consideration is the challenge posed when family transition is coupled with decrease in available resources (such as financial or time resources), as can be the case when parents divorce. Sometimes decrease in resources may be a precipitating factor for the relationship dissolution, though. Ultimately, determining what factors cause another, such as whether divorce causes poorer outcomes in children, is extremely difficult if not impossible (Cowan, 2010). Our task, then, is to be careful to take a critical stance when interpreting the impacts on development from family structure, and to keep in mind that when children are cared for by at least one consistent, nurturing, responsible adult with adequate resources, the potential exists for them to grow and develop successfully in any family setting (AAP, 2003; Sanson & Lewis, 2001). So just where are children in the United States growing up?

DATA ON CHILDREN'S FAMILY CONTEXTS

From early U.S. census reports in the late 1800s, up until the 1970s, we know that between 83 and 87% of children in the United States lived with two parents. From the 1970s through 2009, that number steadily declined, and currently 69% of children live with two parents. During this same time period the percentage of children living with a single mother steadily increased from 9 to 25% (Kreider & Ellis, 2011). Keep in mind that census surveys are self-reports, and there are also changes in people's willingness to accurately report family status. Again we are urged to remain critical consumers of published information and to not leap to assumptions. In addition to these statistics, which point to changes and increases in nonnuclear families, divorce rates have actually dropped over the past

30 years and divorced parents are both maintaining stronger contact with children (Coontz, 2010). Additional results from the 2011 census survey of family life in the United States reflect more variations in the household composition of homes where children reside (under 18):

- 69% of all children live with two parents
  - 87% with both biological parents
  - 11% with one biological parent and one step or adoptive parent
- 27% of all children live with one parent
  - 86% with the mother
- 16% of all children live in blended families
- 4% of all children live with no parent
  - 59% live with a caregiving grandparent
  - 8% live with a foster family

Despite the growing numbers of families that represent structures other than a nuclear family model, the nuclear family persists in society's perception as "normal," with a privileged status. Nonbiological caregiving adults such as grandparents or stepparents are often marginalized, with terms like "real father" or "real mother" used to refer to biological parents only. Likewise, the negative, stereotypical image of the uninvolved, overbearing stepfather or the cruel, neglectful, jealous, or abusive stepmother has endured for generations through children's literature and in movies and television. Legal rights and responsibilities generally only extend to biological parents, regardless of history of parenting responsibility. Even in school and medical care systems, stepparents are often not recognized as an authority figure or a responsible party, regardless of living or marital status with the biological parent (Jones, 2003). Language, systems, laws, and policies that narrowly define family membership and responsibility perpetuate a perceived second-rate status of blended families and can undermine the important role that members of blended families play in children's lives.

Descriptions of Family Structures

A wider array of family structures is described below, along with unique dynamics acting as protective or challenging factors that impact children's outcomes. The purpose of exploring these different family structures is not to convey preference but rather to better understand the differences in children's experiences of family life. Again, it is necessary to emphasize that warm, nurturing parenting with reasonable, consistent, and appropriate discipline (an "authoritative style") is related to positive child outcomes in any family structure.

TWO PARENT HOUSEHOLD

Children living in a two parent household continue to represent the majority of family structures, although by a diminishing majority. Two parent households also vary and can represent both biological parents in a marital or unmarried cohabiting relationship, but can also include stepparents, foster parents, or adoptive parents. The *married parents with biological children* (the nuclear family) structure has been the most widely accepted family structure and for much of our history has been considered the only legitimate definition of family in legal as well as sociopolitical arenas. In recent decades public acceptance and legal definitions have broadened, but there remains a pervasive belief in the value of the nuclear family model. In measures of developmental outcomes, children do fare better when the family unit is characterized by quality parenting processes, relationship stability, and adequate resources. Two-parent biological families tend to provide these key characteristics more often than other family structures (AAP, 2003; Sanson & Lewis, 2001). When children are raised by both biological parents throughout childhood, and when family interactions are characterized by mutual commitment, shared parenting, respectful problem solving, and warmth, children benefit from socialization to these models of successful interactions. In essence, children learn what they live, and the message in such families is about how to supportively engage together over the long term. And while some research indicates that these qualities are more likely to be present in the nuclear family structure, increasingly other family structures continue to demonstrate potential for such healthy socialization as well.

As prevalence of cohabitation with children increases, either among both biological parents or among one biological parent and a partner, and in light of ethnic and cultural differences in parental expectations, it becomes increasingly important to understand the nature of cohabiting families. Researchers suggest that between 40 and 55% of children in the United States will experience living household with cohabiting parents or in parent-partner households over the span of their childhood (Artis, 2007). Researchers also point to some cultural differences in rates of cohabitation. Among Hispanic Americans, for example, cohabitation of parents is a more accepted and widespread experience than in White non-Hispanic or Asian families and does not diminish either parent's commitment to the family and parenting responsibilities (Manning, 2006). Families in which cohabiting parents (biological or other) tend to view each other as equally responsible for children's well-being demonstrate the importance of policies and public perspectives that validate the role of both parents, married or not, in children's lives.

In addition, the increase in the number of cohabiting couples with children is often cited as a breakdown in family values and regarded as undesirable. Both perspectives serve to perpetuate the power and privileged status of the nuclear family model, and detract from the realities of children's actual family experiences. In around half of the families of children born to unmarried parents, the couple was cohabiting, and roughly half of these cohabitating couples remain in a long-term cohabitating family structure (roughly the same percentage as of original marriages which remain intact). The vast majority of cohabitating couples with children report plans to marry but cite current financial instability as a barrier (England & Edin, 2010). In other words, the values of commitment to partner and children are strong among unmarried cohabitating parents; however so are the stressors associated with lower socioeconomic status and lower income. Research comparing outcomes of children with married versus unmarried cohabitating parents, or in stepparent households, is inconsistent. Some studies indicate similar developmental outcomes for children across family type, although the presence of economic hardship and maternal emotional problems are correlated with more negative outcomes (Artis, 2007; Lansford, Ceballo, Abbey, & Stewart, 2001; Ram & Hou, 2003).

BLENDED FAMILY

The term *blended family* refers to adults and children who have become a family through cohabitation, close relationship, or remarriage (sometimes referred to as a *reconstituted family*). "The presence of a stepparent, stepsibling, or half sibling designates a family as blended" (Kreider & Ellis, 2011, p. 1). Blended or step families are the fastest growing form of family structure in the United States (Greeff & Du Toit, 2009). The blend generally involves a biological parent who forms a relationship with a new partner who then becomes an involved, responsible party to the parent's child(ren). The majority of blended families comprise children and a biological mother newly coupled or remarried to a stepfather (Kreider & Ellis, 2011). The stepfather's children might or might not reside with the new family, though with the formation of the new family, both partners become stepparents to each other's children. When existing children are joined together in a new relationship, they become *stepsisters* or *stepbrothers*. Blended families also include children from the new couple; these children are *half-siblings*: one of the new child's biological parents is shared with the original children and the other parent is a stepparent.

Roughly 30% of all children are likely to spend some part of their childhood in a blended family structure (AAP, 2003). While blended family transitions can improve experiences for children by providing additional parenting time and financial resources, "in general, children who are raised in a stepfamily do about as well as do children of single mothers" (AAP, 2003, p. 1551), with some potential experience of stress due to family transition. Since most blended families are formed after a period of single parenting, of which the large majority are single mother families, research attention has focused on the role of stepfathers in the blended family structure. While stepfathers tend to be less emotionally involved and spend less time with stepchildren (compared to a co-residing biological father), taking on the father figure role and investing significant quality time has a positive impact on children's outcomes (Parent, Saint-Jacques, Beaudry, & Robitaille, 2007).

Sources of strength and resilience that are identified by blended families include (Greeff & Du Toit, 2009):

- Quality of relationships and time spent together as a family
- Open and caring communications
- Social support and extended family
- Positive outlook

Professionals working with children in blended families can support healthy family functioning by recognizing the important roles stepparents and stepsiblings have in children's lives. Consider encouraging active participation in program and school activities, and asking the family about which members should be included on information sheets and notices from the program or school. These are ways to validate all family members (not just a narrow definition of *mother* or *father*).

SINGLE PARENT HOUSEHOLDS AND TWO HOUSEHOLDS

Many single parent households are created when couples with children divorce or separate. Some are created when unmarried or non-cohabitating couples have a child but do not choose to reside together. And some are created when single people have children and choose to raise them on their own. In general, the tasks of parenting alone, plus shouldering all financial responsibilities for maintaining a household, present a significant workload for a single parent. Having access to an available network of resources to support single parent families is a key determinant of positive child and family outcomes. Networks include quality child care, social support, family-friendly employer policies, safe housing, adequate financial resources, and more.

Being raised in a single parent household (single father or mother) is commonly cited as a potential detriment to children's development, primarily due to an increase in parent stress or depression and reduced economic resources and employment (AAP, 2003; Leininger & Ziol-Guest, 2008; Ricciuti, 2004). However, there is wide variety in the income and social resources among single parent families, and a growing body of research reveals that children in single parent families, even for long periods of childhood and adolescence, develop typically on academic and behavioral measures when the following parenting factors are present (Ricciuti, 2008):

- Maternal competence and positive parenting skills
- Maternal education level
- Strong positive expectations for children's development
- Emphasis on the value of schooling

Extensive evidence exists showing that all families, but especially more vulnerable families, fare better when social and economic resources are adequate and available. Thus it is essential that professionals be aware of and link families into community networks and resources to support single parents in developing the above factors.

GAY AND LESBIAN PARENTS

Gay and lesbian couples and individuals may enter into parenthood via a number of avenues, including through a heterosexual relationship (subsequently "coming out"), a surrogate agreement, in-vitro fertilization, artificial insemination using a known donor or an anonymous donor bank, adoption, or foster care placement. No other category of family structure has impacted both the legality of parenthood and society's psyche about parenthood in the ways that same-sex parenthood has. While assisted conception has certainly been used by heterosexual couples, married couples, and single women, conception among same-sex parents is the most obvious contradiction to "traditionalist" ideas about conception being strictly a biological process between a man and a woman. "Instead, [assisted fertility] opens up the jarring prospect that procreation, as a social, as opposed to biological, phenomenon can be separated from the different-sex couple" (Struening, 2010, p. 84). The idea of people becoming parents without conceiving, gestating, giving birth, or necessarily adopting has confounded family law courts when they are faced with custody battles over children born through surrogate or assisted conception. While some rulings maintain a firm line between genetic material and offspring, others have expanded the borders of "family" to consider:

- Intent to bring the child into the world
- Daily caregiving actions
- Meaningful relationships from children's perspective
- Support for meeting children's needs
- The seminal "best interest of the child" standard

What these cases demonstrate is the potential for legal systems to respond to social trends, changes in technology, and the way in which humans interact together. While notoriously slow to respond, the courts are increasingly finding and creating precedents for a broader definition of families—a promising trend, and one that validates the strength of same-sex couples and parents.

Perhaps due to the intensity of scrutiny and conflict among social, religious, and political groups concerning gay and lesbian parenthood, the research on outcomes of children raised by gay and lesbian parents is expanding greatly. Numerous studies have emerged addressing concerns about children's attachment, academic achievement, experiences within the family, and the children's own sexual identity development. Summaries of numerous studies across diverse samples have provided clear and compelling evidence that gay and lesbian parents can provide as nurturing and

While today's families come together through a variety of paths, research shows that children benefit from loving, supportive relationships in any family structure.

healthy an upbringing as heterosexual parents can, including the following findings (APA, 2005; Gartrell & Bos, 2010; McCann & Delmonte, 2005; Patterson, 2006):

- Gay and lesbian parents are as deeply committed to parenting and family well-being as heterosexual couples and many spend more time involved with their child(ren)'s home and school life.
- Children of gay and lesbian parents exhibit secure attachment with both parents.
- Gay and lesbian parents tend to equally divide household and child care tasks.
- Gay and lesbian parents tend to make more conscious efforts to provide their child(ren) with interactions with adults of the opposite sex through family and friendship networks (as a counterpart experience to same-sex parents).
- Children of gay and lesbian parents develop typically in all areas of development, including gender identity and behavior and academic competence.

The American Academy of Pediatrics likewise summarized numerous studies in creating a technical report and policy statement in support of gay and lesbian parents, with the following: "The weight of evidence gathered during several decades using diverse samples and methodologies is persuasive in demonstrating that there is no systematic difference between gay and nongay parents in emotional health, parenting skills, and attitudes toward parenting. No data have pointed to any risk to children as a result of growing up in a family with 1 or more gay parent" (Perrin, 2002, p. 343). Responding to the increases in family diversity, to the significant evidence for the healthy development of children raised by gay and lesbian-parents, and to evolutions in public acceptance of many kinds of families, numerous health, medical, and social service agencies have publicized policy statements over the past decade in support of gay, lesbian, and bisexual people becoming parents through surrogate, adoptive, or unassisted and assisted fertilization. Statements from the American Academy of Pediatrics, American Bar Association, American Psychological Association, and the Child Welfare League of America (to name just a few of the 14 organizations cited in a report by the National Center for Lesbian Rights) affirm the legitimacy and ability of gays and lesbians to meet the important "best interest of the child" standard (NCLR, 2006).

While children of gay or lesbian parents report having experienced anti-gay sentiment or homophobic bullying that was very upsetting, these encounters do not negatively impact children's overall development more than bullying or isolation of children of heterosexual parents. However, the overall negative psychological and social impact on children of bullying related to any number of issues remains a major cause for concern among professionals. Research reports from interviews of children reveal that school staff routinely ignore or in other subtle ways promote teasing and bullying (including physical abuse), and that educators can be less prepared to appropriately handle homophobic teasing than other forms of teasing, perhaps due to the pervasive view that heterosexuality is normal and homosexuality is abnormal (Fairtlough, 2008; Ray & Gregory, 2001). Adequate training, administrative policy and support, and personal preparation can help professionals develop effective strategies to manage negative sentiment and ensure physical and psychological safety for all children and families.

ADOPTIVE FAMILY

Children entering adoptive families often come from adverse backgrounds and have experienced significant family transition or trauma. Children placed for adoption may have been orphaned, abandoned (often due to extreme family poverty), or removed from their biological families for reasons of abuse or neglect. Not surprisingly, many of these children suffer from developmental delays, particularly in physical and psychological health. Behavioral challenges have been cited as a long-term issue for many adoptive families (Houston & Kramer, 2008), though within several years post-adoption, most children's developmental delays have seen significant improvement and development is within normal range (Palacios, Roman, & Camacho, 2010). Listen to the story of Heather's family in this **video** as her mother talks about Heather's adoption and developmental progress.

Increasing numbers of foster children are being adopted into the foster family especially due to changes in federal legislation that, prior to the mid-1990s, historically discouraged foster family adoption (Houston & Kramer, 2008). Recognizing the goal of expedient permanent placement for at-risk and foster children was a key driving force for the passage of adoption legislation in the 1990s. In addition, the growing popularity of international and intercultural adoption adds a unique layer of complexity to the adopted child's transition in terms of change from original family and change from home country and culture. International adoption is appealing to many families for a variety of reasons including the desire to provide stability and a loving family to a child from an impoverished, institutionalized, or high-risk life, and because of somewhat easier procedures (Hollingsworth, 2003). More internationally adopted children tend to come from orphanage institutions, a situation that can increase the likelihood of internalizing and externalizing behavior problems (Palacios, Roman, & Camacho, 2010).

Many adoptive families, whether they are same-race or interracial or intercultural, report facing uncomfortably invasive questions and comments from strangers and family members. Adoptive children report wondering about their history and the complexities of adoptive family life, about bonding, and what forming a family through this way means to them. When outsiders, peers, family friends, or family members ask probing questions or make hurtful comments, the wounding and resulting insecurity can deeply hurt children and parents (Singer, 2010). As Janice's story illustrates:

> When we finally decided to adopt Kalee, it was after years of trying to conceive. We experienced a lot of grief and pain during those years, but as soon as Kalee came into our lives we really felt whole in our hearts again. She is absolutely the missing piece of us and together we couldn't be more of a real family than if she had come into our lives through any other way. Even now that Kalee is 8 and we've been together for 7 years, I still feel crushed inside when people feel the need to point out that she is adopted and imply, through various infuriating and hurtful comments, that we are less of a family because of it. So what if she looks a little different than us?! My mother had blonde curly hair and I have dark hair and that doesn't make us less of a family. Kalee spent a year growing without us, but she will absolutely be my real daughter for the rest of her life. It does help me to have a scripted response that I say every time, so I can feel like I make my point but still dismiss the comment. I guess people's insensitivity will always hurt inside. I just wish I could shield Kalee from feeling this.

Some comments are not intentionally hurtful and some comments *are* teasing and bullying. Questioning children about why they look different from their parents, about their "real mother," about why they were given away, whether they were sold, or how they like being adopted is common. Some children report being teased outright about being unloved, unwanted, and not part of a "real family." Such comments reveal persistent, deeply ingrained discrimination against family structures that do not match the biological nuclear family model. Supporting children and families in preparing for such questions or comments with planned responses, even if they choose not to share any personal information (ignoring the comment or saying "that's private") can be useful in redirecting inappropriate comments, reducing bias, empowering children to maintain their privacy, and preserving children's sense of identity within their family.

There is compelling evidence that ongoing support and services aids families and adopted children in adjusting, forming into a strong family unit, and remediating any developmental delays (Houston & Kramer, 2008; McDonald, Propp, & Murphy, 2001). However, while child and family outcomes improve over time, in general, post-adoption services and agency follow-up are limited to 1½ to 3 years. Early childhood program and school professionals are in a unique position to provide information about social service contacts and social support networks for adoptive families throughout childhood.

GRANDPARENT CAREGIVERS

In 2010 nearly 3 million children lived with a grandparent who was responsible for the household and family, and for nearly 1 million children the parent was not present in the home (U.S. Census Bureau, 2010). Grandparents take on parenting responsibilities (also called *kinship* care) for a variety of reasons—when parents are incapable of providing adequate care, often due to substance abuse, mental illness, poverty, abandonment, or incarceration (Connor, 2006; Sands, Goldberg-Glen, & Shin, 2009). Sometimes these arrangements are made informally and grandparents have had ongoing contact and relationships with grandchildren, and sometimes arrangements are made in crisis points with little preparation. These cases involve similar dynamics as those faced by foster children and families (discussed below), as the large majority have faced significant negative family upheaval. The majority of children struggle with additional psychological, emotional, and developmental needs (Kelley, Yorker, Whitley, & Sipe, 2001). However, children removed from parents' care and placed with grandparents tend to exhibit fewer behavior problems than children placed in nonrelative foster care (Poehlmann, 2003).

Most grandparents who are in a parenting role for grandchildren express mainly positive and mixed feelings about the experience, citing both deep emotional connection to and enjoyment of grandchildren as well as increased stress, health problems, role ambiguity, and lack of energy to keep up with children (Dolbin-MacNab, 2006). Grandchildren tend to report positive perspectives on grandparent caregiving, especially in the wake of abandonment by parents, when the grandparent provides much needed consistency (Sands, Goldberg-Glen, & Shin, 2009). Grandchildren also tend to demonstrate healthy attachment and bonds with grandparent

Extended family members often take on parenting or guardianship roles informally or formally through adoption, sometimes in place of biological parents and sometimes as shared support.

caregivers and extended family, though they remain pained by parents' inability or unwillingness to care for them. Functionality of the grandparent-headed family is dependent on circumstances surrounding assumption of care, family economics and stability, length of kinship care, relationship with grandchildren's parents, and access to social and health care resources (Poehlmann, 2003). Peer support groups and assistance accessing needed services and resources have demonstrated significant positive improvements in grandparent caregiving and can strengthen child outcomes (Kelley, Yorker, Whitley, & Sipe, 2001).

Professionals working with children being raised by grandparents may need to carefully consider legal constraints when a biological parent maintains (or parents maintain) legal custody but the grandparent is the primary caregiver. Clearly developing strong reciprocal relationships with the main caregiver is important for supporting children's success in school. However, some parents who are not caring for their children (for a variety of reasons) still maintain legal rights to decision making, signing paperwork, and even record and information flow. Ideally all parties are able to work together, but if not, professionals need to be aware of legal requirements and limits. Grandparents raising their grandchildren might may be confident interacting with programs and schools, having had prior experience raising their own children. Others might be particularly anxious about their parenting abilities, how well they will be welcomed at school, and how active a role they should take. We can smooth the start of relationships by not assuming that grandparents are playing only an ancillary role, or by effectively dismissing their responsibility for children.

FOSTER FAMILY

Children living in foster homes are generally at risk for negative developmental outcomes due to the variety of stressors that have precipitated their coming into foster care arrangements. Removing children from their biological or legal parents is always precipitated by a family crisis that might involve serious abuse or neglect, parental incarceration or death, substance abuse, mental illness, or another serious threat to children's welfare (AACAP, 2005). Foster families are agency-approved family residences that may comprise nonrelatives, relatives, or families who intend to adopt (CWLA, n.d.). Foster care is generally defined as a temporary measure until stability can be regained, either through reuniting with biological parent(s) or through adoption.

Foster children are considered a high-needs group due to traumatic family background, and they are unique in that placement in a foster home is intended to be a temporary measure. While 16% of validated abuse cases result in removal of children from the home, in some communities 40% of young children (under the age of 4) in validated abuse cases are removed (Heller & Smyke, 2002). Chronic health conditions, as well as acute medical conditions, are common, as are developmental delays. Behavioral challenges stemming from family trauma and removal from the family are up to seven times more likely in foster children (Younes & Harp, 2007). In young children, eating, sleeping, and toileting behavioral problems are frequent and require skillful and sensitive caregiving responses at home and in child care programs. Often foster families are not provided with complete histories on children's background or health and medical needs, which can impede assessment and design of intervention plans for home and programs or school. For children placed in foster care (or relative care) due to a parent's incarceration, there are added burdens of social stigma associated with parents' criminality, the logistical difficulty of maintaining contact, and a higher incidence of shame and erosion of the parent–child relationship (Cunningham, 2001). These are areas where training and special preparation for family and professionals are warranted when engaging with foster children.

Ideally, foster families are carefully screened and trained and are provided with initial and ongoing support, though there is some discrepancy in whether these measures actually occur, despite the unique challenges of nurturing children in crisis. Aside from the needs of foster children, foster families face several challenges, including (Heller & Smyke, 2002; Younes & Harp, 2007):

- Complex caretaking needs of children in crisis (including medical and psychological health care)
- An ambiguous role, legally and functionally (responsible but not an ultimate authority)

CLASSROOM STORY CORNER

How Could She Be Asked to Do All This?

As an Infant Mental Health specialist located in a mid-sized urban area, I primarily work with young children under 4 who have been removed from custody of their parent and placed in an alternate family setting. Most of my cases are infants of single mothers who are in treatment programs, incarcerated, or have been charged with abuse/neglect. Many of my family placements are with extended family members, though I worry about the stability of families sometimes in these situations. The behavior of the mother can stem from her own inadequate childhood experiences, so looking to grandparents to foster (usually grandmothers) can sometimes pose a challenge. But our agency prefers kinship placements because they tend to be easier to process and last longer than foster care. I don't like sounding biased when I raise concerns, but my perspective is to be aware of risks and protective factors.

Like for (let's call her) Lucia, for example. Lucia was a young mother herself, and now her 23-year-old daughter, Brenda, was also a mother of 4 children and a newborn born with Fetal Alcohol Syndrome. Brenda has a couple of arrests for substance use and was recently arrested again. Lucia had already taken in Brenda's older three children at Brenda's first arrest. When she was released, Brenda moved in with a new boyfriend and had the two younger girls, leaving the older children with her mother. Now that she's incarcerated again, the infant and toddler have also gone with Lucia. Now in her early 40s Lucia struggles with the responsibility of all five children and trying to keep her job and harbors a good deal of resentment toward her daughter about it. Sometimes she tells me the kids are "rotten like their mother" but the children have not shared negative feelings during therapy, and she appears to be doing the best she can at home with them. The older children have stabilized for the most part and are faring well enough in school. The toddler is struggling with aggressive behaviors and a lot of emotional outbursts, both of which are more than Lucia feels she can handle with the newborn.

But there are a number of other extended family members who are so helpful with the children and are a major source of support. Fortunately we were able to enroll the two babies in an Early Head Start program which also provides supports for Lucia. The teachers working with the toddler and I are working closely with Lucia and our team to help understand her behaviors in the context of her experience and give them both strategies to cope with what they are going through. Sometimes I wonder how could one grandmother be asked to do all this? This isn't even a very extreme case for our region. I know we're low on trained foster families, especially for multiple siblings and special needs. But it really is easy to see how overwhelming some situations are for kinship or foster families. If we didn't have the IT (Interdisciplinary Team) and supports for and from all of the extended family members involved, I would worry much more about kids like these. Our team is so good at helping families identify resiliency sources in their lives. It comes from a philosophy based in strength and resilience values.

- Temporary nature of placement, which can result in reduced depth of attachment
- Lack of support from social service agencies needed to meet children's diverse needs
- Emotional toll of foster parenting, including accepting the rights of biological parent(s)
- Negative impact on biological children of foster parents, as much time and attention is needed to provide stability for foster children

Assisting foster families in working through the many challenges they face is an interdisciplinary task, and often there are inadequate resources to fully develop needed supports. While the need for foster families increases, the availability of qualified placement families is decreasing. This leads some researchers to worry that the system designed as a resource for children in crisis is, itself, in crisis (Heller & Smyke, 2002). The majority of foster families undertake the challenging task out of genuine desire to make a positive difference in the lives of vulnerable children. Most families report overall positive impact on their own lives as a result of fostering, though home life for biological children and parents inevitably alters dramatically (Younes & Harp, 2007). Professionals can have a positive impact on supporting foster family functioning by being aware of interdisciplinary resources and supporting foster family's access to them.

Curricular Connections

MATERIALS

Diversity among families has become a popular topic in children's literature, and there are many quality titles to choose from. Simple photograph books using family-portrait-style images can be used to spark children's thinking about many family configurations, as well as a possible design and creation of their own class or group family book. More complex stories of family transitions are available, and they can help spark dialogues and help children feel that they are not alone in facing transitions. Look for text that is simple, clear, concrete, and honest. Topics like divorce, incarceration, death, remarriage, and adoption are sensitive ones and sometimes can make us feel unsure of how to invite or respond to dialogue. Using literature is a way to segue into guided explorations, to familiarize a group with certain circumstances, or invite specific conversations. Recent articles provide checklists and annotated booklists to assist professionals in selecting and using quality, appropriate literature to enhance children's appreciation for diverse families and perspectives. These resources include those by Birkmayer, Cohen, Jensen, and Variano (2005), NAEYC (n.d.), and Morgan (2009) and web sources like *Little Parachutes: Picture Books to Help Children with Life's Challenges* (www.littleparachutes.com).

Invite families to share items, photos, and stories from their lives and any family history they might have access to. Items might be artifacts used in current family traditions or rituals, handmade items that mark family events, or mementos that remind children or family members of their home life. Photos and stories might document family historical highlights or might be images from current daily life together. Here, too, professionals need to be aware of children's basic family background information in order to decide what is appropriate to ask families to share and what limits will be important to set as a way to ensure all children are included in the process. For children who are adopted or estranged from biological parents, the lack of family history might be a source of stress, and professionals need to plan ahead for how to support these children.

ENVIRONMENT

Create areas in the program or school setting that allow children and families to create displays of photos and items from their lives. This might be a shelf, countertop, tabletop, or corner of a room or hallway. Consider a space that allows for supervision if artifacts are family property so that children can be guided to explore and appreciate the items but not to misuse or misplace them. Family displays can be themed or might simply comprise artifacts that are of significance to the family. It helps to have family members describe the artifact so that a brief explanation can be included as a tool to engender dialogue among the program or school community. Some display materials might be considered controversial, and staff should be clear about the purpose and potential of the displays, as Wayne's story illustrates:

> Our school decided that we needed to promote more feeling of connectedness among our families, so we decided to make a photo project of family portraits and stories that would be installed along our main hallway. We were all really excited about it and that our principal was able to get some grant funding for materials. We offered families a voucher to have a portrait taken at our local studio or have a large print made of their own picture. Pretty much all of our families seemed really into the project and immediately photos began coming in. We had them all arranged in a specially made frames along the hallway wall, keeping them covered until the big unveiling reception. We knew that we had some "non-traditional" families, you know, gay parents and interracial couples, but I guess we didn't really think it would be a problem for anyone.
>
> Well, we managed to gather photos for every child, so we knew no one was left out (even though we took a photo of a couple of children as they were dropped off by a family member, to at least have something). We had our unveiling, which went pretty well. But by the next day the principal and me and some other teachers started getting pretty heated complaints about how we were promoting homosexuality and mixed relationships. I really didn't know how to

handle the comments and was so surprised that some people took the project like that. A couple of families heard some of the comments and I know it was really hurtful. We had done this project with just the opposite intent—really in the spirit of celebrating each of our children and families. I know the saying "you can't please all the people all the time," but thinking back we probably could have tried to prepare ahead of time for some of that. It still is a good project and we will do it again. In some ways it was OK that those comments and biases came out so we could talk about them and try to make a difference through the dialogues. It sure was a learning experience for us all.

INTERACTIONS WITH CHILDREN

There is nothing as personal to a child as his family, and children are keenly sensitive to negative perceptions about family members. Professionals must be careful and deliberate in the ways we talk about families in general and specific family members. Sometimes we make sweeping comments like "Bring these notes home to your moms and dads," or we plan craft activities to recognize Mother's Day, Father's Day, or Grandparent's Day without realizing the impact on children whose mother, father, or grandparents are not present in their lives or recognizing those who have multiple mothers or fathers. Often my teacher education students comment that most of the children live in a "typical family,"—so why can't they plan "down the middle" for the majority? Some even say it is unfair to children not to celebrate these kinds of days. But as we know, the nuclear family model is not necessarily the majority and it is becoming less so all the time. As family mobility, immigration, and relocation continue to increase, we see fewer children with close connections to extended family. That is not to say that we should ignore children who are close with both parents and extended family, nor that we should ignore familiar holidays. But we should identify ways to alter how we integrate family focused activities into our practice. Perhaps each of the above-mentioned holidays could be reframed in broader terms to be a moment to appreciate any special family member. Maybe we decide to have three "Families Day" holidays instead of one for each specific member and use that time to identify and describe many things that we love about certain family members.

In addition to rethinking the types of learning experiences we plan for children that might revolve around an exclusionary and narrow definition of family, we also need to reconsider the terms we use to refer to families. As you internalize a broader framework for recognizing families, let your language shift also from talking about *the family* to *families*. Shift from *mother* and *father* to *parent* or *caregiver*. Share with children positive, loving stories of different family configurations, with an emphasis on concepts of connections, relationships, and interactions as defining features of families. Let children engage with you in the process of conceptualizing what families mean to us today.

Before engaging in classroom projects centered around holidays like Father's Day or Mother's Day, it is important to know the contexts within which children are growing up, to anticipate possible questions other children or families might have, and to promote positive valuing of all families.

INTERACTIONS AMONG CHILDREN

We know that young children are intense observers of their world and particularly curious about differences. Sometimes they hold inflexible ideas about the world—also a developmental norm and often shaped by family or societal biases. We need to be aware of the potential for negative interactions when children think concretely or narrowly about family while noticing other children who live in a different family structure or style from them. It is not uncommon for a preschool child to definitively tell another "You can't have two daddies," or "You can't be that baby doll's mommy because you look different." While the child doesn't intend to be hurtful—but rather is stating what she knows about the world—these words are especially confusing and hurtful for a child in a blended family, with gay parents, or in an adopted family. Professionals need to be prepared to foster dialogue from comments like these to encourage children to rethink their frameworks of family. However, we can't just rely on responses to these impromptu comments from children. Appreciation of human diversity must be purposefully woven throughout the curriculum and daily life of the program or school to make such dialogues more effective. Deliberate preparation and anticipation allow us to be prepared to invite and respond to children's comments and questions about ways that we are different.

LEARNING EXPERIENCES

Exploration of families is a popular theme in early childhood programs and has the potential to be an effective getting-to-know-us and community-building topic. But a "families" topic can also potentially exclude, if a narrow definition of families is used or if children have experienced significant family transitions. Valuing our diversities does not mean ignoring them but rather supportively and sensitively cultivating a group climate that allows for sharing and noticing both similarities *and* differences without negative judgments. Focusing on daily routines and the experiences of everyday life allows all children (even those who live with nonbiological parents or in temporary housing) to see similarities among each other and the context of transitions. Some important considerations for embarking on a class exploration of families:

- Begin by learning about children's basic family background; anticipate potential issues.
- Focus exploration on the concept of all families as well as on the children's own families.
- Use a broad framework for conceptualizing families; encourage identification of "big ideas," such as changes or connectedness.
- Ask children to share any experiences and ideas they are comfortable with about how they think about the form and function of families.
- Provide many ways for children to explore and represent their ideas about families as opposed to having all children complete the same activities (such as a family tree).

Exploring children's concepts and experiences about families is also appropriately embedded in a larger study of self. When children focus on their body, self, relationships, and the cultural and community context of their daily lives, they naturally all have something of value to share and represent while also allowing for realizations about similarities and differences. An "all about me and my family" project can include subtopics and learning experiences in all of the content areas, such as:

- Self and body:
  - Parts: measurements, counting, interactions and connections, simple anatomy

- Functions: ways we move, things we can do, parts we control, parts we don't
- Appearance: seeing-myself portraits, differences and similarities among us, favorite features, "how I change over time" photo journal
- Personality characteristics:
  - How I respond to people: graph a spectrum of responses (quiet or talkative?), acting and role playing
  - How I respond to tasks and problems: my problem solving style, my thinking style, our different strategies
- Things I like:
  - "My favorite _____" lists
  - "Things I love about _____" poems
  - Charting and graphing class differences and similarities
- Important people in my life and family:
  - Drawing and listing important people
  - Making maps of where I live, where they live
  - "What I love about you" or "my favorite things to do with _____" letters, poems, stories, reflections
  - Drawing or describing where we live, making models
- Routines and traditions:
  - Listing and describing things we do every day and once a week
  - Identifying things we do occasionally, like special times or events
  - Comparing and contrasting daily and occasional activities
  - Identifying people we interact with in those activities
  - "My favorite activities" stories, tally chart
  - Listing what kinds of foods we eat
- School life:
  - Things we do at school: activities and sequencing daily routines
  - "My favorite part of the day" stories, drawings, reflections, tally charts and graphs
  - Identifying and describing classmates, teachers, staff
- Community around us:
  - Maps of my house and street, school, popular places (market, library, friends, bus stop, etc.)
  - Descriptions of visits to places we go with family: interview family and people we interact with
  - Creating 3-D model of homes and the community from boxes (food, recycled packing, made from cardboard and tape, etc.)

- Roles people play in the community:
  - Dramatic play/charades
  - Interviews and letters to meet and learn from different people in our community
  - "Places I go and places I don't know" photo exploration
  - Interrelationships with public works systems: guest presentations, field trips, mapping, sequencing (where clean water comes from, where garbage goes, how roads get built, where our food comes from, etc.)

Family Partnerships

Forging meaningful partnerships with diverse families is, in some ways, a two-part process. First, we need to make clear and effective efforts to welcome all families into our professional setting. This effort has to involve all important family members in children's lives. Think about ways to broaden the scope of family involvement as you watch this **video** where extended family members talk about Brianna and then share their close involvement in her life. We need to be purposeful about engaging all families in our programs in ways that are reciprocal and mutually beneficial, and that reaffirm our collaborative role with their children. The following are just a few ideas for ways to reach out and welcome all families:

WELCOME LETTER

If you begin on a specific date, you have the opportunity to reach out to all your families while you are all new to each other. Your first welcome letter or newsletter can set the tone for your future interactions and absolutely sends families a message about your values, goals for your time with their children, what they can expect from you, and what you invite and hope for in relationships with them. Use this opportunity well—you know what people say about a first impression! While a welcome letter or newsletter is a one-way information exchange, your primary goal should be to clearly invite families to interact. You cannot successfully complete the first and most important task, which is to know your children, without information from families on the context within which children live.

- Emphasize for families that you need to learn from them about their children, reinforcing the essential place they hold in their children's lives and education. Tell them why it is so important to know about the larger context of children's lives in order to be able to fully and appropriately support their time in the program or school. Not all families come to us with prior understanding of how essential for their children's success our interrelationships with them are.
- Clearly make a statement about what valuing diversity means to you and how you will encourage awareness and appreciation with their

children. This is a time to briefly let families know that you will support children's questions, thinking, and curiosity about human differences and how you plan to promote appreciation for each other through sharing and exploring differences and similarities. You may want to provide a short example to illustrate what you mean by this. Again, not all families have thought about this ahead of time and some might assume you will ignore or dismiss certain differences. This is a chance to demonstrate to families that you are competent, intentional, and prepared for even the more sensitive and delicate aspects of our work and to position yourself as a resource for them if they are unsure how to handle certain questions or topics.

- Provide families with several specific, concrete examples of ways you need them to engage with you, the program or school, and the group to ensure success for their children. Identify a variety of options, and encourage families to suggest other ways to be involved too.

ONGOING MEANINGFUL ENGAGEMENT

Practice has clearly shown that children are more successful in school, feel more positively about school and themselves as learners, and are more engaged when they have family members who are interested and involved in their school life. Professionals are instrumental in both welcoming and sustaining family involvement though deliberate action and attitude. Too often professionals can tend to minimize the family's role or even to

Welcoming all family members in the early childhood setting is an essential first step in building meaningful partnerships.

attribute challenges with children to negative family qualities. In turn, families might tend to leave children's education "to the professionals" and not see the essential collaborative role they, as families, play. Make your message clear—that children need for families and professionals to work in concert, and provide specific examples of what that means. You might have to make repeated attempts to reach and recruit families, especially if they have previously had negative experiences or are nervous about not fitting in.

Families might feel comfortable engaging with programs and schools on special projects like fund-raisers, book fairs, and community events, or on administrative tasks. Consider including a family presence on governing or advisory boards. Having a role in program or school governance can provide a forum for a new sense of empowerment and purpose, and a contributory role for family members. Parental involvement is often most effective and lasting when families are offered opportunities to take on important roles within the program or school, reinforcing their important role in their children's learning.

Consider identifying specific roles, tasks, projects, or times of day where a family member could engage with the group. Family members have a variety of expertise which can support learning goals, participating in some of the following ways:

- As a special guest teacher
- Demonstrating different professional roles
- Sharing religious knowledge
- Guiding exploration about diverse abilities
- Being a guest story reader or storyteller
- Being a small group leader during content area group time (reading, math, science, social studies, arts)
- Being a "lunch bunch" guide, wherein a family member is designated a certain table or small group with which to promote positive social interactions and discussion about nutrition during lunch time; this might include reading a short story or just enjoying supervising social time
- Being a "ride guide": a family member rides the bus in the morning or afternoon to support positive social interactions, provide additional supervision, or facilitate fun games and storytelling

Many programs and schools will designate a room or part of the building as a family resource center. Part lounge, part information station, part library, the resource room can be overseen by a family member or staff and is a place for families to find support and comfort, and to focus on their needs. Information on family literacy programs, public library events, adult education programs, health and welfare sources, and any freebies that might interest families can be organized and housed here. Coffee, snacks, reading materials, and a few cozy chairs invite family members to stay and share a while. Some family resource rooms include a donated sewing machine, computer and printer, language translation software, community guides, or even tutoring. Consider encouraging voluntary sharing of contact information or self-forming of support groups on a variety of topics.

Encourage families to tell their stories and share important parts of who they are as individuals and as a unit. Supporting and involving all families, but especially those who are not of the nuclear-family structure, takes some deliberate and intentional welcoming and requires planning and preparation. It is important to be clear and honest, and to anticipate any potential for negative backlash so that you can be prepared to efficiently and quickly manage negative experiences. Families need to be welcomed in to programs and schools, but even more importantly, their experiences, once they are involved, need to be positive and supportive.

Summary

DEFINING *FAMILY* IN MODERN TERMS

- The term *nuclear family* has been used to describe a family unit consisting of a married mother and father with children living in the same household. Until the past couple of decades this definition was narrowly viewed as the only legitimate family structure.
- Several major social and legal shifts have changed the way people live and organize their home lives in the United States today.
- These changes have necessitated the rethinking and redefining of what constitutes families today.
- Important considerations now acknowledge that individual families change over time and that the nature of family life has changed societally over decades.

FAMILY STRUCTURES IN THE UNITED STATES

- An important lens through which to look is to think about *families* as opposed to *the family* when framing definitions of family structure.

- A modest majority of children live with two parents (most with biological parents and a smaller percentage within a step or adoptive family structure).
- Despite the growth of other family structures and experiences, the nuclear structure maintains a privileged status.
- Blended families, single parent families, gay and lesbian parents, adoptive families, grandparent caregivers, and foster families each are becoming increasingly part of children's experience of family life.
- Each of the distinct and overlapping types of family structures presents unique considerations, strengths, and needs.

CURRICULAR CONNECTIONS

- The proliferation of children's books and materials that positively represent diverse family structures allows professionals to use these resources to introduce and support children's diverse experiences of family life.

- Dedicating spaces for families to share elements of their family structure, traditions, and experiences also provides the opportunity for sharing diversity and appreciating differences.
- Program activities and interactions should be intentionally inclusive of all the ways that family units are comprised and change, emphasizing cohesive elements throughout transitions.
- Carefully planned, integrated explorations of families as a learning topic can serve to validate all children's experiences and engender community building within groups.
- Activities should be planned to offer a wide range of ways to consider and represent different family experiences.

FAMILY PARTNERSHIPS

- Engaging with families in program and school settings requires that professionals carefully work to welcome and sustain family engagement over time.
- Meaningful opportunities should be provided for families to share important roles within the program or school, as well within the child's group.
- Professionals should have a clearly articulated philosophy and policies on valuing and appreciating family diversity that is shared with families in clear terms.

Chapter Learning Outcomes: Self-Assessment

Use this space to reflect on how well you have achieved the learning goals for this chapter by evaluating your own competency in the topics below. List three to five items that describe key concepts that you have learned from the chapter.

Describe the complexities in definitions of family.	
Explain demographic contexts and trends in family structures.	
Compare characteristics of diverse family structures.	
Practice strategies for promoting appreciation of diverse families with children.	
Create partnerships with diverse families.	

Chapter Activities

DISCUSSION QUESTIONS

1. Reconsider the initial task of generating a definition of family now that you have read the chapter. Compare how your definition is similar or different, and explain why you made changes or retained concepts.
2. Discuss changes in policies such as family leave for adoptive parents, family benefits for cohabitating partners, same-sex marriage or civil unions, and so on, and the impacts on the lives of children and families.

SELF-REFLECTION

Reflect on your own family experiences and describe what your family life was like. Trace any changes or transitions over the course of your life from birth through adolescence. Identify ways that you feel your own family experiences influence your views and definitions of families. Consider how your personal experience and beliefs may impact your values and the ways you work with children and families representing different structures.

TEACHING DISPOSITION

1. In light of the goals of welcoming families and sustaining meaningful engagement, begin to draft a document which you could use to convey your values and goals for engaging with families:

   - Your beliefs about families and family diversity
   - Why family participation is so important to children's outcomes
   - Ways you welcome families to engage with you and their children

2. Using the "All about me and my family" project outlined above as a starting point, create a curriculum map clearly defining learning goals, integrating all content areas, and identifying specific standards from the Common Core Standards (www.corestandards.org) that would be addressed in your project.

IN THE FIELD

Locate a professional in your community who works in any capacity in a family services agency involving adoption or foster care, in child welfare services or family therapy, or who specializes in infant mental health, for example. Interview that person about his or her perspectives on family composition, resiliency factors in families, and what supports are particularly important to healthy family functioning.

Weblinks

Teaching Tolerance online resources include lesson and project plans for integrating explorations of diverse family structures and experiences with young children, including the Family Tapestry project. *http://www.tolerance.org*

"**Welcoming Schools** offers tools, lessons and resources on embracing family diversity, avoiding gender stereotyping and ending bullying and name-calling in elementary schools. It offers an LGBT inclusive approach that is also inclusive of the many types of diversity found in our communities." *http://www.welcomingschools.org/about/*

9 Abilities

An essential part of quality practice is for educators to use systematic observation, assessment, and reflection to really get to know each child in order to individualize experiences to support each child's unique strengths and needs. However, in practice, educators sometimes tend to "plan down the middle," targeting the children within a typical range of developmental expectations. Some educators might feel unprepared to support every child or might view the children outside of the typical range of development as outside of their responsibility. Some look to specialists or paraprofessionals as solely responsible for children outside the typical range of developmental or academic expectations. And while partnering with a specially trained team is an important collaboration, delegating sole responsibility to a specialist can often lead to some children being marginalized or excluded in the classroom.

Best practices in teaching support the meaningful inclusion of all children in the classroom community, with individualized supports.

An important part of shifting this practice is for early childhood professionals to be knowledgeable about diverse approaches to teaching, including those that have typically been considered in the realm of special education. This means seeing each child as an individual and capable of active participation and success in a variety of social, emotional, physical, academic, and intellectual areas. Choosing to recognize the inherent value and worth of each individual, even as abilities might vary from one to another, is a choice to embrace an inclusive, social justice perspective. Working for social justice in our classrooms and communities is the primary overarching value that drives current professional practice. This chapter provides a brief description of the many ways that children develop differently and gives specific strategies for cultivating environments and attitudes in classrooms and programs for young children, attitudes that welcome and support all children's access and active participation.

Early Childhood Inclusion

Current trends in early care and education strongly promote *inclusion*. "**Early childhood inclusion** embodies the values, policies, and practices that support the right of every infant and young child and his or her family, regardless of ability, to participate in a broad range of activities and contexts as full members of families, communities, and society" (DEC/ NAEYC, 2009, p. 2). Inclusive practices are those that are intentionally designed to appropriately and meaningfully engage all children to their fullest potential within the same learning environment and care setting. Appropriately challenging and supporting children's strengths and needs requires broad planning based on overarching developmental expectations and also individualized adjustments based on knowledge of specific children. Listen to key aspects of what an inclusive classroom looks like in this **video**.

Across the field, a majority of professionals and a vast majority of families report open, welcoming access to early childhood programs for all children as a top priority (Hurley & Horn, 2010). Willingness is a necessary start, but professionals also need specialized knowledge on how to effectively adapt instruction, environment, materials, staffing, schedules, and programming outcomes to fully support each child's development and achievement, including children with diverse abilities (NPDCI, 2011). To support these efforts, professional guidelines identify three core components of high quality early childhood inclusion: access, participation, and support (DEC/NAEYC, 2009).

- A first step towards inclusive practices is a belief in the fundamental principle that all children deserve membership in the community group (be it a classroom, care center, or other early childhood setting) and that differences in abilities are a natural part of human diversity.

LEARNING OUTCOMES

- Define *early childhood* inclusion

- Explain concepts of *ability* and *disability* in a historical and social context

- Discuss the responsibilities of professionals in meeting all children's needs in program and school settings

- Describe categories of differences in ability based on federal legislation

- Practice inclusive teaching strategies which support children with diverse abilities

- Create partnerships with families of children with diverse abilities

- A second step is intentional organization and planning of program and school settings to maximize each child's strengths and capacities and ensure full participation. This may include considering the design of indoor and outdoor spaces so that all children can safely access and fully use play and learning spaces.

- An essential third step in high quality inclusive programming is the identification and implementation of systemic support, including professional development training, scheduled time for collaborations, and structures for family–professional collaborations. Families, community agencies, local businesses, program administrators, and national foundations can be sources of support in different aspects of inclusive programming.

Inclusive programming thus embodies an attitude and skillful, deliberate practice. These essential aspects underscore the complexity and substantial challenges that face early childhood professionals today as we strive towards optimizing development and learning for all children.

IN MY FAMILY

She Belongs With Me

Back when I had my babies [in 1968] it was common practice to take the baby away after birth for a checkup. When they came back with her the doctor informed me that Dianne had not responded well on the test and that he thought she had a birth defect called Down Syndrome. He immediately told me that I should sign her over to an institution because she would never be normal and would put too much strain on the rest of our family. He just said it like he was telling me it looked like it might rain that afternoon. He was so matter-of-fact and had this tone of disgust or dismissal, like Dianne was a rotting piece of fruit spoiling the bowl and with no sense of her as a human being. In fact, sending them away is what most parents did with these cases, he said. Of course I was scared and had no idea what this would mean for our lives. But I knew I couldn't send her to one of those places. Dianne was my baby and no one was going to take her from me.

Over her early years I had to do so much for her, you know, to teach her basic things. I didn't have anyone giving me help or advice, since most parents didn't keep children with differences like this. Honestly, most people's attitude was like they didn't want to be bothered

having to even notice children like this. So I just tried anything I could think of. Like when she was a year [old] I used to get into a crawling position on my hands and knees and I would tie her little hands to mine and legs to my knees and crawl around the floor for a while. She wasn't doing it on her own so I figured I had to show her little body what it felt like. I may not have known exactly what to do for her all the time, but I sure kept trying. There were lots of things like that. I don't know . . . I guess I just tried anything to help her.

Now as an adult Dianne can do a lot of things for herself like many daily living activities. Though I guess she will always live with me and go to a supervised work program for adults like her. Someday she'll move into a group home where someone will provide assistance like I give her. But sure as I'm standing here she always belonged in our family and has had a much more productive life than that doctor ever thought she would! She belongs in our home just as much as she belongs in our community. All of our children do. It still makes me so mad to think about those kinds of times when no one wanted to recognize Dianne as a person, valued the same as anyone else.

Understanding *Diverse Abilities*:
Social and Legal Context

In essence, the term *diverse abilities* refers to all of us. Everyone has abilities and needs, though to varying degrees and in varying ways. The goal of recasting our lens around the term *diverse abilities* as opposed to focusing only on "disabilities," "special needs," or "exceptionalities" is to emphasize the inherent normalcy of humans exhibiting a wide range of performance levels and types of behaviors and skills. Differences among us all are a normal part of human diversity, but what is accepted as typical or normal developmental functioning is socioculturally defined. This means that groups of scientists and researchers have observed thousands of children over many decades and made decisions about the range within which children's development *should* fall, based on average performance emerging from those observations.

Most would argue that this approach is necessary, and our field has certainly been enhanced by such work. But as with any socioculturally defined term and framework, there is potential for bias that can lead to discriminatory practices. While it is true that a large majority of infants and children demonstrate developmental behaviors in a range that is defined as typical, those who are not within this range are consequently defined as atypical, disabled or impaired, at risk for developing a disability; or gifted or talented. This division is both problematic and useful. In order for us to mitigate the problems and maximize the usefulness and purpose of categorizing and labeling abilities, we must think deliberately and critically about the ways we conceptualize developmental and educational expectations, and—just as important—the ways we interact with children based on those expectations.

The potential problems inherent in creating parameters to label what is typical and what is atypical have long cast a shadow over society and educational practice. Historically, the shadow has taken on the shape of deeply exclusionary practices that justified isolation and segregation of children labeled as outside of the normal range of functioning. Prior to major social and legal changes over the past 50 years, children who did not function within a typical range were considered "defective" and were largely removed to isolated residential institutions (Odom & Wolery, 2003). Often these facilities functioned more as warehousing or sometimes like prisons. Dianne's mother reflected on the strong pressure she felt to follow this social expectation. Some children whose development did not follow typical patterns were educated in specialized home-based programs, though still segregated from children whose development followed typical patterns (Darragh, 2010).

Even with gains in acceptance and accommodation over the past 50 years, ours is still a society which values productivity, health, fitness, and achievement, and while current practice largely admonishes institutionalization as an unacceptable form of exclusion, truly inclusionary values and practices are far from deeply ingrained in our psyche or practice. When we use terms such as *disability* and *special needs*, which focus on lack of capability or neediness, we effectively marginalize individuals outside of the "productive members" (Kottak & Kozaitis, 2008). Many people object to such *deficit-perspective* terms, especially individuals and families who have experienced the discrimination that has been so prevalent throughout our history. Indeed, it is due to the tireless, passionate work of families with children who were marginalized and excluded that we have laws which make discrimination based on ability illegal.

SOCIAL AND LEGAL RIGHTS: HISTORICAL ECHOES

The current legislation ensuring specialized services for children with diverse abilities has historical roots emerging out of the civil rights movements of the 1950s and 1960s. The intense and violent struggles for racial equality started in the streets and played out in the courts, shedding light on the inhumanity and unconstitutionality of segregation. The earliest court cases that provided equal access to educational opportunities for children of color, notably *Brown v. Board of Education of Topeka Kansas* in 1954, were important predecessors in the slowly developing climate of advocacy and equity for marginalized groups (Darragh, 2010). Court decisions continuing to rule in favor of equal access to end segregation set a clear precedent that would prove useful in challenges to the exclusion of children with diverse abilities from schools and public programs.

Civil advocacy movements and landmark Supreme Court decisions translated into legislative provisions for marginalized groups with the Civil Rights Act, Title IV, in 1964 and **The Elementary and Secondary Education Act** (ESSA) in 1965. The ESSA and important subsequent amendments through 1968 represented the first federal agenda focused on educational services for children with diverse abilities. This law placed responsibility for services with schools as opposed to separate institutions which had previously been the primary setting for services. Throughout these years of Lyndon Johnson's presidency, other efforts to reduce inequity included the Head Start grant program, designed to provide free quality preschool programming to children from families with limited income. As federal agencies were established to oversee accessibility to services and grant programs, similar programs for infants and toddlers facing risk factors (ability or limited family resources) were included in legislative amendments.

Families and organizations continued to use the court systems as a vehicle for advocacy, fighting passionately for the right of all children to access meaningful educational experiences in the same public school settings as typically developing children. The next set of important legislation came in the mid-1970s in the form of The Vocational Rehabilitation Act (Section 504 of Public Law 93-112) and the Education for All Handicapped Children Act (**Public Law 94-142**). Echoing civil rights legislation, Section 504 prohibits discrimination from any programs receiving federal funding on the basis of an individual's ability. The definition of *disabilities* in Section 504 is broader and works in concert and sometimes to compliment Public Law (PL) 94-142, though the two laws share most of the same core principles (Salend & Rohena, 2003). But it is Public Law 94-142 which extensively outlines educational access for children with diverse abilities and grants funding for states to provide services.

In 1975 the signing of Public Law 94-142 dramatically changed the landscape of education in the United States and ushered in a new era of responsibility and accountability for what schools must provide to all children (Darragh, 2010; Gollnick & Chinn, 2009). Listen to professionals discuss the application of laws for children with special needs in schools in this **video**.

There are several key provisions in the law:

- Unequivocal access to a *free and appropriate public education* (referred to as the FAPE standard) for all children with disabilities ages 3 to 21, in the least restrictive environment in or as close to a regular education setting as possible
- Protection of the rights of children, youth, and parents and guardians
- Ensured involvement of parents and families in educational decisions
- Requirement for the creation of **individualized education programs**, including integrated plans with goals, objectives, and supports
- Assess to the effectiveness of programs, services, and children's progress
- Provision of funding for appropriate accommodations

These provisions set a new precedent for public educational practice in many ways. This law marked a new level of acknowledgement of the role families play in children's education and sought to afford families a voice in educational decisions for their children. Requiring that children be educated in regular education classrooms or in settings as close to it as possible sent a clear message that the segregated and often substandard environments previously relegated for children with diverse abilities were inherently inadequate and no longer an acceptable option. During this time, Head Start also continued to strengthen the national focus on preschool inclusion as a non-school-based, federally funded, early intervention program with a policy mandate reserving a percentage of program space for children with diverse abilities (Odom, 2002). **Early intervention/early childhood special education** (EI/ECSE) comprises programs and services designed for infants, toddlers, and preschool children with, or at risk for, developmental disability. These programs are organized and administered through state-appointed agencies and focus heavily on family support and education. Individualized plans to strengthen children's development in skills and behaviors foundational to success in school and daily life are essential in EI/ECSE. Programs housed within and administered in schools though state departments of education sometimes overlap in serving preschool age children, though the focus of services tends to emphasize the social, behavioral, and academic skills necessary for success in school (Odom & Wolery, 2003).

Early childhood special education *refers to programs and services specifically designed for children with, or at risk for, developmental delays.*

Emergence of IDEA Legislation

And so a paradigm shift was taking place in the United States over the course of the 1970s and 1980s. The tolerance for segregation that had prevailed decades before was being replaced by policies and practices that recognized the rights of all children to access and benefit from education. By 1990, the right to accessibility had also emerged as a basic civil rights issue in the public sphere outside of education. The passing of the Americans with Disabilities Act (ADA) in 1990 reechoed the struggles of earlier civil rights movements' fight for racial equality. The ADA expressly prohibits discrimination based on ability in employment processes and requires accessibility and/or accommodations in employment settings, public transportation, and communication (telephone) services (Gollnick & Chinn, 2009). Like Section 504, the ADA is an antidiscrimination law and does not provide grant funding for services.

That same year the landmark **Individuals with Disabilities Education Act (IDEA)** law was passed and served as the amendment and update to PL 94-142. IDEA serves as the funding provision for special education services in schools as well as outlining eligibility for services (OCR, 2011).

Underscoring the growing social awareness and acceptance of individuals with diverse abilities, the new IDEA legislation intentionally promoted the use of **person-first language**. For example, consider even the two titles:

- Education for All Handicapped Children Act
- Individuals with Disabilities Education Act

The deliberate shift away from *handicapped children* to *individuals with disabilities* sends a clear message that we see the person, first and foremost, not their ability status. Terms such as *paralyzed child* or *visually impaired child* were replaced with the terms *child with a physical impairment* or *child with visual impairment*. The use of person-first language marks an important shift in public perception of personal value, dignity, and equal acceptance. "Individuals with disabilities are people or individuals first. Their disability is secondary and at times inconsequential in their ability to perform the task they undertake" (Gollnick & Chinn, 2009, p. 171). This strategic and deliberate emphasis continues to be important today as we promote attitudes and practices that see each person as a unique individual with a diverse array of abilities and needs, but always with inherent value.

Amendments to the IDEA law continued in 1997 and 2004 in attempts to clarify, streamline, and extend services. The context of the child's development within the family became an important lens. The role of families was clarified to underscore families as essential partners and key decision makers in children's education and service plans. Stemming from evidence that children at risk for developmental delays benefit from intervention services beginning as early as possible, provisions were added to extend services to infants and toddlers. Part B of the IDEA law targets children and youth age 3 to 21, and Part C focuses on interventions and services for infants and toddlers from birth to age 3 (Bruder, 2010). A new term emerged in Part C corresponding to the least restrictive environment component of Part B, highlighting the *natural environment* of the family, home, and community as the most desirable setting within which to provide services for infants and toddlers (Darragh, 2010).

Of particular importance to early childhood professionals is the trend in the law and in models of high quality practice to emphasize the essential interrelationships between young children and their families. Emphasizing the impact on development of the nested interrelationships within children's lives, Vygotsky's sociocultural theory (Bedrova & Leong, 1996), and Bronfenbrenner's bioecological model (Bronfenbrenner, 1992) have become influential frameworks for supporting children and families. In the bioecological model, children and immediate family are positioned at the core and represent the strongest influence. Radiating outward like the layers of an onion are concentric circles of influence including the child's extended family, care settings, schools, community, political systems, and so on. In sociocultural theory, children's development and learning are inextricably connected and shaped by their social and cultural context. In both views, children's growth and development are very much interrelated with their environments and intimately connected to families. Such perspectives drive early childhood professionals to always maintain this holistic view of development. This translates into the need for high quality, inclusive, early childhood and early intervention practice to focus on the following (Odom & Wolery, 2003; Bruder, 2010):

- Meaningful involvement of families in programs and services for children, including the assessment process
- Validation of the important influence families have on children's development
- Recognition of the influence children have on their families and environments

Systems and practices that support meaningful family involvement in children's education are essential aspects of inclusive programming.

• Resources and supports extended to families to strengthen their capacity to meet the needs of infants and toddlers with diverse abilities, extending beyond services just for the child

• Development of individual plans for services and supports with goals, outcomes, and appropriate assessments

School-based early childhood special education programming and community-based early intervention programs (such as Head Start and Early Head Start for infants and toddlers) continue to evolve over time as practice is shaped by ongoing shifts in attitudes and expectations. Today's view on access to education is framed by a social justice perspective in which we must contextually consider children's and families' lives and the diverse strengths, needs, and resources of each child as an individual and as a valued member of a community.

The Educational Context of *Diverse Abilities* or *Exceptionalities*

While there is value and purpose in reframing the way we think about and talk about children's functioning as along a spectrum of diverse ability points, in school settings there is a specific purpose for using particular terms. In the context of education, diverse abilities are generally referred to as **exceptionalities**. The term refers to a child's functioning in a variety of areas that are interrelated with life inside or outside schools, including:

• Academic achievement
• Cognitive and intellectual development
• Speech, language, and communication
• Emotional or psychological functioning within specific contexts
• Physical and motor functioning
• Health condition
• Social skills and interactions

In the United States, the practice of assessing and labeling children's diverse abilities as exceptional in some way is a relative evaluation: a child's functioning is evaluated in comparison to expectations of learning and development based on a range which is considered normal or typical. Children whose functioning falls above or below the normal range in any particular area(s) are considered exceptional. If the child's functioning is above the normal range, the child may be labeled *gifted and talented*. If the child's functioning is below the normal range, the child may be labeled as *having a disability*.

The IDEA uses the term *child with a disability* to describe or label an infant, child, or youth whose functioning in certain area(s) is below expectation. This term is a necessary cue for access to intervention services and funding under the federal legislation. (IDEA does not address children whose functioning is above the normal range.) Schools and intervention specialists use specific labels for purposes of accessing services and individualized therapies. In this way, the application of a specific label to a child's behavior or functioning is used as a gateway to acquire the supports designed to improve developmental or academic outcomes for the child.

Early childhood professionals are truly in the front row seat when it comes to initial awareness of diverse abilities that might impact the child's functioning in school or program. Given this influential position, it is important that you have a broad awareness of legal, policy, and practice considerations related to children with diverse abilities. This includes overview-level knowledge of descriptions of how children's development can differ from one another or from expectations defined as typical. Your awareness should also include knowledge of how schools and programs are organized to support all children's development and learning. On a cautionary note, however, it is imperative that you use your knowledge of these descriptions to enhance your ability to diversify instruction and to involve interdisciplinary professionals when concerns arise—but not to prematurely label children. The assessment process is complex and multi-faceted, and it must thoroughly engage a variety of sources of screening and support.

CATEGORIES OF DISABILITIES UNDER IDEA

The IDEA includes 13 separate categories of conditions which classify a child as having a disability when two key conditions exist:

1. The child's educational performance is "adversely affected" or negatively impacted by one or more of these conditions
2. The child needs special education and services due to their diagnosed condition (GPO, 2012)

Table 9.1 provides a brief overview of these categories. A diagnosis in one or more of these areas requires state agencies to provide access to services for children from birth through age 21 (NICHCY, 2012).

These categories and descriptions continue to evolve through revisions to the legislation. They serve the purpose of identifying criteria that require

TABLE 9.1 *Description of 13 IDEA Categories of Disabilities (GPO, 2012)*

IDEA Term	Description of Symptoms or Behavioral Evidence
Autism Spectrum (IDEA uses the term *autism*)	Significant delay in the development of social interaction skills, including communication, and can include: • Repetitive movements • Sensory sensitivity • Difficulty coping with changes in routine or environment Under IDEA, if a child has a diagnosis of *emotional disturbance* that is the cause of adverse educational performance, then the classification of autism would not apply
Emotional disturbance	Persistent, significant evidence of one or more of the following: • Inability to learn that is not related to intellectual, sensory, or health issues • Inability to form lasting relationships with peers and teachers • Inappropriate behaviors or feelings in nonstressful circumstances • Pervasive unhappiness or depression • Physical symptoms or anxiety related to personal or school issues • Schizophrenia
Deaf–blindness	Hearing and visual impairment occurring together and causing severe developmental, educational, and/or communication needs that cannot be met by programs specialized for either hearing or visual impairment
Deafness	Hearing impairment which impairs a child's ability to process linguistic input with or without sound amplification
Hearing impairment	Permanent or fluctuating impairment not included under deafness
Speech or language impairment	Communication, language, or voice disorder, such as stuttering
Visual impairment, including blindness	Impairment in vision which adversely affects educational performance even with the use of correction; includes partial sight and blindness
Specific learning disability	Disorder in processes related to language that results in the inability to perform language arts or mathematical functions and can include processing or perceptual conditions or brain injury; does not include learning problems that are the result of other disabilities (such as visual impairment) or the result of cultural or socioeconomic status
Intellectual disability (replacing the term *mental retardation*)	Significantly below average intellectual functioning and deficient adaptive behavior demonstrated during the developmental period
Orthopedic impairment	Severe physical impairment which may include genetic disorders, impairment caused by disease, or conditions such as cerebral palsy

IDEA Term	Description of Symptoms or Behavioral Evidence
Other health impairment	Limited strength or alertness, or heightened alertness to stimuli that diminishes focus on educational environment, which is due to chronic or acute health problem such as: • Asthma • Attention deficit disorder • Attention deficit hyperactivity disorder • Diabetes • Epilepsy • Heart condition • Leukemia • Tourette's syndrome • Sickle-cell anemia • Rheumatic fever
Traumatic brain injury	Injury to the brain caused by an external force that results in diminished ability in motor functioning, mental processing, or behavior; does not include injuries from birth trauma or genetic disorders
Multiple disabilities	Combination of significant impairments that cause severe needs that cannot be met in specialized programming for a single disability; not including deaf-blindness

school action in terms of meeting diverse abilities, and they provide a snapshot framework to enable professionals to recognize the scope of diversity of human abilities. Applying any descriptive label to a child has implications and impacts on the child and family, and professionals must be cautious and deliberate in the process. Assessing a child to determine ability status and to identify service and programming needs is complex and requires a sensitive, collaborative dialogue among professionals and families, reliance on careful observation, and connection to relevant research evidence.

ASSESSING DIVERSE ABILITIES HAPPENS EARLY

It is common for early childhood professionals to be among the first to notice differences in abilities in young children. While some differences in abilities are present from birth, many areas develop over the early years. Some are only noticed as a potential concern as children enter into formal group settings such as child care, preschool, or elementary school. Sometimes a difference is only noticeable in the program or school setting where a child's ability level might pose a problem in terms of the child's performance on tasks or in meeting specific expectations. In the more individual and less formally structured context of a home setting, young children's abilities and functioning might be markedly different from age-mates but those differences might not be as noticeable due to the setting. When children enter structured, formal educational group settings that focus on specific learning skills, social expectations, and self-regulation behaviors, large and small differences in abilities become more noticeable. In addition being in a group provides a ready source of comparisons between children, which can highlight differences.

The process through which a diagnosis is made and a label identified is often initiated by early childhood professionals or parents who observe behaviors that seem outside of an expected range for typical development. An important consideration is that there is also evidence of an adverse effect on the child's educational performance. Bethany's experience is not uncommon among preschool professionals:

> My co-teacher and I began noticing an area of concern with Sasha's communication when she was 3. She often did not follow simple directions even after multiple requests and her speech was fast and generally difficult to understand. She appeared fidgety and like she wasn't paying attention much of the time and did not really engage in whole or small group activities. Other children withdrew from her and she seemed sort of outcast from the class. But when she was using the classroom tablet or by herself doing puzzles, she was quiet, focused, and attentive. In talking with her grandmother (who has custody), we all began to keep track of specific things we observed at home, in the community (Sasha and her grandmother participated in church events twice a week), and at school. We met to review our observation notes and thought it was important to have a Speech-Language therapist also observe Sasha to help identify any concerns but also offer us some strategies.
>
> After several observations, reviews of her pediatrician's notes, visits with Sasha and her grandmother and the teachers, he identified a language processing problem. He was able to schedule twice-weekly therapy for Sasha and worked with us and her family on strategies we could use. He suggested that we integrate visual symbols alongside print on labels and schedules as well as using simple gestures and signs when we talked. And, wow…it was like unlocking a door! The more we could pair verbal and visual information, the more Sasha responded to us and other children. Once we learned to give Sasha information in ways she could understand she responded eagerly. Her speech is slowly becoming more understandable and the other children are interacting more with her. I feel like we all came together and have changed what could have been a rough future for this little girl. It feels really good to see a positive outcome like this.

Sasha is on the road to success developmentally and in school, and the collaborative assessment process had a big part in that. Essential and overarching considerations about identification and assessment process include focusing on the following (DEC, 2007):

- Child- and family-centered context (attention to family's linguistic and cultural background)

- Involving interdisciplinary teams (teachers, specialists, therapists, administrators, families)
- Comprehensive information sharing among team members, especially family members, in language and terminology families understand
- Integration of relevant information from a variety of sources
- Use of authentic assessment measures related to the child's everyday routines

Assessment in the early years is guided by awareness that young children's development progresses through relatively predictable trends though at widely varying paces. In this way, children's development is characterized as universal and also highly diverse. In general, the developmental changes during the early years are more rapid and significant than at any other time in life and are highly influenced by children's internal processes and the context of their lives. Assessment of children, prompted by concern for their developmental progress, relies heavily on observations of children in natural settings and engaged in daily routines, activities, and play. In addition, checklists, discussions with family and others involved with the child on a regular basis, and careful use of reliable and valid screening tools, provide a more complete picture (DEC, 2007).

Early childhood professionals are uniquely positioned to influence children's outcomes, because often, the earlier a child receives intervention, the stronger the positive impact will be. While school systems may be more connected to intervention services and resources, professionals working with preschool age children must be as knowledgeable and prepared as their K–12 counterparts. For many children at risk for developmental delays, the earliest months or first years are the prime window for intervention. For example, there is compelling evidence showing that children exhibiting Autism Spectrum Disorder symptoms demonstrate the most benefit from intensive intervention that begins as early as possible, potentially at 2 years old (NRC, 2001).

However, the overarching premise of inclusion is not just about accommodations for specific children with or at risk for specific types of disabilities. "To benefit all children, including those with disabilities and developmental delays, it is important to implement an integrated, developmentally

The majority of children's diverse abilities can be successfully accommodated in the classroom, program, or school community with individual support or universal modifications that can enhance learning for all children.

appropriate, universally designed curriculum framework that is flexible, comprehensive, and linked to assessment and program evaluation activities" (DEC, 2007, p. 3). All high quality early childhood programming begins with the ultimate goal of equity in access and participation. Designing backwards from this goal allows access to be built in to the curricular and programmatic structure. Several important professional agencies have collaborated to create a framework to guide inclusive practice and define the essential elements of early childhood curriculum.

Guidelines for Inclusive Practice from the Division for Early Childhood

The landscape of early childhood education continued to change in response to legislative changes (IDEA and No Child Left Behind), program and learning standards and related accountability, and evolving research on best practices. To provide guidance and advocacy for high quality inclusive practice, the Division for Early Childhood of the Council for Exceptional Children (DEC) convened a joint working group with members of the National Association for the Education of Young Children (NAEYC) to create a position statement on early childhood inclusion. The 2009 statement outlines recommendations in curriculum, assessment, and program evaluation in inclusive programs serving young children. The statement outlines how high quality early childhood programming involves carefully developed curricula that are deliberately designed for appropriate developmental expectations and are flexibly tailored to each child's strengths and needs. In particular, the principles of *Universal Design for Learning* are highlighted as a framework for inclusive practice.

UNIVERSAL DESIGN FOR LEARNING: EQUITY PRINCIPLES, FROM ARCHITECTURE TO EDUCATION

The civil rights movement sparked a response in laws and policies from the 1960s through the 1990s to promote access for individuals with diverse abilities. Emerging out of the implementation of those laws was a concept and related practices in architecture called *universal design* (UD). In building, environment, and product design, UD focuses on intentional planning for full accessibility and participation, with an emphasis on equitable, meaningful, and full inclusion of all people. The process involves carefully considering all potential users' needs from the earliest phase of design and development so that access is embedded eloquently and naturally and benefits all users (Stockall, Dennis, & Miller, 2012). Examples are lowered sinks in bathrooms, automatic door openers, lowered curbs at crosswalks, textured sections of sidewalk at crossing points, and larger rubber handles on implements. These features might be considered solely for individuals with particular diversities, but such embedded features actually provide access and ease of use for a wide array of users. As such, UD is a way to serve all people in a more effective, integrated way, which reduces segregation and separation. This approach to planning deliberately for the widest audience has proven successful in product development and marketing and also in the **Universal Design for Learning** (UDL) framework (CAST, 2011).

Much like designing spaces for equal access, curricula can be deliberately designed for full participation by all children and families. Three essential considerations drive universal design as applied to the curriculum development process: multiple means of representation, multiple means of expression, and multiple means of engagement (CAST, 2011; DEC, 2007; Stockall, Dennis, & Miller, 2012). These three considerations focus specifically on learning and on children's experiences of their learning environment.

- *Multiple means of representation:* This relates to how children gather and perceive information. All individuals access information and experiences differently based on personal background, processing styles, skills, and interests. This makes it essential that educators present information and content in different ways, (such as through hearing, seeing, or manipulating), at different levels of complexity, and in a variety of adjustable formats (print size, sound volume). Professionals plan for variation in questions, directions, expectations, and learning plans to acknowledge different abilities. The goal is to adjust learning opportunities to widen the access to content.

- *Multiple means of expression:* This relates to how children organize ideas and plan and perform tasks to express what they know. Just as children access information and experiences differently, they also process and demonstrate their knowledge and thinking in different formats, structures, and levels of complexity. It is important to plan for variety in how children can appropriately show what they know, feel, and wonder about. Among the wide array of options (such as written, spoken, and dramatic play, sociodramatic play, graphic arts, technology applications, and so forth), children should be given equally valued options and support in selecting choices. Keep in mind that some children may be more easily overwhelmed with too many choices and therefore can be offered a carefully selected smaller array. The goal is to offer and value many formats for children to share what they are thinking.

- *Multiple means of engagement:* This relates to how children get interested and actively involved in learning experiences. Just as children access and share information differently, they also have different interests and motivations, and get excited about different aspects of experiences. An important focus for professionals is to create and validate many options for capturing children's interests, curiosity, and preferences. Professionals provide and adjust challenges and supports as needed to capture and sustain engagement (scaffolding). The goal is to tap in to children's internal motivations and drives in order to maximize attention and involvement in learning experiences.

High quality inclusive programming for young children begins with intentional design to broadly promote access and meaningful participation for all children, but programs might also need to individualize through accommodations and modifications. **Accommodations** are adjustments, sometimes minor, to materials, schedules, routines, or formats of instruction and assessment that allow equal access and participation. **Modifications** are more involved alterations or alternatives to expectations of children, criteria for successful performance, assessment format, or instructional approach and level (DEC, 2007). Accommodations or modifications are based on individual children's strengths and needs and are developed and implemented in collaboration with program teams and families. Developing an overarching curriculum framework and individualizing for instruction and assessment are essential components of quality early childhood practice.

CURRICULUM AND ASSESSMENT CONSIDERATIONS

Well-designed early childhood programs knit together curriculum and assessment into one cyclical framework. *Curriculum* refers to the broad learning goals for children (in essence, the "what" that children will be doing) and should address all areas of development, as well as content area knowledge and skills. State and national learning standards are integrated into these overarching goals, though they are not the sole source of the curriculum (DEC, 2007). Many learning standards documents, such as the common core content standards, address the scope and sequence of key content coverage (English language arts and mathematics) but do not include comprehensive goals for foundational knowledge and skills or for all of the developmental domains (physical, socioemotional, cognitive). Thus, inclusive early childhood program curricula are designed to be comprehensive and adaptable: comprehensive to address all areas of development and learning, and adaptable to include all children. The curriculum plan outlines the ranges of learning and development outcomes as well as the sequence of developmental expectations and learning experiences needed to achieve the outcomes. It is especially important that curricula for young children be firmly rooted in authentic and engaging daily activities, routines, play, and nurturing relationships. These experiences are centered on children's interests and the context of their lives, both of which are essential elements of meaningful learning.

Assessment refers to the collection of evidence of children's progress and includes data on individual children and groups or entire programs. Assessment is systematic and ongoing, occurring at regular intervals throughout the course of children's learning. Sources of evidence might include observations, checklists, performance tests, work samples, reflection notes, photos, videos, notes and reports, or tests. Assessment evidence informs decisions about individual children's strengths, needs, and progress and also drives curricular decisions. Gathering assessment data allows professionals to evaluate children and program progress and tailor planning to ensure all children are meeting appropriate goals.

An important consideration in both curriculum planning and assessment is that accommodations and modifications be made as needed, based on individual children's diverse abilities. Adjusting the timing, format for responses, or outcomes based on children's strengths and needs does not undermine the program or assessment, but rather acknowledges the diverse ways that children learn and develop. In turn, knowledge of individual children's strengths and needs guides instructional approaches and decisions including:

- Type of interaction (child directed, adult or peer mediated, teacher directed)
- Material selection
- Schedule or pace of activities

CLASSROOM STORY CORNER

Family Partnerships for Lucien

Observing the kindergarten class during small group time and through the transition to lunch, it quickly became clear that Lucien's behavior was not in the same range as the other children. He moved around the room while all of the other children were sitting working on literacy activities in small groups. He would crawl under the table, lay sideways in his chair, push his book off the table, or just crawl under the easel in the corner and sit there. The teachers occasionally called him back to the table or redirected him to the task. Sometimes they ignored his behaviors. At the end of September, his teachers were hoping for more focus from him and shared their perspectives:

Lucien has to stay behind for a couple of minutes at the start of recess about twice a week to make up for refusing to listen to teachers or stay on task for more than a minute or two. He is a little younger than the other children here, but his issues are more about attention and that he has no prior structured learning experience. He was at a day care that didn't have an organized program, and so he really has no prior experience with a structured routine or organized academic learning. After a few months where we weren't able to improve his behavior, we became concerned about his learning progress falling behind.

I'm not really too worried when a child doesn't know all his letters, but more worried when he can't stay involved with a small group activity for 10 minutes. At first when we talked to his mom and began discussing having a specialist screen him, she was very resistant. I understand her concern about having a label follow him around through school. We wanted to remain collaborative and not alienate her, so we didn't push too hard. But we did invite her to observe and we took some video footage to help her understand just how his behavior was undermining his ability to get the full benefit from kindergarten. Once she saw him in comparison to the other children and could see what he was missing, she agreed to screening and then to accessing additional services. Lucien has a para[professional] come in the classroom every morning and helps keep him on task and explain tasks to him using specific prompts and cues. We have all designed and implemented a positive behavior support plan which includes positive reinforcement, specific verbal and visual cues, focused skill building on appropriate behavior, and practice sessions. It's only been a month, but we have all seen some real improvements in Lucien's ability to stay on task and interact productively with peers. I have also learned some good strategies from the team to use with Lucien and also the other children, which are proving helpful. Mom's been especially pleased and is now really involved with the team. It's definitely a success story.

- Multisensory formats (visual, auditory, body-kinesthetic)
- Frequency and type of reinforcement

From design to implementation and revision, inclusive curriculum and assessment is complex and labor intensive work. It demands a genuine, antibias attitude, sophisticated knowledge of universal and individual children's development, and awareness of broad resources, partnerships, and support networks. Careful, intentional design and reflective implementation increase children's positive outcomes, and embedded supports from the initial design phase make more effective use of limited resources. Challenging as it might be, this approach represents the best we can offer children and is well worth the effort in the end.

Curricular Connections

Aside from a fundamental belief that all children are valuable and capable members of the community, modifying and adapting programming is the core of supporting success for children with diverse abilities. Modifications might come in the design of the space, furniture arrangement, schedules, specialized materials, teaching approaches, communication modes, and individualized instructional support. Planning for differences and adaptations prior to implementing instruction is a key part of quality instruction, as described in this **video**. Effectively planning for differences results in a **differentiated classroom**, defined as (Hoover, 2011, p. 5):

With appropriate adaptations, supports, and equipment, families and professionals alike emphasize the importance of providing access for all children to high quality inclusive programs.

A classroom that contains structures and procedures designed to deal simultaneously with the variety of factors that students bring to the learning environment (e.g., varied preferences for learning, varied experiential backgrounds, cultural/linguistic diversity, range of reading levels, self-management abilities, time-on-task levels).

A key starting point in differentiated programming is that professionals begin relationships with children by carefully assessing children's development and performance to understand who each child is developmentally and academically, the family context, and how children learn and think about their world (Duhaney, 2003). Using assessment tools and methods to learn about each child is the first step in designing instruction and appropriate programming and should always be analyzed in the context of the child's life within his family, program setting, and community. Assessment methods designed to learn about children new to your program might include:

- Family visits and questionnaires
- Reviews of portfolio or files from previous programs
- Observations of children at play
- Listening to children's dialogue
- Observation of children completing typical tasks
- Analysis of children's functioning within different settings and during different tasks
- Developmental checklists

It is important to think about assessment as a cycle of three parts:

1. Initial assessment that guides programming decisions and instruction
2. Ongoing assessments that document children's developmental progress and inform next steps (formative)
3. Assessments at the end of key learning experiences or end of a school year that provide a big picture evaluation (summative) and lead to decision making for the next level

Appropriate, authentic assessment is a starting place, but it is also interwoven throughout the other curriculum connection areas below, as assessment information will also inform the goals and outcomes of adaptations.

A major benefit of exploring diverse instructional strategies is the potential benefit for all students, not just those with specific or identified differences. This is important for two reasons: a young child's learning needs might not be formally identified yet and high quality inclusive practice is about diversifying learning experiences and environments globally and individually. In other words, varying instructional strategies reaches diverse learners and maintains interest more effectively for all children, while personalizing for specific children meets unique needs. Designing a universally accessible curriculum and differentiating instruction is necessary for some children—and benefits all children (Dunn & Perez, 2012). It really is a win–win!

MATERIALS

The universal design framework provides an important lesson for modified materials that can benefit all users. The use of assistive technology and devices is an essential aspect of quality practice for children with diverse abilities who are not benefitting optimally from traditional materials.

IDEA legislation further acknowledges the importance of assistive technology by requiring professionals to integrate recommendations for assistive technology in children's Individualized Family Service Plans or Individualized Education Plans (IFSP or IEP). "Assistive technology embraces all devices and equipment that can help young children with disabilities to develop and use their skills to the best of their potential" (Judge, 2000, p. 125). Sometimes modifications or adjustments to materials are a simple process that professionals can complete themselves. Examples of simple adjustments include adding larger grips to handles or handheld tools (art, drawing, digging, eating, and so forth) or making picture boards to support communication. Examples of more complex, specialized equipment to support greater needs can include mobility equipment, communication devices, and computer programs.

ENVIRONMENT

Design and organization of the learning space must reflect the strengths and needs of the children to provide equitable access and optimal utilization. Be careful not to crowd the floor plan or walking pathways if children use mobility devices. If a child does have mobility differences, consider placing her desk or cubby close to the door or walkway.

Likewise be aware that children's attention and focus can be easily distracted by crowded walls or lots of visual stimulation around the space. Make deliberate choices about what and how many things are hung on walls or displayed on shelves. Some children might be easily overwhelmed with many items to choose from, so limiting toys and materials helps focus attention and target learning experiences. Placing children's desks or quiet area near the teacher's space can allow for closer supervision and fewer distractions. Using headphones is a simple strategy to reduce noise distraction for children who are more successful at focusing on a task when distractions are minimized. Headphones allow the child to be in control of auditory input without isolating the child from the group.

In general, children benefit from consistency in routines and schedules, though professionals should also adjust and allow for flexibility. While consistent routines provide stability, adjusting to maximize and support learning and play experiences also gives children an opportunity to develop flexibility and adaptability. But for some children the comfort of expectation, predictability, and routine is extremely important, and changes can prompt emotional outbursts and significant distress. Take care to let children know when changes are happening, emphasizing a new plan and sensitively coaching them on how to navigate their emotions through changes.

INTERACTIONS WITH CHILDREN

All children have a right to individualized instruction that can help them receive maximum benefit of the school or program experience. For children who are accessing additional supports through IDEA-related services, specific plans or adaptations can be implemented by you or additional staff. All children also have the right to confidentiality about any diagnoses or IEPs. Ethical practice requires that professionals maintain confidentiality appropriately and, when conversations about children's diverse abilities is legitimate, that professionals remain respectful of children and families. It is important to be careful in interactions with and around children to avoid labeling or otherwise classifying children by ability status.

Developing warm, caring relationships with children is an important first step in effective teaching. For children with challenges in maintaining attention, strong relationships with teachers often prompt more consistent and effective responses to behavior management cues, which also increases focus and productivity (Duhaney, 2003). Take time to learn about children's personal interests and the things that are important in their lives, and integrate activities that highlight personally meaningful topics and events into the classroom. Help children feel noticed and valued for who they are by:

- Learning children's names quickly and using them often
- Knowing names of children's close family members
- Noticing and celebrating positive meaningful events in children's lives
- Focusing on and emphasizing positive behaviors in all children, not just using a few "model" students
- Providing opportunities for children to share their strengths; purposefully integrating children's personal interests and strengths into the classroom (for example, if a child loves monster trucks, drawing comics, sports, music, horses, or a story character, find ways for him to share his passion in group learning experiences so he feels he has something legitimate and valuable to offer the group)
- Speaking to children on their level (face-to-face, using eye contact, smiling, using clear and understandable language, using a calm and even tone) to convey respect and awareness for who they are and what they know
- Listening patiently and with genuine interest to what children say and trying to understand what they mean when their words seem different than what they are trying to communicate
- Learning children's nonverbal communication cues (facial expressions, body posture, gestures) by watching carefully and using context cues such as environment, materials in use, others involved; for example, a child saying "eee-eee" might mean "I need to use the potty" if she is near the bathroom and tensing her body, or she might mean "Give me that" if gesturing to a nearby toy on the shelf

INTERACTIONS AMONG CHILDREN

Developing social skills and the ability to interact as a meaningful part of a group are key tasks of the early years. Being in a group of peers provides opportunities for children to manage and balance their own drives and needs against the needs and interests of others and to develop reciprocity and interaction skills. Positive social interaction, turn taking, reciprocal communication, and teamwork are all skills that are a part of successful learning in classroom settings. When children have difficulty developing productive, reciprocal, and prosocial interactions and relationships among peers, their learning and socioemotional development can suffer.

Teachers begin by cultivating and modeling warm, supportive relationships with all children and clearly conveying the expectation that children also treat each other respectfully. But more than just modeling, adults also need to provide clear examples of specific behaviors that convey respect and friendship. Saying "Be kind" is vague for young children. Instead, label specific attitudes and behaviors by saying things like "Taking turns is how we are fair" or "Asking someone to join your play is what friends do." When children are given interactive learning opportunities that promote engagement at a variety of levels and formats, they can participate in their own ways but still be a part of the group.

Children generally benefit from mixed-ability groups in which children's strengths and needs are both valued and supported. Ability grouping may be used infrequently and for specific experiences targeting developmental or instructional outcomes that can be enhanced through such grouping. However, ability grouping can be problematic for a number of reasons. Children often recognize the levels and develop insecurity about being in lower level groups. In addition, in homogeneous groups, children are not able to learn from more abled peers—or benefit from sharing their own strengths to clarify or guide their peers' learning process.

LEARNING EXPERIENCES

Current practices consider all children, regardless of developmental level or academic functioning, to be capable of learning and making significant progress towards learning goals and standards. Some discord exists in our field as to the appropriateness or viability of widely applied academic learning standards; these concerns emerge mostly out of concern for the essential role of play in young children's learning, the individual nature of development, and the varying abilities and needs of children. Professionals do agree, however, on the importance of supporting clear program and developmental goals and providing individualized and developmentally appropriate programming for all children.

To plan and support appropriate learning experiences, early childhood professionals rely on robust knowledge of typical and atypical developmental expectations and knowledge of individual children's capacities. Responsive instruction and programming always includes differentiation in terms of:

- Materials
- Instructional approaches
- Pacing of instruction

Differentiating is a key part of planning for children's learning and development and should include plans for children developing within a typical range and those who are below and above that level. Individualizing instruction adds another important layer to planning in which professionals systematically adjust learning experiences on an individual basis. While each child will have unique strengths, needs, and preferences related to learning, examples of broad categories of developmental and learning differences and examples of considerations and instructional strategies are included in Table 9.2.

TABLE 9.2   *Diverse Abilities Instructional Strategies*

Diverse Ability Area	Instructional Strategies and Considerations	What Children Can Learn About This Diversity
Attention and focus on learning tasks	• Integrate opportunities for focused physical movement in lessons, transitions, and throughout the day to expend excess energy. • Minimize loud background noise and environmental distractions. • Provide cues and supports to organize information, directions, and task steps (graphic organizers, planners, step sequence cards).	• Sometimes a person's body is busier and needs to move. • Sometimes a person's brain notices more things at one time. • People organize information in different ways.
Cognitive and intellectual development	• Selecting a variety of books and materials at different complexity levels on the same topic allows all children to explore the same topic together. • Give instructions and direction using varied level of vocabulary and steps.	• People think about things in different ways. • People finish tasks at their own pace or in their own time.
Speech, language, and communication	• Use simple, clear directions. • Speak in an adequate tone of voice and articulate clearly. • When available, use a voice amplification/distribution device. • Provide visual and auditory cues and directions (signs, symbols, verbal cues). • Model patient active listening and teach children to wait for others to finish speaking.	• Some people listen with just their ears and other people listen with their ears and a small device. • Some people communicate with words and other people use their hands, gestures, written notes, or a machine that talks for them. • People speak different languages.
Emotional or psychological functioning	• Maintain a calm voice and demeanor. • Use calming redirection cues (e.g., "Let's take a breath and work out a solution together.") • Provide a safe spot in the room for expressing strong emotions. • Offer materials for safely expressing physical aggression such as handheld squish balls, clay or dough for squeezing or punching, or exercise bands for stretching.	• Everyone has a range of feelings. • We all have different ways of expressing feelings. • Sometimes we need help to express our feelings safely.

(Continued)

TABLE 9.2 *(Continued)*

Diverse Ability Area	Instructional Strategies and Considerations	What Children Can Learn About This Diversity
Physical and motor functioning	• Ensure access to and around in the environment (ramps, lifts, bar-style door handles, open pathways). • Arrange desks or tables to allow ease of flow among activities (with children using mobility support positioned on a clear pathway). • Use hook and loop tape, magnets, and rubber grippers on materials to support coordination. • Reconsider rules or expectations such as "Raise your hand to speak"; consider an alternative cue to request attention.	• People's bodies move in different ways. • Many people move around in the environment using just their body and many other people move around using their body and a device or equipment to support a part of their body.
Health condition	• Know the physical limitations the condition imposes on the child; for example, what activity level is too strenuous. • Be aware of cues of limitations such as shortness of breath, flush, posture changes, onset of seizure, and so forth. • Provide a quiet or small, semiprivate space if children need rest or medication administration if a nurse's room is not available. • Maintain close communications with families to ensure updates on children's health.	• Sometimes a part of a person's body needs medicine or extra support to work properly. • Everyone's body gets a little sick now and then; sometimes a person's body takes longer to get well. • Health conditions (such as those listed under IDEA) are not contagious and you cannot get sick from playing with our friend.
Social skills and interactions	• Provide structured opportunities for dyad or small group interactions. • Coach children on specific steps for social interaction. • Use simple picture cues and directions for social exchanges. • Practice social interactions in structured learning experiences. • Provide the child with self-talk prompts to cue herself (for example: "First I ask if I can join the group. I make eye contact. Then I wait for a response."). • Practice with children responses for when inappropriate social exchanges occur (for example: "We keep our hands to ourselves," or "I don't like it when you call me names like that.")	• Some people prefer small quiet groups or working alone sometimes. • Some children are learning how to play and work together appropriately. • We can all help each other follow the rules of our classroom community by using clear and friendly reminders.

An additional consideration, which continues to emphasize the social justice approach to teaching, is to be open with children about the many ways that we all differ in thinking, physical appearance and functioning, emotional processes and expressions, and communicating. On the one hand it is important to protect children's privacy and confidentiality, but it is also important to cultivate a supportive, caring community who recognize and appreciate that each one of us has shared and different experiences. Children notice differences, and when we try to ignore them (even in the name of privacy), we run the risk that children will fill in gaps from our silence with misconceptions. Children often think that people with illness or chronic health conditions are always contagious or always going to get progressively more sick or even die. Children may assume that people who speak sign language don't think the same way as other people or don't have understandable ideas to share.

Family Partnerships

All early childhood practice requires a heavy emphasis on family connections and collaborations. Families with children who are developing outside of the typical range are especially important partners in their child's growth, development, and learning. Young children's development is influenced most strongly by their family context and the communities in which they live. Successful programming for any child requires reciprocal relationships with families. As the child's first teacher, the family holds a wealth of information and resources to guide and support children's development in settings outside the home.

Not only is working collaboratively with families a hallmark of quality practice, it is also required by IDEA legislation, advocated by major professional organizations, and integrated into most program policies. Families must be knowledgeable and active decision makers in children's learning plans and supporting services. It is so important for professionals to always remember and be sensitive to the complex and, at times, overwhelming position families are in when they navigate complicated systems and paperwork. Listen to this interdisciplinary team and family discuss the importance of building parent trust in this **video**.

An important first consideration in partnering with families is to ensure that communications, reports, and assessment data are framed in format, terms, and language that are understandable to family members. If they are to be major decision makers in forming learning plans for their children, family members need to be appropriately informed and supported in understanding the context of children's learning and the process of goal-setting.

Building strong relationships with families begins with professional teams seeking family input and carefully listening to family perspectives, goals, and expectations for their children. Key steps in relationship building include:

- Inviting families into the program or school setting to become familiar and comfortable with these contexts
- When possible, completing a home visit to connect with families in their familiar, comfortable surroundings

- Encouraging families to share stories involving their child
- Sharing positive program and school experiences; if you have concerns, be sure to share these in between positive reflections, to begin and end on a positive note
- Affirm with families that your role is to support children *and* families as an entwined unit
- Integrate family photos, stories, and artifacts from children's homes into the classroom environment and curriculum
- Provide opportunities for families to participate in program events and in the classroom with children

As with the principles of the Universal Design for Learning, all children benefit from strong family–program partnerships. However, for children with diverse abilities or particular needs, these partnerships are especially important for optimizing children's outcomes.

Summary

EARLY CHILDHOOD INCLUSION

- Inclusive practices are those that are intentionally designed to appropriately and meaningfully engage all children to their fullest potential within the same learning environment and care setting.
- Inclusive practices involve making adjustments or adaptations to physical or temporal (schedule) environments, materials, and interaction approaches in order to diversify instruction and interactions with children.

UNDERSTANDING *DIVERSE ABILITIES*: SOCIAL AND LEGAL CONTEXT

- *Diverse abilities* is a term used to more inclusively describe all people and to represent the ways in which each of us has different strengths and needs.

- Widely used frameworks of development that identify normal or typical ranges and, comparatively, abnormal or atypical development, are both useful and troubling.
- Developmental milestones and broadly applied expectations help us understand how children will grow and develop and allow us to design appropriate settings and learning experiences.
- Developmental expectations have also been used to marginalize or exclude some children who are not "keeping up" with expectations.
- Until advocacy efforts and federal legislation began to assert rights for children and adults with disabilities in the 1960s, exclusionary policies and practices were common.
- Over several decades and evolutions, the Individuals with Disabilities Education Act (IDEA) has become a major force in guiding and funding programming specifically tailored

to meet the needs of children with a variety of defined disabilities.

- IDEA calls for access to free and public education for all children, regardless of ability status.

THE EDUCATIONAL CONTEXT OF *DIVERSE ABILITIES* OR *EXCEPTIONALITIES*

- Assessing and labeling children's diverse abilities as exceptional in some way is a relative evaluation: a child's functioning is evaluated in comparison to expectations of learning and development based on a range which is considered normal or typical.
- The IDEA uses the term *child with a disability* to describe or label an infant, child, or youth whose functioning in certain area(s) is below expectation; the term is used as a cue to access services and supports.
- The IDEA includes 13 separate categories of conditions that classify a child as having a disability when two key conditions exist: first, the child's educational performance is adversely affected or negatively impacted by one or more of these conditions, and second, the child needs special education and services due to his diagnosed condition.
- The process through which a diagnosis is made and a label identified is often initiated by early childhood professionals or parents who observe behaviors that seem outside of an expected range for typical development.
- Assessment of children, prompted by concern for their developmental progress, relies heavily on observations of children in natural settings and engaged in daily routines, activities, and play.

GUIDELINES FOR INCLUSIVE PRACTICE FROM THE DIVISION FOR EARLY CHILDHOOD

- The joint statement between the Division for Early Childhood of the Council for Exceptional Children and the National Association for the Education of Young Children (DEC/NAEYC, 2009) outlines recommendations for curriculum, assessment, and program evaluation in inclusive programs serving young children and advocates using strategies from the Universal Design for Learning framework.
- Inclusive early childhood program curricula are designed to be comprehensive and adaptable: comprehensive to address all areas of development and learning, and adaptable to include all children.
- Assessment evidence informs decisions about individual children's strengths, needs, and progress and also drives curricular decisions.

CURRICULAR CONNECTIONS

- Using assessment tools and methods to learn about each child is the first step in designing instruction and appropriate programming and should always be analyzed in the context of the child's life within their family, program setting, and community.
- Designing a universally accessible curriculum and differentiating instruction is necessary for some children and benefits all children.
- For children who are accessing additional supports through IDEA-related services, there may be specific plans or adaptations implemented by you or additional staff.
- Current practices consider all children, regardless of specific developmental level or academic functioning, to be capable of learning and making significant progress towards learning goals and standards.
- Responsive instruction and programming always includes differentiation in terms of materials, instructional approaches and pacing of instruction.

FAMILY PARTNERSHIPS

- As the child's first teacher, the family holds a wealth of information and resources to guide and support children's development in settings outside the home.

- Working collaboratively with families is not only a hallmark of quality practice; it is also required by IDEA legislation, advocated by major professional organizations, and integrated into most program policies.

- Building strong relationships with families begins with professional teams seeking family input and carefully listening to family perspectives, goals, and expectations for their children.

Chapter Learning Outcomes: Self-Assessment

Use this space to reflect on how well you have achieved the learning goals for this chapter by evaluating your own competency in the topics below. List three to five items that describe key concepts you have learned from the chapter.

Define early childhood inclusion.	
Explain concepts of ability and disability in a historical and social context.	
Describe categories and assessment of differences in ability.	
Discuss the responsibilities of professionals in meeting all children's needs in program and school settings.	
Practice inclusive teaching strategies which support children with diverse abilities.	
Create partnerships with families of children with diverse abilities.	

Chapter Activities

DISCUSSION QUESTIONS

1. Some professionals working in schools today talk about seeing "exclusion in the inclusive classroom"—where children with diverse abilities are combined in one classroom but their unique needs and strengths are not addressed or accommodated. In essence, children are placed in the general education classroom but are not meaningfully included. Discuss the complexities of meaningful inclusion and identify examples that might represent what professionals call "exclusion in the inclusive classroom."

2. In small groups, identify several issues involved in the assessment and labeling of a child with a specific disability (use the IDEA categories or another framework). Consider the implications of labeling from a variety of perspectives.

SELF-REFLECTION

Thinking back on your own years in K–12 schools, do you recall noticing students with diverse abilities or were you aware of special education classrooms or programs? How were ability differences or special needs handled in your schools?

TEACHING DISPOSITION

1. Imagine you are the parent of a child who has just entered kindergarten. After two months of school you child's teacher calls a conference in which he tells you that your child is behind the other children in academic skills and lagging behind district standards. You sit, somewhat stunned, while he tells you that he really thinks you should approve the request to have your

child screened for special education services. Discuss with a classmate how you imagine you would be feeling about this meeting and your thoughts about screening and labeling.

2. Inclusive, responsive practice is challenging and complex. List five major concerns you have or challenges you anticipate facing and list two or three possible sources of support or resources to assist you.

IN THE FIELD

Using websites, phone books, or school district information sources, create an annotated resources list of at least eight community agencies in your area that provide services for children with diverse abilities or special needs. Consider health and medical, educational, social, and family support programs to create a broad base of resources to support your practice.

Weblinks

The Division for Early Childhood of The Council for Exceptional Children (DEC): An international membership organization for those who work with or on behalf of young children with disabilities and other special needs. *www.dec-sped.org*

The Early Childhood Technical Assistance Center provides resources and supports to improve state early intervention and early childhood special education service systems, increase the implementation of effective practices, and enhance the outcomes of these programs for young children and their families. *http://www.ectacenter.org*

10

Supporting Individual Learners

Developing a solid knowledge of the many facets of human diversity is an important first step toward becoming a culturally competent professional. This exploration must also include awareness of terms and frameworks for creating differentiated experiences that engage all learners and reflect cultural, intellectual, and learner diversity. We all interpret our world and experiences in different ways. Sometimes our perceptions and interpretations are impacted by our background of experiences and influences. Sometimes our processing, learning, and representing of ideas is heavily influenced by the particular ways we think about things in our world. Understanding differences in learning and thinking styles and approaches is essential for focusing on appropriately guiding children's perception and learning. This chapter presents frameworks of thinking and learning styles, with connections to how diversified practice ensures equity in early

Validating and supporting multiple ways of thinking, learning, and representing ideas is a key part of ensuring all children have opportunities for meaningful learning.

childhood education. Equity in teaching includes using effective practices to diversify educational settings and differentiate instruction to reflect children's differences culturally and as learners.

Differences in Learning Styles

Ensuring learning success for children in child care and classroom settings requires that professionals be intentional and deliberate in all decisions and interactions with and for children and families. In order to optimize development and maximize each child's potential, we have to understand the varied processes of learning and how teaching can support them. A key component of this knowledge is to become familiar with theories and models of different ways people think or process information, and to recognize how individuals differ in learning tasks. One approach to developing this knowledge is to explore the key ideas involved in theories of diverse learning styles, while emphasizing that many styles will be represented in any given group of learners (Nilson, 2010). Understanding learning and thinking styles is key to developing differentiated instruction practices to ensure success for all children.

Learning style refers to ways in which individuals learn new material, and it encompasses thinking, emotional, and psychological behaviors that impact how a person takes in, engages with, and responds to learning experiences and environments (Felder & Brent, 2005). Multiple intelligence theory is an evolving framework that describes nine different ways that people take in, process, and use information and experiences within their cultural context (Gardner, 2006). These theories relate to how we learn and demonstrate new knowledge and skills as well as how we internalize habits and approaches to learning. Think about how the 1st grade teacher in this **video** is providing a variety of ways to think about and share information.

There are literally dozens of theories and models with an even larger array of products centered around assessing student learning style for the purpose of tailoring instruction for individual students (Litzinger, Lee, Wise, & Felder, 2007). However, with limited time and resources, becoming familiar with the concepts of thinking style can help focus professionals on diversifying their practice, not on assessing children's style and narrowing instruction to one style preference (Pashler, McDaniel, Rohrer, & Bjork, 2009).

Before you begin teaching others, learning about different thinking styles is all about you. The study of learning styles is generally best used as a means of assessing your own processing style to focus your efforts on balancing your styles (Nilson, 2010). Your preferences or style will impact how you interact with others and how you teach. Among educators there is a popular phrase used as something of a warning to teacher education students: "Who you are is how you teach." This isn't necessarily a problem unless you have strong biases—in any of the aspects of diversity we have explored in this text—of which you are not aware and are not balancing in your professional work.

CLASSROOM STORY CORNER

Ati's Story

I have a love–hate relationship with August. Well, OK. Not quite hate, but high stress anyway. Every August I recreate my first letter home to the families of the children in my new class. It's my favorite time because I am excited to begin making relationships, but also stressful because I know there is so much I have to learn about them. And after all these years, I know one thing for sure: there will be an incredible array of differences among my new group. Even if they sometimes appear to be similar at first glance, the differences among us are always stunning!

My first correspondence home has a lot to cover but a singular focus: I need my families to know where I stand on our differences and our shared connections, and also what I expect from them along the same lines. So I always begin the year with a welcome letter. But it's not a shallow "Hi, we're going to have a great year, don't forget to pack extra clothes" kind of welcome letter. This is my big chance to welcome the families into a journey that will be deeply complex, sometimes confusing, awakening and revealing, and almost certainly into new territory. It's an invitation to journey into responsive, culturally competent, inclusive, intentionally diversified practice—and it's usually all new to them. It's a lot to take on in one August letter. But without that first moment of explanation, invitation, and advocacy, my whole year wouldn't make sense.

I always start my letter by welcoming them on the journey with me and assuring them that what we will learn will be lessons for life, not just for 1st grade. Set against the context of an increasingly complex and diverse world, I emphasize my values of promoting acceptance and appreciation for each and every one of the families as skills children will need to be successful in tomorrow's world. I talk about how "family" includes children and the people they live with but also people near and far who are important and influential to them. I point out many of the ways we all differ in our looks, language, habits, beliefs, behaviors, resources, and strengths, and how finding similarities makes us a community. I share a story about how I felt when I had been excluded and rejected because of how I was different, and the far-reaching impact even one moment of that can have on a child. And then I begin my statement of how our year will be spent developing

- Awareness of each other's strengths
- Compassion for differing needs (we all have them!)
- Celebration of our uniqueness
- Appreciation for our similarities
- Resiliency in the face of challenge
- The ability to engage collaboratively in a diverse group

I make it clear that each person in our newly forming class community, which includes families and friends, is an equal member and has a right to be treated with fairness and kindness. I define what equity means to me. To accomplish this I let my families know that my curriculum will not include emphasis on any one culture's beliefs, ideas, or practices but will reflect both children's lives and the larger world around us. And I let them know that we all will strive towards the same goals but reach them from different paths (different learning styles, languages, and ability levels). I explain that this means that the materials, learning activities, assessments, and events in our class are deliberately selected to reflect and enrich each of us. At some point in each day we will be hands-on and messy, reading alone and out loud, using tools and instruments to measure and experiment, making and watching videos, and drawing things we've learned. I end my letter by posing to them the challenge and invitation to be my partner in giving our children this transformative, character-shaping experience.

I am sure there are more than a few families over the years who have thought about moving their kids out of my class at that moment. Ha! But you know what? I back up the spirit of that letter every day in the classroom and in my daily outreach with families. I include families in my regular assessments of children's progress, and every two months I share updated reports that include a profile of how I see their children preferring to learn. They might have doubts that August day they get my letter, but by October they know what an incredible thing this is for their children. My partnerships with them are as meaningful to me as my relationships with the children. And I wouldn't change a bit of that stressful August policy-writing experience. That is the moment that defines me as an educator.

Being a strongly verbal thinker and teaching using mostly whole group discussion will inevitably leave most of your children unengaged and frustrated (Felder & Henriques, 1995). You certainly will have excluded Dual language learners and children with some auditory or social processing challenges. Teaching only in your preferences or strengths will result in narrow, ineffective instruction (Felder, 2010). Even with the best intentions to be an effective professional, you may fall into this narrow focus if you are not aware of how preferences impact thinking, learning, and responding to our world.

With the array of differences in learning and thinking, just as with the many ways that people differ culturally, you must be able to diversify and adjust your approaches to reach all children. Through this lens, the goal of cultural competence encompasses knowledge of diverse thinking styles as well as individual cultural background, which you then build on to modify your instructional approaches to reach all kinds of learners. The process of tailoring instruction and interaction approaches to different learning styles and diverse backgrounds is called **differentiation** (Tomlinson & McTighe, 2006). The essential core requirement of successfully differentiating in meaningful ways and to truly engage learners is that professionals must know children well (Ginsberg, 2005). Knowing children begins with our exploration of human diversity and the accompanying, honest self-awareness, and continues with a deliberate effort to learn about each child we work with.

A brief overview of two models of learning and thinking is presented here, along with examples of differentiating practice with young children. The goal of this overview is to encourage you to think broadly about the many ways children experience and learn about their world. While the assessment instruments, which are paired with many theories and models, have not

Providing opportunities for children to work in groups and alone is one way to support different styles and intelligences through classroom design.

yet demonstrated strong validity and reliability, and their use as a screening tool with children isn't universally accepted as a good use of instructional time, The Felder-Silverman Index of Learning Styles test stands out with good reliability and validity, making it one of the stronger models (Felder & Spurlin, 2005; Litzinger, Lee, Wise, & Felder, 2007; Nilson, 2010). As demonstrated by the self-tests you will take after the overviews, learning style preferences and the eight multiple intelligences are present in each of us but vary in strength and in the ways the preferences impact our behaviors.

THE FELDER-SILVERMAN MODEL OF LEARNING STYLES

A popular framework for understanding thinking processes in the learning environment is the concept of individual learning styles. Learning styles have been characterized as the ways that we process experiences and integrate them into our knowledge base (Cuthbert, 2005; Felder & Brent, 2005; Kolb, 1984). Definitions of learning styles often include broad categories of thinking, such as *concrete* or *abstract*, and categorizing perception and processing in modalities such as *visual*, *auditory*, *verbal*, or *tactile/kinesthetic*. While the Felder-Silverman Model was designed for and is most researched with engineering students, it translates well into any educational setting. The model builds on earlier theories and models and classifies learners' preferences in four areas, plotting preference along a spectrum in each category (Felder, 1996). Four key questions drive decisions about how learners are placed in each category, as outlined in Table 10.1 (Felder, 2005; Felder & Henriques, 1995).

TABLE 10.1 *Felder-Silverman Model of Learning Styles*

Key question used to categorize learning style	Dimensions of learning style categories	Descriptions of learner behaviors based on categories
1. What is the preferred way of perceiving information?	Sensory	Attends more to facts and hands-on procedures; attuned to lights, sounds, and tactile sensations; methodical and concrete in problem solving.
	Intuitive	Tuned in to insights, memories, and broad ideas; innovative problem solvers; comfortable with abstract concepts and theories.

Key question used to categorize learning style	Dimensions of learning style categories	Descriptions of learner behaviors based on categories
2. Which modality is preferred for sensory information?	Visual	More easily understands drawings, diagrams, pictures, charts, and graphs.
	Verbal	Able to process written and spoken information more readily.
3. How does the learner prefer to process information?	Active	Prefers to engage with information through hands-on or physical activity or active discussion.
	Reflective	Prefers to think introspectively about information before acting or making decisions.
4. How does the learner move towards understanding information?	Sequential	Thinks in small, logical, incremental steps; thinking progresses in linear way.
	Global	Thinks in holistic "big picture" ways; uses a systems approach to thinking; prefers to understand how new information connects to existing knowledge.

Understanding Sensory/Intuitive Learning

The sensory/intuitive category builds on decades of work by Jung and echoes the categories of the popular Myers-Briggs Type Indicator (MBTI) personality test (Felder & Henriques, 1995). Sensory perceivers patiently focus on details and are frustrated with complications or ambiguous rules. These children take time and may be slow to complete tasks, but they attend to details, are more comfortable memorizing facts, and readily apply structured procedures to solve problems. They respond best when information and learning experiences are connected to authentic applications and examples are used to make abstract ideas concrete. Intuitive learners are more motivated by discovering through innovation, exploring theories, and using imaginative and abstract thinking. Intuitive learners dislike repetition and strict rules and tend to complete tasks more quickly, though with less attention to detail and potentially more errors.

Differentiating Early childhood professionals need to recognize that these children are internally motivated to respond differently to more or less structure, rules, and expectations of attention to detail. Balancing your approach may involve providing time for some children to attend to details in their work and cueing them to notice the whole, while providing more scaffolding and cues to engage other children in taking time to focus on parts and details. Provide specific real-world examples along with a big picture view, making connections to sequences in learning. All children benefit from being provided with the context of learning experiences, so tell children the purpose or goals before, during, and at the completion of learning experiences.

Understanding Visual/Verbal Learning

The visual/verbal category is similar to many other theories of learning that emphasize different modalities that learners use to take in and process information. A distinction in Felder-Silverman's model is that visual/verbal and tactile/kinesthetic are separated into different categories and measured separately (Felder & Henriques, 1995). The visual/verbal category is probably the most easily understood and familiar. Visual learners understand and remember new information when it is presented in graphic form through charts, graphs, diagrams, time lines, and in video or demonstrations. Verbal learners better process and remember new information when it is shared in spoken or written words. Among children who are still developing formal reading skills, verbal preference centers on spoken words and directions.

Differentiating Pairing picture cues with words (like photos with labels or schedules) gives all children additional support as they learn conventional literacy skills and is especially powerful to connect both modalities. Color-coding written text and circling key phases, focusing on context cues in story illustrations, and selecting more visually rich materials (such as children's magazines and high quality picture books) help connect visual and written text. Use graphic organizers (for example, concept webs or Venn diagrams) to provide visual structure for information. An important point for early childhood educators to remember is that quality of interactions among members of the learning community, among both adults and children, is one of the most powerful predictors of children's outcomes. Specifically, all children benefit most from verbal interactions that are characterized by:

- Attentive listening and responses that extend dialogue (longer exchanges)

- Adult modeling of increasingly complex and novel vocabulary
- Authentic, natural conversations that convey interest and caring
- Open ended questions and critical thinking prompts
- Extending children's comments to build on ideas and expand vocabulary
- Patient conversational partners who give children time to think as they speak (don't jump in and finish sentences for children or talk through pauses)

Understanding Active/Reflective Learning

This category aligns closely with Kolb's (1984) groundbreaking work in learning styles as well as with the introvert–extrovert category of the MBTI, and relates to kinesthetic descriptions (Felder & Spurlin, 2005). While all children are naturally active and hands-on learners, some children need more time to think about things and work alone. Active learners are most engaged when they are able to either physically do something to experiment with, act out, or dialogue with others about new ideas. They prefer to try out ideas and materials to learn about them, and gravitate towards group activities that allow for active exploration and problem solving. Reflective learners prefer to think about information before engaging, thinking through problem solving strategies prior to beginning, and are most comfortable processing new information and experiences initially alone, or introspectively.

Differentiating Balanced instruction does not necessarily mean evenly divided among different strategies, and this category is a prime example (Felder, 2010). Equally dividing instructional time with young children into half active, social learning opportunities and half quiet individual tasks would not appropriately reflect *both* individual learning styles and who young children are developmentally. Instead, the balance will always be more heavily active, hands-on, social learning experiences interspersed with meaningfully planned time for individual reflection and thinking. Even the small effort of pausing for more than a few seconds after posing a question to children and telling them to "think about that for a few moments before you respond" and then letting them make a sign that they are ready to share an idea (hand up, finger on nose, hands on shoulders, etc.) helps give "think time" to reflective learners, but also encourages all children to think. Using a "think-pair-share" structure for individual-small group-whole group reflection and discussion is another effective way to reach children along this spectrum of preference. This weighted balance of more active experiences with some reflective experiences responds to children's naturally active state, but also encourages development of the skill of thinking things through.

Understanding Sequential/Global Learning

This category is about the process the learner uses to develop meaningful understanding of new concepts. At one end of the spectrum the learner strings together details in a logical progression to form overarching ideas. At the other end, the learner's understanding of the main ideas evolves in big jumps (the big picture perspective), and she needs to understand connections and relationships to be able to understand supporting details (Felder & Brent, 2005). Sequential learners are able to easily follow strings of ideas in logical order to work their way through solving problems or building understanding. However, lacking a clear sense of the overarching context of their learning can impact their ability to consistently and appropriately use new information. Global learners more easily see ultimate goals or solutions, though they might not be able to fill in all of the steps that lead to the solution. This can pose challenges for their ability to repeat or replicate results.

Differentiating All children, especially global learners, benefit from learning experiences that are contextualized and clearly connected to other content, learning experiences, and daily life. Equally, all children, especially sequential learners, benefit from cohesively designed learning content that logically builds on prior knowledge and creates a foundation for future learning (Voltz, 2003). Consider using an expanded KWHL+ chart to contextualize and outline a sequence for learning. (KWHL+ stands for: **K**now, **W**ant to know, **H**ow to find out, **L**earned, and **more [+]** to learn.) A KWHL+ is created as a group at the start of a topic where learners collaboratively identify:

What do we already Know (prior knowledge)?	What do we Want to know more about?	How can we explore our questions?	What have we Learned?	What + (more) do we want to learn next?
Children fill in these sections before, during, and at closing of a topic of study.				

To further support connections, state and restate the purpose for learning experiences at the beginning, middle, and end of lessons, and refer back to the KWHL+ chart frequently. Helping children see connections between content and learning experiences and understand the purpose of their learning supports understanding for children along the sequential/global spectrum (Felder, 1996) and is good practice for all children.

Learning and Representing Through Multiple Intelligences

Historically, much of school experiences and expectations revolved around ability to think and learn through linguistic and mathematical processes. Reading, writing, computing numerically, and organizing information logically still make up the majority of the school day. Concerned by the experiences of children who demonstrated keen thinking and strong competencies in other areas but who struggle or were labeled as "failing" in school, Howard Gardner researched and developed a broader framework for considering the many ways people are smart. While his work was fueled by an interest in how people exhibit strength and competency in different ways, his framework was about more than talent or special skill. Specifically, he focused on creative problem solving and the mental processes individuals engaged in as they solved authentic and complex problems (Gardner, 2006). How people experience their world, the frames they use to structure their thinking, and the strategies and methods they use to solve problems are driven by individual intelligence(s).

Gardner has defined eight distinct intelligence areas, although the theory is flexible and evolving, with additional intelligence areas currently under review and research. Gardner's current list of intelligence types are summarized in Table 10.2 (Gardner, 2006).

In Gardner's work you can see some parallels to the learning styles theories in terms of general definitions of categories (though there are

All children benefit from active, hands-on learning experiences, but for children who are particularly tactile or kinesthetic learners, these experiences are essential for learning abstract concepts.

TABLE 10.2 *Summary of Gardner's Multiple Intelligences*

Intelligence type	Characteristics of this intelligence in action
Verbal/linguistic (word smart)	Well-developed language skills and a sensitivity to the sound, meaning, and rhythm of words
	Listens, speaks, reads, or writes as preferred ways to process experiences
Differentiating	Use words to understand and express ideas, such as by talking through problem solving steps or creating word cues or rhymes.
	Children with communication delays in one or more language area might have strengths in another and still be a strong verbal/linguistic thinker.
	Verbal thinkers might need to talk through problems to understand complex concepts (think-pair-share, turn-and-talk, or listen-discuss-decide can be helpful).
Logical/mathematical (number smart)	Ability to think abstractly in concepts and to discern numerical patterns
	Orderly, sequential ways of thinking about problems and knowledge of how objects function (physics)
Differentiating	Organize materials and information into orderly patterns or linear sequence.
	Dual language learners benefit from opportunities to understand and express ideas through charts, graphs, or numeracy processes.
	Integrate use of flow charts, graphic organizers, and diagrams in learning and representing new content or concepts.
Musical (music smart)	Appreciation for or the ability to produce rhythm, pitch, and tone quality
	Songs, rhymes, or rap are vehicles for interpreting and remembering information
Differentiating	Intentional music selection can be used to impact emotions and mood or guide physical activities and might be particularly useful for children with challenges regulating emotions or coordination.
	Music is deeply connected to cultural roots and used as a way to create shared identity and connect particular cultural communities; for example, in the unique styles characteristic of music from different parts of the world (popular Bollywood music and videos from India, rhythmic African drum compositions, Mexican Mariachi folk) to distinct styles more popular in regions of the U.S. (Appalachian string groups, highly rhythmic urban hip hop or rap).
	Vibrations made by music recordings or instruments provide an opportunity to feel rhythm for children with hearing impairments (touching a drum as it's struck or holding a balloon near a source of sound).

Intelligence type	Characteristics of this intelligence in action
Visual/spatial (art smart)	Thinking in pictures or images or the ability to visualize abstractly Awareness of how one's self and the physical world are oriented in the surrounding spatial environment Individuals often create mental pictures or imagery while listening; what might seem like staring off into space or doodling might actually be creating important visual cues to process information
Differentiating	Use graphic representations such as charts, graphs, and pictures to help children understand, remember, and express ideas. Children with organizational focusing or detail recall challenges can benefit from graphic organizers and charts as a structure to focus thinking. Dual language learners and all young children who are developing formal literacy skills can benefit from graphic and picture cues such as picture labels on shelves or schedules. Children with a variety of communication challenges can successfully share ideas through picture boards or card rings (a set of sturdy or laminated mats or cards with pictures of relevant items like blocks, coats; Images for common activities such as drinking, using the bathroom, playing outside, going home; and emotional states like feelings, wanting to be alone or join a group, or tired).
Body/kinesthetic (body smart)	Ability to use and control one's movement, or a sensitivity to handling and manipulating objects Use of information gathered from their fingertips, by hands-on learners, to identify, classify, or recognize materials; might use movement or dance to represent and express ideas More attuned, as kinesthetic learners, to the physical environment and sensitive to stimuli around them
Differentiating	Integrate manipulatives in all learning experiences across content areas to support the active, hands-on nature of all young children. Offer small hand-held squish balls or stretch a large rubber band around a child's leg and the chair leg to allow for tactile stimulation. Offer frequent movement breaks during seat work sessions to allow children to stretch and move their bodies (games like Simon Says maintain focus while allowing for movement). Use body movements related to content, such as charades-style gestures to pantomime land forms (one hand in a fist and the other circling it in wave motions for island and water) and parts of speech (pump arms for verbs/action words or put hands overhead to make a pointy roof for noun/place). Use textured paint on handouts or diagrams or sandpaper cutouts (like sandpaper letters and numbers) to allow fingertips to feel the drawings and shapes.

(Continued)

TABLE 10.2 *(Continued)*

Intelligence type	Characteristics of this intelligence in action
Interpersonal (we/people smart)	Awareness and sensitivity to the moods and motivations of other people
	Comfortable interaction in groups, attuned to the moods and desires of the people around them, naturally capable of influencing peers
	Interested in social interactions and engaging with others; socio-dramatic play a particular favorite activity
Differentiating	Give time to interact with peers in order to process and think about learning experiences; in other words, they may "talk it out" with others to clarify their learning.
	Support children's social leadership skills by offering peer leader roles and opportunities for children to guide and teach.
Intrapersonal (me smart)	Self-awareness and a connection with one's own feelings and thought processes
	Awareness of goals and internal motivation
	Takes in information and experiences and processes internally
Differentiating	Give time to think, reflect, and internally work out problems before representing ideas (through verbal, visual, or interpersonal means).
	Include time to plan, set goals, and reflect, or to journal about experiences individually.
	Connect learning experiences to emotional states or moods to link internal states with learning.
Naturalist (nature smart)	Appreciation and ability for recognizing, sorting objects in nature
	Interest in life cycles and patterns in nature
	Strong capacity to identify species categories and attribute classifications of natural plants, minerals, and animals
Differentiating	Encourage the process of scientific inquiry to engage with learning experiences and materials (observe, predict, pose questions, test, observe, reflect).
	Support classification activities to work through problems (of any sort, not just related to natural materials or phenomena).

more defined here) and the emphasis on different processing modalities. For example, compare the active/reflective category in the Felder-Silverman Model with the kinesthetic and interpersonal/intrapersonal intelligences in Gardner's theory. Note that all of the descriptions include similar terms and behaviors. Despite some differences in configurations, most theories of learning and thinking styles include more similarities than differences, reflecting some of the universal behaviors that we exhibit as learners.

CLASSROOM STORY CORNER

Making it Work

After my welcome letter with my explanation of what teaching for social justice means to me goes home, I spend the first few months of the year using get-to-know-you topics as the frame for our curriculum. Like everyone else, I feel the pressure to keep on track with my district's curriculum expectations. But I have worked really hard to focus my children's learning on making meaningful connections to each other and still acquiring essential knowledge and skills. These relationships are so important to building awareness and appreciation for diversity, and it really does work to meet standards too! We begin with a few weeks of an All About Me theme which moves into Families, and finally we branch out into Communities around Thanksgiving. We don't spend all day every day on theme-related lessons, but we do integrate all content areas and easily address learning standards through the cohesive theme lens. For example, exploring self and family includes:

- Blending skin tones using color mixing and proportions
- Measuring, counting, and comparing (ourselves and family members)
- Writing stories, letters, and interviewing families
- Drawing self and family portraits
- Sharing stories in oral and visual poster presentations
- Analyzing video clips of differences in family lifestyles
- Charting and graphing data from investigations
- Reading journals of family stories, including historical narratives
- Mapping family travels and immigration
- Making inferences about traditions from details in family stories
- Documenting and creating dramatic play around family traditions (cooking, festivities, daily routines)
- Dramatic play and story-writing about family member occupations

There is so much opportunity to embed meaningful learning and skill development into integrated projects like these. And it just makes so much sense to the kids; I can't imagine splintering off all those experiences. Within these broader topics I'm able to engage the children in such a variety of experiences, and each child's personal need for more challenge or more support is met because experiences are naturally personalized through small group and individual activities. This is the only way I can feel like I am really differentiating (varied approaches to learning experiences) and individualizing (tailoring to each child's strengths and needs).

One of the most significant opportunities, though, is for me to really listen to children's developing ideas about themselves and their world. Even with a fairly similar looking community, there is always some diversity present when we take the time to look and listen. For example, this year I have a child who is adopted and a different race than her adoptive parents. Early in the Families study I was doing a read-aloud with a few books about family differences and the children were making a comparison chart. Jakob randomly blurted out "When people are adopted they get angry." This was such an interesting, biased comment; I knew we had to explore this idea. I responded that I looked forward to talking more about our ideas about families, wrote a quick anecdotal record and finished the reading. Afterwards, I asked small groups to create four questions to ask when interviewing families about their unique experiences. I prompted Jakob's group to think about a question that would invite people to talk about ideas and feelings about family transitions and changes. Many children in the class have experienced transitions, from blended families to births and deaths. They naturally wondered about feelings about all that and also had their own to share. Here is one exchange I recorded:

AUSTIN: Well, we could ask if they liked their new sister.

BRANDI: Or we could ask if they had a grandma who died like mine did.

JAKOB: Or if they were mad about moving.

TEACHER: Jakob, I remember how you mentioned you think people might be angry when they are adopted.

JAKOB: Yeah. Well, my mom's friends adopted a boy and he was mad. He said adopted kids get mad sometimes about being adopted.

TEACHER: I see. That's a good connection. …

BRANDI: [breaking in] But also they could be glad because now their new parents love them. Gabby's adopted and I go to her house sometimes. She has a whole bunch of toys and her own room. Her mom is just her mom, like mine. She's not mad.

TEACHER: So it sounds like there are different feelings about changes in families and some are the same as yours and some are different. Those are all important feelings someone might have.

JAKOB: I guess I forgot about Gabby. I wonder why some kids are mad and some aren't.

TEACHER: That's a great point and reminds us that people have different feelings about changes. Can you all think of a way to ask our families about that?

Just from their small group question-planning they realized a couple of significant things: people have different experiences of family transitions and people share their feelings in a variety of ways. They realized they had to be careful about making assumptions, but they also realized they could make some inferences from observations. I love how this kind of learning prompts them to think like researchers and allows them to think about important things in their world in different ways.

Using Learning Styles and Multiple Intelligences Effectively

Nearly all people have abilities in several or all of these areas. Many people have modest or strong preferences for one or a couple of these ways of thinking, and we will use different intelligences depending on the content or type of learning experience. Often we are not fully aware of our preferences or not aware of how preferences can impact our own learning, teaching, and interactions with others. Understanding your own thinking or intelligence preference(s) is important because your preference(s) can heavily influence how you present information and engage children in learning. It is not uncommon for teachers to frame learning experiences through their own ways of thinking and learning (remember "who you are is how you teach"). The problem begins when teachers rely too myopically on one or two styles, missing students who would benefit from a different intelligence or processing style.

Researchers have identified variations in processing and learning approaches based on contexts inextricable to the learner, including:

- The situation surrounding the learning experience
- Previous experience with the content
- Cultural background of the learner

While testing students for learning style type and tailoring instruction to their type might be somewhat debated, there is universal support for teachers' use of learning styles frameworks to broaden and differentiate teaching approaches (Cuthbert, 2005; Pashler, McDaniel, Rohrer, & Bjork, 2009; Sternberg & Zhang, 2005; Tomlinson & McTighe, 2006). Watch the process these teachers go through as they manage the planning, implementation, and reflection on their MI learning centers classroom structure in this **video**. The ways children process information about their world and how they represent their thinking vary widely. It makes sense that a variety of instructional approaches are necessary for different learning situations (for example, different content or learning objectives), and having a wider array of instructional strategies will improve your ability to reach diverse learners. In addition, it makes sense that exposure to learning strategies in all of the preference types provides learners with an opportunity to strengthen areas that are not naturally preferred, thus making them more successful in any learning setting. Teachers need to skillfully design learning experiences that integrate the variety of learning and thinking styles and intelligences to ensure that all children's preferences are maximized and expanded. Consider the variety of learning and representation opportunities in integrated projects:

In this play-based classroom, teachers skillfully nurture and capture children's literacy ideas through drawings, dictation, drama, dialogues, and constructions.

- Interest-based topics tap in to internal motivation.

- Hands-on investigations allow for tactile input and handling of materials.

- Group work promotes dialogues and working through ideas together.

- Reflective journaling invites internal dialogues and connections to self.

- Highly applied experiences give children opportunities to practice skills in a meaningful context.

- Researching through books, websites, field visits, and interviews encourages language and interpersonal skills.

- Structuring project work using an inquiry model (question, research, investigate, reflect, share) helps organize children's thinking and activities.

Teachers can align practice in many ways with key theories about how children's learning, thinking, and representing differ. The key is to diversify learning experiences to provide many ways for children to experience information and to give all children opportunities to strengthen a variety of learning and thinking styles. These points reemphasize how this exploration of human diversity is threefold, with its focus on self-reflection, awareness of individuals, and understanding of how groups engage together.

ATTITUDE TO ACTION, BELIEF TO BEHAVIOR 10.1

Identifying Your Preferences

In order to strengthen your own learning and better understand how to diversify your teaching, take a few moments to identify your intelligence area preferences. By answering a short list of questions about how you prefer to spend free time, how you solve problems, and ways you prefer to experience the world, you can reveal important biases which are a natural part of who you are. Remember that biases are normal and not problematic by themselves. Problems only arise when professionals are not aware of or making efforts to reduce their biases or preferences and children are being excluded or marginalized as a result.

Visit the Literacy Works website (literacyworks.org) and search for MI assessment for overviews of the multiple intelligences and a free interactive self-test that returns immediate feedback on your intelligence strengths.

Also, visit Felder and Solomon's Index of Learning Styles pages through the North Carolina State University website to explore descriptions of learning styles and take an interactive Index of Learning Styles. This online self-test yields immediate results of where your preferences lie on the four categories and can be accessed at http://www4.ncsu.edu/unity/lockers/users/f/felder/public/ILSpage.html.

Print or make a note of your results and compare them to your own ideas about how you like to think and learn. Recall learning experiences that were particularly meaningful to you and moments when you felt empowered and capable as a learner. For example, do you remember being especially excited about a large, complex group project or listening to an inspired teacher tell stories of historical events and days gone by? Was one of your fondest memories getting lost in a new book as you lounged in a cozy chair in the library? Or perhaps PE, recess, or cooking and woodshop were highlights of your school day? Think about what learning moments are on your personal highlights reel and how they are connected to your learning styles and intelligences reports. Try to connect three attributes of these experiences with your intelligences and learning styles to identify elements of the learning environment or instructional strategies that were especially effective in supporting you as a learner.

One of my best learning moments	What type of learning or intelligence style was I using?

Summary

UNDERSTANDING INDIVIDUAL LEARNERS

- *Learning style* refers to the ways in which individuals learn new material. It encompasses thinking, emotional, and psychological behaviors that impact how a person takes in, engages with, and responds to learning experiences and environments.
- Multiple intelligence theory is an evolving framework that describes nine different ways that people take in, process, and use information and experiences within their cultural context.
- The study of learning styles is generally best used as a means of assessing your own processing style in order to focus your efforts on balancing your styles.
- The process of tailoring instruction and interaction approaches to different learning styles is called *differentiation*.

THE FELDER-SILVERMAN MODEL OF LEARNING STYLES

- The model builds on earlier work, integrating components from several models into a broader picture of variations in learning preferences.
- Four areas of difference in learning style are outlined:
  - Sensory–Intuitive
  - Visual–Verbal
  - Active–Reflective
  - Sequential–Global

MULTIPLE INTELLIGENCES

- Sparked by numerous examples of successful people who were once school "failures," Howard Gardner identified eight distinct ways of processing and representing thinking.
- His theory recognizes that, historically, schools have focused on linguistic and logical ways of thinking and learning, ignoring the many other ways that children think.
- His eight intelligences are:
  - Verbal/linguistic
  - Logical/mathematical
  - Musical
  - Visual
  - Body/kinesthetic
  - Interpersonal
  - Intrapersonal
  - Naturalist

USING LEARNING AND THINKING STYLES EFFECTIVELY

- Responsive, diversified practice involves recognizing the many ways people differ and responding appreciatively and sensitively to adjust your interactions, programming, and dispositions.
- Effective instruction builds on sensitivity to diversity through evidence-based practice: selecting research-based instruction, systematic pre-assessment, programming, post-assessment, and ongoing decision making based on evidence of effectiveness.

Chapter Learning Outcomes: Self-Assessment

Use this space to reflect on how well you have achieved the learning goals for this chapter by evaluating your own competency in the topics below. List three to five items that describe key concepts you have learned from the chapter.

Describe theories of different preferences in learning and thinking styles.	
Explain current recommendations for integrating learning and thinking styles research into practice.	
Practice research-based strategies for differentiating instruction, including *Response to Intervention*.	

Chapter Activities

DISCUSSION QUESTIONS

1. Reflecting on your own experiences as a learner, as well as on the results of your learning styles tests, discuss the following questions:

   - What do I know about my own learning?
   - How do the results of my learning/ intelligence styles inventories reflect my educational experiences?
   - How can understanding how I think and learn impact my success as a student?
   - How can these reflections improve my teaching?

2. Working in small groups, identify 3 to 5 challenges to culturally responsive, evidence-based practices that you feel are moderate to major obstacles. Brainstorm potential solutions or resources that can support remediation of these challenges.

Challenge	Solution or Resources for Support

SELF-REFLECTION

Gather the self-tests or notes you made as you completed the intelligence and learning styles test throughout this chapter. Compare and analyze the results as you consider the following:

1. Describe the ways the results were either surprising or what you expected.

2. If the results from different tests are consistent, reflect on how the results compare with your own impressions of your ways of thinking and learning. Do they feel "right" to you?

3. If the results are inconsistent across tests, try to explain why you think that might be. Do you use many different ways of processing? Did you struggle with selecting preferences in the questions? Do you feel unsure about how to define your preferences or ways of thinking?

4. Now think about what the results might mean for how you share, convey, or teach information to others. What connections can you make between your internal processing style and how you engage with other people?

Using your survey results and your reflections, create a "T-chart" to compare how your style and preferences influence your own thinking and learning, as well as your teaching and interacting with others.

Influence of My Personal Style	
How my preferences impact my learning and thinking (problem solving)	How my preferences impact my teaching and interacting with others
Example: My MI preferences are strongly skewed towards verbal-linguistic and my visual is quite low.	*After reflecting on my practice in light of my results, I realize that I do a lot of talking and discussion activities. I don't integrate as many opportunities for charts, graphs, or videos.*

TEACHING DISPOSITION

Visit the HighScope website's Assessment section. Select "Child Assessment" from the links on the left. Select either the Infant/Toddler COR or Preschool COR link (www.highscope.org). Open the Observation Items to read sample notes from teacher using the HighScope Child Observation Record assessment instrument. Read and choose three of the anecdotal records noted under different levels. Identify what kinds of developmentally appropriate, varied instructional support you could plan for the child noted in the anecdotal record to develop several learning styles or intelligence areas. Based on the observation note, their current level, and the outcomes in the next level, what would you do with this child to support their development? Consider interactions, materials, activities, and supports. Use the chart below to practice making your assessment data-driven instructional decisions.

Anecdotal Record (reprint)	Developmental Indicator and Level	Instructional Plans
11/3 At snack, Shayna points and says the word "Milk," indicating that she wants more milk.	Initiative: Making Choices and Plans; Level 2	To support Shayna extending the length of her sentences when making a choice, I will model using a short sentence when Shayna uses one or two word phrases and wait for her to repeat my words. I will pair my verbal cue with a gesture.
		For example: *Shayna, I hear that you want more milk. Can you say "I want more milk" and make the hand sign for milk like this (model)? When you say "I want more milk" I can pour you more milk.* (Then I will wait for her to respond, repeating the sentence and gesture if necessary.)

IN THE FIELD

Observe a classroom setting (through a field visit or video segment) and identify as many different examples as you can of environmental design or instructional practices that reflect different learning styles or intelligences. Create a chart with the learning style or intelligence category and a brief description of the classroom example.

Weblinks

The HighScope Educational Research Foundation website includes information on curriculum, assessment, research on effective programs, and trainings related to the HighScope program. *www.highscope.org*

The Center for RtI in Early Childhood has information and resources to support appropriate implementation of RtI frameworks in early childhood programs. The website includes information on tiered systems, publications, presentations, and a network of other professionals. *http://www.crtiec.org/*

The Promising Practices Network website is a unique resource that offers credible, research-based information on what works to improve the lives of children and families. *http://www.promisingpractices.net/*

11 Teaching *in* a Diverse World

Successful culturally responsive practices rely on several key elements that involve teachers, families, and organization-wide effort. These elements include genuine interest in and valuing of diversity; critical self-reflection on potential biases; knowledge of everyday experiences of diverse individuals; development of cultural competence and skill; diversifying practices to reflect the experiences and preferences of people you work with; and administrative support (Balcazar, Suarez-Balcazar, & Taylor-Ritzler, 2009). Your self-awareness and knowledge of others has been enhanced throughout this text. You have engaged in numerous activities to spark reflection and action as you identified ways to adjust your practice to meaningfully engage with children and families from diverse backgrounds.

In this chapter you will explore evidence-based, high quality practices, look at examples of teachers'

Honoring and valuing diverse children and families requires formal policies about including and valuing everyone, and informal actions that invite families to share their cultural traditions every day.

decision making and culturally responsive teaching, practice your skills as teacher, and advocate for equity and social justice in education. Your purpose is to reflect on ways to thread diversity and complexity through all aspects of classroom life and to bring all of the previous chapters together into your own action.

From this practical perspective, your final step in this ongoing journey will be to articulate a clear statement of your commitment to appreciating diversity and to determine how you will engage children in exploring and valuing diversity. Tremendous value and power lie in articulating where you stand on diversity issues in your personal and professional life—both for you and the families you work with. In essence, you are creating a starting point for engaging in dialogue, reflection, and advocacy about what valuing diversity is all about.

Research on What Works for All Children

Effective instruction builds on solid theoretical foundations, quality research, and sensitivity to diversity through evidence-based practice. **Evidence-based practice**, as applied to early childhood education, is defined as "a decision-making process that integrates the best available research with family and professional wisdom and values" (Buysse & Wesley, 2006, p. xiv). This means recognizing that evidence-based practice is a way of making decisions that synthesizes quality research outcomes with family and professional judgment. Thinking about evidence-based practice as one set of rules, standards, or a particular product is problematic in education and doesn't adequately take into account the widely differing goals, needs, opportunities, and strengths of children, families, teachers, and communities. Thus, in order to appropriately respond to each child, evidence-based practice requires professional judgment, knowledge of individual children and families, and review of research data on effectiveness.

Responsive, diversified practice involves recognizing the many ways that people differ—and responding appreciatively and sensitively in order to adjust your interactions, programming, and dispositions. Knowledge of diversity includes appreciating how people differ in the ways they talk, in what they believe, what resources they have access to, what they look like, what their home and family life feels like, and even in how they think. "For all people, language, ethnic and racial history, experience with political and economic oppression, sense of opportunity, values, and perceptions converge in the response to teaching and learning" (Ginsberg, 2005, p. 220). Consider the importance of using effective practices as you listen to this **video** clip.

The **Response to intervention (RtI)** framework has become a widely used model of innovation in individualized, evidence-based practice. A key

- Discuss how evidence-based decisions inform culturally and individually relevant practice

- Identify instructional strategies that support diverse learners

- Practice strategies for meaningfully including all children and valuing diverse families

- Create a personal statement about what valuing diversity means in your work

purpose of RtI (already familiar to the field of early childhood education) is identifying and addressing individual needs before they evolve into later developmental problems or disabilities (NAEYC, n.d.). Because it focuses so heavily on each individual child, RtI is uniquely suited to work for children from diverse backgrounds.

RESPONSE TO INTERVENTION (RtI)

Across the nation and across all areas of education, RtI has taken center stage in recent years as a guiding framework and system for ensuring success for all children. RtI is widely cited as helpful for children needing specialized support, including dual language learners, children with identified disabilities and without formal diagnosis, children struggling to meet benchmark standards, and children from underresourced homes (Bayat, Mindes, & Covitt, 2010; Gettinger & Stoiber, 2007; Greenwood, Bradfield, Kaminski, Linas, Carta, & Nylander, 2011). With roots dating back to the 1970s and with initial applications in K through 12 and special education programs, RtI has since gained popularity as a program- or school-wide effort to ensure success for young children (Jackson, Pretti-Frontczak, Harjusola-Webb, Grisham-Brown, & Romani, 2009) and is demonstrating promise as a means of addressing behavioral challenges in young children.

Even more important when applying RtI to early childhood settings is the system-wide approach that involves families, specialists (such as speech-language pathologists, reading specialists, developmental psychologists, and so forth), classroom professionals, and administration in a meaningful way. RtI is a broad framework that integrates multiple avenues of support to leverage resources into collaborative problem solving teams (Bayat, Mindes, & Covitt, 2010). Think of RtI as a framework or a system; it is not a single-classroom, one-teacher program.

RtI is a multitiered system of support. Programs are designed with several levels of instruction, and individualizing is embedded in each level and based on an assessment-instruction-assessment structure (Bayat, Mindes, & Covitt, 2010). Instruction is based on a research-supported curriculum and delivered deliberately through high quality practice. Assessment is implemented with all children at initial, formative (during), and summative (end point) stages. Resulting data are used to guide instructional and service decisions (Jackson, Pretti-Frontczak, Harjusola-Webb, Grisham-Brown, & Romani, 2009).

The most popular model is a three-tier structure that increases in intensity and individualization as a child progresses "up" the hierarchy, representing an increased need for individualized instruction and support. The application of tiers of instruction is also flexible across developmental or educational outcomes and will vary based on each child's functioning in each outcome (NAEYC, n.d.). For example, a 1st grader might need tier 2 or tier 3 instruction while working on addition and subtraction problems, but the same 1st grader might be successful in tier 1 instruction in socio-emotional, language, and physical development and learning outcomes. Or a toddler might need tier 2 support to develop hand-eye coordination but be developing well with tier 1 language activities. This dynamic, flexible, individualized approach is especially useful for maximizing strengths and targeting support when working with children from diverse backgrounds. In addition, children might be recommended for additional diagnostic screening if tier 3 interventions are not resulting in progress, but a child might be referred for special education services screening at any time based on family and support team recommendation (NAEYC, n.d.).

Visit the Center for Response to Intervention in Early Childhood at http://www.crtiec.org/ for resources and information on each tier of implementation. Figure 11.1 is an example of a visualization of an RtI structure with

FIGURE 11.1 *Three-tier RtI Structure*

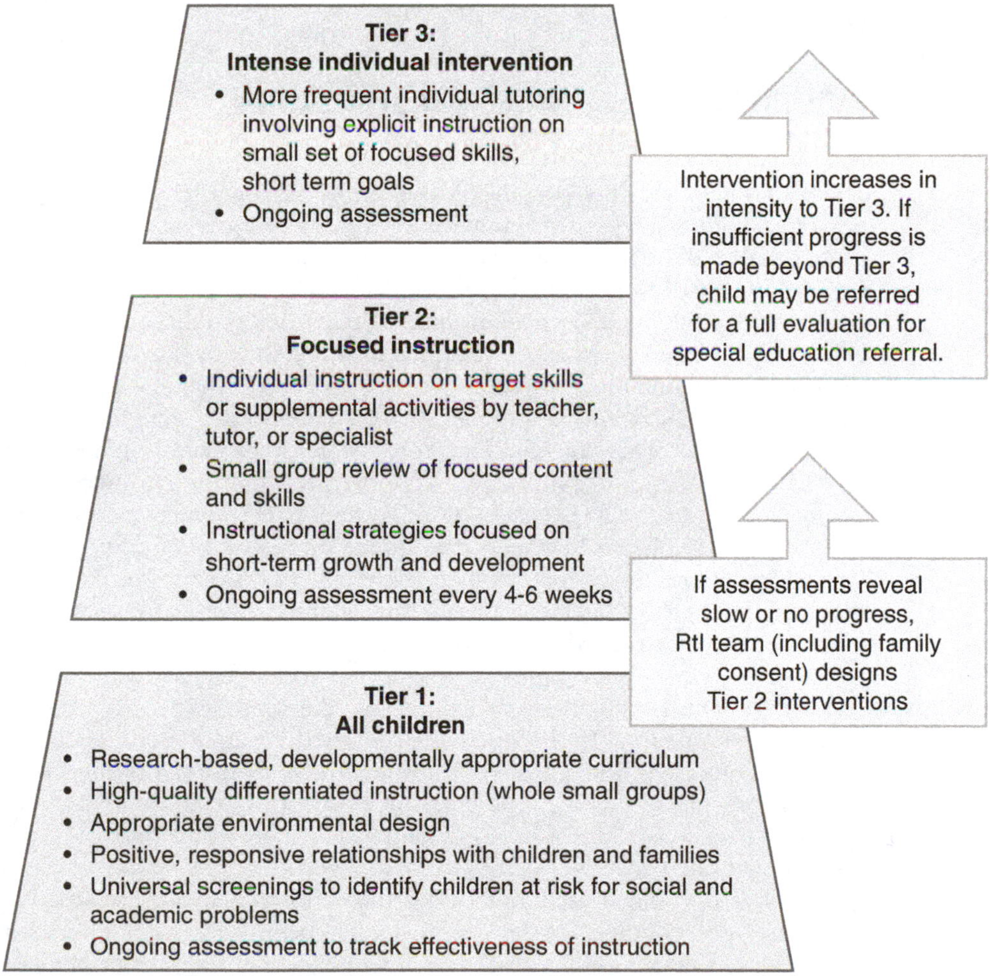

Tier 3:
Intense individual intervention
- More frequent individual tutoring involving explicit instruction on small set of focused skills, short term goals
- Ongoing assessment

Intervention increases in intensity to Tier 3. If insufficient progress is made beyond Tier 3, child may be referred for a full evaluation for special education referral.

Tier 2:
Focused instruction
- Individual instruction on target skills or supplemental activities by teacher, tutor, or specialist
- Small group review of focused content and skills
- Instructional strategies focused on short-term growth and development
- Ongoing assessment every 4-6 weeks

If assessments reveal slow or no progress, RtI team (including family consent) designs Tier 2 interventions

Tier 1:
All children
- Research-based, developmentally appropriate curriculum
- High-quality differentiated instruction (whole small groups)
- Appropriate environmental design
- Positive, responsive relationships with children and families
- Universal screenings to identify children at risk for social and academic problems
- Ongoing assessment to track effectiveness of instruction

key practices for early childhood education applications. Notice in particular how ongoing assessment is present at all levels. Frequently assessing the effectiveness of instruction is an essential part of RtI implementation.

One essential element of RtI implementation is the frequent, systematic collection and use of data to inform decision making at each stage of implementation. Standardization and fidelity of implementation in instruction and assessment are crucial in order to obtain reliable results that can accurately and appropriately be used to inform decisions. The Center for RtI in Early Childhood (www.crtiec.org) has designed assessment tools and procedures and target developmental indicators as a resource for professionals creating RtI implementation plans for use with infants and toddlers, preschool, and early elementary age children. The work on translating RtI principles and practices for use with young children continues to evolve through research and reflection. For more information on Individual Growth and Development Indicators, including assessment systems, visit Kansas University's Juniper Gardens Children's Project which is linked from the Center for RtI in Early Childhood's webpage.

EVIDENCE-BASED, HIGH QUALITY EARLY CHILDHOOD CURRICULA

The National Association for the Education of Young Children (NAEYC) describes high quality curriculum for young children as the "scope and sequence of skills that guide instruction that is explicit and systematic as well as developmentally and culturally appropriate" (NAEYC, n.d., p. 5). There are several early childhood curriculum models that have demonstrated strong evidence for effectiveness and appropriateness and that are suitable options for tier 1 programming (instruction for all children). The research-based early childhood programs and models that have demonstrated effectiveness in improving outcomes for children in terms of overall development, not just school success, are particularly important for supporting success for young children from diverse backgrounds. The RAND research group maintains a database of information and evidence on research-based programs for children and families that includes early childhood curricula. Programs designated as "proven" and "promising" are outlined, along with criteria for evaluation at www.promisingpractices.net.

A strong example of a proven program in continued use with diverse children is the HighScope Curriculum by the HighScope Educational Research Foundation. HighScope was designed as an experimental lab school serving preschool children from underresourced neighborhoods of Ypsilanti, Michigan, in 1962. The curriculum (a list of developmental indicators, active constructivist-based learning activities, child and program assessment tools) is now widely used in over 20% of Head Start programs as well as other programs across the country. A major longitudinal research study, ongoing for over 50 years, has been tracking progress for 123 African American children at risk for intellectual delay from families of low socioeconomic status from 3 years old through middle adulthood. The study has tracked academic success, school success, and quality of life indicators. Findings from this Perry Preschool Study have consistently demonstrated significant gains in academic outcomes, reduction in special education services, increased employability and income, reduction in criminal activity, and stronger relationship longevity for program participants. Numerous additional rigorous research studies have demonstrated HighScope program effectiveness for decades. The HighScope model includes several important components that make it a good fit for implementation with RtI tier 1:

- Validated assessment instruments implemented systematically (generally every few months)
- Research-based core curriculum encompassing all developmental and academic areas
- Staff training and professional development support
- Daily structure centered around developmentally appropriate learning activities
- Emphasis on development of self-regulation and decision-making
- Specific curriculum models for infants, preschool, and elementary ages

In addition, HighScope is effective with children from diverse backgrounds because of the emphasis on authentic materials and experiences that reflect each child's experiences in their own home and communities. HighScope

The highly interactive, developmentally aligned HighScope curriculum has been demonstrating positive results for over 50 years, particularly in early intervention settings.

teachers explore and integrate meaningful ideas, artifacts, and events into the daily program and support and extend children's representations of their lives through language, creative expression, sustained dramatic play, routines, and symbolic representation activities. Children's thoughts and ideas, conveyed in their own language and at their own level, are the starting point from which teachers take the lead and extend thinking and learning. HighScope's resources include a number of bilingual family guides, informational booklets on the curriculum and Child Observation Record, and information-gathering materials. These materials allow professionals to ensure robust two-way communications with families and support the development of the strong partnerships that are so essential to children's success.

In this **video**, visit a HighScope classroom and explore the philosophy and practice of HighScope programs. Identify three examples of what you would consider best practices in effective, culturally relevant early childhood education in the descriptions or classroom scenes.

Video example (classroom scene or description)	How does this demonstrate best practice?	How is this culturally relevant and how does it value diversity?
Classroom includes verbal and visual cues for schedules, materials, and labels.	*Instead of using only words, the word/picture pairing promotes literacy and autonomy.*	*It includes dual language learners and prereaders, and supports multiple ways of thinking.*

Bringing It All Together

Now it's your turn to make the leap from theory to practice! In this section, three practical scenarios will be presented as a model of how early childhood professionals are working in real life. After each model, a similar classroom scenario will be presented for you to take on the role of the professional and make your own decisions for practice. Take time to carefully consider what you have learned about best practices research, what you know about children and yourself as a new professional, and what you can appropriately infer about the children's family context. This activity isn't about finding the "one right answer"! It is about the process professionals go through to make sound decisions for children's learning and development.

Infant-Toddler Classroom Models and Practice

Model 1: Infant and toddler classroom example

Ali, Johanna, Sareet, and Cory are a teaching team in a mid-sized infant and toddler center in an urban area. They have come together for the first monthly team meeting of the year. In this meeting they are reflecting on the families and children enrolled in their care and developing their initial plans for individual children and the group as a whole. All families have been provided with a program handbook of policies and expectations and have been asked to complete a detailed information form, providing as much background as possible about their child and family.

Ali starts by reviewing the roster of children and the family information that was gathered when they enrolled. Important Information is shared, which includes both what children are doing now as well as family goals and expectations over the year in each area. A sample of the summaries the teachers review is shown in Figure 11.2. This information is designed and presented to families for two purposes:

1. As a way to learn about children before they enter the program so the program and environment can be tailored to individual children's preferences and needs

2. As a venue for families to share important goals, plans, expectations and hopes for their children and for family perspectives to be validated and valued

The discussion about 30-month-old Sean centers on the family's routines and goals for him, especially relating to different perspectives about independence and autonomy in feeding and sleeping. The team takes time to brainstorm ideas for supporting the family's goals, facilitating healthy development, and appropriately including his grandmother as an important caretaker. Below in Figure 11.2 is an excerpt from Sean's family's intake form.

FIGURE 11.2

Family Intake Form for Sean

Dear families,

We believe that very close partnerships with families and teachers is essential for children's best outcomes at our program. We value families as children's first and primary teachers and strive to align our practice with your goals for your children while sharing with you our knowledge base about best practices in early care and education.

Please use this form to share as much information as you can about your child's habits, routines, preferences, and activities in the areas noted below. In the first open space, please share where your child and you are currently; in the second space please share your family's goals and expectations about where you would like your child to be heading in the coming year in terms of their skills and development in those areas.

(Continued)

Routine, habit, developmental area	Where your child is currently	How you expect your child to develop over the year
Example: *Feeding*	[Our toddler], is currently exploring limited table foods in a small bowl with his hands, and he sometimes holds a spoon. His diet is strictly vegetarian and he cannot eat nuts.	We would like [our toddler] to continue practicing using a utensil and expanding the foods he tries, within vegetarian and nut-free options. We will send his lunch in every day, but he can eat school snacks.
Feeding: schedule, foods, preferences, habits, routines, goals	*Sean does not eat dairy or wheat.* *He sometimes holds the utensil or feeds himself, but mostly I feed him.* *He likes a pretty good variety of foods from fruit, vegetables, meat, and grains; mostly traditional Vietnamese foods.*	*I prefer Sean to be fed to keep things cleaner, ensure that he eats enough, and gets through mealtimes more quickly. He can hold the utensils and practice eating sometimes, but mostly he should be fed.*
Sleeping: schedule, preferences, habits at home, needs, goals	*Sean sleeps with me in the main bedroom. He has been in my room since birth and it has been an important source of comfort through our transition moving here. He sleeps well from 8pm–8am. We sometimes take a nap midday, and I lay with him until he falls asleep. We read books and tell stories at bed time.*	*Sean usually needs someone to rub his back or sit with him as he falls asleep for naps. He doesn't really want any stuffed toy or anything. Low background noise can help.* *Sean will continue sleeping in my room until he feels ready for his own room.*
Activities: preferences, rhythms and routines during the day (active times, quiet times); how does your child interact with different people in his/her world?	*Sean's paternal grandmother, who lives with us is a primary caretaker. For some - much of the day she is his main caregiver and contact.* *Sean enjoys quiet activities like puzzles and books. He likes click-together blocks.* *When visiting with cousins, Sean enjoys their play and watches them with great interest.*	*Sean's grandmother will continue to play an important role in his daily life and we would like her to come to school regularly to support his caregiving and interactions. She is partially fluent in English, but Vietnamese is her primary language.* *We want Sean to continue learning Vietnamese while he develops English as well. We will travel to Vietnam to visit family several times a year.*

As the teaching team talks, Sareet creates a list of individualized practices that the team feels are responsive and important for Sean and the group. Their list includes:

- Label shelves and areas of the room in Vietnamese and English.
- Include an extra rocking chair (borrow one from the parent lounge) for when grandmother is in the classroom.
- Explore roles that grandmother could take on that support children's interactions and relationship building, such as storytelling of traditional tales (taking care to allow Sean to engage with children even while grandmother is there).
- Dialogue with family about healthy development of autonomy, while still valuing the family's goals for interdependence (be sensitive to this as their goal, less than independence).

- Follow consistent routine for rest times: soft lullaby music, storytelling, backrub, or rocking as needed.
- Include photo cards of simple images with snap building blocks.
- Send home recorder and ask family to create bilingual stories on tape from favorite books for the classroom listening center.
- Integrate photos from part of Vietnam where family will visit, as well as familiar scenes, and post in classroom or as a classroom book.

Practice 1: Planning for Rachel

Consider how you could individualize practices, materials, routines, and environment for two-year-old Rachel, whose parents are a same-sex interracial professional couple and who have shared the following information on their enrollment form:

Rachel has a good appetite and is willing to try new foods sometimes. She enjoys fruits, noodles, bread, cheese, and some meats. We keep Kosher, so we will send in all of her foods and utensils. She doesn't enjoy strong tasting foods (rich flavors and spices). She insists on using the spoon and fork herself, which often means mealtimes are messy. Mealtimes are an important social time and we insist that Rachel participate in the family mealtime (which regularly includes extended family who live nearby) and is especially important on Friday evening when we observe Shabbat. We encourage talking and enjoying company at the table and want mealtimes at school to be social too.

Rachel has been sleeping independently since she was a few months old and needs to have a dark environment for her naps. She seems to like the white noise machine. She naps for an hour during the day and sleeps well throughout the night. We used the "cry-it-out" method to promote self-regulation, which we believe is an essential skill for her to develop. It is important for us that Rachel continue to develop strong self-regulation skills and learn to recognize the importance of the group's needs and balancing that with her own needs.

Rachel mostly shows little interest in other children and gets frustrated quickly when having to work collaboratively. She is the youngest child in the large family/community network and she enjoys a lot of attention. We spend a lot of time with other adults and she behaves very well in this company. We value manners when speaking to adults and she is starting to use preferred words like please and thank you. We would also like for her to develop stronger interpersonal skills when working with other children. Sometimes she seems to be ignoring us when we talk to her, especially if she is facing away from us or is deeply focused on an activity.

Information about Rachel from parent notes	Ideas to individualize for Rachel (environment, materials, groupings, routines, etc.)

Preschool Classroom Models and Practice

Model 2: Preschool classroom example

The preschool teaching team of the "butterfly" room in a small, rural child care center creates an individualized plan of instruction for each child, which is reassessed and adjusted as needed bimonthly. The teachers carefully consider information from families and from observations to intentionally plan experiences that meet children's needs and maximize their strengths. Their approach to individualizing always begins with a focus on children's interests and strengths to ensure they view children in positive, empowered ways. They use a three-part form to organize their observation notes and plans. A sample of their individualized planning from a mid-year report is shown in Figure 11.3.

FIGURE 11.3

Sample Individualized Planning from a Mid-Year Report

Child's interests, strengths, and needs	Individualizing (instruction, grouping, materials)	Notes
David: • Likes big trucks, active play, using math tools, working in pairs, storytelling performances. • Good at logical thinking, physical coordination activities, problem solving when prompted. • Needs support meeting basic needs (adequate food, clothing), help focusing on sequencing story segments, inserting self into groups, social conflict resolution.	• Put David, Jai, Elli, and Ryshan in small group reading instruction. • Use Literature Circles packet on *Henry Hikes to Fitchburg*. • Follow up with story drama. • Guide group's negotiating through story drama design (anticipate conflicts, prepare prompts). • Use tables, charts, and numbered lists as graphic organizers in small group dialogues about stories. • Create take-home literature packs for weekly loan. • Store high quality snacks in case David comes to school hungry. • Locate spare clothes, pair of shoes, and coat for use as needed.	• Highlight Ryshan's strong interpersonal skills to be a model for group setting interactions. • Focus on collaborative group member roles through literature packet. • Assign David to Henry character in story drama. • Have children make sequence cards for story drama prompts. • David's family is in economic stress, and occasionally he comes to school hungry or talks about being hungry soon after arrival. • Follow up with Sandi [director] re: support programs to help family with food, clothing.

Carlton:

- Likes order and organizing environment, working alone, sensory table.
- Good at creating original fantasy stories, puzzles, list-making.
- Needs help staying at rug during group time, staying on task, following directions, engaging with peers, persevering through challenging tasks, gross motor coordination.

- Once per week, Carlton selects book for rug time sharing.
- Assistant will note length of time on task/rug during group time—goal of 8 minutes.
- Small group work: pair with Jennifer for problem solving tasks.
- Tinted blue water with sea shells and ocean creature figures in sensory table; recommend Onlee to partner for sorting and classifying game.
- Give Carlton the team leader role in making the indoor obstacle course in gym, team with Elli, Jai.
- Create fantasy stories with social role scripts that practice focusing attention during rug time.
- Create checklist of key behaviors together, review with Carlton daily, send home report to mom weekly.
- Include books on loss in book corner, dialogue with school counselor at elementary school for advice.

- Mom is raising Carlton alone; father passed away 6 months ago.
- In previous program, Carlton was given the choice to be at rug for group time or not—almost always opted to be alone on other side of room.
- Initial goal of 5 minutes of focus at rug time mastered in first 6 weeks; new goal of 8 minutes.
- From Carlton's behavior therapist: Use verbal cue "Carlton, now I need you to __" when directing or redirecting him to a task.
- When redirecting, use gentle hand on shoulder, eye contact, and quiet firm voice.
- Recommend center-wide staff training on grief in children.

Onlee:

- Likes outdoor activities, sensory table, science explorations, routines.
- Good at taking things apart to figure out how they work, generating questions (curious), attention to detail.
- Needs help with transitions especially end of day, managing emotional outbursts, staying in classroom (tries to leave), making relationships.

- Keep Onlee in same small group (Kyle, Jai, Sam, Janelle) several times during day.
- Assign Onlee to Wendy as primary [teacher].
- Earn out-of-classroom 5-minute walking breaks with Wendy to visit James [brother]; strive for 2x/day.
- Expand books in classroom library on grandparents as parents, family transitions, moving.
- "Our community" mapping project: map classroom/school/grounds, explore visitor center tourist maps, list/photos of places we go; have parents draw homes with child and send in, make classroom community map.

- Onlee joined class late in fall after removal from home and placement (with brother) with grandmother, who recently moved to U.S. from Mexico. Grandmother speaks Spanish and moderately good English. Grandmother has legal and physical custody of both children, biological mother in out-of-state rehab, no contact with biological father (in Mexico). Grandmother seeking new apartment as current is too small, so anticipate another home transition.
- Onlee sees family counselor 1x/week; counselor's recommendations: focus on consistent core routine, short but scripted procedures for end-of-day (rug story, put home journal in bag, coat/bag on, line up, handshake, dismiss), cool down corner when highly emotional, out-of-room breaks as incentive.

(Continued)

(*Continued*)

Practice 2: Preschool individualizing

Now it's your turn. Look through the notes on three children in Figure 11.4 and begin to make some individualized plans. Think about the following as you plan:

- Small group partners: what characteristics would you want to pair with the focus child to support his or her needs?

- Materials: what adaptations or additions would you make to classroom materials based on focus child's interests, strengths, and needs?

- Routines: does the focus child need adjustments to schedules or routines?

- Instructional content: how can you maximize the focus child's motivation by integrating his or her interests wherever possible?

- Resources: what resources (materials or people) do you need to access to meet the focus child's needs?

FIGURE 11.4

Practice Individualizing

Child's interests, strengths, and needs	Individualizing (instruction, grouping, materials)	Notes
Thalia: • Likes story time, messy art projects, block building, chalk drawing on pavement during recess; is friends with Myra. • Good at taking care of others (especially Myra), drawing story sequences with some writing, creating elaborate structures with a lot of symmetry. • Needs help with developing English (progressing well, only slightly behind expectations), separating from teacher to engage with peers, managing emotional outbursts of crying and withdrawing from group (usually when she gets overstimulated by classroom activity level).		• Father, brother, Thalia, and grandmother recently moved from El Salvador; mother remained in El Salvador to care for ill grandfather. • Family lives temporarily with an aunt, plans to move by end of year. • Grandmother speaks Spanish only, but other family members speak English fairly well.
Naim: • Likes talking about family events (often religious), drawing pictures for his mom, dictating stories, small group interactions. • Interested in marble roll station, making structures with snap-together blocks, art. • Needs space for regular prayer, help to resolve interpersonal conflicts when disagreements arise with peers, help integrating himself into peer group free play outside (often left out and sits alone).		• Naim's family is Muslim. Naim's mother picks him up from school and wears a hijab. Other children often ask questions about her attire and their family's religion. • Naim chooses to maintain prayer schedule of family, including prayer during program. • We (teachers) need more information/staff training on Muslim faith and traditions to help with children's many questions.

ATTITUDE TO ACTION, BELIEF TO BEHAVIOR 11.3

Classroom Model and Practice

Model 3: Differentiated lesson plans

Here are sample lesson plans from 2nd grade and kindergarten classrooms in a diverse, economically stressed community. After the basic lesson outline, the teachers use the section on differentiating to map out important adjustments to the lesson that can meet the varying needs for support and challenge in the classroom. Review the lesson plans and differentiation section and think about how these adjustments help ensure learning for a wider array of children.

Sample lesson plan 1

Lesson title	About me: Poetry exploration
Assessment of prior learning	This activity was a tie-in to our poetry unit. It was also meant to serve as a means of self-reflection, allowing the children to think about how they view themselves.
Purpose/goal	To help children connect a story, *The Colors of Us*, that was read to them, with thinking about how they view themselves and then writing about it.
Measurable objectives	Create a 5+ line "About Me" or "I Am" poem.
Common Core Standard	W.2.5. With guidance and support from adults and peers, focus on a topic and strengthen writing as needed by revising and editing. W.2.8. Recall information from experiences or gather information from provided sources to answer a question (Who are you?). L.2.2. Demonstrate command of the conventions of standard English capitalization, punctuation, and spelling when writing.
Materials	*The Colors of Us*, by Katz Paper Pencils
Overall procedures	1. Read aloud 2. Pair/share and class discussion and reflection 3. Independent writing
Introduction/ anticipatory set	Today, we are going to explore how we might seem to be all the same but how we are also very different from each other!
Body of activity	1. Students join me on the rug. 2. Students listen to *The Colors of Us*. 3. Students share what they enjoyed or took away from the reading. 4. Children share with a partner one word they would use to describe themselves. 5. As a class, we brainstorm adjectives that we could most use to describe ourselves or each other. 6. Children break out into independent sessions for creating their own "About Me" poem.
Conclusion/wrap up	As children complete their poems, they will be able to share them with their peers. Poems will be added to their poetry books/collections, which will be assembled into a class poetry book.

(Continued)

Differentiation	
Above level	**Children are always challenged to write more poems or to, in this instance, create a different type of poem style about themselves once first poem is completed. Check for spelling. Add additional details or more descriptive words.**
Below level	**Children will have a model to base their learning on if stuck with getting their ideas moving.**
Different modalities	**Read aloud, discussion, writing (linguistic, interpersonal).** **Bring mirrors to prompt connection to appearance (visual, intrapersonal).** **Cue to check "My Family" books for ideas and self-reflection (visual, intrapersonal).** **Graphic organizer (word map, elaborate to phrase, combine to poem; logical).**
Cultural considerations	**Have a variety of descriptive words available for skin tone.** **Use "My Family" books for reference/description of religious and family traditions.**
Extensions into next step	The children will be revisiting this text to think and investigate further what makes us all individuals and unique from one another. We will be conducting peer-to-peer interviews and then write newspaper articles about it, and this will all tie back into that, starting with how we view ourselves and then extending it to think about others.
Assessment/ evaluation	The children's ability to create a logical, creative, and reflective poem about themselves will be assessed; will be viewed along with their other poetry as well. A 4-point scale for effort, ideas, creativity, and number of descriptive details will be used.

Sample lesson plan 2

Lesson title	**Exploring squid with kindergarteners (child-initiated project on oceans)**
Assessment of prior learning	Brief discussion about prior project activities, notes of children's responses Connection to children's ocean project and aquarium visit last week
Purpose/goal	Develop curiosity about the natural world. Explore the roles of scientist, explorer, and investigator. Learn basic knowledge about structure of a squid. Investigate a topic of interest through active exploration.
Measurable objectives	Manipulate tools (magnifying glass, pincers, scissors). Find and identify basic squid body parts: body, fins, eye, tentacles, sucker/teeth ring, beak. Compare observations of squid to observations of octopus.
Materials	Whole squid Tools: tweezers, magnifying glasses, pans, pointed cotton swabs, scissors Photos, video clip of squid in ocean Stuffed and plastic models Soap/lemon for cleanup
Overall procedures	Introduce purpose/goal, tools, and basic procedure for opening squid body, locating beak and sucker/teeth; guide open-ended hands-on exploration and dissection if interested; wrap-up with reflection prompts for dialogue.

Introduction/ anticipatory set	"Last week when we went to the aquarium a group of you asked if we could hold and touch the octopus. Greisan's mom was able to bring in a whole squid, which is a lot like an octopus but a little different. She is going to share how scientists explore the natural world." Share pictures of live squid and sketch of interior of squid, and demonstrate use of tools. "Did you know that squids don't have any bones, but they have a LOT of teeth? Squid don't eat with their teeth. Do you want to see how they eat?" Invite children to explore at science stations in the project room. Invite children to play with squid models and books in the classroom if they prefer not to handle the actual squid.
Body of activity	Children explore squids. In small groups, guide identification of body structures and parts, using photos, video clips, and sketches. Facilitate connections through dialogue, charting comparisons among creatures. Create a few verses of squid song and actions (tune of "row, row, row your boat") "Squid, squid, swim so fast Shooting through the sea Giant eyes, glowing eyes In the dark I see. Squid, squid, swim so fast Shooting through the sea Ten arms, my tentacles Bring the fish to me. Squid, squid, swim so fast Shooting through the sea No bones, one big beak And tiny rows of teeth" . . . and so forth.
Conclusion/wrap up	Clean up squid when each group has finished. Gather children. "What did you notice and find out when you were investigating the squid?" Write dictation of their comments. Encourage children to draw sketches in their project journal of what they saw.
Differentiation	
Above level	**Provide reference books to extend depth of exploration.** **Introduce and use expanded vocabulary.** **Identify additional body parts and organs.**
Below level	**Focus on open exploration, not naming structures.** **Or, 1 to 1, assist in locating basic body structures at child's request.** **Model use of tools.** **Use simple reference photos.**

(Continued)

(Continued)

Different modalities	**Whole squid or models (tactile, visual)** **Acting out how squid behave (kinesthetic)** **Photographs of live squid (visual)** **Anatomy guide and anatomy sketch (logical)** **Description of materials and procedures (verbal)** **Team or individual stations (inter/intrapersonal)** **Squid song and actions (musical, kinesthetic)** **Discuss connections to other similar sea life such as octopus (naturalist)**
Cultural considerations	**Emphasize that children can explore the models and photographs in the class-room (Alaina's vegan family objects to her touching actual animal).** **Several children have not used these tools before; provide support and model use.** **Two children are dual language learners; provide extra photos and watch video, label basic parts in home language.**
Extensions into next step	Revising KWHL chart Revisiting project documentation with children to identify interest in other creatures
Assessment/ evaluation	Photos, notes, observation (use of tools, identification of parts) Quotes of children's dialogues List of children's comments (dictation) Drawings Added notes to KWHL chart

Practice 3: Differentiating lesson plans

Now it's your turn. Review the basic lesson outline for these 1st grade lesson plans and note differentiating, imagining several ways that you could add differentiation to the plan. Think about children with linguistic differences, fine motor development differences, different experiences of community, and so forth. Make notes on your lesson expansions in the differentiation section towards the end of the plan.

Lesson title	**Creating how-to videos**
Assessment of prior learning	This activity allowed me to see if the class truly understands what it takes to write a how-to book. Their instructions have to be clear and detailed for someone to learn from their how-to book.
Purpose/goal	Develop expository writing skills. Learn to write for the audience. Use technology to publish written work.
Measurable objectives	Children will show they can write clear step-by-step instructions on how to do something. They will test their instructions with a partner where the partner will act out the instructions. From there they will edit what is not clear, and revise as needed.
Common Core Standard	W.1.7. Participate in shared research and writing projects (e.g., explore a number of how-to books on a given topic and use them to write a sequence of instructions). W.1.6. With guidance and support from adults, use a variety of digital tools to produce and publish writing, including in collaboration with peers.

Materials	How-to step-by-step organizer paper Pencil White construction paper x 20 Crayons Scissors Flip camera
Introduction/ anticipatory set	Children have been learning how to write how-to books on something they are experts on. To take their writing to the next level, I will introduce creating a video from their how-to writing. They will need to complete an editing checklist of their how-to book before they are able to create their video.
Body of activity	1. Students join me on the rug. 2. We will review why we write how-to books and the important details we need to add. 3. I will introduce making a video to them. 4. I will show them the example video I made about my how-to book on "how to make a peanut butter and jelly sandwich." 5. I will explain that each of them will have a chance to make their how-to book into a video, but they have to complete a checklist before they do. 6. I will hand each of them the checklist that leads them through their how-to book to see if it's the best it can be. 7. Once they feel their checklist is completed, they will come to me so I can check it. 8. When they have an edited, easy to read how-to book, they can begin their video. 9. They will need two pieces of construction paper (one for their background, the other for their pieces). 10. Once they have created their movable pieces, they will join me in the hall to record. 11. First we will do a practice shot to get them used to reading and moving their pieces at the same time. 12. Then we will record their video.
Conclusion/wrap up	After everyone has completed his or her video, we will discuss why a how-to video can make our how-to books more clear (steps are easier to follow when we have movable pieces to show).
Differentiation	
Above level	
Below level	
Different modalities	
Cultural considerations	

(Continued)

Extensions into next step	During snack time, when children are at their desks, I will show their how-to videos. We will talk about how helpful it is to not only read a how-to book but see their how-tos demonstrated.
Assessment/ evaluation	Students will be assessed on their how-to book by the checklist. This checklist allowed the students to evaluate their own how-to books and edit them where needed. Once they have completed the checklist, I will go over it with them and point out anything they might have missed.

Lesson title	School community helper interviews
Assessment of prior learning	Children have been learning about how our community works as a team to run smoothly. Our school is made up of many jobs, some we might not know about. This activity allows me to see children's understanding of the importance of teamwork within a community.
Purpose/goal	Students will be able to conduct an interview to further investigate a question. They will have to come up with questions that will get them to the answer the class wants to know (How do you help our school? How can we help you?).
Measurable objectives	Children will show that they understand the assignment by asking questions that are relevant to our goal.
Common Core Standard	SL.1.1. Participate in collaborative conversations with diverse partners about 1st grade topics and texts with peers and adults in small and larger groups.
	SL.1.1a. Follow agreed upon rules for discussions (e.g., listening to others with care, speaking one at a time about the topics and texts under discussion).
	SL.1.1b. Build on others' talk in conversations by responding to the comments of others through multiple exchanges.
	W.1.8. With guidance and support from adults, recall information from experiences or gather information from provided sources to answer a question.
Materials	Paper Pencil Clipboard Camera Flip video camera
Introduction/ anticipatory set	Today we will be able to learn more about the different jobs it takes to keep a school functioning. Not only do our community members help us, but we can help them in return. We will be professional interviewers and learn more about our important role in our school.
Body of activity	1. Students will join me on the rug as we list the many community helpers we have in our school. 2. I will then partner up the students and assign them someone to interview (I will already have prepared the school employees and determined a time they are available to be interviewed). 3. Once each student has a partner and a person to interview we will go back to our desk to come up with interview questions.

	4. They will work with their partners to come up with questions that will help them answer how school employees help our school and how we can help them in return.
	5. Students will be guided in writing appropriate questions when needed.
	6. Students will need to decide who is going to ask what question in their interview. (They must have at least four questions.)
	7. Once students have their questions, throughout the day they will go to their interviews.
	8. When they go to their interview, they will each have a clipboard with their questions attached.
	9. Students will write down the answers they are given under each question.
	10. Once interview is completed, they will take a picture with the interviewee for documentation.
Conclusion/wrap up	After everyone has completed his or her interviews, I will type up the questions and answers and put them together in a book. Once the book is completed, we will join together on the rug, and students will talk about their interviews. We will discuss the answers that were given and talk about how it is our job to help the employees of our school.
Differentiation	
Above level	
Below level	
Different modalities	
Cultural considerations	
Extensions into next step	To show our school community how much we appreciate what they do for us, we will write letters thanking them and telling them how we will help them every day.
Assessment/ evaluation	Students will be assessed by how relevant their questions are to the task at hand. They will also be assessed on their behavior and appropriateness during the interview (Were they on task?).

ALTERNATIVE IDEAS FOR HOLIDAY-THEMED ACTIVITIES

As a final practice activity, consider these alternatives for classroom holiday activities that Alex has developed for his kindergarten class. In the final row in Figure 11.5, identify a specific holiday practice you are familiar with and develop alternative ideas for supporting the meaningful learning goals while being more inclusive of all children and families.

FIGURE 11.5

Alternative Ideas for Holiday-Themed Classroom Experiences

Holiday	Potentially Exclusionary Activity	Learning Goals	Alternative Experiences for Organized Classroom Plans (still always welcoming children's emergent conversations about their home experiences)
St. Valentine's Day	Party with sweets, and friendship or love message exchanges	Identify qualities of friendships. Share feelings with people you care about.	Friendship Fridays: select classmate's name from a hat and write a positive note expressing something you like and appreciate about them; or write favorite things about classmates or loved ones on strips of paper and make an ongoing paper chain; string it around the room
Christmas	Crafts themed on Christmas trees, St. Nicholas/Santa Claus; Christmas carol singing	Make connections to family traditions. Explore social cultural and/or religious meaning of various winter holidays.	Sharing and reading personal stories, creating drawings and artwork, and representing through dramatic play authentic family customs, events, and traditions during the winter season. Read calendars and picture books, and watch video clips about diverse family customs, making connections to children's own traditions (similarities/differences diagram).

Your ideas

IN MY FAMILY

A Letter Changed Everything

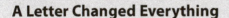

Being in school was regularly punctuated by awkward moments when I had to be asked to leave the classroom so the rest of the children could celebrate either a birthday or one of the many holidays throughout the year. I would see the trays of cupcakes, plates of cookies, or bags of decorations come in as I was ushered down the hall to the office. There I would sit, listening to the clicking of typing or overhearing phone conversations. Eventually I would be called back in to the classroom and I'd walk past the garbage bin by the door overflowing with wrappers, streamers, and other evidence of a party.

My family's religious beliefs didn't allow me to celebrate holidays or birthdays. We did observe a solemn gathering for acknowledging Christ's death. However, that obviously wasn't one of those school events. So for me, I always felt singled out, left out, clearly "other," and I was not immune to all the looks of pity or disdain

I saw from teachers and the other kids. More than once I remember teachers whispering over my head as they walked me back to the classroom about "how sad his parents would do that to him." I pretty much hated having to go to school a lot of the time. And I know my parents felt stressed about it.

Well . . . except for 3rd grade. My 3rd grade teacher, Ms. Carter, had a policy about diversity, and she sent home a welcome letter in the beginning of the year with her beliefs and plans laid out. My parents talked about it at dinner when the letter came. They mentioned that the teacher said she knew there were different beliefs and family backgrounds in our class and that to prepare for our differences she had made a policy designed to include everyone. Ms. Carter's policy was that each person's family experiences were different; we might share some things but we also do things differently. She wrote that in her classroom, being fair meant that everyone was included in the life of the classroom all the time. She said that fairness was the first rule of her room.

Since she knew that some families celebrate certain holidays, some celebrate other holidays, and some don't celebrate any formal holidays, Ms. Carter made a plan that there wouldn't be any organized celebrations of any holidays. She wrote about how children should always feel welcomed to talk about what was happening in their lives outside of school, including religious or holiday traditions. Sharing important parts of our family lives would be a valued part of being a class together and a big way for us to learn to appreciate each other. The difference in her room was that there wouldn't be parties, crafts, or class plays centered on certain holidays or religions that would potentially exclude some children. I could tell by my parents' conversation that they were more relaxed about this school year than they had been before.

That year in Ms. Carter's room was my favorite time at school. No one whispered about me and my family's beliefs. I never had to leave the room when the rest of the class was doing something together. I was just as "right," just as important, as everyone else. I also learned a lot about other kids' home traditions when we talked about what we did on weekends and over school breaks. At lunchtime it was like we were storytellers, taking turns highlighting things we did with family and friends outside of school. I didn't realize that some of my classmates' religious beliefs sounded a lot like some of my family's. Before that I thought we were so different. It was just cool to get to learn about other ideas and family stuff in this . . . relaxed way. My parents talked a lot more to Ms. Carter than to other teachers I've had. I really think it was all because of that letter she sent home at the beginning. School was a whole different place for me because of that little letter.

A Commitment to Valuing Diversity in Education

Experiences, realities, and internalized sense of identity are vastly and qualitatively different among different cultural groups. In particular, individuals who are classified as outside of the dominant culture (by their own self-identity or by a label placed on them by others) have a very different experience of "in-group" or "out-group" existence and of the vast inequities operating within social groups (de Freitas & McAuley, 2008). Similarly, teachers often label as successful and more capable children whose learning and thinking style are a "good fit" with the classroom structure, while children whose styles differ are often assessed as unsuccessful or incapable of learning (Tomlinson & McTighe, 2006). To further exacerbate the divide, children who have had multiple experiences of being outside the "chosen circle" or privileged group suffer negative internalizing behaviors (withdrawal and self-doubt) or externalizing behaviors (inattention, disrespecting others).

Minimizing differences can appeal to many students and teachers, especially those from the White middle-class or those from the dominant group, because it feels more comfortable than acknowledging that the foundation of dominant or White privilege is rooted in and perpetuated by racism and classism. Facing the reality of the power/privilege structure means confronting the idea that each member of the dominant group plays a role in, and benefits from, discrimination against nondominant members (Derman-Sparks & Ramsey, 2006). Only when we honestly and critically examine the roots of this discomfort can we actually move forward toward developing a more aware teaching force that is equipped to develop in our young the capacity to envision and create a more equitable society. A recommendation for preservice professionals is to "embrace discomfort as part of the ongoing emotional labour of confronting one's privilege" (de Freitas & McAuley, 2008, p. 433). So then, for early childhood professionals, the once-neutral awareness from the early childhood years now may be an adult awareness laced with discomfort, guilt, pain, and confusion.

Yet somewhere in the span between children's natural curiosity and adult awareness of the socio-politico-historical context of differences lies the potential to realize and reprogram realities of inequity and power in society. For early childhood professionals, the journey of exploring diversity involves looking at self, others around you, and society as a whole. It exposes raw nerves and deeply entrenched norms that include systematic unfairness. In order to be able to guide children's development of positive attitudes about human diversity and equity and genuinely form essential partnerships with families, adults working with children and families are ethically obligated and compelled to take up the task with depth and commitment.

Teaching intentionally for social justice lays essential foundations for children to develop positive attitudes and behaviors toward the rich diversity in today's world.

LINKING VALUES, ACTIONS, AND ADVOCACY

Throughout this text you have explored human diversity through a personal lens as well as professional perspectives. Your task now is to make essential connections between personal and professional aspects of diversity—the heart and the mind of this work—to culminate this part of the ongoing journey towards engaging children and families in their own journey of valuing diversity and advocating for social justice.

Being a culturally competent early childhood professional requires that you feel prepared and competent to support and appreciate differences among children and families. As stated in the beginning of this chapter, the final element of culturally responsive practice is administrative support. One way each of us serves as an advocate to guide and inform administration is through clear articulation of values and commitment to practice. To set the stage for embracing and valuing diversity, it is important that you prepare a statement or policy about your goals regarding diversity awareness and appreciation. This statement can serve as a starting point for conversation with families as well as a proactive explanation of how you will handle sensitive situations. The purpose of writing the statement is to clearly articulate your beliefs and values regarding diversity and education. In this way, you demonstrate that you are competent, intentional, and prepared for even the more sensitive and delicate aspects of your work and you position yourself as a resource for others who might feel unsure about how to handle certain questions or topics about differences.

ATTITUDE TO ACTION, BELIEF TO BEHAVIOR 11.4

Articulating Your Commitment

Take a few moments to think about how your values and beliefs emerge into your practice, being especially aware of the impact your actions have on others. How are your actions (discipline, educational expectations, parent contacts, classroom celebrations, etc.) impacted by your values? Construct your own diversity policy statement, which can be shared with families as a welcoming letter and explanation of what "valuing diversity" means to you. Describe your beliefs and knowledge of diversity and how you will encourage awareness and appreciation with children. This is a time to explain how you will support children's questions, thinking, and curiosity about human differences and how you plan to promote appreciation for each other through sharing and exploring differences and similarities. Consider how you will validate and respond to children's questions or comments about differences and how you plan to extend conversations and thinking about diversity. Think about some of the scripts you have created to respond to bias and the stories you have read about family and classroom experiences relating to diverse children and families. Figure 11.6 includes ideas and prompts to organize your approach to crafting a statement.

(Continued)

(Continued)

FIGURE 11.6

Worksheet to Start Diversity Philosophy Statement

Idea prompts	Idea details	What my own values look like in practice
What specific choices have I made in my classroom design plans that are evidence of my values?	Center-based? Group meals? Peace table? Time out chair? Parent information board? Desks in rows?	
What specific learning materials, toys, displays, books, posters, computer/tablet games do I have in the classroom that reflect my values or culture?	Do I always use farm animals as the only example of "animals"? Would children from some settings connect better with dogs, cats, and birds as examples of "animals"?	
	Are toys or images of "homes" always a single-family looking house (boxy base, triangular roof, yard, fence, and so on)?	
What are my classroom rules? What behaviors warrant discipline and what does the discipline look like?	Do I expect children to take care of one another?	
	Do I explain what being responsible for yourself looks like?	
	Do I isolate children who misbehave or don't follow rules?	
How do I handle family traditions or holidays?	Do I require all children to perform a holiday play (held in December to coincide with Christmas and/or Chanukah but called "holiday" to seem neutral)?	
	Do I plan holiday-themed crafts during the school day?	
What ways do I connect with families?	Newsletter, notes, two-way journals, parent volunteers, home visits?	
Do I tend to favor certain kinds of instruction (verbal, visual) or management style (structured, unstructured, in-between)?		
What image do I picture to describe "teaching"? How do I talk about my role as a teacher?		

Summary

RESEARCH ON WHAT WORKS FOR ALL CHILDREN

- Evidence-based practice requires that teachers are knowledgeable about relevant research data on instructional effectiveness, that they are knowledgeable about individual children and families, and that they are able to use sound professional judgment in order to appropriately respond to each child and family.
- RtI is widely cited as helpful for children such as dual language learners, children with identified disabilities and those without formal diagnosis, children struggling to meet benchmark standards, and children from economically stressed families, who need specialized support.
- RtI is a multitiered system of support, meaning that programs are designed with several levels of instruction and individualizing is embedded in each level and based on an assessment–instruction–assessment structure.

- RtI is structured around the use of high-quality curricula with strong assessment instruments and procedures.
- The HighScope program is an example of a high quality, research-based, early childhood curriculum, with an integrated validated assessment instrument, designed for either infant/toddler, preschool, or elementary age children.

LINKING VALUES, ACTIONS, AND ADVOCACY

- Working for social justice means developing awareness of the ways that children and families differ, appreciating these differences, and adjusting settings and practices to support all children.
- The work of exploring personal backgrounds and biases often involves discomfort, though it is essential that professionals be willing to work through these feelings to recognize the ethical obligation to advocate for equity and social justice.

Chapter Learning Outcomes: Self-Assessment

Use this space to reflect on how well you have achieved the learning goals for this chapter by evaluating your own competency in the topics below. List three to five items that describe key concepts you have learned from the chapter.

Discuss how evidence-based decisions inform culturally and individually relevant practice.	
Identify instructional strategies that support diverse learners.	
Practice strategies for meaningfully including all children and valuing diverse families.	
Create a personal statement about what valuing diversity means in your work.	

Glossary

Academic language   Linguistic styles and vocabulary that are part of content area knowledge (math, science, social studies, and so on) but that differ from conversational language.

Acceptance   Allowing something or someone to exist but not necessarily having positive feelings about them or it.

Accommodations   Adjustments, sometimes minor, to materials, schedules, routines, or formats of instruction and assessment that allow equal access and participation.

Acculturation   The pressure to conform to the dominant culture at the expense of one's own individual cultural identity.

Appreciation   Valuing, rating highly, and admiring others for the ways in which they are diverse and unique.

Awareness   A neutral state of simply noticing how people are different.

Biases   The ways we tend to think about things; biases occur naturally through personal experience.

Bioecological model   A framework created by Urie Bronfenbrenner for understanding human development. The biolecological model describes many layers of direct and indirect influence in children's lives and also recognizes the bidirectional nature of influences.

Christian normalcy   Ways in which White, European-influenced, Christian values and practices are so historically and deeply ingrained that many people don't even realize the bias.

Code switching   The capability of bi- or multilingual children to switch language, depending on the place and the person with whom they are communicating.

Colorblindness   *Choosing* to ignore skin color and cultural diversity to minimize the differences among people.

Cross-cultural communication   Recognizing specific behavioral differences between cultures, such as eye contact, smiling, personal space, physical contact, gender expectations, solving problems, directness of speaking, and more, and using a communication style that is appropriate for the audience.

Cultural competence and **cultural intelligence**   The knowledge, skills, attitudes, and behaviors that integrate sensitivity and appreciation for cultural differences into everyday actions.

Culture   Ways of thinking, norms, and values that are expressed in artifacts and everyday behaviors.

Differentiated classroom   Structures and procedures that accommodate a wide range of strengths, styles, and needs.

Differentiation   The process of tailoring instruction and interaction approaches to different learning styles and diverse backgrounds.

Discrimination   Negative attitudes prompting negative actions, policies, or organizational practices towards a target group or groups.

Diversity   Variety; the ways people or things are different.

Dual language learner A child whose home language is other than English.

Early childhood inclusion Practices that are intentionally designed to appropriately and meaningfully engage all children to their fullest potential within the same learning environment and care setting.

Early intervention/early childhood special education (EI/ECSE) Programs and services designed for infants, toddlers, and preschool children with, or at risk for, developmental disability. These programs and services focus heavily on family support and education along with individualized plans to strengthen children's development.

Elementary and Secondary Education Act (ESSA) The first federal agenda focused on children with diverse abilities. ESSA required schools to provide services for children with disabilities.

Enculturation The process of learning one's own cultural norms and expectations, which are internalized through experience.

Equality Having the same access to services and institutions.

Equity Fairness and having one's unique needs recognized and met.

Ethnicity (ethnic) One's sense of membership with a national origin, usually connected to origin of one's ancestry.

Ethnocentrism The belief that one's own race, nationality, or heritage is superior to others.

Ethnographic research A form of qualitative research that involves immersed observations and direct interviews. Ethnographic research can involve the researchers living in the community of individuals being studied.

Evidence-based practice A way of making decisions which seeks to synthesize quality research outcomes with family and professional judgment.

Exceptionalities Children's functioning in all areas of development and academics when outside the range of typical expectations.

Extended family Relatives other than parents and siblings. Extended family can include grandparents, aunts and uncles, cousins, and more.

HighScope Perry Preschool Study It is a long-term research study of 123 African American children from low income homes, 58 of whom were randomly assigned to a high quality preschool program at ages 3 and 4 between 1962 and 1967.

Identity Our concept of who we are. Identity is connected to beliefs and behaviors.

Individualized education programs Integrated plans with goals, objectives, and supports tailored to the unique strengths and needs of children diagnosed with a disability.

Individuals with Disabilities Education Act (IDEA) The law that updates and amends PL 94-142 and provides funding for special education services extended through schools.

Institutional racism Racism that occurs when agencies perpetuate unofficial policies and practices that promote differential outcomes based on racial classification, or when they fail to take action to equalize opportunities and promote equality in systems and policies.

Learning style The ways in which individuals learn new material and that impact how a person takes in, engages with, and responds to learning experiences and environments.

Macrosystem The outer layers of influence that are less direct and that exert less influence on children's development.

Microsystem The inside layers of influence on a child, including the stronger and closer relationships that have a greater degree of influence on and are more influenced by the child.

Modifications More involved alterations or alternatives to expectations of children; criteria for successful performance, assessment format, or instructional approach and level.

Monotheistic   Believing in one omnipotent god.

Multicultural education   Strategies to meaningfully integrate students' diverse backgrounds into the school environment and adapt instruction to support learner diversity.

Nuclear family   Married mother, father, and biological children living in the same household.

Oppression   A phenomenon that occurs when negative beliefs and actions that target a particular group or groups are part of a larger social system and structure.

Person-first language   Language that places intentional focus on positioning individuals first and descriptive characteristics second, as in *child with visual impairment*.

Pluralism   The acceptance of individuality, multiple perspectives, cultures, or diverse people within a shared social context.

Polytheistic   Believing in more than one god or goddess.

Prejudice   Prejudgments and inaccurate assumptions (usually negative) about individuals from a particular group. Prejudice is not based on actual knowledge of the individuals.

Public Law 94-142   The part of the Education for All Handicapped Children Act that extensively outlines educational access for children with diverse abilities and grants funding for states to provide services.

Resiliency   The ability to compensate for challenges and risk factors and to create positive outcomes in spite of those challenges.

Response to intervention (RtI)   A broad framework of multitiered support systems that leverages the resources in collaborative problem solving teams in order to individualize instruction for each child.

Scaffolding   The dynamic process whereby a child's experience with a challenging task is shaped by interactions, verbal cues, and careful prompts from a more knowledgeable partner.

Script   A short, prescribed statement used to maximize a teachable moment; a script is a particularly useful tool to prepare for use in stressful or uncomfortable situations.

Social justice   Relating to the equitable distribution of advantage, resources, and power.

Social referencing   A behavior, seen during the first year, in which an infant will look to the expression of a trusted caregiver to determine how to respond to an unfamiliar experience.

Socioeconomic status (SES)   A widely used gauge of family financial stability. SES includes measures of income, parent employment, neighborhood resources, and parent education level.

Standard English   The format of English spoken by a professional, educated, middle-class group. Standard English carries more prestige than other structures of English.

Tolerance   See **Acceptance**.

Universal Design for Learning   An approach to planning and instruction that is deliberately inclusive of the widest possible audience and takes into account wide variety in abilities.

References

AACAP (American Academy of Child & Adolescent Psychiatry). (2005). *Facts for families: Foster care*. Washington, DC: AACAP.

AAP (American Academy of Pediatrics). (2003). Family pediatrics: Report on the task force on the family. *Pediatrics, 111*(6), 1541–1571.

Abo-Zena, M. M. (2012). Faith from the fringes: Religious minorities in school. Retrieved from Phi Delta Kappan website at http://www .kappanmagazine.org

Addy, S., & Wright, V. (2012). *Basic facts about low-income children*. National Center for Children in Poverty.

Ansell, E. B., Rando, K., Tuit, K., Guarnaccia, J., & Sinha, R. (2012). Cumulative adversity and smaller gray matter volume in medial prefrontal, anterior cingulate, and insula regions. *Biologic Psychiatry, 72*(1), 57–64.

APA. (2005). *Lesbian and gay parenting*. American Psychological Association Lesbian, Gay, and Bisexual Concerns Office. Washington, DC.

Apfelbaum, E. P., Sommers, S. R., & Norton, M. I. (2008). Seeing race and seeming racist? Evaluating strategic colorblindness in social interaction. *Journal of Personality and Social Psychology, 95*(4), 918. doi: 10.1037/ a0011990

Arnsten, A., Masure, C., & Rajita, S. (2012). This is your brain in meltdown. *Scientific American, 304*(4), 48–53.

Artis, J. (2007). Maternal cohabitation and child well-being among kindergarten children. *Journal of Marriage and Family, 69*(1), 222–236.

Atwater, S. A. (2008). Waking up to difference: Teachers, color-blindness and the effects on students of color. *Journal of Instructional Psychology, 35*(3), 247–253.

Baca Zinn, M., Eitzen, D. S., & Wells, B. (2008). *Diversity in families*. Boston, MA: Pearson.

Balcazar, F., Suarez-Balcazar, Y., Taylor-Ritzler, T. (2009). Cultural competence: Development of a conceptual framework. *Disability and Rehabilitation, 31*(14), 1153–1160.

Ball, J., & Simpkins, M. (2004). The community within the child: Integration of indigenous knowledge into First Nations childcare process and practice. *American Indians Quarterly, 28*(3/4), 480–498.

Banks, J. A. (2006). *Cultural diversity and education: Foundations, curriculums, and teaching* (5th ed.). Boston, MA: Pearson Education, Inc.

Batalova, J., & McHugh, M. (2010). *Top languages spoken by English language learners nationally and by state*. Washington, DC: Migration Policy Institute. Retrieved March 25, 2013, from http://www .migrationinformation.org/ellinfo /FactSheet_ELL3.pdf

Bayat, M., Mindes, G., & Covitt, S. (2010). What does RtI (Response to Intervention) look like in preschool? *Early Childhood Education Journal, 37*, 493–500.

Bedrova, E., & Leong, D. J. (1996). *Tools of the mind: The Vygotskian approach to early childhood education*. Upper Saddle River, NJ: Pearson/Merrill Prentice Hall.

Bennett, C. I. (2011). *Comprehensive multicultural education* (7th ed.). Boston, MA: Pearson Education, Inc.

Bennett, M. J. (2009). Defining, measuring, and facilitating intercultural learning: A conceptual introduction to the intercultural education double supplement. *Intercultural Education, 20*, S1–S13.

Bergen Jr., T. J. (2001). The development of prejudice in children. *Education, 122*(1), 154–161.

Bergner, G. (2009). Black children, White preference: Brown v. Board, the doll tests, and the politics of self-esteem. *American Quarterly, 61*(2), 29–332.

Birkmayer, J., Cohen, J., Jensen, I., & Variano, D. (2005). Children's books about family relationships and experiences. *Beyond the Journal, Young Children on the Web*. 1–5. Retrieved from the National Association for the Education of Young Children website at http://www.naeyc.org/files/yc/file /200505/07Birckmayer.pdf

BLS (Bureau of Labor Statistics). (2012). Employed persons by detailed occupation, sex, race, and Hispanic or Latino ethnicity. Retrieved on February 18, 2013, from http://www .bls.gov/cps/cpsaat11.pdf

Bowker, J. (2006). *World religions*. New York: NY: DK Pub.

Bredekamp, V. S., & Copple, C. (1997). *Developmentally appropriate practice in early childhood programs* (2nd ed.). Washington, DC: NAEYC.

Breuilly, E., O'Brien, J., & Palmer, M. (1997). *Religions of the world* (Rev. ed.). New York, NY: MacDonald Young Books.

Bronfenbrenner, U. (1979). *The ecology of human development*. New York, NY: Harvard University.

Bronfenbrenner, U. (1992). Ecological systems theory. In R.Vasta (Ed.), *Six theories of child development: Revised formulations and current issues* (pp. 187–249). Philadelphia, PA: Kingsley.

Bronfenbrenner, U., & Morris, P. (1998). The ecology of developmental processes. In W. Damon & R. Lerner (Eds.), *Handbook of child psychology: Volume 1: Theoretical models of human development* (5th ed.). Hoboken, NJ: John Wiley & Sons Inc.

Bruckman, M., & Blanton, P. W. (2003). Welfare-to-work single mother's perspectives on parent involvement in Head Start: Implications for parent-teacher collaboration. *Early Childhood Education Journal, 30*, 145–150.

Bruder, M. (2010). Early childhood intervention: A promise to children and families for their future. *Exceptional Children, 76*(3), 339–355.

Bucher, R. D. (2010). *Diversity consciousness: Opening our minds to people, cultures and opportunities* (3rd ed.). Upper Saddle River, NJ: Pearson Education, Inc.

Buysse, V., & Wesley, P. (Eds.). (2006). *Evidence-based practice in early childhood education*. Zero to Three: National Center for Infants, Toddlers and Families, Washington, DC.

CAEP (Council for the Accreditation of Educator Preparation). (2012). Commission of standards and performance reporting: Draft recommendations for the CAEP board. Retrieved on March 10, 2013, from http://caepnet.org/commission/standards

Callaway, A. (2010). Literature review: The growing need to understand Muslim students. *Multicultural Perspectives, 12*(4), 217–222.

Campbell, D. E., & Putnam, R. D. (2012). America's grace: How a tolerant nation bridges its religious divides. *Political Science Quarterly, 126*(4), 611–640.

CAST (Center for Applied Special Technology). (2011). What is Universal Design for Learning? Retrieved from the National Center of Universal Design for Learning at http://www.cast.org/udl/index.html

CCSSO (Council of Chief State School Officers). (2011, April). Interstate teacher assessment and support consortium (InTASC) model core teaching standards: A resource for state dialogue. Washington, DC: Author. Retrieved from http://www.ccsso.org/intasc

Cherlin, A. (2010). One thousand and forty-nine reasons why it's hard to know when a fact is a fact. In B. Risman (Ed.), *Families as they really are*. New York, NY: W.W. Norton and Co.

Connor, S. (2006). Grandparents raising grandchildren: Formation, disruption and intergenerational transmission of attachment. *Australian Social Work. 59*(2), 172–184.

Cook, C., Powell, A., Sims, A., & Eagger, S. (2011). Spirituality and secularity: Professional boundaries in psychiatry. *Mental Health, Religion & Culture, 14*(1), 35–42.

Coontz, S. (2010). The evolution of American families. In B. Risman (Ed.), *Families as they really are*. New York, NY: W.W. Norton and Co.

Copple, C., & Bredekamp, S. (Eds.). (2009). *Developmentally appropriate practice in early childhood programs* (3rd ed.). Washington, DC: National Association for the Education of Young Children.

Corrigan, J., Denny, F. M., Eire, C. M. N., & Jaffee, M. S. (1998). *Readings in Judaism, Christianity, and Islam*. Boston, MA: Pearson Education, Inc.

Cowan, P. (2010). When is a relationship between facts a causal one? In B. Risman (Ed.), *Families as they really are*. New York, NY: W.W. Norton and Co.

Crosnoe, R., Leventhal, T., Wirth, R., Pierce, K., & Pianta, R. (2010). Family socioeconomic status and consistent environmental stimulation in early childhood. *Child Development, 81*(3) 972–987.

Cross, B. E. (2003). Learning or unlearning racism: Transferring teacher education curriculum to classroom practices. *Theory into Practice, 42*(3), 203–209.

Cunningham, A. (2001). Forgotten families—the impact of imprisonment. *Australian Institute of Family Studies. 59*(4), 35–38.

Cuthbert, P. (2005). The student learning process: Learning styles or learning approaches? *Teaching in Higher Education, 10*(2), 235–249.

CWLA (Child Welfare League of America). (n.d.). Practice areas: Family foster care. Retrieved on August 8, 2012, from http://www.cwla.org/programs/fostercare/default.htm

Danby, S. (2008). The importance of friends. *Early Childhood Matters, 108*, 36. Bernard Van Leer Foundation.

Darragh, J. (2010). *Introduction to early childhood education: Equity and inclusion*. Upper Saddle River, NJ: Pearson.

De Freitas, E., & McAuley, A. (2008). Teaching for diversity by troubling whiteness: Strategies for classrooms in isolated white communities. *Race, ethnicity and education, 11*(4), 429–442.

DEC (Division for Early Childhood). (2007). Promoting positive outcomes for children with disabilities: Recommendations for curriculum, assessment, and program evaluation. Missoula, MT: DEC.

DEC (Division for Early Childhood of the Council for Exceptional Children), NAEYC (National Association for the Education of Young Children), & NHSA (National Head Start Association). (2013). *Frameworks for response to intervention in early childhood: Descriptions and implications.*

DEC/NAEYC. (2009). *Early childhood inclusion: A joint position statement of the Division for Early Childhood (DEC) and the National Association for the Education of Young Children (NAEYC).* Chapel Hill: The University of North Carolina, FPG Child Development Institute.

Derman-Sparks, L. (1993). Empowering children to create a caring culture in a world of differences. *Childhood Education, 70*(2), 66–71.

Derman-Sparks, L., & Ramsey, P. G. (2006). *What if all the kids are white?* New York, NY: Teachers College Press.

Derman-Sparks, L., & The Antibias Curriculum Task Force. (1989). *The Antibias Curriculum: Tools for empowering young children.* Washington, DC: NAEYC.

Dolbin-MacNab, M. (2006). Just like raising your own? Grandmothers' perceptions of parenting a second time around. *Family Relations, 55*(5), 564–575.

Duhaney, L. M. G. (2003). A practical approach to managing the behaviors of students with ADD. *Intervention in School and Clinic, 38*(5), 267–279.

Dunn, A., & Perez, L. (2012). Universal Design for Learning (UDL) in action: The smart inclusion toolkit. *Teaching Exceptional Children, 45*, 2. Retrieved from the Council for Exceptional Children website at http://tecplus.org/articles/article/9

Eamon, M. K. (2001). The effects of poverty on children's socioemotional development: An ecological systems analysis. *Social Work, 46*(3), 256–266.

Earl, M. (2001). Shadow and spirituality. *International Journal of Children's Spirituality, 6*(3), 277–288.

Eberly, J. L., Joshi, A., & Konzal, J. (2007). Communicating with families across cultures: An investigation of teacher perceptions and practices. *The School Community Journal, 17*(2), 7–26.

Eck, D. L. (2007). Prospects for pluralism: Voice and vision in the study of religion. *Journal of the American Academy of Religion, 75*(4), 743–776.

Edwards, J., & Farghaly, A. (2006). *Locating culture in unexpected places.* Proceedings of the CATESOL State Conference.

England, P., & Edin, K. (2010). Briefing paper: Unmarried couples with children. In B. Risman (Ed.), *Families as they really are.* New York, NY: W.W. Norton and Co.

Espinosa, L. M. (2005). Curriculum and assessment considerations for young children from culturally, linguistically, and economically diverse backgrounds. *Psychology in the Schools, 42*(8), 837–853.

Evans, G., & Rosenbaum, J. (2008). Self-regulation and the income-achievement gap. *Early Childhood Research Quarterly 23*, 504–514.

Fairtlough, A. (2008). Growing up with a lesbian or gay parent: Young people's perspectives. *Health & Social Care in the Community, 16*(5), 521–528.

Felder, R. (1996). Matters of style. *ASEE Prism, 6*(4), 18–23.

Felder, R. (2010). Are learning styles invalid? (Hint: no!) On Course newsletter, September 27, 2010. Retrieved from the On Course Newsletter website at www.oncourseworkshop.com/learning046.htm

Felder, R., & Brent, R. (2005). Understanding student differences. *Journal of Engineering Education, 94*(1), 57–72.

Felder, R., & Henriques, E. (1995). Learning and teaching styles in foreign and second language education. *Foreign Language Annals, 28*(1), 21–31.

Felder, R., & Spurlin, J. (2005). Applications, reliability and validity of the Index of Learning Styles. *International Journal of Engineering Education, 21*(1), 103–112.

Fitzgerald, H. E., Mann, T., Cabrera, N., Sarche, M., & Qin, D. (2009). Development of infants and toddlers in ethnoracial families. *Infant Mental Health Journal, 30*(5), 425–432. doi: 10.1002/imhj.20222

Fuentes, Y. S. (2011). Head Start today: A look at demographics and culture and linguistic responsiveness. Presentation in Advisory Committee for Head Start Research and Evaluation meeting, September 21, 2011. Retrieved on June 7, 2013, from the Office of Planning, Research & Evaluation website at http://www.acf.hhs.gov/programs/opre/resource/head-start-today-a-look-at-demographics-and-culture-and-linguistic.

Gall, T., Malette, J., & Guirguis-Younger, M. (2011). Spirituality and religiousness: A diversity of definitions. *Journal of Spiritualty in Mental Health, 13*(1), 158–181.

Gallas, K. (1998). *Sometimes I can be anything: Power gender and identity in a primary classroom.* M. Cochran-Smith & S. L. Lytle (Eds.). New York, NY: Teachers College Press.

Gardner, H. (2006). *Multiple intelligences.* New York, NY: Basic Books.

Garrick Duhaney, L. (2003). A practical approach to managing the behaviors of students with ADD. *Intervention in School and Clinic, 38*(5), 267–279.

Gartrell, N., & Bos, H. (2010). US national longitudinal lesbian family study: Psychological adjustment of 17-year-old adolescents. *Pediatrics, 126*(1), 1–9.

Gennetian, L. A. (2005). One or two parents? Half or step siblings? The effect of family structure on young children's achievement. *Journal of Popular Economy, 18*(1), 415–436.

Gettinger, M., & Stoiber, K. (2007). Applying a response to intervention model for early literacy development in low-income children. *Topics in Early Childhood Special Education, 27*(4), 198–213.

Ghiso, M. P. (2013). Every language is special: Promoting dual language learning in multicultural primary schools. *Young Children, 61*(1), 22–26.

Gillanders, C. (2007). An English-speaking prekindergarten teacher for young Latino children: Implications of the teacher-child relationship on second language learning. *Early Childhood Education Journal, 35*(1), 47–54.

Ginsberg, M. (2005). Cultural diversity, motivation, and differentiation. *Theory into Practice, 44*(3), 218–225.

Gollnick, D. M., & Chinn, P. C. (2009). *Multicultural education in a pluralistic society* (8th ed.). Upper Saddle River, NJ: Pearson Education, Inc.

Gomez, R.A. (1991). Teaching with a multicultural perspective. *ERIC Digest.* ED339548. Urbana, IL: Clearinghouse on Elementary and Early Childhood Education. Retrieved from ERIC Digest website at http://files.eric.ed.gov/fulltext/ED339548.pdf

Gonzalez-Mena, J. (2008). *Diversity in early care and education: Honoring differences* (5th ed.). New York, NY: McGraw-Hill; Alexandria, VA: NAEYC.

Gordon, J. (2005). Inadvertent complicity: Colorblindness in teacher education. *Education Studies, 38*(2), 135–153.

Gorski, P. C. (2008). The myth of the "culture of poverty." *Educational Leadership, 65*(7), 32–36.

GPO (Government Printing Office). (2012). Title 34: Education. Part 300—Assistance to states for the education of children with disabilities. 71 FR 46753, Aug. 14, 2006, as amended at 72 FR 61307, Oct. 30, 2007. Retrieved from the U.S. Government Printing Office website at http://www.ecfr.gov/cgi-bin/text-idx?c=ecfr&sid=96025ad40230ae0f4a530ec51d0519ca&rgn=div5&view=text&node=34:2.1.1.1.1&idno=34#34:2.1.1.1.1.1.36.7

Greeff, A., & Du Toit, C. (2009). Resilience in remarried families. *The American Journal of Family Therapy, 37*(2), 114–126.

Greenwood, C. R., Bradfield, T., Kaminski, R., Linas, M., Carta, J., & Nylander, D. (2011). The Response to Intervention (RtI) approach in early childhood. *Focus on Exceptional Children, 43*(9), 1–22.

Griffith, R. (2008). Beyond diversity and multiculturalism: Pluralism and the globalization of American religion. *OAH Magazine of History, 22,* 24–27.

Guerino, P., Harrison, P., & Sabol, W. (2010). Prisoners in 2010. Bureau of Justice Statistics. NCJ236096. Retrieved on February 12, 2012, from the Bureau of Justice Statistics website at http://bjs.ojp.usdoj.gov/index.cfm?ty=pbdetail&iid=2230

Halim, F. (2006). Pluralism of American Muslims and the challenge of assimilation. *Journal of Muslim Minority Affairs, 26*(2), 235–244.

Hamm, B., & Banks, A. (2008). Study shows racial diversity across U.S. faiths. Pew Forum on Religion and Public Life. Washington, DC. Retrieved from the Pew Research Religion & Public Life Project website at http://www.pewforum.org/Religion-News/Study-Shows-Racial-Diversity-Across-US-Faiths.aspx.

Hanley, J. H. (1999). Beyond the tip of the iceberg: Five stages toward cultural competence. Retrieved from The International Child and Youth Care Network website at http://www.cyc-net.org/reference/refs-culturalcompetence.html

Harper, S. N., & Pelletier, J. (2010). Parent involvement in early childhood: A comparison of English language learners and English first language families. *International Journal of Early Years Education, 18*(2), 123–141.

Haycock, K. (2001). Closing the achievement gap. *Educational Leadership, 58*(6), 6–11.

Haynes, J. (2008). *Religion and politics.* New York, NY: Taylor & Francis e-Library.

Heller, S., & Smyke, A. (2002). Very young foster children and foster families: Clinical challenges and interventions. *Infant Mental Health Journal, 23*(5), 555–575.

Hemphill, C., Vanneman, A., & Rahman, T. (2011). *Achievement gaps: How Hispanic and White students in public schools perform in mathematics and reading on the National Assessment of Educational Progress.* Washington, DC: National Center for Educational Statistics.

Hernandez, D. J., Denton, N. A., & Macartney, S. E. (2008). Children in immigrant families: Looking to America's future. *Society for Research in Child Development, 22*(3), 1–23.

Hoff, E., Laursen, B., & Tardiff, T. (2002). Socioeconomic status and parenting. In M. Bornstein (Ed.), *Handbook of parenting,* (2nd ed.). Mahwah, NJ: Laurence Earlbaum Associates.

Hollingsworth, L. (2003). International adoption among families in the United States: Considerations of social justice. *Social Work, 48*(2), 209–217.

Hoot, J. L., Szecsi, T., & Moosa, S. (2003). What teachers of young children should know about Islam. *Early Childhood Education Journal, 31*(2), 85–90.

Hoover, J. (2011). *Response to Intervention Models.* Boston, MA: Pearson.

Houston, D., & Kramer, L. (2008). Meeting the long-term needs of families who adopt children out of foster care: A three-year follow-up study. *Child Welfare, 87*(4), 145–170.

Hout, M., & Fischer, C. (2002). Why more Americans have no religious preference: Politics and generations. *American Sociological Review, 67*(2), 165–190.

Huaqing Qi, C., & Kaiser, A. P. (2003). Behavior problems of preschool children from low-income families: Review of the literature. *Topics in Early Childhood Special Education, 23*(4), 188–216.

Huerta, M., & Jackson, J. (2010). Connecting literacy and science to increase achievement for English language learners. *Journal of Early Childhood Education, 38,* 205–211.

Humes, K. R., Jones, N. A., & Ramirez, R. R. (2011). *Overview of race and Hispanic origin: 2010* (2010 Census Briefs #C2010BR-02). Washington, DC: U.S. Census Bureau. Retrieved from http://www.census.gov/prod/cen2010/briefs/c2010br-02.pdf

Hurley, J. J., & Horn, E. M. (2010). Family and professional priorities for inclusive early childhood settings. *Journal of Early Intervention, 32*(5), 335–350.

Hyun, E. (2007). Cultural complexity in early childhood: Images of contemporary young children from a critical perspective. *Childhood Education, 83*(5), 261–267.

Jackson, S., Pretti-Frontczak, K., Harjusola-Webb, S., Grisham-Brown, J., & Romani, J. (2009). Response to intervention: Implications for early childhood professionals. *Language, Speech, and Hearing Services in Schools, 40,* 424–434.

Jones, A. (2003). Reconstructing the stepfamily: Old myths, new stories. *Social Work, 48*(2), 228–236.

Joshim, H. Y. (2007). Because I had a turban. *Teaching Tolerance, 32,* 46–48.

Judge, S. (2000). Accessing and funding assistive technology for young children with disabilities. *Early Childhood Education Journal, 28*(2), 125–131.

Kail, R. (2007). *Children and their development* (4th ed.). Toronto, Canada: Pearson Prentice Hall.

Keat, J. B., Strickland, M. J., & Marinak, B. A. (2009). Child voice: How immigrant children enlightened their teachers with a camera. *Early Childhood Education Journal, 37*(1), 13–21.

Kelley, S., Yorker, B., Whitley, D., & Sipe, T. (2001). A multimodal intervention for grandparents raising grandchildren: Results of an exploratory study. *Child Welfare, 80*(1), 27–50.

Kids Count. (2008). *2008 Kids Count Data Book.* Annie E. Casey Foundation.

Kids Count. (2010). *2010 Kids Count Data Book.* Annie E. Casey Foundation.

Kolb, D. A. (1984). *Experiential Learning.* Englewood Cliffs, NJ: Prentice Hall.

Koppelman, K. (2011). *Perspectives on human differences.* Boston, MA: Pearson.

Kosmin, B. A., & Keysar, A. (2009). American religious identification survey (ARIS 2008). Hartford, CT: Trinity College.

Kottak, C. P., & Kozaitis, K. A. (2008). *On being different: Diversity and multiculturalism in the North American mainstream* (3rd ed.). New York, NY: McGraw-Hill.

Kowalski, K. (2003). The emergence of ethnic and racial attitudes in preschool-aged children. *Journal of Social Psychology, 143*(6), 677–698.

Kozulin, A., Gindis, B., Ageyev, V., & Miller, S. (2003). *Vygotsky's educational theory and practice in cultural context.* Cambridge: Cambridge University Press.

Kreider, R., & Ellis, R. (2011). Living arrangements of children: 2009. *Current population report*s, 70–126, U.S. Census Bureau, Washington, DC, 2011. Retrieved from the United States Census Bureau website at www.census.gov

Lansford, J., Ceballo, R., Abbey, A., & Stewart, A. (2001). Does family structure matter? A comparison of adoptive, two-parent biological, single-mother, stepfather, and stepmother households. *Journal of Marriage and Family, 63*(3), 840–851.

Lee, S. M. (2001). Using the new racial categories in the 2000 census. Census 2001: Annie E. Casey Foundation.

Leininger, L., & Ziol-Guest, K. (2008). Reexamining the effects of family structure on children's access to care: The single father family. *Health Sciences Research, 43*(1), 117–133.

Liang, X., & Zhang, G. (2009). Indicators to evaluate pre-service teachers' cultural competence. *Evaluation and Research in Education, 22,* 17–31.

Litzinger, T., Lee, S. H., Wise, J. C., & Felder, R. (2007). A psychometric study of the Index of Learning Styles. *Journal of Engineering Education, 96*(4), 309–319.

Lofaso, A. (2009). *Religion in the public schools: A road map for avoiding lawsuits and respecting parents' legal rights.* Americans United for Separation of Church and State. This book was downloaded free of charge at religioninthepublicschools.com.

Love, J., Kisker, E., Ross, C., Raikes, H., Constantine, J., Boller, K., . . . Vogel, C. (2005). The effectiveness of Early Head Start for 3-year-old children and their parents: Lessons for policy and programs. *Developmental Psychology, 41*(6), 885–901. doi:10.1037/0012-1649.41.6.885

Mahathera, N. (1982). Buddhism in a nutshell. Vajirarama, Colombo, Sri Lanka. Retrieved on August 14, 2013, from the Access to Insight website at http://www .accesstoinsight.org/lib/authors /narada/nutshell.html

Manning, W. (2006). Cohabitation and child well-being. *Gender Issues, 23*(3), 21–34.

Marks, L. (2004). Sacred practices in highly religious families: Christian, Jewish, Mormon, and Muslim perspectives. *Family Process, 43*(2), 217–231.

McAllister, C. L., & Thomas, T. (2007). Infant mental health and family support: Contributions of Early Head Start to an integrated model for community-based early childhood programs. *Infant Mental Health Journal, 28*(2), 192–215. doi:10.1002 /imhj.20129

McCann, D., & Delmonte, H. (2005). Lesbian and gay parenting: Babes in arms or babes in the woods? *Sexual and Relationship Therapy, 20*(3), 333–347.

McDevitt, T. M., & Ormrod, J. E. (2010). *Child Development and Education* (4th ed.). Upper Saddle River, NJ: Pearson Education, Inc.

McDonald, T., Propp, J., & Murphy, K. (2001). The postadoption experience: Child, parent, and family predictors of family adjustment to adoption. *Child Welfare, 80*(1), 71–94.

McSherry, W., Cash, K., & Ross, L. (2004). Meaning of spirituality: Implications for nursing practice. *Journal of Clinical Nursing, 13*(8), 934–941.

Merino, S. M. (2010). Religious diversity in a "Christian nation": the effects of theological exclusivity and interreligious contact on the acceptance of religious diversity. *Journal for the Scientific Study of Religion, 49*(2), 231–246.

Morgan, H. (2009). Picture book biographies for young children: A way to teach multiple perspectives. *Early Childhood Education Journal, 37*(3), 219–227.

NAEYC (National Association for the Education of Young Children). (1995). Responding to linguistic and cultural diversity recommendations for effective early childhood education. Retrieved from http:// www.naeyc.org/files/naeyc/file /positions/PSDIV98.PDF

NAEYC (National Association for the Education of Young Children). (2005). Screening and assessment of young English-language learners. Retrieved from http://www.naeyc .org/files/naeyc/file/positions /ELL_SupplementLong.pdf

NAEYC (National Association for the Education of Young Children). (n.d.). Children's books about families. Retrieved from http:// tyc.naeyc.org/articles/pdf /Childrensbooksaboutfamilies.pdf

NCES (National Center for Educational Statistics, U.S. Department of Education). (2010). Early Education and Child Care Arrangements of Young Children. Retrieved on February 18, 2013, from http://nces .ed.gov/programs/coe/pdf /coe_cfa.pdf

NCES (National Center for Educational Statistics, U.S. Department of Education). (2012). *Digest of Educational Statistics, 2011* (NCES 2011-001), Introduction and Chapter 2; U.S. Department of Education, National Center for Educational Statistics, Schools and Staffing Survey, Teacher Data Files, 2007–09.

NCIIP (National Center on Immigrant Integration Policy). (2010). ELL Information Center Fact Sheet Series: No. 3.

NCLR. (2006). Policy statements supporting adoption by gay, lesbian, and bisexual people. San Francisco, CA: National Center for Lesbian Rights. Retrieved from www .nclrights.org

Nesheiwat, K. M., & Brandwein, D. (2011). Factors related to resilience in preschool and kindergarten students. *Child Welfare, 90*(1), 7–24.

NICHCY (National Dissemination Center for Children with Disabilities). (2012). IDEA—The Individuals with Disabilities Education Act. Retrieved from http://nichcy.org/laws/idea

Nieto, S., & Bode, P. (2012). *Affirming diversity: The sociopolitical context of multicultural education* (6th ed.). Boston, MA: Pearson Education, Inc.

Nilson, L. (2010, November 18–21). The truth about learning style. Keynote address at the *International Lilly Conference on College Teaching*, Oxford, OH.

NPDCI (National Professional Development Center on Inclusion). (2011). *Competencies for early childhood educators in the context of inclusion: Issues and guidance for states.* Chapel Hill: The University of North Carolina, FPG Child Development Institute: Author.

NRC (National Research Council). (2001). Educating children with autism. C. Lord & J. McGee (Eds.), Washington, DC: National Academies Press. Retrieved from the National Academies Press website at http://www.nap.edu/openbook .php?record_id=10017&page=R1

Nsamenang, A. B. (2008). Culture and human development. *International Journal of Psychology, 43*(2), 73–77.

Nye, B., Hedges, L. V., & Konstantopoulos, S. (2004). Do

minorities experience greater lasting benefits from small classes?: Evidence from a five year follow-up of the Tennessee class size experiment. *Journal of Educational Research, 97,* 94–100.

OCR (Office for Civil Rights). (2011). Protecting students with disabilities: Frequently asked questions about Section 504 and the education of children with disabilities. Retrieved on November 5, 2012, from the U.S. Department of Education website at http://www2.ed.gov/about/offices /list/ocr/504faq.html

Odom, S. (2002). Learning about the barriers to and facilitators of inclusion for young children with disabilities. In S. Odom (Ed.), *Widening the Circle.* New York, NY: Teachers College Press.

Odom, S., & Wolery, M. (2003). A unified theory of practice in early intervention/early childhood special education: Evidence-based practices. *The Journal of Special Education, 37*(3), 164–173.

O'Flaherty, B., & Shapiro, J. S. (2002). *Apes, essences, and races: What natural scientists believed about human variation 1700–1900.* Discussion paper no. 0102-24. Department of Economics, Columbia University, New York, NY. Retrieved from Academiccommons.columbia .edu/download/fedora_content /download/ac:113662/CONTENT /econ_0102_24.pdf

Olavarria, M., Beaulac, J., Belanger, A., Young, M., & Aubry, T. (2009). Organizational cultural competence in community health and social service organizations: How to conduct a self-assessment. *Journal of Cultural Diversity, 16,* 140–150.

Onchwari, G., Onchwari, J., & Keengwe, J. (2008). Teaching the immigrant child: Application of child development theories. *Early Childhood Education Journal, 36*(3), 267–273.

Orlova, N. (2003). Teaching American little-c culture to prospective teachers of English. In *Theory and Practice in English Studies.* Vol. 1. Proceedings from the seventh Conference of English, American and Canadian Studies, 179–183. Brno: Masarikova Univerzita. ISBN 80-210-3283-9.

Palacios, J., Roman, M., & Camacho, C. (2010). Growth and development in internationally adopted children: Extent and timing of recovery after early adversity. *Child: Care, Health & Development, 37*(2), 282–288.

Papadopoulos, I., Tilki, M., & Ayling, S. (2008). Cultural competence in action for CAMHS: The development of a cultural competence assessment tool and a short cultural competence training programme. *Contemporary Nurse,* Special TCN issue, *28*(1-2), 129–140.

Parent, C., Saint-Jacques, M., Beaudry, M., & Robitaille, C. (2007). Stepfather involvement in social interventions made by youth protection services in stepfamilies. *Child and Family Social Work, 12*(3), 229–328.

Pashler, H., McDaniel, M., Rohrer, D., & Bjork, R. (2009). Learning styles: Concepts and evidence. *Psychological Science in the Public Interest, 9*(3), 105–119.

Patterson, C. (2006). Children of lesbian and gay parents. *Current Directions in Psychological Science, 15*(5), 241–244.

Payne, R. K. (2005). *A framework for understanding poverty* (4th ed.). Highlands, TX: Aha Publications, Inc.

Payne, R. K. (2009). Poverty does not restrict a student's ability to learn. *Phi Delta Kappan, 90*(5), 371–372.

Percy, M. S. (2003). Feeling loved, having friends to count on, and taking care of myself: Minority children living in poverty describe what is "special" to them. *Journal of Children and Poverty, 9*(1), 55–70.

Perrin, E. (2002). Technical report: Coparent or second-parent adoption by same-sex parents. *Pediatrics, 109*(2), 341–344.

Peterson, B. (2004). *Cultural intelligence: A guide to working with people from other cultures.* Boston, MA: Intercultural Press, Inc.

Pew Research Center. (2008). U.S. religious landscape survey. Pew Forum on Religion and Public Life. Washington, DC. Retrieved from religions.pewforum.org/

Peyton, M. R., & Jalongo, M. R. (2008). Make me an instrument of your peace: Honoring religious diversity and modeling respect for faiths through children's literature. *Early Childhood Education Journal, 35*(1), 301–303.

Poehlmann, J. (2003). An attachment perspective on grandparents raising their very young grandchildren: Implications for intervention and research. *Infant Mental Health Journal, 22*(2), 149–173.

Powell, B., Bolzendahl, C., Geist, C., & Steelman, L. (2010). *Counted out: Same-sex relations and Americans' definition of family.* New York, NY: Russell Sage Foundation.

Powlishta, K. K., Serbin, L. A., Doyle, A. B., & White, D. R. (1994). Gender, ethnic, and body type biases: The generality of prejudice in childhood. *Developmental Psychology, 30,* 526–536.

Pungello, E. P., Iruka, I. U., Dotterer, A. M., Mills-Koonce, R., & Reznick, J. S. (2009). The effects of income, race, sensitive parenting and harsh parenting on receptive and expressive language development in early childhood. *Developmental Psychology, 45,* 544–557.

Ram, B., & Hou, F. (2003). Changes in family structure and child outcomes:

Roles of economic and familial resources. *The Policy Studies Journal, 31*(3), 309–330.

Ramsey, P. G. (2004). *Teaching and learning in a diverse world* (3rd ed.). New York, NY: Teachers College Press.

Ray, V., & Gregory, R. (2001). School experiences of the children of lesbian and gay parents. *Family Matters, 59*, 28–34.

Ricciuti, H. (2004). Single parenthood, achievement, and problem behavior in White, Black, and Hispanic children. *The Journal of Educational Research, 97*(4), 196–206.

Rigg, A., & Pryor, J. (2007). Children's perceptions of families: What do they really think? *Children and Society, 21*(1), 17–30.

Robinson, C. C., & Clardy, P. (2011). It ain't what you say, it's how you say it: Linguistic and cultural diversity in the classroom. *Journal of Cultural Diversity, 18*(3), 101–110.

Rogoff, B. (2003). *The cultural nature of human development.* Oxford, UK: Oxford University Press.

Salend, S., & Rohena, E. (2003). Students with attention deficit disorders: An overview. *Intervention in school and clinic, 38*(5), 259–266.

Sands, R., Golberg-Glen, R., & Shin, H. (2009). The voices of grandchildren of grandparent caregivers: A strength-resilience perspective. *Child Welfare, 88*(2), 25–45.

Sanson, A., & Lewis, V. (2001). Children and their family contexts. *Family Matters, 59*(4), 4–9.

Schulz, M. M. (2009). Effective writing assessment and instruction for young English language learners. *Early Childhood Education Journal, 37*(1), 57–62.

Schwartz-Henderson, I. (2013). An informed approach for teaching children who are living with poverty. *Childcare Exchange, 35*(3), 48–54.

Schweinhart, L., Montie, J., Xiang, Z., Barnett, W. S., Belfield, C., & Nores, M. (2005). *Lifetime effects: The HighScope Perry Preschool Study through age 40*, 194–215. Ypsilanti, MI: HighScope Press.

Sensoy, O., & DiAngelo, R. (2009). Developing social justice literacy: An open letter to our faculty colleagues. *Phi Delta Kappan, 90*(5), 345–352.

Shady, S. L. H., & Larson, M. (2010). Tolerance, empathy, or inclusion? Insight from Martin Buber. *Education Theory, 60*(1), 81–96.

Shibley, M. A. (2011). Sacred nature: Earth-based spirituality as popular religion in the Pacific Northwest. *Journal for the Study of Religion, Nature, and Culture, 5*(2), 164–185.

Sims, M., & Hutchins, T. (2001). Transition to child care for children from culturally and linguistically diverse backgrounds. *Australian Journal of Early Childhood, 26*(3), 7–11.

Singer, E. (2010). The 'W.I.S.E. Up!' tool: Empowering adopted children to cope with questions and comments about adoption. *Pediatric Nursing, 36*(4), 209–212.

Smith, T. (2002). *Religious diversity in America: The Emergence of Muslims, Buddhists, Hindus, and others.* National Opinion Research Center. GSS Social Change Report No. 47.

Sternberg, R. J., & Zhang, L. (2005). Styles of thinking as a basis of differentiated instruction. *Theory into Practice, 44*(3), 245–253.

Stockall, N. S., Dennis, L., & Miller, M. (2012). Right from the start: Universal design for preschool. *Teaching Exceptional Children, 45*(1), 10–17.

Strohschein, L., Roos, N., & Brownell, M. (2009). Family structure histories and high school completion: Evidence from a population-based registry. *Journal of Sociology, 34*(1), 83–103.

Stronge, J. H. (2002). *Qualities of effective teachers.* Alexandria,

VA: Association for Supervision and Curriculum Development.

Struening, K. (2010). Families "in law" and families "in practice": Does the law recognize families as they really are? In B. Risman (Ed.), *Families as they really are.* New York, NY: W.W. Norton and Co.

Subedi, B. (2006). Preservice teachers' beliefs and practices: Religion and religious diversity. *Equity & Excellence in Education, 39*(3), 227–238.

Tomlinson, C. A., & McTighe, J. (2006). Integrating differentiated instruction and understanding by design. Alexandria, VA: Association for Supervision and Curriculum Development.

Trumbull, E., Rothstein-Fisch, C., & Hernandez, E. (2003). Parent involvement—according to whose values? *School Community Journal, 13*(2), 45–72.

Tucker, C., Kojetin, B., & Harrison, R. (1995). *A statistical analysis of the CPS supplement on race and ethnic origin.* Washington, DC Bureau of Labor Statistics.

UNESCO (United Nations Educational, Scientific, and Cultural Organization). (1995). Declaration of principles on tolerance and follow-up plan of action for the United Nations Year for Tolerance. Records of the General Conference, 28th session, Vol. 1.

U.S. Census Bureau. (2010). American fact finder: Grandchildren characteristics. 2010 American Community Survey.

U.S. Census Bureau. (2012). Income, poverty, and health insurance coverage in the United States: 2011. U.S. Census Bureau. Retrieved on March 13, 2013, from http://www.census.gov/prod/2012pubs/p60-243.pdf

U.S. Department of Health and Human Services. (2013). Annual update of the HHS Poverty Guidelines. Dated January 18, 2013, FR DOC. 2013-01422. Retrieved on March 13, 2013, from the Federal Register website at https://www.federalregister.gov/articles/2013/01/24/2013-01422/annual-update-of-the-hhs-poverty-guidelines

U.S. Department of Health and Human Services. (n.d.). Retrieved from the Office of Head Start website at http://www.acf.hhs.gov/programs/ohs/ on March 13, 2013

Vandenbroeck, M. (2000). Self-awareness, cultural identity and connectedness: Three terms to (re) define in anti-bias work. *EECERA Conference on Diversity, Complexity, and Multiple Perspectives* (pp. 1–9). London, England.

Vandenbroeck, M. (2008a). The challenge for early childhood education and care. In L. Brooker & M. Woodhead (Eds.), *Developing positive identities* (p. 26). Early Childhood in Focus 3. UK: The Open University.

Vandenbroeck, M. (2008b). Beyond color blindness and tokenism. In L. Brooker & M. Woodhead (Eds.), *Developing positive identities*. p. 28. Early Childhood in Focus 3. UK: The Open University.

Vanneman, A., Hamilton, L., Baldwin Anderson, J., & Rahman, T. (2009). Achievement gaps: How Black and White students in public schools perform in mathematics and reading on the National Assessment of Educational Progress. Washington, DC: National Center for Educational Statistics.

Vaught, S. E., & Castagno, A. E. (2008). "I don't think I'm racist": Critical race theory, teacher attitudes and structural racism. *Race, Ethnicity and Education, 11*(2), 95–113.

Voltz, D. (2003). Personalized contextual instruction. *Preventing School Failure, 47*(3), 138–143.

Vygotsky, L. S. (1962/1986). *Thought and language*. Cambridge, MA: MIT Press.

Wardle, F. (1998). Meeting the needs of multiracial and multiethnic children in early childhood settings. *Early Childhood Education Journal, 26*(1), 7–11.

Weaver, G. R. (1986). Understanding and coping with cross-cultural adjustment stress. In R. M. Paige (Eds.), *Cross-cultural orientation*. New conceptualizations and applications. Lanham, MD: University Press of America.

Williams, K. C., and Cooney, M. H. (2006). Young children and social justice. *Young Children, 61*(2), 75–82.

Wood, D. (2003). Effect of child and family poverty on child health in the United States. *Pediatrics, 112*(3 Part 2), 707–711.

York, S. (2003). *Roots & Wings*. Upper Saddle River, NJ: Pearson.

Younes, M., & Harp, M. (2007). Addressing the impact of foster care on biological children and their families. *Child Welfare, 86*(4), 21–40.

Yow, W. Q., & Markman, E. M. (2011). Young bilingual children's heightened sensitivity to referential cues. *Journal of Cognition and Development, 12*(1), 12–31.

Zeece, P. D. (1998). "Can God Come Here?" Using religion-based literature in early childhood settings. *Early Childhood Education Journal, 25*(4), 243–246.

Index